Evil Corporations

This book elaborates and interrogates the idea of evil corporations from a diverse range of disciplines.

There has long been awareness of systemic harms inflicted by corporations, but this awareness has rarely led to any effective legal means to prevent and/or respond adequately to them. Lawyers and legal theorists appear to be stuck asking the same questions, and giving the same ineffective answers. Part of the problem, this book maintains, is the relative lack of theoretical interrogation into the nature of corporations as responsible, moral agents. To break this stasis, this book draws upon philosophies of wickedness in order to ask whether or not corporations are, or can be, evil. With contributions from a range of different disciplines, including law, cultural theory, theology, and philosophy, it offers a novel account of how and why corporate wrongs are caused, whilst exploring the extent to which the legal system itself facilitates such wrongdoing.

The book targets a broad international audience with research interests in corporate crime. This will be of particular interest to those within the legal discipline, including corporate law, criminal law, corporate crime and law and humanities scholars.

Penny Crofts is Professor at the Faculty of Law, University of Technology Sydney, Australia.

Evil Corporations

Law, Culpability and Regulation

Edited by Penny Crofts

Routledge
Taylor & Francis Group
a GlassHouse Book

First published 2025

by Routledge
4 Park Square, Milton Park, Abingdon, Oxon OX14 4RN

and by Routledge
605 Third Avenue, New York, NY 10158

Routledge is an imprint of the Taylor & Francis Group, an informa business

a GlassHouse book

This research was funded by the Australian Government through the Australian Research Council Discovery Early Career Research Awarded (Project number DE200100881), examining 'New Approaches to Corporate Legality: Beyond Neoliberal Governance'.

British Library Cataloguing-in-Publication Data
A catalogue record for this book is available from the British Library.

Library of Congress Cataloging-in-Publication Data
Names: Crofts, Penny, editor.
Title: Evil corporations: law, culpability, and regulation/Penny Crofts.
Description: Abingdon, Oxon [UK]; New York, NY: Routledge, 2024. |
Includes bibliographical references and index.
Identifiers: LCCN 2024002692 (print) | LCCN 2024002693 (ebook) |
ISBN 9781032513126 (hardback) | ISBN 9781032514932 (paperback) | ISBN 9781003402534 (ebook)
Subjects: LCSH: Corporation law—Criminal provisions. |
Corporations—Corrupt practices | Corporate power. | Guilt (Law)
Classification: LCC K1315 .E95 2024 (print) | LCC K1315 (ebook) |
DDC 345/.0268—dc23/eng/20240129
LC record available at https://lccn.loc.gov/2024002692
LC ebook record available at https://lccn.loc.gov/2024002693

ISBN: 978-1-032-51312-6 (hbk)
ISBN: 978-1-032-51493-2 (pbk)
ISBN: 978-1-003-40253-4 (ebk)

DOI: 10.4324/9781003402534

Typeset in Sabon
by Deanta Global Publishing Services, Chennai, India

Contents

Notes on Contributors

Elise Bant is Professor of Private Law and Commercial Regulation at the University of Western Australian Law School, a Professorial Fellow at the University of Melbourne and a Fellow of the Australian Academy of Law and Consultant to HFW Australia. Professor Bant's main areas of teaching and research interests lie in the fields of unjust enrichment and restitution law, property, contract and consumer law, civil remedies, equity and trusts. She is author of *The Change of Position Defence* (2009) and co-author (with Justice James Edelman) of *Unjust Enrichment* (2016), editor of two collections of essays, co-author of a leading Australian casebook on Remedies and has published over 70 articles, chapters and other scholarly works in her specialist fields. Elise has conducted extensive Australian Research Council grant research with Professor Jeannie Paterson on the regulation of misleading conduct at common law, in equity and under statute. She has also been awarded an ARC Future Fellowship to examine corporate liability for serious civil misconduct.

Simon Bronitt is the Head of School and Dean of Sydney Law School commencing July 2019. In 2021, he was elected as a Fellow of the Australian Academy of Law. Drawing on comparative and interdisciplinary perspectives, Professor Bronitt has published widely on criminal justice topics ranging across terrorism law and human rights, comparative criminal law, covert policing, family violence and mental health policing. Recent publications include *Law in Context (5th ed., 2024)* and *Federal Proceeds of Crime Laws (2024)*.

Liz Campbell is the inaugural Francine V. McNiff Chair in Criminal Jurisprudence at Monash Law and is Adjunct Professor at her alma mater, University College Cork, Ireland. Her socio-legal research looks at how the criminal law deals with misbehaving corporations, as well as the use of biometrics (like DNA and face-recognition technology) in the criminal process. She was appointed to the Australian Law Reform Commission's Advisory Board for its Review into Australia's Corporate Criminal

Responsibility Regime and is a member of the Law Council of Australia's Foreign Corrupt Practices Working Party.

Hui Chia is a PhD candidate at Melbourne Law School and recipient of the James and Valerie McNiff Scholarship, which is awarded for research in the field of medical jurisprudence. Her thesis investigates the question of legal liability for harms caused by the use of Artificial Intelligence (AI) in healthcare. She has published on the topic of autonomous AI and interdisciplinary work in the field of AI and law. She has also published on several topics in corporate law, including the complexity of corporate legislation and empirical analysis of shareholder resolutions.

Stephanie Collins is Associate Professor of Philosophy at Monash University, Australia. Her research develops theories of collective agency and collective responsibility. Her books are *The Core of Care Ethics* (2015), *Group Duties: Their Existence and Their Implications for Individuals* (2019) and *Organizations as Wrongdoers: from Ontology to Morality* (2023).

Vicky Comino is a highly regarded corporate law scholar at the T.C. Beirne School of Law, University of Queensland. Her book, *Australia's 'Company Law Watchdog': ASIC and Corporate Regulation*, is the definitive text on corporate regulation in Australia. She is regularly sought out for media comment and her work has been cited by the courts and in government reports (e.g., the Final Report of the Banking Royal Commission), demonstrating her ability to produce research with real world impact. Vicky has also maintained her professional links with the legal profession and with industry, including serving as Chair of the Queensland Law Society Committee for the accreditation of Business Law Specialists.

Penny Crofts is Professor at the Faculty of Law, University of Technology Sydney. She is an international expert on criminal law and models of culpability. Her research in the area of socio-legal studies, coalescing around issues of justice in criminal law in practice and theory, makes a distinctive contribution to critical evaluations of criminal legal models of culpability and enforcement. Her analysis of criminal legal models of wickedness has contributed to a jurisprudence of blameworthiness. She was appointed to the Australian Law Reform Commission's Advisory Board for its Review into Australia's Corporate Criminal Responsibility Regime. The symposium for this book was funded by the Australian Research Council grant 'Rethinking Institutional Culpability: Criminal Law, Philosophy and Horror' (DE180100577).

Mihailis E. Diamantis is the Ben V. Willie Professor of Excellence at the University of Iowa College of Law, United States, where he researches corporate crime. He holds a JD from Yale and a PhD in philosophy from New York University. Before joining Iowa's faculty, he practised white-collar defence in New York and clerked for the Chief Judge of the US Court of Appeals for the Ninth Circuit.

Olivia Dixon is Senior Lecturer at the University of Sydney Law School where her research focuses on corporate crime, with a particular interest in enforcement. She has written on diverse topics such as the criminal code, corporate culture, whistleblowing, data brokers and sanctions. She was a member of the advisory panel for the Australian Law Reform Commission (ALRC) Report into Corporate Criminal Responsibility and has recently co-authored *Corporate Misconduct and White-Collar Crime in Australia: Federal Regulation, Investigation Powers and Enforcement*.

Jacinthe Flore is Lecturer in History and Philosophy of Science based in the School of Historical and Philosophical Studies at the University of Melbourne, Australia. She is the author of *A Genealogy of Appetite in the Sexual Sciences* (2020) and *The Artefacts of Digital Mental Health* (2023).

Joanna Kyriakakis is a Senior Lecturer at Monash University Faculty of Law, Australia. Her work focuses upon corporate accountability for international crimes.

James Martel teaches political theory in the Department of Political Science at San Francisco State University, United States. His most recent book is *Anarchist Prophets: Disappointing Vision and the Power of Collective Sight* (2022). Other books of his include *The Misinterpellated Subject* (2017) and *Divine Violence: Walter Benjamin and the Eschatology of Sovereignty* (2011). He writes on anarchism, critical legal theory, critical race studies and comparative literature, among other fields.

Jeannie Paterson is a Professor of Law and Director of the Centre of AI and Digital Ethics at the University of Melbourne, Australia.

Timothy D Peters is Associate Professor of Law, School of Law and Society, University of the Sunshine Coast, Australia; Adjunct Research Fellow, Law Futures Centre, Griffith University, Australia; and President of the Law, Literature and Humanities Association of Australasia. He is author of *A Theological Jurisprudence of Speculative Cinema: Superheroes, Science Fictions and Fantasies of Modern Law* (2022), co-editor of the forthcoming *Routledge Handbook of Cultural Legal Studies* and the recipient of an Australian Research Council Discovery Early Career Researcher Award (project number DE200100881) funded by the Australian Government, examining 'New Approaches to Corporate Legality: Beyond Neoliberal Governance'.

Honni van Rijswijk is Senior Lecturer in the Faculty of Law, University of Technology Sydney and writes on law and literature, collective culpability and technology. Honni's monograph, *Law and the Girl at the End of the World*, is forthcoming with Routledge.

Luke Russell is Associate Professor of Philosophy at the University of Sydney. He works in the area of moral philosophy and has written on evil, forgiveness, virtue and vice. Luke's books include *Real Forgiveness* (2023), *Being Evil* (2020), and *Evil: A Philosophical Investigation* (2014).

Lisa Siraganian is J.R. Herbert Boone Chair in Humanities and Professor of Comparative Thought and Literature at Johns Hopkins University, United States, and author of *Modernism and the Meaning of Corporate Persons* (2020), winner of the MSA Book Prize and the MLA's Matei Calinescu Book Prize, *Modernism's Other Work: The Art Object's Political Life* (2012), and editor of *The Norton Anthology of American Literature, Tenth Edition, Volume D* (1914–1945) (2022).

Marc Trabsky is Associate Professor in Law, and an Australian Research Council DECRA Fellow at La Trobe University, Australia. He is the author of *Law and the Dead: Technology, Relations and Institutions* (2019), *Death: New Trajectories in Law* (2023) and the co-editor of the *Routledge Handbook of Law and Death* (2024).

Rebecca Wallis is Lecturer at the T.C. Beirne School of Law, University of Queensland, Australia. Her teaching and research interests are in criminal law and procedure, the law of evidence and in the structure and operation of the criminal justice system. She is concerned with how legal and regulatory theories play out in practice to shape the operation of the justice system in intended and unintended ways. Rebecca holds a Bachelor of Arts and a Bachelor of Laws from the University of Queensland, and a Master of Arts in Criminology and Criminal Justice (Hons) and PhD from Griffith University.

Acknowledgements

Evil Corporations is a product of a two-day symposium hosted by the Faculty of Law, University of Technology Sydney, and funded by the University of Technology Sydney and by a grant from the Australian Research Council entitled 'Rethinking Institutional Culpability: Criminal Law, Philosophy and Horror' (DE180100577). I planned the symposium for years and invited my favourite leading experts with a challenge to think about 'evil corporations' in a scholarly and creative way. The contributions to this book more than met the challenge. Some were unable to make the final symposium, but helped along the way, including Steve Tombs, Alecia Simmonds, Anthea Vogl, David Carter and Dave Whyte. Others attended the symposium and contributed to knowledge and general happiness but were unable to publish in the book, including Cameron Tonkinwise, Jason Schultz, Nicole Graham, Eugene Schofield-Georgson, Michael Austin, Zoe Townsden and Kate Falconer. I would like to thank all attendees for giving up their time and for bringing a spirit of generosity and creativity to the event. The symposium was, of course, intellectually rigorous, but it was also a great deal of fun. Scholarly connections and new friendships were formed. The symposium shows the continuing need and significance of meeting in person and the capacity of transdisciplinary work to challenge boundaries and provide new ways of thinking.

I cannot thank Katrina Mathieson enough for her tireless support and energy in helping me organise the symposium and finalise the book. I would like to give a shout out to Claire van Vuuren at Bloodwood Restaurant, who hosted our delicious symposium dinner. I express gratitude to my partner Molly Tregoning, who understands the ups and downs of academic work and the time it takes. A shout out also to Juno and Faith, who happily chat about villains with me, even though they choose the good.

Penny Crofts

Introduction

*Penny Crofts**

There has long been awareness of massive systemic harms inflicted by corporations, harms that in recent times have exponentially increased. However, this awareness has rarely led to any effective legal means to prevent and/or respond adequately to these harms. Lawyers and legal theorists appear to be stuck asking the same questions, yielding the same ineffective answers. Part of the reason for the apathetic legal response to corporate harms is the insufficient theoretical interrogation into the nature of corporations as responsible, moral agents. This includes whether the harms caused by corporations due to the acts of a few 'bad apples', structures enabled and required by law, or are corporations inherently evil?[1] To break this stasis, this book considers corporate culpability by focusing on the question of whether corporations can be evil from diverse disciplines including law, theology, literature, philosophy and political science. *Evil Corporations* contributes to a technical account of how and why corporate wrongs and harms are caused, exploring the extent to which the legal system facilitates corporate wrongdoing. The essays presented here offer normative accounts of whether corporations can and should be regarded as responsible and culpable agents and how this might be evidenced and reflected in law.

Whilst the concept of evil is often associated particularly with religious discourse,[2] there are many important and persuasive secular models of wickedness, including early influential ideas from the ancient Greeks of evil as lack or dearth.[3] Furthermore, definitions of evil are contingent, changing across time and place. In *Evil in Modern Thought*, Susan Neiman asserts that

*The research for this chapter was funded by the Australian Research Council for the project 'Rethinking institutional culpability: criminal law, philosophy and horror' DE180100577.

1 Douglas Litowitz, 'Are Corporations Evil?' (2004) 58 *University of Miami Law Review* 811.

2 See for example, Thomas Aquinas, *On Evil* (2003, Oxford University Press 1274); Brian Davies, 'Introduction' in Brian Davies (ed.), *Thomas Aquinas: On Evil* (Oxford University Press 1274); Augustine, *The Confessions of St Augustine* (Edward Pusey tr., Collier Books 1961).

3 Aristotle, *The Nicomachean Ethics* (J. Thomson tr., Penguin 2004); Todd C. Calder, 'Is the Privation Theory of Evil Dead?' (2007) 44 *American Philosophical Quarterly* 371; Mary Midgley, *Wickedness: A Philosophical Essay* (Routledge 2001).

DOI: 10.4324/9781003402534-1

in the 18th century, the concept of evil referred both to acts of human cruelty and instances of human suffering, which included natural disasters such as earthquakes and floods.[4] Accordingly, natural evil did not require a responsible moral agent, although some theists argued that natural disasters such as the 1755 Lisbon earthquake was a punishment and warning from God.[5] The Lisbon earthquake led Voltaire to argue that any rationalistic defence of God in light of such horrendous suffering was unbearable. Contemporary models of evil require responsible moral agents, which Neiman argues is a shift from blaming God for the state of the world to taking responsibility for it on our own.[6] There have been further shifts in conceptions of evil in response to various challenges and events. The mass atrocities of the first half of the 20th century resulted in a rethink of conceptions of evil,[7] and there was a revival of interest in the study of evil after President George W. Bush's State of the Union address in 2002 attributing responsibility for the attack on September 11 to the Axis of Evil.[8] *Evil Corporations* argues that the proliferation of harms caused by corporations is likewise a challenge to update our models of evil. Corporations are entities created by humans and law, and it is vital and urgent that we take responsibility for the actions of these entities.

In contemporary philosophy, some thinkers are sceptical about the label of evil. For example, political theorist Phillip Cole argues that the label of evil does not give us any explanatory insight into why a person has done something, instead it places them as a character in a mythological narrative of a battle of good and evil.[9] For Cole, labelling a person evil puts them outside the borders of humanity, precludes any possibility or necessity of communication, and justifies and requires extreme measures. Whilst Cole's arguments are salient, he focuses on only one model of wickedness, that of a mythical, monstrous wickedness, outside the borders of humanity. This model is present in contemporary legal narratives, constructing (some) terrorists, paedophiles and those who perpetrate particularly heinous crimes as monstrous, resulting in extreme (legal) measures to these threats.[10] There are, however,

4 Susan Neiman, *Evil in Modern Thought* (Scribe 2002) 3.

5 Ibid., Ch 4.

6 Ibid. 4.

7 Hannah Arendt, *Eichmann in Jerusalem: A Report on the Banality of Evil* (Penguin 1994); Zygmunt Bauman, *Modernity and the Holocaust* (Polity 1989); Stanley Milgram, *Obedience to Authority* (Harper and Row 1974).

8 John Hamm, '"High Crimes and Misdemeanours": George W. Bush and the Sins of Abu Ghraib' (2007) 3 *Crime Media Culture* 259; Luke Russell, 'Evil-Revivalism versus Evil-Skepticism' (2006) 40 *The Journal of value inquiry* 89; Richard Bernstein, *The Abuse of Evil: The Corruption of Politics and Religion since 9/11* (Wiley 2006).

9 Phillip Cole, *The Myth of Evil* (Edinburgh University Press Ltd 2006).

10 Todd Calder, 'Evil, Ignorance and the 9/11 Terrorists' (2004) 20 *Social Philosophy Today* 53; Penny Crofts, 'Monsters and Horror in the Royal Commission into Institutional Responses to Child Sexual Abuse' (2018) 30 *Law and Literature* 123; Dave MacDonald, 'Ungovernable

other, different models of wickedness, that do not require a supernatural agent or inhuman humans.

Although arguments by sceptics are an important reminder of the way in which the rhetoric of evil can dehumanise and demonise, many moral philosophers assert the need for a coherent account and evaluation of terrible events and people. For example, in *The Death of Satan: How Americans have lost their sense of evil*, Delbanco argues that although the 20th century has a 'rich repertoire of evil', producing spectacles of unparalleled cruelty, we have a 'crisis of imagination', with 'no language for connecting our inner lives with the horrors that pass before our eyes in the outer world'.[11] Although not the subject of Delbanco's book, as we know from innumerable government inquiries, media reports and examples recounted in this collection, corporations are responsible for many of the horrors that occur in our world. And yet, the language with which we as a community, and in legal circles specifically, engage with corporate harms lacks the depth of moral discourse. We tend instead to frame many corporate harms as accidents, tragedies or disasters, as though there is no responsible agent to hold accountable.[12] This leaves us in an intractable situation – if there is no responsible agent, then these harms cannot be prevented – and yet – as shown in this book, many of the harms caused by corporations *are* eminently preventable. *Evil Corporations* contributes to the argument of the urgent need to develop a nuanced account of corporate responsibility and culpability.

This need for an examination of corporations as moral entities is reflected and reinforced in moral philosophy. When teasing out ideas about evil, moral philosophers tend to focus on individuals – particularly those who have caused harms – whether criminals, people who made (bad) decisions during extreme events such as war and/or fictional characters. Despite including fictional creatures in analyses of evil, most moral philosophers do not engage with corporate entities as moral creatures. The legal treatise writer Coke influentially asserted that corporations are *persona ficta*, created in the imagination of the law.[13] Given engagement with other fictional creatures in philosophies of wickedness, such as Satan, Iago and Hannibal Lecter, one could argue that the very fictionality of corporations likewise renders them a subject for analysis.[14]

Monsters: Law, Paedophilia, Crisis' (2012) 12 *Griffith Law Review* 585; Penny Crofts, 'Monstrous Wickedness and the Judgment of Knight' (2012) 21 *Griffith Law Review* 72.

11 Andrew Delbanco, *The Death of Satan* (Farrar, Straus and Giroux 1995) 3.

12 Jana Macfarlane Horn, 'Accident, Scandal, Disaster: The Media Framing of Corporate Crime' [2023] *Crime, Law and Social Change*.

13 Sir Edward Coke, *The Third Part of the Institutes* (Garland Publishing Incorporated 1628).

14 See for example, Delbanco (n 11); Francois Flahault, *Malice* (Liz Heron tr., Verson 2003); Midgley (n 3); JC Oleson, 'Contemporary Demonology: The Criminological Theories of Hannibal Lecter, Part Two' (2006) 13 *Journal of Criminal Justice and Popular Culture* 29.

At the same time, accounts of the reality of corporate entities have seen some engagement with questions of moral responsibility and group agency.[15] Chapple develops List and Petit and applies their ideas to a philosophical argument about the moral responsibility of corporations.[16] Stephanie Collins's recently published book *Organizations as Wrongdoers*, explicitly engages with the question of corporate blameworthiness from a philosophical perspective.[17] In this collection, Luke Russell considers the question of whether corporations do evil or can be considered as evil, within the discipline of philosophy. On the most part however, there is an anthropocentric and individualistic bias in philosophies of wickedness – as though individuals are the only moral agents. This individualistic bias is likewise reflected and reinforced in criminal legal doctrine and theory.[18] The criminal law was constructed around the archetypal legal subject – the responsible human being.[19] Thus even though corporations have long been recognised as legal subjects, it has proven very difficult to even imagining applying criminal law to the bulk of corporate wrongdoing. Honni van Rijswijk and I have argued elsewhere that this failure to criminalise corporate harms is horrific, because a central justification for criminalisation is public harm, and corporations cause a proliferation of mass harms.[20] *Evil Corporations* is not an argument against individual responsibility. Individual responsibility is still very important for accounts of corporate responsibility, as shown by contributions by Liz Campbell, Tim Peters and Lisa Siraganian in this collection. Rather, *Evil Corporations* is an attempt to address the balance and add depth and nuance to accounts of culpability so that they include corporations. Given that we have created corporations it is urgent that we construct meaningful narratives of responsibility for the harms that corporations cause.

Most definitions of evil have some form of harm at their centre. For example, in his summary of philosophies of wickedness, Calder argues that harm is an 'essential component of evil'.[21] Theorists like Kekes argue that harm of

15 Christian List and Philip Pettit, *Group Agency: The Possibility, Design, and Status of Corporate Agents* (Oxford University Press 2011); Anders Strand, 'Group Agency, Responsibility, and Control' (2013) 43 *Philosophy of the Social Sciences* 201.

16 Chris Chapple, *The Moral Responsibilities of Companies* (Palgrave MacMillan 2014).

17 Stephanie Collins, *Organizations as Wrongdoers: From Ontology to Morality* (Oxford University Press 2023).

18 Celia Wells, *Corporations and Criminal Responsibility* (Oxford University Press 2002).

19 Ngaire Naffine, 'Our Legal Lives as Men, Women and Persons' (2004) 24 *Legal Studies* 621.

20 Penny Crofts, 'The Horror of Corporate Harms' (2022) 38 *Australian Journal of Corporate Law* 23; Penny Crofts and Honni van Rijswijk, *Corporate Harms: A Horror Story* (Routledge Forthcoming).

21 Todd Calder, 'The Concept of Evil' in Edward Zalta (ed), *The Stanford Encyclopedia of Philosophy* (Winter, 2016).

evil must be serious and excessive.[22] Other theorists emphasise the quality of the harm. For example, Claudia Card argues that wickedness involves 'intolerable harms'[23] – that is, harm that makes life not worth living from the point of view of the victim, including severe physical or mental suffering, and deprivations. Luke Russell asserts that wickedness 'must be appropriately connected to an actual or possible extreme amount of harm'[24] – a definition which includes the equivalent of attempts in criminal law, where an accused intended but did not succeed in causing the prohibited harm. Given the centrality of harm to philosophical definitions of wickedness, the failure to consider corporations as moral entities is particularly stark. Corporations are capable of causing, and do cause, systemic harms on an industrial scale. For example, critical criminologist David Whyte asserts:

> [a]fter taking into account studies from across disciplines and after treating official data with the necessary analytical revision, at least 50,000 people die every year as a result of working in the United Kingdom alone. That's more than 1,000 a week. And, according to established research by the restrained UK safety watchdog, the Health and Safety Executive (HSE), as many as three-quarters of those workers are killed because of criminal breaches of the law. Put differently, the number of people criminally killed by their employer *every week* in the United Kingdom is roughly comparable to the number killed by interpersonal murder are *every year*. Globally, there are many times more people killed by illness and injury at work and by the toxic environmental consequences of profit-making every year than are killed in wars and conflicts. And yet, studies of safety crimes are few and far between, and are dwarfed by the burgeoning literature in terrorism and political violence studies, or indeed the literature on war crimes.[25]

Corporations cause a proliferation of harms that radically exceeds the capacity of individuals – except perhaps a (fictional) nefarious and ambitious super-villain.[26] Given this capacity for harm, the question of whether corporations can be conceptualised as evil is urgent. As a society we are increasingly dependent on corporations, they are becoming more and more capable of causing ever larger harms, and yet it seems less and less likely that they will be held accountable at law.[27]

22 John Kekes, *The Roots of Evil* (Cornell University Press 2005) 1–3.

23 Claudia Card, *The Atrocity Paradigm: A Theory of Evil* (Oxford University Press 2002) 16.

24 Luke Russell, *Evil: A Philosophical Investigation* (Oxford Univeristy Press 2014) 61.

25 David Whyte, 'Still Dying for a Living' (2013) 53 *British Journal of Criminology* 1206, 1206–1207.

26 Timothy D Peters, 'You Are Bad Guy, but This Does Not Mean You're Bad Guy: The Office of the Villain in Despicable Me, Megamind and Wreck-It Ralph' (2023) 73 *Saeculum* 165.

27 Scott Veitch, *Law and Irresponsibility: On the Legitimation of Human Suffering* (Routledge 2007).

Part of the reason why a narrative of corporations as evil is essential is that criminal law, whether national or international, is an expressive system of blaming – that is, criminal trials make findings as to *guilt*.[28] Criminal law is a powerful moral discourse, communicating right and wrong, backed by legitimate sanctions of the state. A common argument against criminalising corporate wrongdoing is that criminal law is a toothless tiger, and corporations do not overly worry about the application of criminal law. On the contrary, there is a power in the label of crime – beyond the sanctions attached. This was shown in the Australian Royal Commission into Misconduct, Banking, Superannuation and Financial Services, where the banks did everything they could to avoid the label of criminal, much preferring to be regarded as immoral or incompetent.[29] There is, accordingly, an expressive power in the label of criminal which corporations prefer to avoid. In fact, in his chapter, Mihailis Diamantis argues strongly in favour of prosecutors using this expressive aspect of criminal law to stigmatise wrongdoing by corporations and to restate and protect society's basic norms. Criminal law communicates that some behaviour is categorically prohibited.[30] Whilst imposing a finding of guilt on an offender expresses that the behaviour was wrong, the failure to criminalise corporate harms is also a message. That is, instead of harms being conceptualised as wrongs, they can be reduced to a cost–benefit analysis,[31] whereby a corporation will decide if it can afford to compensate those who are harmed, or worse, the cost of harms may simply be externalised.[32] Likewise, in their chapter, Hui Chia and Jeannie Paterson emphasise the normative potential of the law, arguing that civil law also has an expressive function, with tort sending a message that the defendant wronged the plaintiff. Chia and Paterson lament the absence of negligence as a standard of product liability, arguing that the strict liability regime reduces harms to a cost–benefit analysis rather than a normative assertion that the production and distribution of dangerous products is reprehensible and will not be tolerated.

28 In relation to international criminal law, see, for example, Joanna Kyriakakis, *Corporations, Accountability and International Criminal Law: Industry and Atrocity* (Edward Elgar).

29 Penny Crofts, 'Strategies of Denial and the Australian Royal Commission into Misconduct in the Banking, Superannuation and Financial Services' (2020) 29 *Griffith Law Review* 21.

30 Joel Feinberg, 'The Expressive Function of Punishment' (1965) 49 *Monist* 397; HM Hart Jr, 'The Aims of the Criminal Law' (1958) 23 *Law and Contemporary Problems* 401; John C Coffee, 'Does Unlawful Mean Criminal? Reflections on the Disappearing Tort/Crime Distinction in American Law' (1991) 71 *Buffalo Law Review* 193.

31 Gregory Gilchrist, 'The Expressive Cost of Corporate Immunity' (2012) 64 *Hastings Law Journal* 1.

32 Gregg Barak, *Unchecked Corporate Power: Why the Crimes of Multinational Corporations Are Routinized Away and What We Can Do about It* (Routledge 2017).

There are all too many arguments against corporations being held to account in criminal law. Much of the focus is on issues of mechanics – of how to impose existing criminal law doctrine that was developed around the archetypal legal subject, that is, the responsible human being, to corporations. In part, this is a movement away from quantitative models of wickedness (which focus on harm) to qualitative models (which focus on motive, intention and desires). Criminal law reflects and reinforces what Midgley has labelled a positive model of wickedness – the intentional or knowing infliction of evil.[33] Whilst the criminal legal system claims to enshrine subjective blameworthiness as central to accounts of culpability, the exceptions far outnumber the rule.[34] Nevertheless, much of the focus of criminal law theory regarding corporate culpability is how best to attribute fault or *mens rea* to corporations.[35] How can we determine what a corporation knew or intended? In this collection different answers and techniques are proposed.[36]

A precursor to dealing with the question of mechanics of how to apply criminal law to corporations is the question of whether and how corporations can be evil. Moral philosophy spends some time seeking to distinguish between the bad and the wicked.[37] In contrast, criminal law tends to focus on the bad, rather than the wicked – that is, whether an accused is sufficiently blameworthy to justify the application of criminal sanctions. Indeed, wickedness can exceed criminal law categories.[38] This issue may arise for corporate harms, which due to their sheer size, number and type, can exceed existing categories of harm recognised by the criminal legal system *and* the capacity of the criminal legal system to investigate or prosecute.[39] *Evil Corporations* aims to interrogate the question of whether corporations can be sufficiently blameworthy to justify the imposition of criminal sanctions. It does this by teasing out types of corporate harms and how they come about, and whether and how corporations can be blameworthy. It proffers a meaningful engagement with corporations as agents capable of making choices – whether good

33 Midgley (n 3).

34 Celia Wells, 'Swatting the Subjectivist Bug' [1982] *Criminal Law Review*.

35 See for example, Elise Bant, 'Culpable Corporate Minds' (2021) 48 University of Western Australia Law Review 352; ALRC, 'Corporate Criminal Responsibility: Discussion Paper 87' (Australian Law Reform Commission 2019) https://www.alrc.gov.au/publication/discussion-paper-87/; Ernest Lim, 'A Critique of Corporate Attribution: "directing Mind and Will" and Corporate Objectives' (2013) 3 Journal of Business Law 333; Elise Bant, 'The Culpable Corporate Mind: Taxonomy and Synthesis' in Elise Bant (ed.), *The culpable corporate mind* (Hart 2023).

36 For example, see Bant, Comino, Crofts, Siriganian and Trabsky in this volume.

37 For example, Claudia Card critiques Mary Midgley's failure to adequately distinguish between the bad and the wicked. Card (n 23).

38 Crofts, 'Monstrous Wickedness and the Judgment of Knight' (n 10).

39 Crofts, 'The Horror of Corporate Harms' (n 20); Crofts and van Rijswijk (n 20).

or bad.[40] Philosophy can assist with teasing out and thinking through the implications of choices and the application of different models of evil.

Evil Corporations is a result of a symposium held in December 2022 at the University of Technology Sydney (UTS), funded by the University of Technology Sydney and the Australian Research Council. I invited theorists and specialists from a range of different disciplines, including legal theorists, cultural critics, philosophers, criminal law experts and corporate law specialists, challenging them to think through ideas about corporate/group responsibility with a twist of wickedness. For the corporate and criminal law theorists, this required adding a twist of evil to their thinking. Moral philosophers were challenged to think through whether corporations could be moral agents and what this might mean. The symposium was fun, highly productive and constructive, with all invitees pushing the parameters of their work and providing feedback to each other. The resulting book has a theoretical depth and coherence that is – like the corporation itself – more than the sum of its individual parts. The chapters speak to each other but are not necessarily in agreement. Instead, the aim of the symposium was to start a conversation about different ways of thinking through questions of corporate culpability.

There are, accordingly, multiple definitions of evil within this collection, disagreement about whether corporations are inherently evil, how and why corporations harm and some scepticism as to the label of evil. For example, in the opening chapter, James Martel asserts that the raison d'être of archism is death itself – which he regards as the definition of evil.[41] Many of the chapters make some reference to Hannah Arendt's idea of the banality of evil,[42] whether to emphasise thoughtlessness, lack of care, the sheer ordinariness of corporate harms and/or the ways in which bureaucracies make people cogs in administrative machinery and dehumanises them. The book contributes to thinking through corporate responsibility with a particular resonance for legal conceptualisations and responses to corporate wrongdoing. A common theme in *Evil Corporations* is that of the vast harms caused by corporations, and the critique that these harms are framed as an acceptable cost of economic wellbeing. This then leads Timothy D. Peters to ask whether these harms are an aberration, functioning in breach of law, or if they are simply an instance of corporate law 'working'.[43] If nothing else, this theme highlights an urgent need to respond and reimagine corporate responsibility.

40 Chapple (n 16); Penny Crofts, 'Crown Resorts and the Im/Moral Corporate Form' in Elise Bant (ed.), *The culpable corporate mind* (Hart 2023); Collins (n 17).

41 Martel in chapter 1 of this volume, 29–30.

42 Arendt (n 7).

43 Tim Peters in chapter 9 of this volume.

The Structure of Evil Corporations

Part 1 of *Evil Corporations* interrogates whether corporations are doomed to be evil. **James Martel** starts the collection with a continuation of his ideas from *Anarchist Prophets: Disappointing Vision and the Power of Collective Sight*, arguing that capitalism is the purest manifestation of what he labels *archism* – a parasitical system based on hierarchy and false projections of authority onto screens of God, nature or reason. Martel points out that archism is justified by a Hobbesian anarchic threat that in the absence of law, the state, and other archist institutions, we would be killing each other.[44] Consistent with Fisher's assertion that it is easier to imagine the end of the world than the end of capitalism,[45] Martel argues that archism is so pervasive that it does not have or need a name – we do not see it as a choice, rather it is a given. In providing a name, Martel is emphasising that archism is a choice – and thus we can (and should) make different choices. This is particularly because for Martel, capitalism, and thus corporations, are always evil – 'rotten to the core, perfectly violent and without redeeming features. Worse yet, it implies that it has a form of malice that is often disguised by blandishments, that it seeks only destruction and its own power over that of all others.'[46] For Martel, liberalism supplies capitalism with a benign face – but this is a false promise, enshrining and protecting hierarchy.

In contrast to Martel, **Luke Russell** argues that corporations can do evil but are not doomed to be evil. Russell adopts a psychologically thin account of evil that does not require malice or intent, instead placing harm at the centre of his definition of evil as a culpably wrong action that is 'appropriately connected to an actual or possible extreme amount of harm.'[47] Russell draws upon philosophical arguments that groups of humans can function as agents, and thus corporations can be moral agents that are responsible in and of themselves for harms that they have caused. Many theorists have argued that corporations are inherently evil, including Martel's claim that archism is inherently destructive, Tombs and Whyte's assertion that corporations are criminal and should be abolished, and Glasbeek's argument that corporations are a menace.[48] In contrast, Russell emphasises the philosophical

44 James Martel, *Anarchist Prophets: Disappointing Vision and the Power of Collective Sight* (Duke University Press) 21.

45 Mark Fisher, *Capitalist Realism: Is There No Alternative?* (Zero Books 2009) https://ebookcentral.proquest.com/lib/uts/detail.action?docID=954706.

46 Martel, p. 20 of this volume.

47 Russell, p. 42 of this volume. This is an application of Russell's arguments developed in Russell, *Evil: A Philosophical Investigation* (n 24); Luke Russell, *Being Evil: A Philosophical Perspective* (OUP 2020).

48 Steve Tombs and David Whyte, *The Corporate Criminal: Why Corporations Must Be Abolished* (Taylor & Francis 2015); Harry J Glasbeek, *Capitalism: A Crime Story* (Between the Lines 2018).

distinction between evil actions and evil persons to argue against corporations as essentially evil, that is, that they are not 'strongly and highly fixedly disposed to perform evil actions, a corporation that we should not hope to reform, but one that should be contained and isolated or destroyed.'[49] In contrast, Russell offers some hope by arguing that corporations are more flexible in their disposition than human beings, and thus, can be reformed or changed. These arguments link to Comino's concluding analysis in this collection that changes to culture are possible.

Stephanie Collins also offers an optimistic account of corporations that is highly original. Collins argues that corporations can be agents in their own right – a 'corporation can have a vice that no role-bearers have, and a corporation can fail to have a vice that all role-bearers have.'[50] In keeping with her argument that corporations can be moral agents, she seeks to articulate the criteria of what it would mean to be a good or bad corporation. Collins draws upon a neo-Aristotelian framework to consider the telos of corporations. Picking up on contemporary arguments about corporate purpose, Collins adopts an instrumental approach, arguing that the virtue or vice of a corporation should be evaluated by how well it serves human flourishing. That is, instead of regarding corporate flourishing as intrinsically valuable, we evaluate corporations as good or bad based on their contribution to human flourishing. The advantage of Collins's approach is also that it allows for corporate diversity, in terms of what corporations do and the purposes that they serve. We can then evaluate whether a specific (type of) corporation serves human flourishing (e.g., nursing homes versus mining companies) and also whether they have gone off-script from their original purpose.

Part 2 articulates some of the many harms by corporations, and contributes to arguments of how these harms come about, which is explored further in Part 3. In Chapter 4, **Joanna Kyriakakis** makes a strong argument for the creation of an offence of ecocide in international criminal law. Kyriakakis notes that international criminal law is especially concerned with evil – indeed, Claudia Card built her model of evil around atrocities which form the basis of core international crimes.[51] In *Corporations, Accountability and International Criminal Law: Industry and Atrocity*, Kyriakakis advocates the application of international criminal law to corporations,[52] an argument that she extends in this chapter by exploring the role of corporations in ecocide: the mass destruction of the environment which may irreparably damage the social survival of groups. She argues that by failing to address ecocide, international law risks becoming complicit in the structural environmental

49 Russell p. 44 this volume.
50 Collins p. 49 this volume.
51 Card (n 23).
52 Kyriakakis (n 28).

violence of modern industrial societies. In keeping with Martel's insights, Kyriakakis argues that 'devastating environmental damage is an inherent product of modern industrial societies',[53] and that international criminal law is needed to intervene to shift the normative boundaries of what is acceptable in the pursuit of economic growth. An advantage of the international forum is that it may bypass weaker state regulations and impose an overall standard of care.

In Chapter 5, **Marc Trabsky** and **Jacinthe Flore** continue with the idea of acceptable harms through an analysis of corporate responsibility for the opioid epidemic. Trabsky and Flore note that at least half a million people have died in the United States due to the opioid epidemic since 1999. In *Death: New Trajectories of Law*, Trabsky argued that legal institutions have not only witnessed but have reified the economic value of death in the 21st century,[54] an argument that is consistent with Martel's contention in Chapter 1 that capitalism is a death cult. Trabsky and Flore argue that in the practice of developing, manufacturing and marketing drugs, pharmaceutical companies are 'always already entangled with an economisation of life and death'.[55] Rather than conceptualising death as a negative of bio-politics, Trabsky and Flore are at pains to stress that death is normalised as allowable by the state.

In Chapter 6, **Hui Chia** and **Jeannie Marie Paterson** continue the theme of allowable or acceptable harms through their analysis of Ethicon for the nasty harms that its pelvic mesh caused. Chia and Paterson argue that product liability regimes arose in response to outrage at injuries caused by unsafe products, but that it was difficult to prove knowledge or intention by the corporation. As a consequence, strict liability models were introduced to ease the burden on plaintiffs so that they could mount a case for compensation without proving corporations intended the harm. The intention of the scheme was that this would encourage corporations to make their products safer. A defence of a state-of-the-art or unforeseen risks is available – that is, corporations will not be liable if they can prove that the defect in their product could not have been discovered given the state of scientific and technical knowledge at the time the goods were supplied. Chia and Paterson point to pelvic mesh to highlight the perverse effect of the state-of-the-art defence – it can encourage corporations to neglect developing scientific knowledge about potential safety risks to improve their chances of relying on the defence. Rather than discouraging corporations from producing and distributing dangerous products, product liability regimes encourage corporations to regard injuries as a cost of doing business. As Chia and Paterson note, women are particularly negatively affected by this cost–benefit analysis because they are cheaper to

53 Kyriakakis p. 69 this volume.
54 Marc Trabsky, *Death: New Trajectories of Law* (Routledge 2023).
55 Trabsky and Flore p. 80 this volume.

compensate than men. Given the legislative regime, this cost–benefit analysis if completely rational, and horrific.

Olivia Dixon continues the idea of corporations undertaking a cost–benefit analysis with her focus on how location-sharing data prioritises profit over privacy, security and physical safety. Chapter 7 reads almost as a dystopian fantasy that is increasingly becoming a reality, with price discrimination and undermining of physical safety. Dixon argues that part of the problem is that we, as consumers, thoughtlessly accept terms and conditions. But, ultimately, she slates responsibility home to the state and legislation, which encourages a cost–benefit analysis.

Contributors to Part 3 meditate on the mechanics of evil corporations, that is, how harms come about. My chapter starts with the premise that evil corporations are a staple of the horror genre and interrogates how audiences recognise that those corporations are evil. The horror genre wallows in our worst fears and taboos. Although evil corporations in horror may inflict a proliferation of supernatural harms (such as a zombie apocalypse), the workings and reasons of evil corporations are all too understandable and recognisable. They cause harms for instrumental reasons (such as the pursuit of profit) and insulate themselves from any knowledge or responsibility for harms to values that we as a society hold dear. Horror films represent literally how corporations externalise harms through design and architecture. In horror, corporations are regarded as evil, not because they intend to cause harm to a particular person, but rather they pose a generalised threat to humans and the environment. Criminal law and philosophy need to update categories to recognise posing a generalised threat as a form of subjective culpability.

In Chapter 9, **Timothy D. Peters** considers the question of responsibility with his analysis of corporations and the way that they create distance between action and consequences. Peters argues that the exercise of corporate power is constitutively vicarious, that is, it is always exercised on behalf of another. This means that there is a structural irresponsibility at the core of the corporate form – no action is ever fully reducible to a particular agent or actor. Through an analysis of the role of office, Peters explores the way that employees can be involved in the wrongs of a corporation in a way that they would never defend as an individual. The corporation separates individuals from his or her actions and is thus constitutively irresponsible. Peters' argument that models of corporate responsibility are just an extension of the constitutive vicariousness of corporations also speaks to Part 1, and the idea that corporations are inherently evil. Peters tentatively proposes that instilling a form of corporate obligation as a result of being part of the world may be a solution.

In Chapter 10, **Lisa Siraganian** explores the intersection of individual and corporate responsibility through an analysis of HBO's *Succession* (2018–). Siraganian is particularly interested in thinking through legal models of collective knowledge and wilful blindness, and how these are manifested in practice. Siraganian argues that whilst there is knowledge within the corporation of a culture of crime and cover-ups, only Tom and Greg have the 'office' of designated sin-eaters. Siraganian points to the way that they incorporate past wrongs of the corporations, and act as though they are impotent and it is something happening to them, when there are things that they could do. They are contaminated by, and rewarded for, their knowledge. Siraganian argues that far from an easy tallying up and apportioning of collective corporate knowledge, it is instead 'a complex and reflexive psychological, social, and political drama'.[56]

In Chapter 11, **Liz Campbell** continues with the issues of corporate knowledge and individual responsibility with an analysis of the misuse of legal professional privilege. Campbell argues that evidence is important because it is needed to prove corporate wrongdoing, and yet corporations have a powerful and distinctive capacity to control information (also flagged by Elise Bant in her chapter), in terms of the structure of the corporation, the sheer volume of information and the mis/use of legal privilege. Legal professional privilege is one of many procedural protections that were developed to protect the rights, dignity and freedom of the ordinary citizen against the arbitrary power of the state. But how can and should these protections work for corporations, some of which may well be larger and/or have more power than the state?[57] Campbell uses two case studies to highlight systemic use by corporations through (individual) lawyers of legal professional privilege to obscure the nature of corporate behaviour and block enforcement actions.

Part 4 concludes with tentative recommendations as to future engagement with corporations. **Mihailis E. Diamantis** critiques the tendency of many academics and prosecutors to use a sanitised law and economic language when describing corporate wrongdoing. Diamantis argues instead in favour of normative language. In keeping with arguments that he has developed elsewhere about branding miscreant corporations,[58] Diamantis argues that prosecutors should use stigmatic language which would validate victims of corporate crime, stimulate public outrage and encourage or shame corporations to obey the law. He turns to the horror genre to excavate tools to overcome the usual obstacles for talking about corporate responsibility. Horror film 'portrays morally inert, morally ambiguous, and morally ambivalent entities as evils that are to be condemned, feared, and resisted'. Zombies may not be moral agents, but films like *Night of The Living Dead* 'leave no ambiguity about the stance we should adopt toward them.'[59] Prosecutors should start

56 Siraganian, p. 171 this volume.

57 Penny Crofts and Honni van Rijswijk, *Technology: New Trajectories in Law* (Routledge 2021).

58 W. Robert Thomas and Mihailis Diamantis 'Branding Corporate Criminals' (forthcoming) 92 *Fordham Law Review*.

59 Mihailis Diamantis, p. 204 this volume.

acting like corporate crime is evil to instil repugnance and disgust for harms inflicted by corporations in a cost-benefit analysis.

In Chapter 13, **Honni van Rijswijk** and I also turn to horror to interrogate corporate responsibility for past harms. Given the potential immortality of corporations, it is vital to think through corporate responsibility for past wrongs. We use the haunted house as a conceptual metaphor to explore the afterlives of slavery. Along with others, we argue that slavery was not incidental to corporations and capitalism, but instead is a key part of capitalism. *In re African-American Slave Descendants Litigation*,[60] the courts adopted a linear approach to time that foreclosed any arguments that the descendants of slaves were disadvantaged – instead holding that the harms were in the past and limited in time by the lifespan of the victims who suffered directly under conditions of slavery. This belies the intergenerational trauma of slavery which affects the past, present and future – and the extent to which the legal system was imbricated in practices of slavery. It also fails to take into account the material benefits of slavery that form the foundations of corporations. We draw upon popular culture representations of the haunted house to consider what is required in response to past wrongs. A true accounting of the benefits and harms of slavery may seem to be immeasurable but denial is insufficient – the haunting will continue and worsen. We argue, at a minimum, corporations and the legal system must investigate their role, acknowledge past injustices and seek to compensate those afflicted by past wrongs.

In Chapter 14, **Elise Bant** builds on her arguments that corporations manifest their states of mind through their systems of conduct, policies and practices. Bant argues that corporations utilise systems of conduct to enable them to achieve their corporate purposes and this is the only way that corporations can engage purposefully with the real world. Bant applies her theory of system intentionality to the real-life example of banks charging fees for no services, which she argues was not due to omission or failure, but a choice by the banks manifested through systems, policies and practices. She then draws persuasively on Kafka's *The Trial*, to note that 'none of the Court's members, employees or agents actually understands fully how the system operates'. And yet, the Court is geared to operate, consistently and in a co-ordinated way to achieve its ends. This analysis dovetails in a nuanced way with some of the issues pointed to by Siraganian and Campbell in their chapters.

In Chapter 15, **Rebecca Wallis** and **Simon Bronitt** also propose a system's approach to corporations and corporate harms. Drawing on complex adaptive systems theories, they examine how corporations are structured and function across micro-, meso- and macro-levels in ways that are both highly adaptive and highly resilient to change or intervention. A complex adaptive

60 *In re African-American Slave Descendants Litigation* 471 F.3d 754, 762–763 (7th Cir. 2006).

systems perspective has implications for the design of regulatory responses by providing a framework within which to identify and map key systemic drivers and risks of corporate misconduct at the level of individuals, departments, corporations and within the state and broader society. Rather than viewing corporations as 'unnatural' beings beyond redemption, the authors remain cautiously optimistic that a complex adaptive systems perspective can guide the further development of responsive regulation that can more effectively hold corporations responsible for the wrongs and harms they cause.

Vicky Comino concludes the collection with an exploration of how corporate culture can change for good. Comino notes that her arguments are consistent with Bant's ideas about system intentionality as a way of understanding how regulators can and should regulate corporate culture, particularly if they wish to address the drivers of wrongdoing within corporations. Comino points to changes to the Commonwealth Bank of Australia's governance, culture and accountability structures and practices under an enforceable undertaking with Australian Prudential Regulatory Authority. The focus of the regulator was not on formal policies, but on the instantiated, de facto, real policies and how they are embedded, audited and buttressed through practices throughout the organisation. Comino is cautiously optimistic of the capacity of regulators to achieve real change to corporate culture.

Evil Corporations highlights significant harms caused by corporations, ponders how these harms come about, and suggests ways to prevent and respond to corporate wrongdoing.

Part 1

Doomed to Be Evil?

Chapter 1

Can Capitalism Ever Be Other Than Evil?

James R. Martel

Introduction

Even to ask the question of whether capitalism is evil is a subversive move insofar as it uses a moral and theological term, evil, to apply to what is normally – or maybe more accurately normatively – understood as a purely rationalist and mechanical operation. Capitalism is not supposed to have a moral quality per se. In its own self imagining, it is about efficiency, profit seeking, competition and, if you ask a neoliberal, freedom. Even so, it seems to me a highly appropriate thing to question whether capitalism does in fact represent an evil force in the world insofar as I believe that capitalism is itself a theological construct. This is not an unprecedented claim. In his essay fragment 'Capitalism as Religion', Walter Benjamin describes this relationship. He tells us that capitalism is a religion but one of a very particular sort. He writes:

> Capitalism is a purely cultic religion, perhaps the most extreme that ever existed. In capitalism, things have a meaning only in their relationship to the cult; capitalism has no specific body of dogma, no theology.[1]

Here, Benjamin shows that, as a religion without a theology, capitalism is eminently flexible. Having no dogma or ideology, capitalism is indifferent to, that is to say, tolerant of, virtually any political or economic formation so long as it allows for the 'cult' of capitalism itself. For this reason, capitalism is fine with various liberal and fascist political forms. It can even tolerate some degree of socialism so long as it itself is never in any real jeopardy.

Critically, it is vital that capitalism appears entirely secular, that is to say that its theological roots be a secret. Benjamin tells us that '[capitalism's God]

1 Walter Benjamin, 'Capitalism as Religion', in Marcus Bullock, Michael W. Jennings, eds, *Walter Benjamin: Selected Writings Vol 1, 1913–1926*, (Harvard University Press 1996): 288–291.

DOI: 10.4324/9781003402534-3

must be hidden from it'.[2] To expose the cult, the theological core, would be to remove capitalism's disguise, rendering it far too vulnerable. Capitalism is a religion that does not wish to be known as such yet, in a sense, it is the most purely religious (or cultic) faith precisely because it has nothing but that faith, that occult theological quality to sustain it and render it coherent.

But does any of that make capitalism *evil*? We may not like it, but to call something evil implies something more than dislike. It implies that something in effect is rotten to the core, perfectly violent and without redeeming features. Worse yet, it implies that it has a form of malice that is often disguised by blandishments, that it seeks only destruction and its own power over that of all others. In what follows, I will argue, again based in part on what Benjamin has to say, that capitalism is indeed evil and irreparably so. I will do so by connecting capitalism to archism, a term that Benjamin doesn't use (in general it's not a term that you hear very often, as I'll explain further) but which I think is very close to his idea of mythic violence. Archism is the name I would use for the contemporary system of political and economic organisation across the globe. It is a system based on hierarchy and domination. As already noted, it is so all-pervasive that it does not normally have (or want) a name and that in fact its lack of a name is part of how it keeps its power. I will argue that capitalism is perhaps the key mode of archism, which I will be opposing to anarchism, and, as such lies at the heart of what is both a theological and, more particularly, evil phenomenon.

Benjamin on Mythic Violence

To begin this enquiry, let me briefly spell out what Benjamin means by mythic violence and how that might connect to questions of capitalism and archism. In his well-known essay 'Toward the Critique of Violence', Benjamin tells us that mythic violence is a form of projection and arrangement of power that largely dominates the world today. It is 'mythic' because it bases its authority on non-existent truths, truths that are either openly theological or offer a disguised theology in the form of secularism (i.e., nature, the state, reason, etc.). Perpetrators of mythic violence project their desires onto these blank (because they are non-existent) screens and what returns is meant to be unimpeachable, not subject to contestation or alteration. Mythic violence is 'violent' (although the term in German, *Gewalt*, does not only mean violence in a literal sense but more like force or assertion of power) because, insecure about its non-existent sources of authority, it must dominate and kill, not just one time but over and over again to continually demonstrate as much to itself as to its subjects and victims, that it is indeed real and true. Benjamin says of this that:

2 Ibid. p. 289.

> If violence, violence crowned by fate, is the origin of law, then it may be readily supposed that where the highest violence, that over life and death, occurs in the legal system, the origins of law jut manifestly and fearsomely into existence. [The purpose of capital punishment] is not to punish the infringement of law but to establish new law.[3]

Here, we can see that the law, in this example, does not exist to serve the population but rather only itself. Through violence, the law 'jut[s] manifestly and fearsomely into existence', but not in a way that establishes its power once and for all. Its claim to have metaphysical or supernatural origins is the source of its power but it is also the basis for its ongoing and permanent vulnerability as it can never become real enough to stop its need to kill again and again. And furthermore, the practice of mythic violence isn't just about law, it is about all forms of power and control in the world, capitalism very much included.

For Benjamin, mythic violence is opposed by divine violence, that is to say, the violence that comes from God. For Benjamin, divine violence does not bring new truths into the world. Rather, it simply undoes the lies that mythic violence attributes to it (including its secularised forms). Human beings are not themselves sources of divine violence, but they can benefit from its interference with mythic violence in order to determine what they collectively wish to believe (or not believe) as they see fit. Being an actual deity, God's exercise of divine violence is not insecure and is therefore not about itself at all.

As Benjamin tells us in a critical statement:

> Mythic violence is blood-violence over mere life for sake of violence itself; divine violence is pure violence over all of life for the sake of the living.[4]

Here, we see the crux of Benjamin's understanding of mythic violence. It is an empty, nihilistic and parasitical force that rules over the human beings under its control (that is to say, just about all of us). It reduces those under its control to 'mere life', even as divine violence ensures that this same category of persons also constitute what Benjamin calls 'the living'. As long as we exist under conditions of mythic violence, we are reduced to being mere life yet we always have the possibility of resistance, thanks to the intervention of divine violence and mythic violence's own vulnerability and so we are simultaneously also always part of the living.

3 Walter Benjamin, 'Critique of Violence', in Marcus Bullock, Michael W. Jennings, eds., *Walter Benjamin: Selected Writings Vol 1, 1913–1926*, (Harvard University Press 1996): 236–252, p. 242.

4 Ibid., p. 250.

At this point, I would like to introduce that other term, archism, into this discussion because I think that if mythic violence answers the 'why and how' question that we can pose about the sources and nature of modern political and economic institutions and practices, the term archism answers the related 'what' question. Archism is a term that covers multiple modes of power. It is above all a metaphysics of hierarchy, a way to organise time and space (so that the future is better than the present and one particular space, say the White House, is better than another) as well as the persons who occupy that time and space (so that Kim Kardashian is better than you or I). Each of us is ranked from top to bottom, put in our place and ordered by the regimes of archism in all of its various guises.

It is useful to speak of archism and not only mythic violence, I find, for several reasons. For one thing, archism more accurately describes a system and a relationship of power that unites its key institutions, the state, the law and, as I will argue further, above all, capitalism itself. Furthermore, to speak of archism inherently brings up its other which is anarchism. The term anarchism actually changes its meaning when it is contrasted to archism as such. Rather than merely referring to the European and North American-based leftist tradition of Bakunin, Kropotkin and Goldman, anarchism in this light means something more like not archism, which is to say, all practices that differ from archism itself. When archism does not have a name, we cannot make this contrast because anarchism appears as just one mode of politics among many. But when we juxtapose it to archism, we see that in fact many of the forms that we thought were varieties of politics – even widely divergent and mortally opposed varieties like liberalism and fascism – turn out to be variations within the larger category of archism and so not so different as we may think (for many communities of Black and Brown folk living in places like the United States, there may be effectively little difference at all between these systems; for others, there may be a big difference in terms of the impact that these systems have on their lives but not when it comes to capitalism).

It is anarchism which emerges, by making this juxtaposition (or constellation if we want to use a Benjaminian term) as being really different. In their recent book *The Dawn of Everything,* the Davids Graeber and Wengrow show that archism (although they do not use that word it is surely the phenomenon that they are describing) is only one of an infinite number of ways that human beings can and have organised themselves, both politically and economically.[5] Their entire book is devoted to showing how archism was not inevitable and that an infinite variety of other forms have dominated the vast majority of human history. Some of these other forms have bad features too but it seems safe to say that archism is among the worst of these options

5 David Graeber and David Wengrow, *The Dawn of Everything: A New History of Humanity* (Allen Lane 2021).

in no small part because it is driven (via the logics of mythic violence) to stamp out all competitors, all varieties save the ones that permit it its own untrammelled power in the world. I therefore think that the contrast between archism and anarchism is not a binary. Archism is one thing, anarchism is everything else. Archism is about mere life and anarchism is the name for the myriad practices performed by the living.

The Political Theology of Capitalism

Based on this brief analysis, I would like to turn my attention now to capitalism in particular as a form of archist power. My claim here is that capitalism is not merely *a* form of archism but possibly *the* form. Other modes of archism, including the state, are forms that I think archism could readily dispense with (for a while it looked like the state was going away, although it seems to have made a comeback). Capitalism, on the other hand, is so basic to archism, such a precursor to elements like the state itself, that it could not really exist, could not function, without this central modality. This is because capitalism is central to the hierarchies that archism produces and protects. It is what generates and sustains those hierarchies. It is capitalism, including its earliest forms like mercantilism, that leads to the ultraviolence of colonialism, genocide, the slave trade and other related matters. It is capitalism and its related ideologies that assign our role in society from lowest to highest and also ensure that we deal with those hierarchies, not as organised communities, but as isolated individuals, picked off one by one and thereby kept in our place.

Thinking of capitalism as the acme of archism helps to guide our thinking in several important ways. First of all, it exposes the ruse of neoliberalism which often seeks to palm off state functions to other parts of the archist network within which we are all suspended. So, for example, there is a neoliberal version of the call to defund the police. This version, though, does not restore power to the communities that it rules over (that would be the anarchist solution). Instead, it seeks to privatise policing through mercenary armies, rent-a-cops and Karens and vigilantes across the nation and beyond. Furthermore, locating capitalism at the centre of archism also serves to show how a doctrine like libertarianism, which seeks to do without the state but not without the market, to deregulate the economy entirely, is not fundamentally any different from liberalism itself insofar as with or without the state, archism will always be triumphant.

If capitalism does in fact lie at the centre of archism, how and why is that the case? What elements of capitalism, taken as a form of political theology (including the magical notion of the 'invisible hand'), have put it in such a central position? Earlier, I discussed the way that for Benjamin capitalism is a religion but I did not specify (nor did he) what the core article of faith, the source of its cultic nature, actually was or is. I think the answer to that question is hierarchy itself. For all of its talk of freedom of competition and the invisible hand, capitalism is a theology of hierarchy. Precisely reflecting the core basis of archism itself, it is based on the idea that some external viewpoint oversees a vast taxonomisation and ranking of people. The mechanism for this reproduction of hierarchy is the market. What shakes out through the mechanism of the market is, in fact, people's moral and theological standing (as Jessica Whyte demonstrates in her recent and brilliant book).[6] In a sense, the market demonstrates the 'truth' of each of us, our core value and worth and in a form of instant karma, we are rewarded or punished accordingly by our resultant economic status.

To understand this better it helps to look to the original theology (taken in a more literal sense) that has led to the modern archist form of capitalism. In a very important sense, the contemporary form of capitalism is a secularised version of Calvinism and Puritanism as conveyed by figures like John Locke and Jean-Jacques Rousseau. Insofar as Locke, in particular, is a major figure in forming modern liberalism, his own Puritan origins are a big factor in the way he understood relations of property, class and other modes of being.

The Puritan revolution that swept through England in the 17th century was above all a revolution about the nature of the interpretation and manifestation of God's Word on earth. English Puritanism was more of a spectrum than a monolith. The main differentiating question concerned the degree to which inspiration by the Holy Spirit (a central concern for all Puritans) was literal. For many Puritans, it was held that the apostles were the last generation to be genuinely inspired by the Word of God and that it was the role of contemporary Christians, aided by their clergy, to understand and apply that prophetic sense. For more radical Puritans, and even extending beyond the Puritans themselves to the Quakers led by George Fox, the Word of God was directly accessible to each person, directly transmitted by the Holy Spirit itself.[7]

Although these positions varied widely and led to great internal debate and consternation, the one unifying point was the belief that the Scriptures contained the Word of God and the Holy Spirit (although in practice the Quakers went beyond this, given the belief that the Holy Spirit's transmission of the Word is prior even to Scripture itself, wherein it was held that 'though the Bible were lost, it might be found in the Mouth of George Fox.')[8]

This understanding of a separate but identical form of transmission of truth produces a kind of diminished individualism for the Puritan subject.

6 See Jessica Whyte, *The Morals of the Market: Human Rights and the Rise of Neoliberalism* (Verso Press 2019).

7 Geoffrey F. Nuttall, *The Holy Spirit in Puritan Faith and Experience* (Basil Blackwell 1947), pp. 28–29.

8 Ibid. p. 26.

Each person receives the Holy Spirit separately but what they actually take in is always the same and in fact they are ranked by the degree to which they respond to and correctly 'read' the Holy Spirit. This sets up an external viewpoint (that of God) which ranks all human actors but which is itself exempt from that very same judgement. Individualism is diminished here because the standard by which to judge each individual comes neither from themselves nor from their community but is an external yardstick that they cannot control or determine.

We can see emanations of this way of thinking in the work of Jean-Jacques Rousseau whose concept of the General Will is quite similar to the power of the Holy Ghost (separate messaging but only one correct message which can be applied better or worse depending on the individual subject's devotion to the public). This also tracks with a tendency by Locke himself to argue, on the one hand, that all people are formally equal but that in practice great inequalities are also permitted. We see this, for example, in his treatment of gender where, after acknowledging that Adam and Eve are formally equal, he goes on to say: 'though as a helper in the Temptation as well as a Partner in the Transgression, Eve was laid below [Adam], and so he had accidentally a superiority over her, for her greater punishment'.[9] Eve's lower status is an 'accident', because it comes, not from something innate in women but rather as a result of Eve's own (bad) choice. This choice however saddles all future women with an inferior status to men even as Locke once again can claim them to be formally equal. Here again, individualism is produced, not as a way to allow for a plethora of different understandings per se – that is the path of anarchism itself – but rather to test, as it were, various human subjects to see which of them was truly 'elect', which could demonstrate God's favour in them (and why).[10]

Locke takes a lot of his own doctrine from an earlier Puritan thinker and cleric, Richard Hooker. In his *Two Treatises,* he cites Hooker repeatedly. Like Hooker, Locke bases human equality on mutual love as well as on the love that God has for all of creation:

> This *equality* of Men by Nature, the Judicious *Hooker* looks upon as so evident in it self, and beyond all question that he makes it the Foundation of that Obligation to mutual Love amongst men, on which he Builds

9 John Locke, *Two Treatises of Government* (Cambridge University Press 1965), 1:44, p. 172.

10 In *Subverting the Leviathan,* I argue that Hobbes is actually quite different from this model, reflecting his own refusal of Puritan political values. For Hobbes, there is no central truth to discern, the Holy Spirit is only a metaphor for individual interpretation and he welcomes and expects a plethora of responses which serves as a counterweight to the authority that he formally gives to the sovereign. See James Martel, *Subverting the Leviathan: Reading Thomas Hobbes as a Radical Democrat,* (Columbia University Press 2007).

> the Duties they owe one another, and from whence he derives the great Maxims of *Justice* and *Charity*.[11]

But there is a darker side to this love. Hooker himself sees that love as serving to justify human inequality wherein the love of God serves to bind us together into effectively one being, some parts of which clearly are held above others. Hooker himself writes:

> Far more comfort it were for us ... to labour under the same yoke, as men that look for the same eternal reward of their labours, to be joined with you in bands of indissoluble love and amity, to live as if our persons being many our souls were but one, rather than in such dismembered sort to spend our few and wretched days in a tedious prosecuting of wearisome contentions.[12]

It is precisely this sort of thinking that allows Locke this notorious line in the *Second Treatise*:

> Thus the grass my horse has bit, the turf my servant has cut, the ore I have digg'd in any place where I have a right to them in common with others become my Property, without the assignation or consent of any body. The Labour that was mine, removing them out of that common state they were in hath fixed my Property in them.[13]

This sentence is possible, or rather its contradictions are not fatal in terms of Locke's own internal reasoning, because the servant's labour is effectively melded into the master's being. The same force of love, that same distant perspective that judges and unites us together in love permits our hierarchies to be non-oppressive, Locke reasons, because it is all in the service of a common goal; the realisation of God's truth on Earth. Here, the master, having better reason, is more able to discern the truth than either the servant or his wife and thus they benefit from being drawn into his macrobody.

This, then could be said to be the original political theology that led to capitalism. It perfectly serves the requirements of liberalism, the political philosophy that arose alongside capitalism itself (along with its later arrival and dark counterpart of fascism) because it permits a sense of egalitarianism and promise – that is to say an appearance of genuine individualism – even as it effectively isolates and depoliticises us each from the other. Similarly, the

11 Locke (n 9), 2:5, p. 270.

12 Richard Hooker, *Ecclesiastical Works (The Works of That Learned and Judicious Divine Mr. Richard Hooker)* (D. Appleton & Company 1851), p. 152.

13 Locke (n 9), 2:28, p. 289.

appearance of maximal choice – a centrepiece of capitalist triumphalism – is itself really just a form of pseudo choice constrained within and by the limits of capitalism itself. Such a state of affairs permits capitalism itself (and hence archism) to run rampant and unopposed in the world. Liberalism supplies capitalism with its benign face; it offers supposed rights (which are really just whims that the state may or may not allow for), claims of equality and so on all of which are a thin cover over its real business – which is the business of archism as well – fomenting and protecting hierarchy.

But how did a theology that was about expressing truths about God become evil? It is really when this doctrine becomes secularised, as the key form of archism, that it starts to approach its true potential as evil because without that overarching substrate of God's love, capitalism becomes merely the rationale for hierarchy without any assuaging features (akin to Weber's 'iron cage').[14] If Locke, citing Hooker, could genuinely say that capitalism was just because it was fulfilling the realisation of God's truth on Earth, once that divine feature is removed (even as the rest of capitalism works in precisely the same way), what you get, as Benjamin tells us too, is the religion without the God. A secularised form of archism, then, holds onto the idea of some externality as a necessary corrective to the community as such but, as with Benjamin's notion of mythic violence, the void that was once God now gets filled by the desires of the archons themselves. With an empty void now serving as the centrepiece and source of authority and power, what results is necessarily nihilistic, arbitrary and ultimately evil.

You can see this evil in so much of what capitalism is and does. In our own time, Michel Feher explains that neoliberalism is not, as so many people think, about efficiency and profit but rather about being creditworthy, as he puts it.[15] To prove that they are worthy of credit, to avoid being 'discredited', neoliberal subjects have to actually overcome their own economic interests and engage in forms of self and other destruction to demonstrate their abnegation to market principles, once again placing a form of nihilism over and above any kind of actual human interest.[16] Thus neoliberalism, which is perhaps the most naked form of capitalist archism yet, will often lead to decisions that hurt investment and profitability. This explains all of the administrators who effectively gut and destroy their companies in order to show how ruthless they can be and even more so the way that capitalism has destroyed all traditional forms of life, and even despoiled the planet. But I don't think that earlier forms of capitalism were any less evil; surely those

14 Max Weber, *The Protestant Ethic and the Spirit of Capitalism,* (Routledge 2001), p. 123.

15 Michel Feher, *Rated Agency: Investee Politics in a Speculative Age,* (Routledge 2018).

16 See also Michel Feher, 'Disposing of the Discredited: A European Project', in William Callison, Zachary Manfredi, eds., *Mutant Neoliberalism: Market Rule and Political Rupture,* (Fordham University Press 2019): 146–176.

that it enslaved and murdered saw capitalism then for what it was just as so many Black and Brown people in the United States today, for one example, know capitalism and archism for what it is in our own time.

Indeed, I would go a bit further and say that if hierarchy is the chief product of Puritanism, a darker form takes hold in the secular, archist version where hierarchy serves, not God but nothing at all, a form of nihilism unto death (an idea that connects to Marc Trabsky's chapter as well). As the acme of archism, capitalism is, you could say all about death instead of about life; really it is a death cult. A parasite upon the living, archism in general has no life of its own. It depends upon that life but does not partake of it. It's chief agents, the archons, are of course alive themselves but archism as such is not. Made of nothing but death, archism seeks out death and destruction even as it also offers itself as the only solution to the very problems that it itself has generated. Its core is hierarchy but its chief result, and maybe its true raison d'être, is death itself. To me, that is pretty much the definition of evil.

Can There Be Any Good Capitalists or Capitalism?

Here, I can imagine a reader asking, surely not all capitalists are evil? Surely there are some firms and individuals that are genuinely concerned for human welfare and the like? What about Canada, Denmark and Sweden, all of those places where capitalism seems to have a kinder, gentler face? What about green capitalism and non-profits? The first thing to say is that in fact capitalism is equally ruthless in every country in the world so the idea of a benign capitalism is just another part of the way that archism hides its true face. Benjamin gives us a sense of how this disguise actually works and also how it is that there can be genuinely good deeds within a capitalist form that is otherwise oriented towards nothing but enforcing hierarchy and death. His essay, 'Toward the Critique of Violence', is not about capitalism per se but about law. Yet in that essay, Benjamin says something about law that I think can be applied to capitalism too. He tells us that the law wishes to think of itself as benign but that in fact the only way that it can manifest itself is via violence and oppression. Thus, he writes:

> The assertion that the ends of police violence are always identical or even connected to those of general law is entirely untrue. Rather, the 'law' of the police really marks the point at which the state, whether from impotence or because of the immanent connections within any legal system, can no longer guarantee through the legal system the empirical ends that it desires at any price to attain. Therefore, the police intervene 'for security reasons' in countless cases where no clear legal situation exists, when they are not merely, without the slightest relation to legal ends, accompanying the citizen as a brutal encumbrance through a life regulated by ordinances, or simply supervising him. Unlike law, which acknowledges in the

'decision' determined by place and time a metaphysical category that gives it a claim to critical evaluation, a consideration of the police institution encounters nothing essential at all. Its power is formless, like its nowhere-tangible, all-pervasive, ghostly presence in the life of civilized states. [17]

Here, we get a better sense of a disconnect between what could be called the idea of law and its practice. This distinction is not merely a matter of academic discourse but actually performs a critical function for the law itself. Were it not for this benign disguise, the law could not promote itself as being anything other than the violent, self-regarding and mythical creature that it is. But if the law were not, at the same time, murderous, it could not exist at all.

Here again, we see a parasitical relationship arising. The law *needs* for there to be non-exploitative, non-violent forms of law precisely so that it can continue to kill with impunity. It can point to those practices and say 'See? The law is good. It is for you, not for itself'.

Yet, whether we are talking about such practices within the field of law or within capitalism or even the state, in all three cases, I think that this good side comes, not from archism at all but rather from anarchist life, from the living themselves who live under archism's domination. As already noted, archism is not itself alive and is therefore not about life at all but about death. It requires the variety and magic of life to draw from both to give itself a semblance of life and also to be able to point to positive practices which it then claims as its own, disguising its own violence and death-seeking in the process.

One of the many conceits of archism is that were it not for the kind of organisational forms that it provides, we would all be murdering each other within ten minutes. This is certainly the case in terms of how liberalism, for one, depicts anarchism. When liberals imagine anarchism, they often invoke an image like Mad Max or Lord of the Flies, describing total chaos so that the words anarchy and chaos are often seen as synonymous. Yet, it is in fact archism itself that is chaotic. The random assignation of value to certain people over others which must then be defended with all of the resources of state and law that are available, means that arbitrariness itself is enshrined in archist practices with a concomitant degree of violence necessary to preserve that order. Archism, through its various ideologies and maybe most especially through liberalism, then projects that chaos and violence outside of itself onto anarchism, onto the living themselves.

Anarchism is once again the name that I would give to all of the myriad and varied forms of political, social, economic and legal self-organisation that occurs at all levels of human interaction. That is really what constitutes

17 Benjamin (n 3), p. 243.

the living in the first place. The living are those who create collective beliefs, structures and knowledges. In the same way that workers collectively know everything that there is to know about a particular workplace whereas their managers only know what their limited forms of knowledge-gathering can know, so too do the people as a collectively already know what they need to know to organise and run their own lives. Archism works very hard to ensure that the living never get an opportunity to talk to one another without the medium of archism itself; whenever they do get an opportunity to do so, as in most early periods of political revolutions, people very quickly and dramatically transform their way of political and economic life before (so far) being beaten back into submission. Yet even under non-revolutionary conditions, even while they are also being reduced to mere life by mythic violence, the living remain engaged, in whatever capacity that they are permitted to, producing the very 'goodness' that archism uses as proof of its own virtue and necessity.

For this reason, I would say that everything that appears to be good that capitalism may produce comes, not from capitalism itself which is evil, rotten to the core and irremediably so, but rather from the anarchist ferment of life itself. Capitalism takes credit for it, claims that such things could not exist without its own overarching structures and then once again uses those things to 'prove' that it is benign after all.

And therein lies a further vulnerability of capitalism and of archism more generally. Capitalism needs anarchist life to exist at all but the opposite is not true. People do not need archist overlords, they don't need bosses, administrators, managers, political representatives and the like. They only need access to one another, to forums which are genuine spaces of political and economic decision making and action. Capitalism could not survive the loss of this parasitical relationship but the living surely could. Under such circumstances, the living return to the status of being about themselves, about one another and in this way avoid the evil that is capitalism. If we take back all that is good and all that has been stolen from us, whether by capitalism, by the law or the state or any of the other myriad archist institutions, the nothingness that is archism is that much more exposed, vulnerable and without the power that it can only generate via lies and violence. In such cases, the living can engage on its own terms expressing its own interests and we could therefore revert to the normal stage of human existence that Davids Graeber and Wengrow describe in *The Dawn of Everything*. Archism, capitalism very much included, would return to the nothing that it always was and we could reprise a fuller expression of the kinds of myriad identities and freedoms that are in fact the human birthright even if archism does not ever want us to realise that.

Chapter 2

Can a Corporation Be Evil?

Luke Russell

Morally Blameworthy Corporations

The terrorist attacks of 11 September 2001 promoted a revival of interest in the concept of evil.[1] President George W. Bush called the terrorists evil and warned the world about a so-called Axis of Evil. This led to a sceptical response from some quarters, with critics claiming that the concept of evil is outdated, medieval and belongs in the world of horror fiction rather than reality.[2] According to this view, there is no such thing as evil, and we would be better off dropping the concept. A number of philosophers whom we might call evil realists have argued back against this sceptical response.[3] They say that evil is not merely a fiction, that some things in the real world are evil, and that a secular concept of evil has a useful role to play in contemporary moral discourse. Philosophical defences of the concept of evil have predominantly been focused on examples of actions performed by individual human beings. The serial killer Ted Bundy was an evil person, for example, and his sadistic murders were evil actions. There has been some discussion of evil groups, which has focused on ideologically bonded collectives which commit atrocities, with Nazis and the Holocaust being the paradigm. But one interesting and common example of putative evil has been neglected by philosophers; namely, an evil corporation. In contrast, the notion of an evil

1 Luke Russell, 'Evil-Revivalism Versus Evil-Skepticism' (2006) 40 *The Journal of Value Inquiry* 89.

2 Phillip Cole, *The Myth of Evil* (University of Edinburgh Press 2006) 215; Inga Clendinnen, *Reading the Holocaust* (Text Publishing 1998) 104; cf. Lance Morrow, *Evil: An Investigation* (Basic 2003) 12.

3 Todd Calder, 'Towards a Theory of Evil Acts: A Critique of Laurence Thomas's Theory of Evil Acts' in Daniel Haybron (ed.) *Earth's Abominations: Philosophical Studies of Evil* (Rodopi 2002) 51; Claudia Card *The Atrocity Paradigm* (Oxford University Press 2002); Eve Garrard, 'Evil as an Explanatory Concept' (2002) 85 *The Monist* 320; Daniel Haybron, 'Moral Monsters and Moral Saints' (2002) 85 *The Monist* 260; Susan Neiman, *Evil in Modern Thought* (Scribe 2003); Paul Formosa, 'A Conception of Evil' (2008) 42 *The Journal of Value Inquiry* 217.

DOI: 10.4324/9781003402534-4

corporation has recently attracted the attention of legal scholars.[4] In this chapter I will attempt to bring philosophical work on the concept of evil into dialogue with recent legal discussion of evil corporations. I will ask what it would mean to say that a corporation is evil, and compare this to the more familiar claims that an action is evil and that a human being is an evil person.

A useful starting point is to note that science fiction and horror movies frequently feature what fans describe as evil corporations. Examples include the Weyland-Yutani corporation in the *Alien* franchise, Omni Consumer Products in *Robocop* and Umbrella Corp in *Resident Evil*.[5] Of course, the fact that something regularly appears in movies does not count as evidence that it actually exists. *Back to the Future* does not provide evidence that time travel is possible any more than *Ghost* gives us a reason to believe in ghosts. If we rely too heavily on fictional examples of evil, then we play into the hands of sceptics who believe that evil is just a mythological fantasy.[6] Nonetheless, the trope of the evil corporation in fiction helps us to get a grip on what an evil corporation is supposed to be, and many things that are explored in fictions do have real-life counterparts. According to the journalist Angela Allan, the cliché from fiction is that of 'faceless, heartless, and soulless corporations conspiring against their employees and consumers' due to 'unlimited greed'.[7] These fictional corporations engage in deception and inflict massive harm on innocent victims in order to maximise their profits. The idea that there might be such corporations in the real world does not seem to be metaphysically fanciful, to say the least. There are plenty of examples of real-life corporations that have been described as evil. The *New York Times* has called the East India Company the 'original evil corporation',[8] the tobacco industry giant Philip Morris was described by a judge as having acted from evil motives,[9] and the journalist Rebecca Grant reports that Monsanto has been labelled 'the world's most evil corporation'.[10] Famously, Google's original motto was 'Don't be evil', which seems to acknowledge that 'the actors within a corporation, as well as the corporation itself, had the propensity to be evil or otherwise'.[11] With this evidence in view, it might be

4 Penny Crofts and Honni van Rijswijk. 2020. 'Negotiating "Evil": Google, Project Maven, and the Corporate Form' (2020) 2, *Law, Technology, and Humans* 75; Penny Crofts, 'Aliens: Legal Conceptions of the Corporate Invasion' (2022a) 34 *Law & Literature* 387.

5 Crofts (n 4) 388.

6 Cole (n 2) 215.

7 Angela Allen, 'How the 'Evil Corporation' Became a Pop-Culture Trope', (2016) *The Atlantic*. https://www.theatlantic.com/business/archive/2016/04/evil-corporation-trope/479295/

8 William Dalrymple, 'The Original Evil Corporation' *The New York Times* (Sept 4, 2019). https://www .nytimes .com /2019 /09 /04 /opinion /east -india -company .html accessed 9/4/2024.

9 Judge Slaps $10bn Damages Bill on "Evil" Philip Morris *WARC* (25/03/2003). https://www .warc .com /newsandopinion /news /judge -slaps -10bn -damages -bill -on -evil -philip-morris /en -gb /13383 accessed 9/4/2024

10 Rebecca Grant, '"World's most evil corporation" Monsanto buys weather big data company for $930M' https://www.reuters.com/article/idUS356200333620131002/

11 Crofts and van Rijswijk (n 4) 75.

hard to see why anyone would reject the idea that a real-world corporation could be evil.

Yet there are a number of reasons why sceptics will doubt this claim. One significant question is whether the people who are calling a corporation 'evil' are merely indulging in playful hyperbole, deliberately using extreme and metaphorical language in order to galvanise their audience or to generate clicks online. It is common for people to use the word 'evil' as an exaggeration for effect. In this mode, you might say that your friend's aggressive cat is evil, or that a particularly rich chocolate cake is evil. One reason that Google's motto 'Don't be evil' generated so much media attention is because of the frisson induced by the word, but there is also a danger that the motto comes across as being flippant or ironic; more Dr Evil than Dr Mengele. In light of this, we must ask whether people are speaking literally and seriously when they say that a particular corporation is evil. We can tell that they are not being ironic in many cases because they want the so-called evil corporation to be held accountable, to be subject to severe punishment, to compensate victims, and possibly to be shut down. These are the practical implications of a literal judgement that something is evil, not a merely playful or exaggerated use of extreme moral language.

Beyond this, there is a deeper worry. It is the thought that a corporation is not really a person, and hence is not a morally responsible agent. A morally responsible agent is something that can be praiseworthy or blameworthy for what it does, something that deserves to be held responsible, something that is culpable. Neither a great white shark nor a battleship is a morally responsible agent. They can possess many morally relevant features, including being dangerous, or harmful, or being worthy of protection, but they are not praiseworthy or blameworthy for what they do. They are things rather than persons, we might say, so a responsible agent is a *someone* rather a something. However, it is not the case that what it takes to be a responsible agent is simply to be a someone or to be a human being. A nine-month-old baby is a someone but is not morally responsible for what she does. Nor is a 99-year old who has severe dementia. According to the standard philosophical account, someone or something counts as a morally responsible agent if and only if it is capable of responding to reasons and choosing how to act on the basis of those reasons.[12] A responsible agent has beliefs about the world, has desires or ends, and makes decisions and forms intentions to act based on those beliefs and desires. The worry is that a corporation is constituted by a collection of individual humans, each of which is a morally responsible agent, but that the corporation itself does not have beliefs or desires, the

12 John Martin Fischer and Mark Ravizza *Responsibility and Control: A Theory of Moral Responsibility* (Cambridge University Press 1998) 33; Dana Nelkin *Making Sense of Free Will and Responsibility* (Oxford University Press 2011) 7.

corporation cannot form intentions, nor act on the basis of reasons.[13] If it is true that only a morally responsible agent could count as evil, we might argue, then a corporation could not literally be evil, even though it could be dangerous and harmful.[14] When ordinary people say that Monsanto or the East India Company were evil, they must be expressing the idea that some of the individual human beings who constituted those companies were evil, just as when someone says 'America is angry' they are really saying that lots of Americans are angry.

This general objection would result in a refusal to ascribe responsibility or blameworthiness for the harmful behaviour of corporations to anything other than individual human office holders or employees.[15] It is worth stating that even if 'identification liability' of individual office holders were the only kind recognised, there would still be scope for condemning and punishing a lot of evildoing in the corporate world. Analogously, many individual Nazi officers were tried and convicted for war crimes regardless of whether the organisation or institution of the Nazi Party was also blameworthy or answerable as a collective. However, I do not think that we should accept the general objection. We should acknowledge that a corporation can be blameworthy. This is not simply a consequence of the fact that a corporation is a person according to the legal fiction. Nor am I arguing that a corporation can be blameworthy for its actions simply on the grounds that it would be morally beneficial for us to be able to blame and punish corporations, although I believe that it would indeed be beneficial.[16] The reason that a corporation can be blameworthy is that a group of humans organised in a certain way can function as an agent.[17] Some of these groups are for-profit corporations in the legal sense, while others might be governments, clubs, societies or churches. It would be far more contentious to claim that a group agent is the kind of thing that can feel an emotion such as compassion or envy, but I accept that a group agent, including a corporation, can deliberate, intend, choose and act, and hence is the kind of thing that can be morally blameworthy for what it has done. Sometimes no individual office holder made a decision to inflict

13 Milton Friedman 'The Social Responsibility of Business is to Increase its Profits' *New York Times Magazine* (1970 September 13) 50; Chris Chapple, *The Moral Responsibilities of Companies* (Palgrave MacMillan 2014) 4.

14 T. Eschmann 'Studies on the Notion of Society in St Thomas Aquinas I. St Thomas and the Decretal of Innocent IV Romana Ecclesia: Ceterum.' (1946) 8 *Mediaeval Studies* 1 35; cf. Crofts (n 4) 393.

15 Crofts (n 4) 393.

16 cf. Christian List and Philip Pettit, *Group Agency: The Possibility, Design, and Status of Corporate Agents* (Oxford University Press 2011) 156.

17 Ibid. 32; Lisa Siraganian, *Modernism and the Meaning of Corporate Persons* (Oxford University Press 2020) 110; Stephanie Collins, *Organizations as Wrongdoers: From Ontology to Morality* (Oxford University Press 2023) 83.

harm on the victims, no individual office holder was culpably reckless and no individual office holder was blameworthy for the results, but the corporation performed the action and is morally answerable for it nonetheless.[18]

It is a separate question as to whether corporations in various jurisdictions are legally answerable for their conduct as corporations. It has long been argued that corporate crime is unjustly neglected and rarely punished.[19] While it may be practically difficult, it is not impossible to hold corporations accountable via punishment. A punishment is the imposition of a burden on a wrongdoer as a reprobative response to the act of wrongdoing.[20] Baron Thurlow was right when he said that a corporation has 'no soul to damn, no body to kick',[21] but not all punishment consists in damning or kicking. Corporations have assets and interests, have public reputations, and have various freedoms accorded to them. It is easy to see how punishments – reprobative burdens – could be placed on this kind of group agent. As a response to wrongdoing by a corporation, that corporation could be formally censured, fined, ordered to pay compensation, publicly shamed and restricted in its operations. Given my claim that corporations are morally answerable for their harmful wrongdoing, I am happy to go along with the thought that the law ought to be used to hold them accountable in these ways, even if the law needs to be changed so as to achieve this outcome.[22]

However, our original question remains unanswered. Now we can phrase it with greater precision: could a corporation be not merely culpable and morally blameworthy, but *evil*? To answer this, we need to think more carefully about the difference between concept of evil and other moral concepts. We need to get clear on what the word 'evil' means.

Corporations as Evildoers

The meaning of 'evil' is contested. It is not merely that different people think that the word applies to different sets of things, although that certainly is true.[23] In the domain of morality, we regularly encounter contestation over the extension of a concept. For example, there is huge disagreement as to which lives are well-lived, which people are honourable, which actions are disrespectful, which actions are obligatory and who counts as virtuous. However, disagreement over the extension of a concept is compatible with

18 List and Pettit (n 16) 166.

19 John Coffee Jr, 'No Soul to Damn: No Body to Kick: An Unscandalized Inquiry into the Problem of Corporate Punishment' (1981) 79 *Michigan Law Review* 386 388; Crofts (2022b) 389.

20 David Boonin, *The Problem of Punishment* (Cambridge University Press 2008) 22.

21 Coffee (n 16) 386.

22 Crofts (n 4) 397.

23 cf. Crofts and van Rijswijk (n 4) 81.

agreement over the basic meaning of that concept. For example, you and I might agree that the meaning of the word 'delicious' is 'tastes very good', but still disagree over which particular things are delicious. The fact that I think that liquorice is delicious and you think that it is not does not show that we disagree about what the word 'delicious' means. When I claim that the meaning of 'evil' is contested, I am not merely acknowledging that, say, you think that slavery is evil, whereas many slave owners disagreed with this judgement. Rather, I am pointing out that there is a lot of disagreement as to which judgement or attitude we are expressing when we use the word evil. In other words, there is disagreement not merely as to *which things* are evil, but also as to *what you are saying about something* when you call that thing 'evil'.

One possibility is that by calling something 'evil' you are simply saying that it is bad. Some people assume that the word 'evil' has distinctively religious origins, or that it buys into a supernaturalist metaphysical worldview. However, when we look at the *Oxford English Dictionary* we discover that originally 'evil' was used as nothing more than a synonym for 'bad'.[24] When you call something evil in this sense, you are not specifying which kind of badness it possesses – moral, rational, aesthetic, prudential – nor are you specifying how bad it is. You are just saying that it is bad in some respect, to some degree. This ultra-broad definition of 'evil' resulted in what now seem to be some rather surprising historical claims about which things count as evil. For example, John Locke says 'We name that Evil, which is apt to produce or increase any Pain, or diminish any Pleasure in us'.[25] The ultra-broad usage of 'evil' to mean nothing more than bad is no longer the standard usage; saying today that a toothache or a stubbed toe is evil would come across as ironic exaggeration. Nonetheless, this usage does persist in some contexts, including in our use of the phrase 'the lesser of two evils', and in the philosophical and theological debate about the so-called Problem of Evil.[26] I take it that this ultra-broad meaning of the word 'evil' is not the one that is in play when we are debating whether a corporation could be evil. It is uncontentious to say that a corporation can be bad and deficient in many ways, including in minor ways. Surely someone who condemns a corporation as evil is saying more than this.

Another possible use of the word 'evil' is to pick out the category of culpable moral wrongdoing. These wrongs are sometimes described as moral evils as opposed to natural evils, which, in contrast, are things that are bad but not morally wrong: cancer, depression, toothaches and suffering caused

24 Luke Russell, *Evil: A Philosophical Investigation* (Oxford University Press 2014) 16.

25 John Locke, *An Essay Concerning Human Understanding*, Peter Nidditch (ed.), (Clarendon 1987) 229.

26 Russell (n 24) 17.

by natural disasters.[27] According to this usage, only responsible agents can do evil, and only actions or things done by responsible agents can be evils. We might still say that agents can be evil in this sense, so long as 'being evil' is taken to mean performing evil actions, just as 'The kids are being naughty' is typically understood to mean that the kids are doing naughty things. Importantly, according to this definition of 'evil', trivial and minor culpable wrongs would still count as evil, alongside more significant wrongs and atrocities.

This definition of evil as culpable wrongdoing fails to accord with most contemporary discussions of evil, and certainly is not representative of the kind of evil corporations that are common in horror and science fiction. The problem is that this definition includes minor culpable wrongdoing as evil. According to most contemporary uses of the word, evil is extreme.[28] As Claudia Card says, '"Evil" is a heavy judgment. Much that is bad is disappointing, undesirable, inferior, even unjust or unfair, but not evil. Many wrongdoings are trivial. Evils never are ...'.[29] Lawrence Thomas agrees, pointing out that an evil act 'must have a certain kind of gravity to it'.[30] The serial killer Ted Bundy lied to his victims about his name and his profession, and lying is a culpably wrong action, but obviously it was not his lying that led people to condemn Bundy as evil. The idea that evil must be extreme is reflected in fictional portrayals of evil as well. Weyland-Yutani from *Alien* is described as an evil corporation not merely because it is morally culpable for minor violations in underpayment of its employees, but because it is 'explicitly willing to sacrifice humans in the quest for profit'.[31]

In light of this, let us reconsider Google's publicity-generating original motto, 'Don't be evil'. Crofts and van Rijswijk have claimed that this motto is impressively aspirational, contrasting it with the supposedly less aspirational motto that replaced it: 'employees ... should do the right thing—follow the law, act honourably, and treat each other with respect'.[32] But if evil refers only to the most extreme cases of wrongdoing, then the original motto is the opposite of aspirational; it is far too weak. 'Don't be evil' rules out only the worst kinds of wrongdoing, saying nothing about the minor culpable wrongs which lack the gravity required to count as evil, not to mention the supererogatory acts of generosity and community-building to which we might aspire. Google having the motto 'Don't be evil' would be analogous to the armed forces having the motto 'Don't commit atrocities'; important,

27 Card (n 3) 5; Neiman (n 3) 268.
28 Russell (n 24) 46.
29 Card (n 3) 7.
30 Laurence Thomas, *Vessels of Evil: Slavery and the Holocaust* (Temple University Press 1993) 77.
31 Crofts (n 4) 401.
32 Crofts and van Rijswijk (n 4) 75.

no doubt, but aimed far too low. In contrast, doing the right thing, acting honourably, and treating others with respect are much more demanding standards.[33]

Most philosophers agree that evil must be extreme and grave, never minor or trivial. There is also widespread agreement that there is an important difference between judging that an action is evil and judging that a person is evil. Not every evildoer is an evil person.[34] There is some kind of escalation involved in the condemning not just the action but the agent as evil. This reflects a more general pattern in evaluations of actions and persons. For example, it is less extreme to say that Dave's comment was racist than to say that Dave is a racist, and less extreme to say that Diane's comment was dishonest than to say that Diane is a dishonest person. Similarly, you don't count as a generous person simply in virtue of performing one generous action, nor do you count as a patient person because you once waited without complaining. The standard explanation of this pattern is to say that these person-level evaluations are judgements on a person's character, not merely judgements on their actions or their motives at a moment in time.[35] People are answerable for what they do, not merely for who they are characteristically, so action-level judgements are still morally important. Nonetheless, what you do or once did does not always reveal who you are. This distinction between act evaluation and agent evaluation should not be overlooked in discussions of evil corporations. We need to distinguish the question of whether a corporation could be an evildoer – that is, an agent that performs an evil action – from the question of whether a corporation could *be* evil in something like the way that a particular human being could be an evil person.

Let us ask first what it would mean to say that a corporation has done something evil. Evil actions are a subset of culpable wrongs, but in virtue of what are evil actions distinct from ordinary, non-evil wrongs? There is a lot of disagreement amongst philosophers in relation to this distinction. One

33 Crofts and van Rijswijk claim that the new motto 'only requires that the subsidiaries and employees "follow the law" and the narrower goals of the corporate form itself' (ibid. 75). I disagree with their interpretation. It is unclear why doing the right thing should be read narrowly to mean merely not breaking the law, rather than doing what is morally right. Moreover, acting honourably and treating people with respect are taken by many virtue ethicists and other moral philosophers to be comparatively demanding and aspirational ethical aims (e.g., Robin Dillon, 'Respect and Care: Toward Moral Integration' *Canadian Journal of Philosophy* (1992) 22 105; Anthony Appiah, *The Honour Code: How Moral Revolutions Happen* (Norton 2010).

34 Card (n 3) 22; Garrard (n 3) 321; Marcus Singer 'The Concept of Evil' (2004) 79 *Philosophy* 185 190; Formosa (n 3) 234; Luke Russell 'Dispositional Accounts of Evil Personhood' *Philosophical Studies* (2010) 149–231.

35 Luke Russell 'Defining Evil Actions: Different Approaches', in Thomas Nys and Stephen de Wijze (eds) *The Routledge Handbook of the Philosophy of Evil* (Routledge 2019) 245–247.

easy option would be to say that evil actions should be defined as extremely harmful culpable wrongs. However, quite a few philosophers have claimed that there is qualitative rather than quantitative difference between evildoing and ordinary wrongdoing.[36] If this were true, then it could not be the case that evil actions are extremely harmful culpable wrongs, because the difference between a fairly harmful culpable wrong and an extremely harmful culpable wrong is merely a quantitative difference. What would make the action evil, on this account, is just that it was more harmful than a non-evil wrong action.

In search of a qualitative difference between evils and ordinary wrongs, some of these philosophers have suggested that the hallmark of evildoing is that it evokes a feeling of horror or incomprehension in victims and onlookers. According to this story, evil actions feel different in the sense that, unlike ordinary wrongs, they make your skin crawl, or make you recoil in terror or disgust, or make you wonder how anyone could do such a thing.[37] In previous work, I have argued that this is a misleading way to characterise the difference between evils and ordinary wrongs. What evokes feelings of horror or incomprehension varies from person to person, and the emotional triggers do not reliably line up with moral severity.[38] The feeling of horror is a fitting emotional response not only to extreme wrongdoing but also to accidental or natural harms, where there is no wrongdoer who is morally responsible for the resultant damage and suffering.[39] Some gory or transgressive wrongs do evoke visceral disgust or horror in an audience despite failing to possess the moral gravity required for evil.[40] Some extremely harmful culpable wrongs tend not to evoke horror or any other strong emotions. Indeed, one reason why it is difficult to get people to take so-called white-collar or corporate wrongdoing seriously is that many of these wrongs are not immediately shocking but seem banal or unremarkable to many people.[41] It is true that these wrongs are horrific (that is, worthy of horror), but often they fail to

36 e.g., Stephen de Wijze 'Defining Evil: Insights from the Problem of "Dirty Hands"' *The Monist* (2002) 85 213; Hillel Steiner 'Calibrating Evil' *The Monist* (2002) 85 184; Garrard (2002) 321; Todd Calder 'Evil and Wrongdoing' in Thomas Nys and Stephen de Wijze (eds) *The Routledge Handbook of the Philosophy of Evil* (Routledge 2019) 218.

37 de Wijze (n 36) 213; Singer Stephen de Wijze 196; Michael Stone, *The Anatomy of Evil* (Prometheus Books 2009) 21.

38 Luke Russell, *Being Evil* (Oxford University Press 2020) 31.

39 Penny Crofts 'The Horror of Corporate Harms' *Australian Journal of Corporate Law* (2022b) 38, 23, 29.

40 Luke Russell 'Evil and Incomprehensibility' *Midwest Studies in Philosophy* (2012) 36, 71.

41 Hazel Croall, 'What Is Known and What Should Be Known about White-Collar Crime Victimization' in Shanna R. Van Slyke and Michael L. Benson and Francis T. Cullen (eds) *The Oxford Handbook of White-Collar Crime* (Oxford University Press 2016) 60; Crofts (n 39) 389.

horrify.[42] If we want the concept of evil action to pick out a kind of moral extreme culpable wrongdoing, and if we want to make sure that white-collar and corporate wrongdoing is not artificially excluded from this category, then we should not define evil action in terms of evoking certain kinds of emotional reactions in an audience.

Some philosophers have looked elsewhere for a qualitative difference between evils and ordinary wrongs. They have tried to identify a psychological hallmark in the evildoer which supposedly distinguishes evil action from non-evil wrongdoing.[43] These philosophers put forward what I have called psychologically thick accounts of evil action. Some have claimed that evil actions are culpable wrongs that are performed out of malice or ill will, such that the perpetrator wants the victim to suffer, and wants this not merely as a means to some other end.[44] (It is worth noting that this philosophical claim employs the more everyday meaning of 'malice' as positive ill will towards the victim, not the broader legal definition of 'malice' which includes recklessness and culpable indifference toward the victim.) Other philosophers have claimed that the psychological hallmark of evil action is the sadistic pleasure that the evildoer takes in the suffering of the victim.[45] Others say instead that the hallmark of evil action is that the evildoer knows that the action is wrong and does it anyway, thus defying morality rather than merely violating moral rules.[46] Others propose that all evil actions are performed by agents who deliberate in such a way that they silence a particularly important set of morally considerations, giving them no weight at all.[47]

Some of these psychologically thick definitions of evil action suggest that it would be unlikely or even impossible for a corporation to do evil. For example, even if we agree that a corporation is an agent that can make a decision and perform an action, we might baulk at the claim that a corporation can feel a sensation or an emotion.[48] So, if an evil action were defined as one in which the agent takes sadistic pleasure, we might conclude that a corporation can perform a wrong action but not an evil action. (Analogously, we might

42 cf. Crofts (n 39) 34. Elsewhere Crofts points out that evil corporations in horror movies 'are almost background noise and are often secondary to the monster (which they may have created or exacerbated) and may not even register' (n 4) 388.

43 Russell (n 4) 79.

44 Thomas (n 30) 76; John Kekes, *The Roots of Evil* (Cornell University Press 2005) 2; Manuel Vargas 'Are Psychopathic Serial Killers Evil? Are They Blameworthy for What They Do?', in S. Waller (ed.) *Serial Killers – Philosophy for Everyone: Being and Killing* (Wiley-Blackwell 2010) 75.

45 Colin McGinn, *Evil, Ethics and Fiction* (Clarendon Press 1997) 62; Steiner (n 36) 189; Roy Perrett 'Evil and Human Nature' *The Monist* (2002) 85 304.

46 John Rawls, *A Theory of Justice* (Clarendon 1972) 439; Perrett (2002) 304; Singer (n 34) 205.

47 Eve Garrard 'The Nature of Evil' *Philosophical Explorations* (1998) 1 53.

48 Chapple, Chris. *The Moral Responsibilities of Companies* (London: Palgrave MacMillan 2014) 131.

say that a charitable corporation can perform generous and beneficial actions but cannot perform a compassionate action because compassion is an emotion.) Perhaps we will run into a similar difficulty in relation to malice-based definitions of evil. If malice were defined such that it necessarily includes emotions, such as schadenfreude, then it is questionable whether a corporation could act out of malice. However, I think it is more plausible to define malice in terms of desires rather than emotions, so I think that a corporation could act out of malice or ill will towards the people whom it harms.[49] But if we did define evil action as malicious culpable wrongdoing, then many of the paradigmatic cases of extremely harmful corporate wrongdoing would not count as evil actions. This is because the paradigmatic evil corporation acts out of greed, not malice.[50] (Again, I am not using the word 'malice' in its broader legal sense which would include culpable indifference as an instance of malice.) In this respect, their greedy motives differ markedly from malice-driven war criminals, terrorists and serial killers. Evil corporations stereotypically show a callous indifference rather than hatred towards their victims, treating them as a means to the end of profit maximisation, or mere collateral damage along the way.

In contrast to all of these philosophers, I have argued that there is not a qualitative difference between evils and ordinary wrongs.[51] I claim that evil actions are simply extreme culpable wrongs. Evil actions can come from virtually any kind of motive, can be malicious or well-intentioned, or may involve a kind of reckless indifference to the victims. Evil actions might or might not evoke feelings of horror in an audience. The evildoer might feel sadistic pleasure, or merely grim satisfaction, or even disgust at what he is doing; indeed, the evildoer could feel nothing at all. This kind of psychologically thin account of evil action has gradually grown out of Hannah Arendt's comments about Adolf Eichmann and the banality of evil.[52] Arendt's claims about evil are unclear in some important respects, and she badly misread Eichmann's actual motives.[53] Nonetheless, some contemporary philosophers agree with Arendt's basic point: we should abandon the idea that all evildoers are stereotypical sadistic villains, that all delight in crushing their victims, and that all are motivated by hatred.[54] Granted, some evildoers are like this, but others are unremarkable bureaucrats who are trying to impress their

49 List and Pettit (n 16) 157.

50 Crofts (n 4) 399.

51 Luke Russell 'Is Evil Action Qualitatively Distinct From Ordinary Wrongdoing?' *Australasian Journal of Philosophy* (2007) 85, 675; Russell (n 24) 120.

52 Hannah Arendt *Eichmann in Jerusalem* (Penguin 2006) 252, 276, 287.

53 David Cesarani, *Becoming Eichmann: Rethinking the Life, Crimes, and Trial of a 'Desk Murderer'* (De Capo Press 2007) 58, 157, 360; Russell (n 24) ibid. 70.

54 Card (n 3) 3; Formosa (n 3) 220; Russell (n 38) 87.

bosses, and who are not thinking clearly about the extremely harmful consequences of their actions.[55]

If we employ a psychologically thin account and define evil actions as extreme culpable wrongs, then there is no obstacle to concluding that corporations can be evildoers and calling for them to be held legally responsible for their evil actions. Advocates of a psychologically thin account of evil action are still required to explain in what sense evils are extreme. The most straightforward option would be to claim that a culpably wrong action must inflict an extreme amount of harm in order to count as evil.[56] If this is correct, we must consider how we will evaluate actions that inflict only a small amount of harm on each one of an extraordinarily large number of victims, such that each individual victim is only mildly upset but the total aggregate of harm is enormous.[57] If this kind of extremely harmful action does not have the moral gravity required to count as evil, then we might claim that an evil action must inflict harm that is extreme for at least one individual victim. A further puzzle remains. What should we say about harmless failed attempts, such as when a misanthropic terrorist tries to murder hundreds of innocent victims but fails to harm anyone because his bomb malfunctions? I think that such failed attempts do have the moral gravity and extremity to count as evil, even though they happen to be harmless.[58] In light of this, I have argued that the relevant kind of extremity is not a straightforward function of the amount of harm that is actually inflicted by the wrong action. In order to count as evil, a culpably wrong action must be appropriately connected to an actual or possible extreme amount of harm.[59] Some harmless actions count as evil because they would have been extremely harmful if things had gone as the agent intended, or as we might have normally expected. That said, most evil actions are in fact extremely harmful. Corporations, as well as individual human beings, can perform culpably wrong actions that meet these conditions, so corporations can be evildoers.

Evil Corporations

Now let us return to the second question: Can a corporation not just do evil, but be evil? What, if anything, is the difference between saying that a corporation is an evildoer and saying that it is an evil corporation? To answer this question, we need to think in more detail about what it takes to be an evil person. I have already pointed out that person-level evaluations are

55 Arendt (n 52) 287.
56 Formosa (n 3) 229; cf. Kekes, John (1998), "The Reflexivity of Evil", *Social Philosophy and Policy*, 15, 1, 216–32; Singer (n 34) 193.
57 Russell (n 24) 51.
58 Ibid. 53.
59 Ibid. 61.

more demanding than action-level evaluations. Saying that a human being is an honest person or a cruel person is a judgement on that person's character. Stepping up from an action-level to a character-level judgement typically involves at least two extra considerations: situational breadth, and fixity of disposition. First, if someone has a particular virtuous character trait – say honesty – then they are disposed to behave in an honest way in a broad range of relevant situations, not just when they are speaking with their friends and family, and not just when they would profit by being honest. Second, if someone is an honest person then their disposition to behave honestly is quite firmly fixed. You can rely on an honest person to tell the truth in the future; they cannot easily be shaken out of this disposition. All of us are aware that someone might perform an honest action on occasion but not be an honest person, precisely because they are not reliably disposed to act honestly across all of the relevant situations and into the future.

Elsewhere I have argued that the claim that a human being is an evil person includes an especially strong judgement about the fixity of that person's disposition towards evildoing. I have called this the write-off intuition.[60] When you declare that someone is evil, you are treating him as a write-off, as someone who cannot be reasoned with, someone who is vanishingly unlikely to change his ways, someone who needs to be contained and isolated or eliminated, someone who is beyond repair.[61] Arguably, this is one of the things that George W. Bush is telling you when he says that the 9/11 terrorists are evil, and what true crime aficionados are expressing when they say that the Golden State Killer is evil; not just that these people have done terribly wrong things, but that we should not pretend that they can be reformed. The write-off intuition allows us to explain why some philosophers maintain that no one is an evil person. According to Philip Cole, we should not judge that any person is evil precisely because we should believe that every single wrongdoer can be redeemed.[62] In contrast, I have argued that most evildoers are not evil people, but that there probably are some people who *are* evil. For example, serial killers and ideologically committed war criminals reveal to us their highly fixed character by repeatedly seeking out extreme wrongdoing, and by rebuffing all attempts at rational engagement.[63] The write-off intuition helps us to see why saying that someone is an evil person is a very high stakes judgement. We ought to be wary of rushing to this conclusion without

60 Ibid. 169.

61 Haybron (n 3) 278; Cole (n 2) 236; Russell (n 34) 244. I do not claim that an evil person must have been innately evil, or 'born evil'. The relevant kind of fixity of character is fixity into the future. For a more detailed explanation, see Russell (n 24) 212.

62 Cole (n 2) 173.

63 Russell (n 38) 127.

having considered the likelihood that this extreme wrongdoer will undergo a change of heart.

When we ask whether a corporation could not merely do evil but be evil, I contend that the latter judgement would require a similar step up in relation to the fixity of its disposition towards extreme culpable wrongdoing. An evil corporation would be not merely a corporation that has done evil, but a corporation that has an evil character, and thus is beyond hope of reform. This would support the claim that not every corporation that does evil is an evil corporation. Obviously, this view about the nature of an evil corporation is debatable. Some critics might claim instead that the conditions required for a corporation to count as evil are radically different from the conditions required for a human being to count as an evil person, and that a corporation might be evil even though it is not an unfixable write-off. However, it is worth noting that some of those who are calling for recognition that corporations can be evil are also very strongly committed to the view that we ought to think of corporations as persons.[64] A corporation, according to the legal fiction, is a non-human person. A corporation can deliberate, choose and act, just as a person can. A corporation is an agent that persists through time, surviving as one and the same corporation even though it changes in various ways, just as a person does. In light of this, there is a strong reason to accept that the idea of an evil corporation should be understood as being closely analogous to the idea of an evil human. I propose that an evil corporation is a corporation that is strongly and highly fixedly disposed to perform evil actions, a corporation that we should not hope to reform, but one that should be contained and isolated or destroyed.

If this is what it means to call a corporation evil, should we conclude that any real-life corporations are evil? This is an open question, but we have some reason to be sceptical. In relation to individual human beings, our views about the flexibility or fixity of character are grounded in our knowledge of human psychology. It is true that many culpable wrongdoers experience remorse and successfully undergo moral reform. The younger they are, the better the chance that they will change. Hopefully we will get better at inducing moral reform as we experiment with different methods of responding to wrongdoing. However, there are some adults who have an established track record of freely chosen extreme wronging and are likely to continue to choose to perform those actions if given the opportunity. We are familiar with stories about wrongdoers seeing the light and suddenly undergoing a wholesale change of heart, but we know that we should not blithely trust serial killers and convicted paedophiles when they say that they are sorry and will not offend again.

When it comes to corporations, though, we cannot just assume that the same human patterns of fixity or flexibility of character will be in place.

64 Crofts (n 4) 391.

Some have argued that the very nature of a for-profit corporation strongly disposes it towards evildoing. If profit-maximisation is the only goal of a corporation, and if profits can often be maximised by completely disregarding the wellbeing of customers and third parties, then we can expect all corporations to drift into evildoing.[65] This view strikes me as being too pessimistic. Many corporations recognise that they have goals other than profit maximisation, and that they work under legal and reputational constraints that give them strong reasons to avoid extreme wrongdoing.[66] In fact, I think that we have reason to believe that the behavioural dispositions of corporations are *more* flexible than the dispositions of human beings. This is because the metaphysical conditions required for the persistence or survival of a human being are much tighter in practice than the conditions required for the persistence or survival of a corporation.[67] We can swap out the parts of a corporation that most strongly influence its behaviour – namely, its office holders and employees – without destroying that corporation. An analogous process is not possible in a human being. An organisation can survive legally as one and the same corporation despite the rapid and thorough replacement of its office holders with new people, as well as radical reform of its policies and practices. Corporation X in 2023 can be qualitatively very different from Corporation X in 2020, even though it is one and the same corporation.

The fact that we can swap out key parts of corporations does not imply that it will always be easy to transform the character of a corporation. A change in senior office holders alone might not change the pervasive culture amongst employees or the behaviour of the organisation as a whole.[68] Sometimes we might even conclude that the industry, not just a specific corporation within it, is morally corrupt, and that attempts to reform via replacement of office holders and employees will simply swap in other corrupt or soon-to-be corrupt parts. Nonetheless, I suspect that thorough behavioural reform is easier to achieve in a corporation that has committed evil acts than it is in a human serial killer or paedophile. Since corporations are more fixable than these adult humans, I think that we ought to be cautiously sceptical of the claim that any given corporation is evil, even though I wholeheartedly agree that there are corporations that are evildoers.

What, then, should we conclude about so-called evil corporations from horror and science fiction movies? They are certainly portrayed as corporations that do evil. It could be argued that we have no idea whether they

65 Steve Tombs and David Whyte *The Corporate Criminal: Why Corporations Must be Abolished* (Routledge 2015) 85; cf. Crofts and van Rijswijk (n 4) 86.

66 Chapple (n 48) 20; Crofts and van Rijswijk (n 4) 78.

67 Chapple (n 48) 185.

68 See Vicky Comino of chapter 16, in this volume.

are supposed to also be evil corporations in the sense that I have spelt out, because what we are told about their fictional worlds does not reveal whether these corporations are fixable or are beyond reform. Yet it is more plausible that these fictional corporations are presented in these films not merely as evildoers, but as irredeemably evil. The narrative function of the evil corporation is not to be a target for possible reform, but to be a faceless antagonist, an immovable force, a hydra-headed greed monster that is beyond repair.[69] If this is true, then these are evil corporations. When we ask whether a real-world corporation is not just an evildoer but evil, we need to consider whether this corporation is similarly unfixable. The practical implications of this judgement are significant. If you think that a particular bank, say, has performed extremely harmful culpably wrong actions in order to maximise profits, but you also think that this bank could be reformed rather than destroyed, then you ought to claim that this bank is an evildoer but is not an evil corporation.

69 cf. Crofts (n 4) 406.

Chapter 3

Corporate Vice

Stephanie Collins

Introduction

Vices are often attributed to corporations. We hear that casinos are 'greedy', mining companies are 'ruthless' or tobacco companies are 'dishonest'. Are such vices reducible to vices of role-bearers?[1] And which traits of corporations are properly labelled 'vices'?

This chapter addresses these questions, starting from recent social ontological literature.[2] I argue that corporations' vices are irreducible to vices of role-bearers. Instead, corporate vice is composed of a complex melange of structures, procedures, cultures, practices, norms and emotions – each of which exists at the irreducibly corporate level. I then propose a standard for corporate vice that follows neo-Aristotelean virtue ethics. The proposal is that a corporation is vicious when it fails to promote that aspect of human flourishing around which the corporation is characteristically or distinctively

1 In other words: is 'nominalism' or 'realism' the correct approach to the corporate vice? According to nominalism, corporate vice exists in name only: corporate vice is nothing more than a collection of vicious individuals. According to realism, corporate vice exists in and of itself: corporate vice is distinct from the vice of its constituent members and the corporation can, therefore, be at fault in way that is different from that of its constituent members. On nominalism versus realism, see Carlos Gómez-Jara Díez, 'Corporate Criminal Liability in the Twenty-first Century: Are All Corporations Equally Capable of Wrongdoing?' (2011) 41 *Stetson Law Review* 41.

2 Recent legal theory has addressed adjacent questions, such as whether current law has the resources to address corporate character and what the notion of 'corporate character' has to offer law. This chapter complements these contributions but focuses more squarely on philosophical issues. Mihailis E. Diamantis, 'Clockwork Corporations: A Character Theory of Corporate Punishment' (2017) 103 *Iowa Law Review* 507. William S. Laufer, 'The Missing Account of Progressive Corporate Criminal Law' (2017) 14 *New York University Journal of Law and Business* 71. Jason Baer, *The Inquiring Mind: On Intellectual Virtues and Virtue Epistemology* (Oxford University Press 2011). William S. Laufer and Matthew Caulfield, 'The Promise of Corporate Character Theory' (2018) 103 *Iowa Law Review* 101. Mihailis E. Diamantis, 'The Law's Missing Account of Corporate Character' (2019) 17 *Georgetown Journal of Law and Public Policy* 865.

DOI: 10.4324/9781003402534-5

oriented. Thus, virtues and vices *exist* irreducibly at the corporate level, but *which* traits are virtues and vices are determined by those traits' contributions to human flourishing.[3]

Before beginning, a caveat. This chapter makes an ontological and moral argument, not a legal one. I assume (in broadly Aristotelean spirit) that the law should be used to encourage corporate virtue. Yet I am neutral on which precise methods the law should use to do this. I take no stand on whether the law should use carrots or sticks, for example, or how exactly the law should punish corporate vice. Of course, regulatory frameworks are important scaffolds for corporate virtue, and a full account of mechanisms for avoiding corporate vice would give specific guidance to the regulatory context. My question, though, is a prior one: what *is* corporate vice?

Corporate Character Traits

Traits of Individuals

For those drawn to ontological parsimony, we might begin by trying to understand corporate vices as vices of individuals. Perhaps a corporation has vice V if and only if the corporation's role-bearers have vice V. Call this the traits-of-individuals view of corporate vice.[4]

The traits-of-individuals view has variations, depending on who counts as a 'role-bearer'. For example, are shareholders of for-profit corporations 'role-bearers'? What about low-level employees, proxy agents or external stakeholders? It's not obvious that we should defer to the corporation's organisational chart – or its own conception of role-bearers – when answering this question. After all, our goal is moral assessment. For the purposes of moral assessment, we should be wary of allowing the corporation to 'forsake' the character traits of certain individuals by quietly omitting to include those individuals within the corporate role chart. There is a moral question, then, about who is a 'role-bearer' for the purpose of using role-bearers' vices as the 'reduction-base' for corporations' vices.

The traits-of-individuals view admits of further variations. It must answer the question of how many, or which, role-bearers need to have a trait, for the corporation to have that trait. Does a corporation have vice V only if *all* members have V, or only if *most* members have V, or only if the *directing* members have V? The last of these options can be associated with the 'identity theory' in criminal law, according to which a corporation is liable

3 This proposal develops an idea from Stephanie Collins, *Organizations as Wrongdoers: from Ontology to Morality* (Oxford University Press 2023), pp. 102–4.

4 I use the cumbersome label 'traits-of-individuals' to distinguish the present nominalist position from an alternative nominalist position considered in the 'Traits of Role-Bearers' subsection.

only when the 'directing mind' has acted with fault.[5] Yet many corporate behaviours might be determined by character traits that are not held by directors, but rather by lower-level role-bearers. Traits of directors need not be dispositive.

I mention these options to illustrate that the traits-of-individuals view is not straightforward, as shown by the different ways that different jurisdictions have sought to grapple with these issues. The view contains complex choice-points. Our responses to these choice-points will likely be influenced by such factors as the corporation's structures, procedures, culture and so on. For example, it would seem natural to say *all* role-bearers' traits matter, and all matter *equally*, in a corporation with a democratic culture. And it would seem natural to say that *proxy agents'* traits should be considered, in a corporation that delegates many decisions to proxy agents. But the questions of whether a corporation has a 'democratic culture', and whether it 'delegates decisions', are questions of the corporation's structures, procedures and culture. These factors introduce a more 'holistic' approach to corporate vice. So, if we were drawn to the traits-of-individuals view because we wished to side-step such messy 'holistic' factors, we might be disappointed. The view is not as parsimonious or simple as it first appears.

Even without adjudicating the above-mentioned choice-points, the traits-of-individuals view is inadequate. Corporate vice is not simply a matter of role-bearer vice – whoever the role-bearers are, and in whatever proportions. A corporation can have a vice that no role-bearers have and a corporation can fail to have a vice that all role-bearers have. Consider dishonesty. It's possible that all role-bearers are scrupulously honest in their private lives – we would ascribe 'honesty' to them considered as humans independent of the corporation – but nonetheless the corporation is vicious, because the role-bearers strictly compartmentalise their home life from their work life. It's also possible that all role-bearers are liars and cheats in their personal lives, while the corporation is structured so as to prevent any lying or cheating when individuals are performing their roles. So moral assessments of individual role-bearers *qua private agents considered independently of the corporation* cannot be where we look when assessing corporate vice.

This may seem obvious, but it is important. We often look to individuals' private lives when assessing corporate character. We might think Tesla is arrogant because we think Elon Musk is arrogant. Or we might think Apple is generous because we think Tim Cook is generous. Indeed, individual vice might be *good evidence* for corporate vice. Musk's individual arrogance might be *good evidence* for the hypothesis that Tesla is also arrogant, because of the *influence* Musk has over Tesla. Yet corporate vice is not *constituted* by

5 This is the dominant model in Australian criminal law, following *Tesco v. Nattrass* (1972) AC 153.

individual vice. When considering Musk as a private individual, his influence over Tesla is best conceptualised as the influence one agent has over another. To test whether Tesla is arrogant, we need to look to Tesla itself – particularly, at attributes I will elucidate in the 'Traits of Corporations' subsection.

Traits of Role-Bearers

The second individual-based view says that corporate character traits are character traits members have *within and because of their roles in the corporation*, or, as I will say, 'qua role-bearers'. This is the 'traits-of-role-bearers' view. The traits-of-role-bearers view has several advocates in the small philosophical literature on collective virtue, so it is natural to extend the view to corporate vice.[6]

The traits-of-role-bearers view has the same smorgasbord as the traits-of-individuals view – a smorgasbord including options for who counts as a 'role-bearer' and what proportion of, or which, role-bearers' traits are relevant. The traits-of-role-bearers view avoids the counterexamples raised above, since it focuses only on facts about role-bearers that are determined by, or otherwise related to, their role in the group. Facts about role-bearers' personal lives do not come into this view's assessment of corporate vice.

As Miranda Fricker points out when advocating the traits-of-role-bearers view, the view is committed to a kind of non-reductionism: 'the individual features in question … are not found at the level of individuals considered independently from the group, for the individuals only have that feature if they are wearing their group-member hat. Some practical identities of individuals are … intrinsically group-involving …'.[7] Because of this, the traits-of-role-bearers view requires an account of when individuals are 'wearing their group-member hat', and of the mechanisms by which individuals can come to exhibit certain character traits *only* when playing their roles. Thus, the role-bearer account will need to be supplemented by a story of corporate-level

6 There are several advocates of the traits-of-role-bearers view. Reza Lahroodi, 'Collective Epistemic Virtues' (2007) 21 *Social Epistemology* 281. Miranda Fricker, 'Can There Be Institutional Virtues?' in T.H. Gendler and J. Hawthorne (eds), *Oxford Studies in Epistemology* (Oxford University Press 2010). T. Ryan Byerly and Meghan Byerly, 'Collective Virtue' (2016) 50 *Journal of Value Inquiry* 33. Miranda Fricker, 'Institutional Epistemic Vices: The Case of Inferential Inertia' in I.J. Kidd, H. Battaly and Q. Cassam (eds), *Vice Epistemology* (Routeldge 2020). Anita Konzelmann Ziv similarly suggests that organisations' virtues are largely a matter of how *members'* virtues 'aggregate and converge'. Anita Konzelmann Ziv, 'Institutional Virtue: How Consensus Matters' (2012) 161 *Philosophical Studies* 87. Likewise in the legal literature: Diamantis argues that '[w]hat matters for corporate honesty is not whether employees are honest round-the-clock, but whether they are honest while on the job'. Diamantis (2019, n 2).

7 Fricker (2010, n 6).

traits, such as the one I will give in the 'Traits of Corporations' subsection, even more strongly than did the traits-of-individuals view.

Yet the traits-of-role-bearers view is still reductionist in spirit, like the traits-of-individuals view was: according to both views, the *character traits themselves* are housed entirely within individuals. These individual-level character traits are *caused*, *supported* or *explained* by corporate-level phenomena, but the traits belong to individuals. To illustrate, Fricker gives an example of an appointments committee that is committed to equal opportunity. Despite each member deriding equal opportunity in their private lives, each member 'goes along' with equal opportunity for committee purposes.[8] Each member is committed to equal opportunity – with associated character traits – in their *capacity as group member*. These commitments are explained by group-level facts (such as corporate procedures, norms or practices). Nonetheless, the commitments – and the character traits themselves – reside within the individuals.[9]

This traits-of-role-bearers view gets something right. When enough role-bearers have a well-entrenched disposition to exhibit a certain character trait while acting within their roles, this will often be *sufficient* for the corporation to have that character trait – particularly in closely-held corporations. Of course, different members can – often, will – exhibit different character traits. Thus, a corporation might come out as partly generous, partly miserly and partly somewhere in between, if different role-bearers exhibit these traits while performing their roles. Yet this complication works in the theory's favour, yielding *gradations* of corporate character: the more members (or the more important the members are) that exhibit a character trait, the more the corporation has that character trait. We might then say that a corporation

8 Fricker (2010, n 6). Both Lahroodi (n 6) and Fricker (2010, 2013, 2020 n 6) use Margaret Gilbert's notion of a 'joint commitment' to explain what it is for an individual to 'go along' with something and therefore exhibit a character trait qua group member. Margaret Gilbert, *On Social Facts* (Princeton University Press 1989). To have a character trait qua group member, on Lahroodi's and Fricker's views, is to be party to a *joint commitment*, together with other members, to exhibit the character trait as a body. Apart from the problems raised in subsequent paragraphs for the traits-of-role-bearers view, I believe the 'joint commitment' version of the view is inapt for large corporations: it's incredibly rare that (enough) members of large corporations will be party to any joint commitments with one another, let alone joint commitments to exhibit certain character traits as a body. So 'joint commitment' accounts of group character traits will produce an implausible dearth of group character traits in the real world, since they require a level of cohesion that overlooks worker alienation.

9 Again, Fricker uses Margaret Gilbert's (n 8) theory of 'joint commitments', on which commitments are group level. But the joint commitments do not arise out of group-level facts like those theorised in the 'Traits of Corporations' subsection ; they rather arise out of individuals' several acts of acquiescing to the joint commitment. The phenomenon of group-level facts that facilitate role-bearer vice is also explored by Penny Crofts, 'The Townspeople of Derry in Stephen King's IT: Bystanders and Responsibility for Evil' in W.S. May (ed.), *Encountering Pennywise: Critical Perspectives on Stephen King's IT*. (University Press of Mississippi 2022).

has many character traits – including many conflicting character traits – to some small degree. 'Full' or 'maximal' exhibition of any given character trait would be rare, requiring all role-bearers to exhibit the trait while performing their roles. Again, this bug may be a feature: on Aristotelian virtue ethics, full virtue (and, we might add, full vice) *is* extremely rare.

The traits-of-role-bearers view is further supported by a metaphysical picture on which corporations are *materially constituted* by role-bearers. On this picture, whenever role-bearers perform their roles, those performances are attributable to the corporation.[10] Note that 'performances' here includes not just behaviours, but emotions, feelings, attention, observation, inclinations and so on. This wide conception of 'performances' is important for a conception of corporate vice on which the vicious person is disposed to behave in certain ways *for* vicious reasons, *with* vicious emotions, *acting on* vicious inclinations, and so on.[11] Human role-bearers are clearly capable of this rich suite of agential performances; thus, on the traits-of-role-bearers view, corporations are capable of them too.

While the traits-of-role-bearers view articulates an important and common basis for corporate vice, it does not provide a *complete* account of corporate vice. This is because role-bearer vice is not *necessary* for corporate vice. Corporations can exhibit a vice despite no role-bearers exhibiting that vice while performing their roles. Suppose one role-bearer is forgetful qua role-bearer, another is miserly qua role-bearer, and another is selfish qua role-bearer. This combination – when combined with the organisation's procedures, structures and so on – can result in *the corporation as a whole* being callous. No member alone is callous qua role-bearer (they are instead forgetful, miserly and selfish), but when the members' traits *interact* with the corporate structures and procedures, the overall result is group-level callousness. Thus, we need more than role-bearer vice, for a full account of corporate vice.

And even if one or more relevant members are callous-qua-role-bearer, it's still true that the callousness is an irreducibly group-level trait if the trait is *multiply realisable* – that is, if the group-level trait *could have been* manifested or constituted by a range of varied individual-level traits, such as forgetfulness, miserliness or selfishness.[12] The corporation's callousness could have been realised in numerous ways at the individual level while remaining the same corporation-level trait, even if it just so happens that the trait was

10 I defend this metaphysics in Collins (n 3).

11 This Aristotelean conception is richer than that theorised by Diamantis (2019, n 2), who conceptualises character as *mere* tendency to behave.

12 Carl Gillett, 'The Metaphysics of Realization, Multiple Realization and the Special Sciences' (2003) 100 *Journal of Philosophy* 591. Christian List and Kai Spiekermann, 'Methodological Individualism and Holism in Political Science: A Reconciliation' (2013) 107 *American Political Science Review* 629.

in fact manifested by callousness in individuals. Moreover, corporate-level facts (such as corporate culture, norms and policy) have an important role in shaping, rewarding and punishing role-bearers' character traits. The corporation's callousness should not be identified with, or reduced to, the particular individual-level character traits that happened to realise it in the actual world, if there were multiple possible individual-level realisers of the same corporate trait.

Traits of Corporations

If corporations' traits are irreducible to members' traits (whether qua private individuals or qua role-bearers), then in what do corporations' traits consist? A broadly functionalist approach to group agency is currently popular among philosophers and legal theorists.[13] On this approach, 'agency is as agency does'. To characterise the agency of corporations – including their vices – we look at whether the corporation functions as an agent over time and circumstances. This is determined by corporate structures, procedures, cultures, practices, norms and emotions – each of which, I will argue, exist irreducibly at the corporate level.

First, consider a corporation's structures. A corporation's structures specify how corporate roles relate, primarily through lines of reporting and delegation.[14] A corporation's structures specify how the corporation's constituent parts (humans) must relate to one another, for the corporation to exist. The structures also specify how the corporation relates to external entities. The relations are representable in an organisational chart or constitution, whether formally written down or not. Following recent analyses of ordinary objects (like tables), the totality of a corporation's structures can be understood as the 'recipe' for how the constituent parts must relate to one another, for those constituent parts to realise the corporation.[15] The recipe

13 In philosophy: Christian List and Philip Pettit, *Group Agency: The Possibility, Design, and Status of Corporate Agents* (Oxford University Press 2011). Bryce Huebner, *Macrocognition* (Oxford University Press 2013). Brian Epstein, *The Ant Trap: Rebuilding the Foundations of the Social Sciences* (Oxford University Press 2015). 2015; Frank Hindriks, 'Collective Agency: Moral and Amoral' (2018) 72 *Dialectica* 3. Stephanie Collins, *Group Duties: Their Existence and Their Implications for Individuals* (Oxford University Press 2019). Collins (n 3). In legal theory: Diamantis (2017 n 2). Diamantis (2019 n 2). Lisa Siraganian, *Modernism and the Meaning of Corporate Persons* (Oxford University Press 2020). Penny Crofts, 'Aliens: Legal Conceptions of the Corporate Invasion' (2022) 34 *Law & Literature* 387. Bant in chapter 14 of this volume.

14 French emphasises structures in his theory of corporate agency. Peter French, 'The Corporation as a Moral Person' (1979) 16 *American Philosophical Quarterly* 207. Peter French, *Collective and Corporate Responsibility* (Columbia University Press, 1984).

15 Koslicki analyses ordinary objects in these terms. Kathrin Koslicki, *The Structure of Objects* (Oxford University Press 2008). I apply Koslocki to organisations in Collins (n 3).

remains constant across changes in the role-occupants (including changes to the CEO), and even across minor changes to the structure itself. A corporation's structure can be vicious by, for example, inhibiting transparency and accountability, or by promoting corruption. Note that viewing a corporation's structure as a locus of vice does not imply or assume that *any* individual role-bearers are vicious: the structure itself can encode vice in how role-bearers are *related*.

Meanwhile, a corporation's *procedures* are the methods the corporation uses to form beliefs, preferences, decisions, intentions and other (functional equivalents of) mental states.[16] Procedures are ways of *operationalising* the structures. Procedures include formal aggregation rules, alongside bargaining, debate, compromise, conversation, command, consultation and so on – as seen within boards of directors, shareholder meetings and stakeholder engagement. A corporation's procedures need not be formal or written down, just as its structure (recipe) need not have a written constitution. Again, the procedures can have vices that are not attributable to any individual role-bearer. These include authoritarianism, managerialism or officiousness – which can be encoded into procedures despite role-bearers' best attempts to resist these vices during role performance.

Another group-level constituent of corporate character traits is the corporate ethos.[17] As theorised by Pamela Bucy, the corporate ethos is gleanable via examination of 'the corporate hierarchy, the corporate goals and policies, the corporation's historical treatment of prior offences, the corporation's efforts to educate and monitor employees' compliance with the law, and the corporation's compensation scheme, especially its policy on indemnification of corporate employees'.[18] As Bucy notes, 'it is not possible to fully, completely, and accurately ascertain a corporate ethos'.[19] Moreover, the elements just listed provide an incomplete picture. Ethos arises from norms of practice and behaviour, unspoken but widely presumed standards of success, habits of attention or prioritisation, assumptions about what is sayable and unsayable, perceptions of what is possible and impossible and other elements that cannot be ascertained purely from the top-down elements mentioned by Bucy. All of these must be examined to ascertain a corporation's ethos – and even then, any assessments about the ethos (particularly by outsiders) are fallible. The result is that we cannot always know whether a corporation is vicious – just as we cannot always know whether a human is vicious.

16 List and Pettit (n 13) emphasise procedures – particularly aggregation procedures – in their theory of corporate agency.

17 See also Comino in chapter 16 of this volume.

18 Pamela Bucy, 'Corporate Ethos: Reformulating Corporate Criminal Liability' (1991) 75 *Minnesota Law Review* 1095, p. 1101.

19 Ibid., p. 1178.

Like vicious structures and procedures, a vicious ethos is not reducible to role-bearer vice. To see this, consider just one aspect of ethos: norms. Cristina Bicchieri has developed the following influential definition of norms:

> A social norm is a rule of behaviour such that individuals prefer to conform to it on condition that they believe that (a) most people in their reference network conform to it (empirical expectation), and (b) that most people in their reference network believe they ought to conform to it (normative expectation).[20]

A social norm can be vicious without any of its individual adherents being vicious. To see this, consider damaging corporate norms, such as norms of overworking. Many people prefer to (in the economist's sense of 'prefer to', i.e., 'will in fact') adhere to such norms, because they believe that (a) most others in their corporation will conform and (b) most people in their corporation believe everyone ought to conform. Yet people might strongly prefer to work in a corporation where (a) and (b) are false, or strongly wish that (a) and (b) were false in their corporation. In this case, the reluctant conformers do not exhibit the relevant vice – say, greed or ruthless ambition – although the norm does.

Finally, consider corporate emotions. On the Aristotelian picture, full-blooded vice requires vicious emotions. This might seem a non-starter for corporations. On a standard picture, emotions include psychological components alongside phenomenal components: judgements and desires alongside 'qualia' or 'what-it-is-like-ness'.[21] We can account for corporations' psychological components (judgements and desires) using the functionalist picture: a corporation's judgements and desires are cashed out, ultimately, in terms of behavioural dispositions and internal mechanisms, including what the corporation rewards and punishes.[22] But what about the phenomenal components? Some argue that corporate phenomenal components are not essential for moral assessments of corporations' emotions: that when we assess corporations' emotions, it is enough to assess the psychological components in functionalist terms.[23] Others argue that corporations lack the phenomenal components, though we can assess the phenomenal components of members-qua-members (along lines described in the 'Traits of Role-Bearers'

20 Christina Bicchieri, *Norms in the Wild* (Oxford University Press 2017), p. 35.

21 Roland de Sousa, 'Emotion' in E.N. Zalta (ed.), *Stanford Encyclopaedia of Philosophy* (Metaphysics Research Lab Stanford University 2014) http://plato.stanford.edu/archives/spr2014/entries/emotion/.

22 Gunnar Björnsson and Kendy Hess, 'Corporate Crocodile Tears? On the Reactive Attitudes of Corporate Agents' (2017) 94 *Philosophy and Phenomenological Research* 273.

23 Ibid.

subsection).[24] Yet another option is that members' phenomenology is attributable to the corporation, when that phenomenology is experienced by members while performing their roles.[25] Without adjudicating between these options, notice that accounts *can* be given of (the moral significance of) corporate emotions, without positing any 'spooky' entity additional to the role-bearers.

In these ways – via structures, procedures, ethos (including norms) and emotions – corporations exhibit character traits irreducible to members' character traits. Of course, corporate traits are not easily discernible, especially to outsiders: corporations regularly engage in window dressing. To assess their structures, procedures, ethos and emotions, we often need deep insider knowledge. Even once we have that knowledge, our moral assessment is not complete. We need to know: *which* traits are virtues? Which are vices? The next section addresses this.

Which Traits Are Vices?

Aristotelianism

The most influential account of vice in contemporary normative philosophy is the neo-Aristotelian conception. On this conception, vice is tied to an entity's 'final cause', end-goal or telos. This is what the object is *for*: A knife's final cause is cutting; a car's final cause is transport; a human's final cause is flourishing as a rational animal. A virtue, then, is a disposition, robust across various situations, to act in certain ways with characteristic motivations, emotions, patterns of attention and so on, in accordance with one's final cause.[26] A vice is a disposition, robust across various situations, to act in certain ways with characteristic motivations, emotions, patterns of attention and so on, in *opposition to* one's final cause. Some contemporary neo-Aristotelians hold that virtues are traits that make an entity a *good instance* of their kind.[27] Others hold that virtues are traits that enable an entity to confront what is *typically difficult* for their kind.[28] Regardless, an assessment of an entity as virtuous or vicious can proceed only once that entity has been categorised into a kind, where one's 'kind' is determined by one's final cause.

24 Deborah Tollefsen, 'The Rationality of Collective Guilt' (2006) *Midwest Studies in Philosophy* 222. Stephanie Collins, '"The Government Should be Ashamed": On the Possibility of Organisations' Emotional Duties' (2018) 66 *Political Studies* 813.

25 Collins (n 3).

26 Rosalind Hursthouse, *On Virtue Ethics* (Oxford University Press 1999). Linda Zagzebski, *Virtues of the Mind* (Cambridge University Press 1996).

27 Jason Baehr, *The Inquiring Mind: On Intellectual Virtues and Virtue Epistemology* (Oxford University Press 2011).

28 Philippa Foot, 'Virtues and Vices' in P. Foot, *Virtues and Vices and Other Essays in Moral Philosophy* (Basil Blackwell 1978).

The trick, then, is to divide corporations into *kinds* according to their *teloi* – or else to specify some telos that is the final cause of all corporations – thus producing a barometer for measuring their virtue and vice. Here, we shouldn't stick too closely to Aristotle, whose division of entities into kinds is notoriously questionable. (He distinguished the telos of women (passive generation) from that of men (active generation), and distinguished the telos of natural slaves (who could flourish only vicariously through their masters' flourishing) from the telos of their masters (who could flourish in their own right).) To divide corporations into kinds, we must consider corporate purpose.

Corporate Purpose

The notion of corporate 'purpose' has a long history, traceable to antiquity.[29] For much of Western history, the legal recognition of a corporation's personhood was granted by the state conditional on the corporation serving a social purpose. It was only in the 19th century that the United Kingdom and United States ended the requirement for corporations to have a social purpose. Many corporations continued to have one *de facto*. Here, 'social purpose' is any activity that benefits those beyond the corporation, other than profit-making. A corporation's social purpose might include charitable donations, provision of public services or improved welfare for stakeholders.[30]

Some legal scholars have argued that such self-determined and self-asserted social purposes are valuable for instrumental reasons: an 'articulated, measurable, and enforceable corporate purpose' enables those who interact with, or participate in, the corporation to know what they are signing up for.[31] So, perhaps a corporation's Aristotelean 'final cause' is its 'social purpose'. If so, a corporation has 'vice' to the extent it fails to live up to – or, perhaps, fails to have – a social purpose. The *specific* virtues to which we should hold a given corporation are whichever traits further (or constitute) its social purpose; the vices we should deride it for are whichever traits impede (or decompose) its social purpose.

This conception of corporations' final causes fails to provide the action-guidance and critical purchase that justify concern with corporate vice: if a corporation's social purpose is *determined and asserted* by the corporation itself, then that purpose can hardly hope to *guide* the corporation. A

29 Leonardo Davoudi, Christopher McKenna, and Rowena Olegario, 'The Historical Role of the Corporation in Society' (2018) 6 *Journal of the British Academy* 17. David B. Guenther, 'Of Bodies Politic and Pecuniary: A Brief History of Corporate Purpose' (2020) 9 *Michigan Business and Entrepreneurial Law Review* 1.

30 Ibid., p. 20.

31 Jill E. Fisch and Steven Davidoff Solomon, 'Should Corporations Have a Purpose?' (2021) 99 *Faculty Scholarship at Penn Law* 1309.

corporation that looks to this purpose for guidance will spin in circles, like a dog chasing its tail. Perhaps more problematically, *others* can hardly condemn corporations for failing to follow purposes determined by corporations' actions: an entity cannot but live up to purposes that have been determined by actions it has already performed. Self-determined and self-asserted purposes, then, are not helpful.

One might object: we value self-determined and self-asserted purposes for humans (provided they don't harm others); so, why not for corporations? In response: virtue ethicists do not sort humans into *kinds for the purposes of determining virtue* by looking at humans' self-determined projects or plans. That is, the virtues and vices that apply to humans – bravery, honesty, greed, pride, etc. – do not arise from chosen projects or plans. They arise from humans' more general status as rational animals. Thus, humans cannot 'pick' which traits are virtues or vices for them *qua* human beings. Since we do not allow humans to do this, neither should we allow corporations to do so.

Instead, we might characterise corporations' final causes in general terms: perhaps what unites the kind 'corporation' – what *all* corporations are 'for' – is to have some social purpose or other. This provides action-guidance, instructing corporations to inculcate a social purpose within their structures, procedures, ethos and so on. And it enables critical purchase, licencing criticism of corporations that lack a social purpose. Indeed, a recent overview of corporate social purpose states that '[o]n the most abstract level ... the purpose of corporations is to facilitate valuable activities, such as the production of valuable goods and services in the case of businesses'.[32] Across interviews with 24 business leaders, these authors found overwhelming consensus that corporations should have a social purpose in this sense – but that corporations themselves should determine exactly which purpose, and how it is pursued.[33] This provides action-guidance and critical purchase, while accommodating corporations' self-conceptions.

This is fine, as far as it goes. But it does not go very far: it allows corporations to do whatever they want, as long as they have some social purpose or other. Sometimes, we have reasonable expectations that a corporation will (continue to) pursue a particular social purpose. Moreover, intuitively, different corporations have *different* final causes: what a bank is for differs from what a school is for, which differs from what a casino is for. This is not just a matter of these corporations having made different *choices*, as one might put on different clothes. It's a matter of them *being* different things: different kinds, constituted in different ways. The catalogue of virtues and vices is

32 Nien-He Hsieh, Marco Meyer, David Robin, and Jens Van 'T Klooster, 'The Social Purpose of Corporations' (2018) 6 *Journal of the British Academy* 49.

33 Ibid.

different for each, and our conception of corporate vice should capture that fact.

Corporate Telos and Human Capabilities

I now make a tentative suggestion that captures the preceding thoughts. My suggestion draws on neo-Aristotelean theory, which lends itself to an 'objective list' account of human flourishing: humans flourish to the extent they have (or, perhaps, 'have the genuine opportunity for') the items on a list of goods. The list might include knowledge, happiness, authenticity, friendship and so on – I am neutral between specific lists.[34] My suggestion is that we can determine the telos of a corporation by asking which item (on the list of objective human goods) is served by that corporation. Thus, a bank's telos might be human autonomy (via financial security); a school's telos might be human knowledge (via education); a casino's telos might be human play (via risk-taking). If these items are on one's preferred objective list of human goods, then these items constitute these organisations' respective purposes – and determine these organisations' distinctive virtues and vices.

This captures much of what goes on when we accuse corporations of being vicious. First, it captures the idea that there are many kinds of corporation, where what it means to be 'vicious' is different for each kind: the kinds are picked out by the different items on the list (or combinations thereof: some corporations serve more than one human good (autonomy and education, say), which implies there are as many kinds of corporation as there are *combinations* of human goods). Each kind has different traits as vices.

Second, the proposal captures the *value* of corporate diversity: the reason why it's good to have a variety of corporations, doing a variety of different things, is because they serve different (combinations of) human goods. It's unlikely that any one corporation will ever serve all items on any reasonable list. Together, though, the variety of corporations can provide a 'patchwork quilt' that covers all items.

34 There are many neo-Aristotelian objective lists. Thomas Hurka, *Perfectionism* (Clarendon Press 1993). Martha Nussbaum, *Creating Capabilities: the Human Development Approach* (Harvard University Press 2011). Guy Fletcher, 'A Fresh Start for the Objective-List Theory of Well-Being' (2013) 25 *Utilitas* 206. Gwen Bradford, 'Problems for Perfectionism' (2017) 29 *Utilitas* 344. One might also consider Lon Fuller's eight principles of the inner morality of law: that laws be general, public, nonretroactive, clear, noncontradictory, practicable, constant and congruent with how laws are administered. Lon Fuller, *The Morality of Law* (Yale University Press 1964), p. 39. I follow H.L.A. Hart (1965) in viewing Fuller's principles as instrumental to *effective legislation* (H.L.A. Hart, 'Book Review: Lon Fuller, *The Morality of Law*' (1965) 78 *Harvard Law Review* 1281) or perhaps encoding thin values like 'reciprocity' and 'respect for autonomy' (Colleen Murphy, 'Lon Fuller and the Moral Value of the Rule of Law' (2005) 24 *Law and Philosophy* 239), but not as encoding a substantive account of the flourishing human (or corporate) life. The latter is the subject of virtue and vice theory.

Third, the proposal avoids the unpalatable idea that corporate flourishing is intrinsically morally valuable: on the proposal, corporate flourishing is valuable as a *contributor* to human flourishing. To be sure, this is somewhat at odds with the general Aristotelian project: that project relativises virtue and vice to the distinctive flourishing of distinct kinds, without necessarily *instrumentalising* the kinds to one another. But corporations clearly are not natural and intrinsically valuable kinds like humans, walruses and oaks. They are artificial and instrumental kinds, like knives and cars. The 'flourishing' knife or car does something *for someone*. The same, I suggest, is true of corporations.[35]

Fourth, the proposal explains why we feel a sense of betrayal when a corporation goes 'off-script', suddenly claiming to serve a new and different social purpose. Our betrayal captures our sense that the particular good that we expected to be fostered by that corporation cannot straightforwardly be compensated by its now serving a different good. After all, the goods on the 'human flourishing' list are incommensurable, under Aristotelian objective list theories.

Fifth and finally, by categorising different types of corporations under different human goods, we can provide more action-guidance and critical purchase than the general 'social purpose' account outlined in the 'Corporate Purpose' subsection. We can also – I hope – reconceptualise our relationship to large organisations in a more positive and constructive light: casinos are not entirely evil; they are good to the extent they enable play. They fall into vice by departing from this purpose, for example by fostering gambling addictions that are anything but playful.

Conclusion

This chapter has analysed corporate vice as a real, important and useful notion. It is real because it is irreducible to vices of individuals. It is important because it serves fundamental needs of human beings, as enumerated on neo-Aristotelian theories which list the goods that make humans flourish. It is useful because it holds different corporations to different standards, while holding corporations accountable for character traits.

35 This proposal resonates with recent calls for 'corporate purpose.' See https://www.ecgi.global/content/corporate-purpose.

Part 2

Corporate Harms

Chapter 4

Ecocide, Evil and the Corporation

*Joanna Kyriakakis**

Introduction

If any field of law can be said to be especially concerned with evil, arguably that title goes to international criminal law. Also referred to as atrocity law, the field addresses crimes that 'shock the conscience of humanity' and represent 'the most serious crimes of concern to the international community as a whole' that 'must not go unpunished'.[1] This at least is the rhetoric, and indeed attention to the discourse of international criminal law is valuable in what it tells us of how actors within the system seek to justify the field's ambit.[2] In truth, what is included and excluded from the field is historically and politically contingent and reflects power relations among states.[3] Nonetheless, there is some basis for the claim that the core international crimes of genocide, crimes against humanity, war crimes and aggression, reflect particularly heinous conduct and are therefore fair contenders for harms that constitute evils, in so much as such a thing exists. Moreover, international criminal law may be seen to construct an evil–virtuous binary, whether explicitly, through

* My thanks to Professor Nicole Graham and participants in Professor Penny Crofts' 'Evil Corporations' symposium for comments on an early draft of this chapter.

1 Rome Statute of the International Criminal Court (opened for signature 17 July 1998, entered into force 1 July 2002) 2187 UNTS 90 ('Rome Statute') Preamble.

2 There is a growing literature that focuses upon the narrative implications of international criminal justice. See, e.g., Anette Bringedal Houge, 'Narrative Expressivism: A Criminological Approach to the Expressive Function of International Criminal Justice' (2019) 19 (3) *Criminology & Crim J* 277; Sofia Stolk, 'A Sophisticated Beast? On the Construction of an "Ideal" Perpetrator in the Opening Statements of International Criminal Trials' (2018) 29 (3) *EJIL* 677; Christine Schwöbel-Patel, 'The "Ideal" Victim of International Criminal Law' (2018) 29(3) *EJIL* 703; Barrie Sander, 'The Method Is the Message: Law, Narrative Authority and Historical Contestation in International Criminal Courts' (2018) 19 *Melb J Int'l L* 299.

3 See, e.g., Christine Schwöbel (ed.), *Critical Approaches to International Criminal Law: An Introduction* (Routledge 2015).

DOI: 10.4324/9781003402534-7

communicative practices,[4] or implicitly, through the individualisation and criminalisation of what might otherwise be understood as system crimes.[5]

Criminalising mass atrocities is a project that has been associated with a number of objectives.[6] Some are common to any criminal justice system, such as deterrence and retribution. Others are unique to the political sphere in which atrocity law operates, such as creating a historical record and ending the impunity that tends to prevail for perpetrators of atrocity crimes. Increasingly, however, international criminal law is justified on expressivist grounds: by reference to the meanings that are communicated to relevant audiences through the social practices constitutive of the criminal law.[7] Expressivist theories focus upon the ways in which criminalisation and punishment serve to shape and restore social values and social solidarity around such values, and to communicate messages about the proper valuation of victims.[8] The law as a performance of values is critical.

It is in part on the basis of the expressive functions of international criminal law that the push to include corporations in the jurisdiction of international criminal courts has been justified,[9] and so too the related effort to introduce ecocide as a fifth international crime.[10] In this chapter I explore present debates in international criminal law on a crime of ecocide from the perspective that ecocide is a paradigmatic state-corporate crime and one, moreover, that emerges inevitably from growth capitalism.[11] In an exploratory spirit, I reflect on ecocide as a potential fifth category of international

4 For specific examples see, Sofia Stolk, 'A Sophisticated Beast? On the Construction of an "Ideal" Perpetrator in the Opening Statements of International Criminal Trials' (2018) 29 (3) *EJIL* 677; Christine Schwöbel-Patel, 'The "Ideal" Victim of International Criminal Law' (2018) 29(3) *EJIL* 703.

5 On system crimes, see André Nollkaemper and Harmen van der Wilt (eds), *System Criminality in International Law* (CUP 2009).

6 Indeed, the project of international criminal justice has been criticised for an over-abundance of aims, some of which may conflict: see, Mirjan Damaska, 'What is the Point of International Criminal Justice?' (2008) 83 *Chi-Kent L.Rev.* 329.

7 On the turn to expressivist theories, see Barrie Sander, 'The Expressive Limits of International Criminal Justice: Victim Trauma and Local Culture in the Iron Cage of the Law' (2015) 5(3) *ESIL Conference Paper Series* 1, 2–4.

8 On expressive theories in the context of international criminal justice, see: Barrie Sander, 'Justifying International Criminal Punishment: A Critical Perspective' in Morten Bergsmo and Emiliano J Buis (eds), *Philosophical Foundations of International Criminal Law: Foundational Concepts* (Torkel Opsahl Academic EPublisher 2019) 167, 192–232.

9 Joanna Kyriakakis, *Corporations, Accountability and International Criminal Law: Industry and Atrocity* (Edward Elgar 2021) 266–271.

10 See, e.g., Darryl Robinson, 'Ecocide – Puzzles and Possibilities' (2022) 20 *JICJ* 313, 317–318; Patrick J. Keenan, 'International Criminal Law and Climate Change' (2019) 37 *BU Int'l LJ* 89; Eliana Teresa Cusato, 'Beyond Symbolism: Problems and Prospects with Prosecuting Environmental Destruction before the ICC' (2017) 15 *JICJ* 491, 505.

11 See 'Ecocide, Capitalism and International Criminal Law' below.

crime in two ways that are prompted by the theme of the book. The first is the perceived 'evil' of ecocide, which might be said to justify its inclusion in the corpus of international criminal law. To explore this idea, among other things I consider how contemporary philosophical literature on the nature of evil might inform debates as to the proper scope of an international crime of ecocide. The second matter to which I then briefly turn is the potential implications of adopting an international crime of ecocide in terms of the ways in which atrocity law might construct the 'evil' and 'virtuous' corporation, in light of the field's tendency toward such binaries.

Ecocide, Capitalism and International Criminal Law

At its broadest, ecocide can be described as 'environmental destruction on a substantial scale'.[12] It is a phenomenon that is linked to state-corporate crime both in the sense that states explicitly condone environmental destruction by corporations (for example, by legalising damage through the provision of concessions or permits) and in the sense that states routinely fail to regulate corporate environmental damage (for example, by failing to pursue corporate reparations or remediation) due to shared state-corporate goals.[13] Some of what is theorised in criminological literature as forms of ecocide constitute harms that are currently lawful. Green criminology accentuates that it is by studying environmental 'crime' broadly that we identify how much serious environmental damage is presently legal and accepted as an 'inherent consequence of industrial activities that are seen to provide significant economic benefits'.[14] A wider perspective also keeps us alert to the function of social power in the perpetration of such violence.[15] Both insights are important to any project of an aspirational nature, which aims to shift normative boundaries, including through reform of the criminal law.[16]

Recent neo-Marxist literature on the phenomenon of ecocide seeks to explain the mechanics of how growth-driven capitalism, and the key social actors within such a system, inevitably produce large-scale environmental destruction.[17] Such works expand upon Marx's treatment of ecology and

12 Rob White, 'Ecocide and the Carbon Crimes of the Powerful' (2018) 37 *U Tas L Rev* 95, 98.
13 These two forms of state-corporate crime are often referred to as state-initiated corporate crime and state-facilitated corporate crime, respectively: Ronald C. Kramer, Raymond J. Michalowski and David Kauzlarich, ''The Origins and Development of the Concept and Theory of State-Corporate Crime' (2002) 48 *Crime & Delinquency* 263, 263–282, 271–272.
14 White, (n 12).
15 Ibid.
16 Ibid.
17 Summarising some of this literature, see: Tim Lindgren, 'Ecocide, Genocide and the Disregard of Alternative Life-systems' (2018) 22(4) *Intl J Hum Rts* 525, 528–531; Michael J. Lynch, Averi Fegadel and Michael A. Long, 'Green Criminology and State-Corporate Crime: The

capitalism to describe the ways in which the global drive for constant economic growth and capital accumulation posited as foundational social goods place ever increasing pressures on the natural environment. This dynamic has been described in terms of a 'metabolic rift'[18] in the exchange between humans and nature, whereby the capitalist mode of production fails to account for the necessary metabolic reciprocity between humans and nature which is required to reproduce natural wealth.[19] Metabolic reciprocity or social metabolism refers to 'the process by which peoples take nutrient matter and energy from their environments, digest, and give back in return'.[20] The ways in which growth capitalism necessitates environmental destruction has also been linked to the system's economic logic which prioritises exchange value (for example, of commodities that can be exchanged on the market) over use value and the implications of this valuation system for the way in which nature is regarded.[21] Limits to productive growth created by nature are barriers to be overcome, rather than accounted for.[22]

The implication of this economic logic is to structurally embed environmental destruction as a recurring and ever intensifying phenomenon.[23] As Lindgren argues, this fact is critical to any debate regarding the role of international criminal law in relation to ecocide:

> Large-scale ecological destruction is a structurally reoccurring phenomenon embedded in the economic logics that buttress and define modern industrial societies and a phenomenon prone to further intensification as modern industrial societies continue to grow beyond their ecological limits. The lack of a crime against ecocide is hence not only a failure to criminalise individual acts of ecocide, but a failure in providing legal barriers against the structural continuation and intensification of ecological harm – barriers that may foster the rethinking of systemically unsustainable and destructive methods of modern human organisation and its asymmetrical, contrary to reciprocal, relationships with nature.[24]

Ecocide-Genocide Nexus with Examples from Nigeria' (2021) 23(2) *J Genocide Research* 236, 241–243.

18 This description of Marx's theory was coined by John Bellamy Foster: see, e.g., John Bellamy Foster, 'Marx's Theory of Metabolic Rift: Classical Foundations for Environmental Sociology' (1999) 105 *Am. J. Soc.* 366–405.

19 Lindgren (n 17) 528–530.

20 Ariel Salleh, 'From Metabolic Rift to "Metabolic Value": Reflections on Environmental Sociology and the Alternative Globalization Movement' (2010) 23(2) *Organization & Environment* (n 17) 206, 206.

21 Lindgren (n 17) 530.

22 Ibid. 530–531.

23 Ibid. 531.

24 Ibid.

By failing to address ecocide, international law risks becoming complicit in the structural environmental violence of modern industrial societies. This is a very real risk given international law's sharing of the same epistemological roots that underpin modern industrial economies,[25] which include the devaluation of social life-systems that are closely entwined with nature.[26]

Environmental violence as a reflection of the devaluation of certain social ways of life also helps explain the link that has been drawn between ecocide and genocide. The link between genocide and ecocide was arguably implicit in the earliest articulation of a concept of genocide by Raphael Lemkin, via the connecting element of culture.[27] Environmental devastation can bring about, in extreme circumstances, threats to the ongoing physical survival of a group. But what concerned Lemkin, and others, is the way in which environmental devastation may bring about a loss of culture so profound that it challenges the social survival of a group.[28] This potentiality has also been tied to the dynamics of the global political economy. For example, Crook, Short and South demonstrate how the destruction of environments as a product of global capitalism has operated as a structural technique of cultural genocide, via policies of ongoing colonisation and imperialism, in relation to particular indigenous peoples.[29] The project to include ecocide as an atrocity crime can thus be understood as a corrective to the way in which our understanding of genocidal violence has become limited to the pursuit of the physical destruction of a group. The ways in which the growth of productive capacity required by capitalism has been pursued globally have also been linked to a North/South divide among states in terms of environmental impacts and material benefits – with an unequal flow of costs and benefits from the Global South to the Global North.[30]

Because of the dynamics described above, ecocide by its very nature will implicate business actors in a way that may well be unique among international

25 Ibid. 536–539.

26 Ibid.

27 Martin Crook, Damien Short and Nigel South, 'Ecocide, Genocide, Capitalism and Colonialism: Consequences for Indigenous Peoples and Glocal Ecosystems Environments' (2018) 22(3) *Theo.Crim.* 298, 305–306. For Lemkin's seminal text, see: Raphael Lemkin, *Axis Rule in Occupied Europe. Laws of Occupation, Analysis of Government. Proposals for Redress* (Carnegie Endowment for International Peace 1944) e.g., 79.

28 Martin Crook, Damien Short and Nigel South, 'Ecocide, Genocide, Capitalism and Colonialism: Consequences for Indigenous Peoples and Glocal Ecosystems Environments' (2018) 22(3) *Theo. Crim.* 298.

29 Ibid.

30 Michael J. Lynch, Averi Fegadel and Michael A. Long, 'Green Criminology and State-Corporate Crime: The Ecocide-Genocide Nexus with Examples from Nigeria' (2021) 23(2) *J Genocide Research* 236, 241–243.

crimes.[31] This fact animates tensions for those who maintain the importance of law's public/private divide.[32] While it has long been accepted that private actors can commit international crimes,[33] a pivot towards such actors in international criminal trials would involve a change in emphasis from the almost exclusive focus to date on government and military actors, who tend to be seen as central to the commission of atrocities.[34] Applying atrocity law to business actors raises unique questions and challenges, not least of which is the question of proving fault where a private person contributes to an atrocity in the context of activity that is otherwise considered legitimate and socially valuable.[35] This concern is reflected in definitional debates in respect of a crime of ecocide, and is taken up further below.

Capturing the 'Evil' of Ecocide

At present, international criminal law does not address environmental harm except in peripheral and highly limited ways.[36] The Office of the Prosecutor of the International Criminal Court has committed to using what tools are available to it to pursue environmental violence,[37] but those will remain limited short of an expansion of its jurisdiction. While a movement towards the introduction of a fifth international crime of ecocide has existed for some time,[38] attention to this idea has surged in recent years, most likely as a

31 An exception might be the war crime of pillage, which is likewise strongly associated with private actors: James Stewart, *Corporate War Crimes: Prosecuting the Pillage of Natural Resources* (Open Society Institute 2011).

32 On the politically constructed nature of this divide, as a mechanism for shielding areas of activity from the allocation of public goals, see: Dan Priel, 'The Political Origins of English Private Law' (2013) 40 *JL & Soc'y* 481.

33 See, e.g., the trials of major industrialists before the American Military Tribunal for international crimes committed during World War II: *United States v. Friedrich Flick* in 6 Trials of War Criminals before the Nuremberg Military Tribunals under Control Council Law No. 10 (1952); *United States v. Carl Krauch* in 7 and 8 Trials of War Criminals before the Nuremberg Military Tribunals under Control Council Law No. 10 (1952); *United States v, Alfried Krupp* in 9 Trials of War Criminals before the Nuremberg Military Tribunals under Control Council Law No. 10 (1952).

34 Carsten Stahn, 'Liberals vs Romantics: Challenges of an Emerging Corporate International Criminal Law' (2018) 50 *Case W.Res.J.Int'l L.* 91, 107–108.

35 Kyriakakis (n 9) 220–230.

36 Ammar Bustami and Marie-Christine Hecken, 'Perspectives for a New International Crime Against the Environment: International Criminal Responsibility for Environmental Degradation under the Rome Statute' (2021) 11(1) *Goettingen J Int'l L* 145, 153–162.

37 ICC Office of the Prosecutor, 'Policy Paper on Case Selection and Prioritisation' (15 September 2016) [41].

38 For a detailed history, see: Anastacia Greene, 'The Campaign to Make Ecocide an International Crime: Quixotic Quest Or Moral Imperative' (2019) 30 *Fordham Envtl L Rev* 1, 2–26.

response to ever-increasing manifestations of planetary decline.[39] This attention has resulted most recently in the production of two expert group opinions on what the elements of such a crime should be.[40] While the prospect of the introduction of such a crime probably remains remote, the groundwork to do so is being laid in increasingly sophisticated and detailed ways.

The case as to *why criminalisation*, and, moreover, why *international criminalisation*, of a category of serious environmental crime has been explored for some time now.[41] Arguments in favour include the claim that ecocide 'satisfies the hallmarks of other international crimes: the harms are devastating, the impacts transcend boundaries, and national regulation is insufficient'.[42] As mentioned above, devastating environmental damage produced by industrial activity often reflects state-corporate collusion in either the production of the harm or in the protection of the perpetrator of the harm (or both), which may be said to animate international criminal law's unique counter-impunity function.[43] This refers to the idea that international criminalisation is warranted because it cannot be left to states to pursue the harm given the stakes for states in maintaining impunity for such conduct. Megret goes further and argues that ecocide may well transcend traditional bases for criminalising certain behaviours internationally, in that it constitutes a 'new category of global crimes that endanger the conditions of global communal life'.[44] Ecocide fills a blind spot of the field by addressing uniquely grave risks to human life writ large.[45]

The fact that devastating environmental damage is an inherent product of modern industrial societies, which may too often be legalised or tolerated by the state, might also press in favour of international criminalisation for reasons relating to the expressive function of international criminal law. As mentioned, it is increasingly accepted that international criminal law has a singular role in signalling the core values of the international community.

39 See, e.g., Ludwik A. Teclaff, 'Beyond Restoration – The Case of Ecocide' (1994) 34 *Nat Resources J* 933, 934–939 (linking attention to the problem of ecocide to the increase in globally catastrophic environmental disasters). Indeed, a significant focus of contemporary literature on ecocide focuses particularly upon climate crime: see, for example, Patrick J. Keenan, 'International Criminal Law and Climate Change' (2019) 37 *BU Int'l LJ* 89.

40 Stop Ecocide Foundation, *Independent Legal Expert Panel for the Legal Definition of Ecocide: Commentary and Core Text* (June 2021); UCLA Promise Institute for Human Rights Definition of Ecocide (2021), available in Robinson, (n 10) Appendix A.

41 See, e.g., Frederic Megret, 'The Problem of an International Criminal Law of the Environment' (2011) 36 *Colum J Envtl L* 195

42 Robinson (n 10) 317. See also, Megret (n 41) 239–240.

43 Making a similar argument in relation to corporate atrocity crime in general, see: Joanna Kyriakakis, 'Corporations before International Criminal Courts: Implications for the International Criminal Justice Project' (2017) 30(1) *LJIL* 221.

44 Megret (n 41) 241.

45 Robinson (n 10) 317.

This expressive effect has been highlighted as a particularly critical reason for the introduction of an international crime of ecocide, in order to shift the normative boundaries of what is acceptable and tolerated in the pursuit of economic growth; in order to shift and cement societal expectations.[46] Its introduction into international criminal law has also been linked to the expressive possibilities of shining a spotlight on the crimes of the powerful[47] and to decolonising international criminal law.[48]

Some of these justifications for introducing an international atrocity crime of ecocide rely substantially on the way in which the crime is defined. There are troubling implications if the definition of the crime is such as to cast the net of culpability too widely. Those accused of international crimes face global stigma, the impact of which needs to be taken seriously. Apart from fairness to those facing the resources and power of the international community of states, there is an independent value in ensuring that international criminal justice remains directed at only the gravest breaches of our shared values in terms of maintaining the legitimacy of the system. The legitimacy of international criminal institutions is linked to their effectiveness in communicating values.[49] Considerations like these may tend one towards preferring conservative limits on the scope of the offence, at least at the international level.[50] At the same time, the crime must be defined in ways that realistically capture the harm that generates the relevant moral outrage in the first place and, if the law's expressive potential is taken seriously, in ways that will meaningfully curb the oftentimes normalised behaviours that threaten humanity. If a crime of ecocide is defined so narrowly that it fails to capture egregious but non-deviant examples of corporate environmental violence, it may do more harm than if it were not to exist at all.

The tension between these considerations is evident in the literature on how a crime of ecocide should be circumscribed. There are two main fault lines running across those debates[51] The first relates to the objective aspects

46 See, for example, Robinson (n 10) 317–318; Keenan (2019); Eliana Teresa Cusato, 'Beyond Symbolism: Problems and Prospects with Prosecuting Environmental Destruction before the ICC' (2017) 15 *JICJ* 491, 505.

47 White (n 12).

48 Lindgren (n 17) 539–543.

49 Richard McAdams, 'The Expressive Powers of Law: Theories and Limits' 136 (HUP 2015) 253–255; Margaret DeGuzman, *Shocking the Conscience of Humanity: Gravity and the Legitimacy of International Criminal Law* (OUP 2020).

50 Robinson (n 10) 321–325.

51 These two issues are not exhaustive. Other key questions include: how the crime ought to be pursued, for example, through a suppression convention or as a crime within the jurisdiction of existing international criminal institutions; how the crime should relate to existing principles of international environmental law; what causation will be sufficient to ground personal responsibility; and how to deal with conduct that is permitted under domestic law.

of the crime; the threshold for severity of harm before it becomes an appropriate matter for international criminalisation. Proposals on this element have included that the environmental damage must be 'widespread', 'long-term', 'severe' or 'extensive', or that it should cause the destruction or loss of ecosystems, or some combination thereof.[52] This impact threshold is critical, in that it will significantly limit or expand the scope of the crime depending upon which standard is preferred, and, in particular, whether they are adopted cumulatively or alternately. Regardless of the precise objective criterion adopted, what is clear is a general consensus that the crime would only capture conduct capable of resulting in quantitatively and qualitatively extreme environmental harms.[53] The second issue relates to the subjective aspect of the crime; the mental element (or *mens rea)* which then grounds personal culpability for creating the risk of actualisation of extreme environmental harm. This second aspect of the crime is particularly critical to the question of business liability. The mental element upon which responsibility for international crimes does and ought to rest has long been a point of discussion in the literature on corporations and international crimes.[54]

Like human rights abuses, environmental damage associated with business often occurs as a consequence of seeking to achieve socially desirable aims such as productivity, development and profit rather than as an intended outcome.[55] Environmental harms may be tolerated on the basis of promises to mitigate those harms through environmental rehabilitation, which is then inadequate or does not eventuate. Examples of this kind include the environmental harm associated with the extractive industries such as the gouging of open-pit mines, the disposal of mine tailings, the production of climate-

52 See, e.g., Stop Ecocide Foundation, *Independent Legal Expert Panel for the Legal Definition of Ecocide: Commentary and Core Text* (June 2021); UCLA Promise Institute for Human Rights Definition of Ecocide (2021), available in Robinson, (n 10), Appendix A; Polly Higgins, *Eradicating Ecocide: Laws and Governance to Prevent the Destruction of Our Planet* (Shepheard-Walwyn, 2010).

53 Importantly, the leading recent expert definition of ecocide posit it as a crime of endangerment, rather than of material outcome: Stop Ecocide Foundation, *Independent Legal Expert Panel for the Legal Definition of Ecocide: Commentary and Core Text* (June 2021) 12.

54 See, e.g., Philipp Ambach, 'International Criminal Responsibility of Transnational Corporate Actors Doing Business in Zones of Armed Conflict' in Freya Baetens (ed.), *Investment Law within International Criminal Law: Integrationist Perspectives* (CUP 2013); Hans Vest, 'Business Leaders and Modes of Individual Criminal Responsibility under International Law' (2010) 8 *JICJ* 851; Norman Farrell, 'Attributing Criminal Liability to Corporate Actors: Some Lessons from the International Tribunals' (2010) 8 *JICJ* 873; International Commission of Jurists (ICJ), *Report of the International Commission of Jurists Expert Legal Panel on Corporate Complicity in International Crimes* (ICJ 2008) Vol. 2.

55 For a recent analysis of the profile of select cases involving allegations of corporate human rights abuses and environmental degradation, see: Wim Huisman and Daniel Sidoli, 'Corporations, Human Rights and the Environmental Degradation–Corruption Nexus' (2019) 22(1) *APJEL* 66.

impacting pollution or the use of outdated technologies, such as gas flaring. Alternatively, environmental damage may be a foreseeable but unintended consequence of hazardous activity, brought about by inadequate attention to risk. Examples of this kind include the 2009 oil spill in Australian territorial waters caused by a well blowout at the Montara oil field[56] and the 2019 Brumadinho dam disaster in Brazil.[57] These kinds of environmental externalities and catastrophic environmental disasters rightly create moral outrage for their devastating impacts and the ways in which the harms could have been avoided.

In the context of atrocity law, the general view is that the unique heinousness of atrocity crimes lies not only in the abject nature of the harm in question but, to a significant degree, in the presence of a high degree of moral culpability. Moral culpability is, in turn, firmly associated with malicious intent in the sense of intending the harmful outcome, even if one does so for instrumental purposes.[58] This idea is reflected, for example, in the default fault standard set out in Article 30 of the Rome Statute.[59] To adopt the same approach in respect of ecocide, however, would limit the crime to those who have sought to bring about extreme environmental damage intentionally, in the sense of having meant to cause that consequence or acting with the awareness that it would occur in the ordinary course of events. This would be likely to significantly curtail the relevance of ecocide to environmental devastation arising from corporate activities where the wrong lies in wilful blindness, toleration of extreme environmental harm, gross negligence or otherwise inadequate attention to risk. The crime would thus have little to no relevance in confronting the structural embeddedness of serious environmental damage as a tolerated, non-deviant and sometimes even mundane risk/product of doing business.

Rightly, there is significant debate over the appropriate *mens rea* element of a crime of ecocide, which reflects awareness that the ordinary standard of intent in this case may not suffice.[60] Proposals vary from, at one end of the spectrum, intent or, at a minimum, subjective recklessness, to, at other end of the spectrum, objective recklessness, 'reasonably foreseeable intent',[61]

56 *Sanda v. PTTEP Australasia (Ashmore Cartier) Pty Ltd (No. 7)* [2021] FCA 237.

57 Luiz Henrique Silva Rotta et al., 'The 2019 Brumadinho Tailings Dam Collapse: Possible Cause and Impacts of the Worst Human and Environmental Disaster in Brazil' (2020) 90 *Int J Appl Earth Obs Geoinformation* 102119.

58 See, e.g., Harmen van der Wilt, 'Mental Blockades in the Recognition of Mens Rea in Corporations', in Grietje Baars and André Spicer (eds), *The Corporation: A Critical, Multi-Disciplinary Handbook* (CUP 2017).

59 According to Article 30, criminal responsibility (unless otherwise provided) depends upon intent and knowledge, which can be demonstrated by an awareness that a consequence will occur in the ordinary course of events: Rome Statute (n 1).

60 Indeed, it has been suggested that the 'mens rea element might be the most disputed element of the concept of ecocide': Bustami and Hecken (n 36) 180.

61 Crook and Short (n 29) 311; Lindgren (n 17) 541.

or even strict liability.[62] Standards on the lower end of the spectrum are likely to encounter particularly robust opposition in international criminal law circles, for reasons set out earlier. However, both recent expert proposals for a crime of ecocide adopt a subjective recklessness standard, though one adopts a 'likely to cause' knowledge standard,[63] while the other adopts knowledge of the 'substantial likelihood' of damage as the standard.[64] There are arguments that support going further than this, however. For example, there are precedents within international criminal law for reducing the fault standard to include a failure to act reasonably in light of known, or knowable, risks. This is the case with command responsibility where the wrong lies in the capacities of the commander to act and their failure to do so, in the context of an expectation that they will exercise a relevant degree of oversight of their troops.[65] Command responsibility may, in fact, have unique relevance to debates around the evils of corporate harms,[66] in the sense that there is a special obligation to prevent foreseeable harms where the actor's positionality in respect of the harm, their power to intervene and their available resources to do so, warrant it. The idea that corporate resources should be directed to prevent certain particularly serious risks from eventuating is gaining traction in debates over the future of corporate crime regulation, as reflected in the serious consideration being given to corporate failure to prevent offences covering human rights abuses or serious economic crime in global business contexts.[67] There are, moreover, ways of signalling the distinct nature of culpability for this type of wrongdoing through the crime label, for example, through the differentiation of dereliction of duty or failure to prevent offences from specific substantive atrocity crimes, and via punishment.[68]

Philosophies of evil might also help justify the adoption of a lowered mental element in the context of ecocide. There are two main approaches that have emerged in contemporary secular philosophical literature as to what

62 Polly Higgins, Damien Short and Nigel South, 'Protecting the planet: a proposal for a law of ecocide' (2013) 59 *Crime Law Soc Change* 251, 262.

63 UCLA Promise Institute for Human Rights Definition of Ecocide (2021), available Robinson, (n 10).

64 Stop Ecocide Foundation, *Independent Legal Expert Panel for the Legal Definition of Ecocide: Commentary and Core Text* (June 2021) 11.

65 While lower than other modes of liability, the mental element for command responsibility remains in a state of uncertainty: see, e.g., Carmel O'Sullivan, 'New court, Same division: The Bemba case as an Illustration of the continued confusion regarding the Command Responsibility Doctrine' (2022) 35 *LJIL* 661, 668–671.

66 See, e.g., Desislava Stoitchkova, *Towards Corporate Criminal Liability in International Criminal Law* (Intersentia 2010) 125–133.

67 See, e.g., Australian Law Reform Commission, *Final Report - Corporate Criminal Responsibility* (ALRC Report 136, 2020) 447–458; UK Law Commission, *Corporate Criminal Liability – An Options Paper* (10 June 2022) Ch. 8.

68 Megret (n 41) 232–233.

differentiates an evil action from morally lesser culpable wrongs. The first encompasses theories that emphasise the psychology of the person doing the harmful act. Psychologically thick accounts of evil focus upon some morally extreme quality in the perpetrator's motives or response to harms as being the hallmark of evil. These include harm motivated by malice (in the sense of desiring the harm to the victim for non-instrumental reasons) or by sadistic pleasure or through a psychological process of silencing moral considerations that ought to make one rule out performing a harmful act.[69] By contrast, psychologically thin accounts of evil reject the proposition that evil actions 'share a narrowly circumscribed set of motives but can be done for all sorts of reasons, and by a very diverse set of moral agents.'[70] Such accounts emphasise the harm itself, its sheer quantitative scale, as the feature that distinguishes evils from lesser wrongs.[71] For example, Claudia Card, in her work on evil arising from an analysis specifically of atrocities, describes evils as 'reasonably foreseeable intolerable harms produced by inexcusable wrongs'.[72] Moreover, in these accounts, culpability is not sacrificed. Instead, it is aligned to the sheer magnitude of the harm that one is expected to act to avoid.[73] Theories of evil thus invite us to consider how the relationship between the objective and subjective elements of a crime interplay. Given the extremely high threshold for an environmental harm to meet the criteria of ecocide, the culpability of the person causing the harm lies in the abject failure of ignoring or tolerating such risk in circumstances where it could reasonably have been avoided; a failure that, moreover, grounds our intuitive or pre-cognitive horror at those who permit such disasters to occur for personal gain.[74]

Notably, psychologically thin accounts of evil share something of a debt to Hannah Arendt's work on the banality of evil.[75] Arendt in her study of the trial of Adolf Eichmann and his role in the Holocaust,[76] famously demonstrated how evil can be 'banal' in the sense that a person can contribute to evil deeds that are structurally enabled through bureaucratic systems by thoughtlessly succumbing their individual agency to the greater animating

69 Luke Russell, *Being Evil* (OUP 2020) Ch. 3.

70 Luke Russell, 'Defining Evil Actions: Different Approaches', in Thomas Nys and Stephen de Wijze (eds), *The Routledge Handbook of the Philosophy of Evil* (Routledge 2019) 251.

71 Russell (n 69) Ch 4.

72 Claudia Card, *Confronting Evils: Terrorism, Torture, Genocide* (CUP 2010) 16.

73 Russell (n 69) 78–84.

74 Defending the relevance of pre-cognitive emotional responses to certain harms as an appropriate measure for identifying evil actions, see Stephen de Wijze, 'Defining the Concept of Evil: Insights from our Pre-cognitive Responses' in Thomas Nys and Stephen de Wijze (eds), *The Routledge Handbook of the Philosophy of Evil* (Routledge 2019).

75 Russell (n 69) 69.

76 Hannah Arendt, *Eichmann in Jerusalem: A Report on the Banality of Evil* (Viking Press 1963).

historical forces of which they are a mere part; forces that, for the perpetrator, render individual instances of violence and individual moral agency superfluous.[77] Arendt's thesis has a unique resonance in the context of corporate crime, which shares features in common with the global phenomena with which Arendt was concerned that render certain people and values superfluous; and which structurally embed and naturalise harms that would otherwise horrify. Arguably, it is the very normality of some atrocities, and not that perpetrators deviate from the ordinary or how they understand their own wrong, that warrants international criminal law's sanction.[78]

The Narrative Implications of Corporate Ecocide

One of the concerns of philosophers who are sceptical about the utility of a concept of evil is the implications of such language for demonising those who do certain acts or cause certain harms. The concern is that the language of evil and of evil-doer can serve to render the subject of such a label beyond the boundary of the human; as monstrous and unknowable; for whom redemption is beyond the pale. This may not only tend to preclude, rather than enable, our understanding of what causes extreme or shocking harms to occur, it may also be used to justify our own treatment of 'evil' persons in ways that go beyond proper moral limits.[79] Similar concerns are reflected in narrative studies of the communicative implications of international trials and how offenders are cast in such trials in order to explain the heinousness of their moral wrong and how they differ from us. For example, Stolk, and others, have demonstrated how international criminal law discourse struggles to move beyond stereotypes to more nuanced representations of perpetrators, of victims and of the harms they produce/suffer. Trial narratives can tend to construct crude binaries of the monstrous and the innocent.[80] To some extent, the rhetoric of the monstrous is reflected in the label sometimes used

77 For a nuanced account of Arendt's theory of the 'banality' of evil and how it links to her earlier work on radical evil, see: Peg Birmingham, 'Hannah Arendt's Double Account of Evil: Political Superfluousness and Moral Thoughtlessness' in Thomas Nys and Stephen de Wijze (eds), *The Routledge Handbook of the Philosophy of Evil* (Routledge 2019).

78 For an excellent defence of this view, see: Saira Mohamed, 'Deviance, Aspiration, and the Stories We Tell: Reconciling Mass Atrocity and the Criminal Law' (2015) 124 *Yale L J* 1628. For a contrary view, see: Itamar Mann, 'Eichmann's Mistake: The Problem of Thoughtlessness in International Criminal Law' (2020) XXXIII (1) *Canadian Journal of Law & Jurisprudence* 145.

79 Setting out and responding to some of these critiques of a concept of evil, see: Eve Garrard, 'Does the Term "Evil" Have any Explanatory Power?' in Thomas Nys and Stephen de Wijze (eds), *The Routledge Handbook of the Philosophy of Evil* (Routledge 2019).

80 Sofia Stolk, 'A Sophisticated Beast? On the Construction of an "Ideal" Perpetrator in the Opening Statements of International Criminal Trials' (2018) 29 (3) *EJIL* 677; Christine Schwöbel-Patel, 'The "Ideal"' Victim of International Criminal Law' (2018) 29(3) *EJIL* 70.

to describe perpetrators of international crimes as '*hostis humani generis*' (enemies of all mankind).[81]

There is also a line of critical thought that challenges the way in which international criminal law is likely to narrate corporate crimes in light of the field's tendency to rhetorical binaries and international law's rootedness in ideologies that underpin modern industrial economies. By contrast to the concern that perpetrators will be cast as monstrous, however, the anxiety is the way in which trial narratives are likely to reinstate the business actor into good society; to affirm their character and to cast their conduct as socially legitimate and well meaning.[82] To illustrate, in their separate analyses of the international criminal trials of leading industrialists after World War II for their role in Germany's atrocities (aggressive warfare, plunder, slave labour and mass murder), Baars, Priemel and Lustig have each demonstrated ways in which enduring narratives produced by those processes served to either downplay the role of industry in the atrocities or went further and constituted apologia for corporate conduct.[83]

The concern that criminal law is more likely to enable and facilitate corporate violence than to censure and curb it, is an enduring one in criminological literature.[84] The risk that international criminal law will align itself with capitalism's violence, rather than provide a mechanism for challenging it, shadows the current effort towards an international crime of ecocide. The scope of the crime is even more critical in light of this risk.[85] As discussed above, within justifiable boundaries, the mental element of ecocide should be such as to capture the heinous wrong that occurs when corporations tolerate

81 For an excellent exploration of the various implications of the use of this rhetoric, see the series of papers making up a special edition of (2018) 47(2) *Netherlands J of L Philosophy* 107–199.

82 Grietje Baars, '"It's Not Me, It's the Corporation": The Value of Corporate Accountability in the Global Political Economy' (2016) 4(1) *Lond. Rev. Int. Law* 127, eg 131–133, 145, 158.

83 Grietje Baars, 'Capitalism's Victor's Justice? The Hidden Stories behind the Prosecution of Industrialists Post-WWII' in Kevin Jon Heller and Gerry Simpson (eds), *The Hidden Histories of War Crimes Trials* (OUP 2013); Kim C. Priemel, 'Tales of Totalitarianism: Conflicting Narratives in the Industrialist Cases at Nuremberg' in Kim C. Priemel and Alexa Stiller (eds), *Reassessing the Nuremberg Military Tribunals: Transitional Justice, Trial Narratives, and Historiography* (Berghahn Books 2012); Doreen Lustig, 'The Nature of the Nazi State and the Question of International Criminal Responsibility of Corporate Officials at Nuremberg: Revisiting Franz Neumann's Concept of Behemoth at the Industrialist Trials' (2011) 43 *NYU. J.Int'l Law & Pol.* 965.

84 See, e.g., Fiona Haines and Kate MacDonald, 'Grappling with Injustice: Corporate Crime, Multinational Business and Interrogation of Law in Context' (2021) 25(2) *Theo. Crim.* 284, 284–285.

85 See, e.g., Lindgren (n 17) 541–542 (advocating the importance of a lowered mental element of 'reasonably foreseeable intent') for a crime of ecocide to achieve goals he advocates as urgent).

or ignore extreme environmental risks. To do otherwise risks sending the message that ecocide is principally aberrant behaviour rather than often non-deviant. Strategies surrounding how corporate prosecutions for atrocity are pursued may also be important. For example, the effort to shine a light on the behaviours of powerful actors could be pursued through an explicit focus in international prosecutorial practices upon global dynamics in the distribution of environmental violence.[86] This need not be in order to cast business actors as monstrous, as beyond the pale of human society. Instead, it is the very mundanity of thoughtlessness and toleration of extreme environmental risk in business contexts that constitutes the evil. The expressive implications of international law continuing to ignore toleration of extreme environmental harms are themselves a message we must grapple with.

Conclusion

Debate over a crime of ecocide occurs at the juncture of atrocity law, and what evils it seeks to address, and capitalism's leading engines, corporations. The debate over this crime raises questions of the degree to which international law can be galvanised to challenge existing impunity for, and outsourcing of, catastrophic environmental damage in the pursuit of development and profit. Understandably, then, a core question within that debate has been the degree to which the mental element standard for such a crime can be legitimately lowered from the usual standard of intent, so as to realistically capture corporate environmental violence when it is extreme but not necessarily deviant. The conceit of this chapter has been that there are reasons not only in international criminal law and corporate crime doctrine that could justify a lowered mental element, to ensure foreseeable extreme environmental harm is part of the crime. But that, moreover, there may be value in international criminal law engaging with philosophies of evil to help explain the qualities of certain wrongs that justifiably invite an elevated moral and legal response.

86 See, e.g., Kyriakakis (n 43).

Chapter 5

Prescription Medicine, Adverse Effects and Economies of Death

Marc Trabsky and Jacinthe Flore

Introduction

The opioid crisis in the United States has been comprehensively documented in scholarly articles, investigative journalism and popular culture since the beginning of the 21st century.[1] More than half a million Americans have died of an overdose from a synthetic opioid since 1999, and approximately 80% of all available opioids around the world are consumed in the United States.[2] Pharmaceutical opioids such as oxycodone, hydrocodone and fentanyl have been synthetically designed since the early 20th century to more effectively manage both acute and chronic pain in comparison to other kinds of painkillers, such as paracetamol, aspirin and ibuprofen. All three classes of synthetic opioids are efficient in treating pain, yet they are also known as highly addictive. Fentanyl, which is commonly used around the world as an anaesthetic for various surgical procedures can be consumed through an intravenous drip, a skin patch, a nasal spray, a tablet or a lozenge, is a synthetic version of morphine and heroin. It is estimated to be around 100 times stronger than morphine and 50 times stronger than heroin.[3] Fentanyl was responsible for contributing to 71,238 overdose deaths in the United States

1 Hulu's *Dopesick* (2021), which was based on Beth Macy's *Dopesick: Dealers, Doctors, and the Drug Company that Addicted America* (Head of Zeus 2018), dramatises Purdue Pharma's role in the US opioid crisis. See also, Joseph Dumit, *Drugs for Life: How Pharmaceutical Companies Define Our Health* (Duke University Press 2012).

2 Olga Khazan, 'The Opioid Epidemic Might Be Much Worse Than We Thought,' *The Atlantic*, 28 February 2020, https://www.theatlantic.com/health/archive/2020/02/more-people-have-died-opioids-us-thought/607165/ accessed 21 July 2023, and Dina Gusovsky, 'Americans consume vast majority of the world's opioids', *CNBC*, 27 April 2016, https://www.cnbc.com/2016/04/27/americans-consume-almost-all-of-the-global-opioid-supply.html accessed 21 July 2023.

3 Department of Justice/Drug Enforcement Administration, Durg Fact Sheet 'Fentanyl', October 2022, https://www.dea.gov/factsheets/fentanyl#:~:text=What%20is%20Fentanyl%3F,than%20heroin%20as%20an%20analgesic accessed 21 July 2023.

DOI: 10.4324/9781003402534-8

in 2021, which was approximately 66% of all drug overdose deaths that year and constituted an increase of 23% overdose deaths since 2020.[4]

The causes of the opioid crisis in the United States have been fiercely contested. The government has pointed to long-term trends in the over-prescription of pharmaceutical opioids for managing chronic pain in the United States, and in 2016, the Centers for Disease Control and Prevention issued guidelines to medical practitioners for prescribing opioids for pain management.[5] Conversely, journalists, scholars and activists have vociferously critiqued the politicisation, privatisation and impoverishment of the healthcare system in the United States, even though the federal government spends more than any other country on healthcare, as the main cause of the opioid epidemic. Prescriptions for opioids are higher in the United States than any other OECD country – 289 million prescriptions for opioids were issued in 2016[6] – and they are routinely dispensed at a low cost in place of more expensive medical interventions for responding to chronic conditions. However, more recently, attention has been shone on the role of pharmaceutical corporations in facilitating, encouraging and profiting from the opioid crisis in the United States.[7]

In Australia, the opioid crisis has not reached the proportions that have been witnessed in the United States. Statistics on drug overdose deaths in Australia are collated by Coroners Courts in each state and territory. The Victorian Overdose Deaths Register, which is unique in Australia, reports annually on all drug overdose deaths in its jurisdiction. In 2021, the Register reported 4,551 overdose deaths in the state of Victoria between 2011 and 2020. In 2011, 362 deaths were reported, which by 2020 had increased to 526 deaths annually.[8] The report classifies the kind of drugs that were

4 Centers for Disease Control and Prevention, *U.S. Overdose Deaths In 2021 Increased Half as Much as in 2020 But Are Still Up 15%*, 11 May 2022, https://www.cdc.gov/nchs/pressroom/nchs_press_releases/2022/202205.htm accessed 21 July 2023.

5 Centers for Disease Control and Prevention, *CDC Guideline for Prescribing Opioids for Chronic Pain – United States*, 2016, Morbidity and Mortality Weekly Report, Volume 65, Number 1, 18 March 2016.

6 US Department of Health & Human Services, *Facing Addiction in America: The Surgeon General's Report on Alcohol, Drugs, and Health* (US Department of Health & Human Services 2016) 1–14.

7 See Barry Meier, *Pain Killer: An Empire of Deceit and the Origins of America's Opioid Epidemic* (Hodder & Stoughton 2020) and Patrick Radden Keefe, *Empire of Pain: The Secret History of the Sackler Dynasty* (Pan Macmillan 2021).

8 Coroners Court of Victoria, *Victorian Overdose Deaths 2011–2020* (29 July 2021) 5. See also, Melissa Davey, 'Prescription drugs involved in 82% of overdose deaths, Victoria coroner says', *The Guardian Australia*, 21 March 2015, https://www.theguardian.com/australia-news/2015/mar/21/prescription-drugs-involved-in-82-of-overdose-deaths-victoria-coroner-says accessed 21 July 2023; 'Pharmaceutical drugs driving rise in Victorian overdose deaths', *The Guardian Australia*, 5 April 2015, https://www.theguardian.com/australia-news/2016/apr/05/pharmaceutical-drugs-driving-rise-in-victorian-overdose-deaths accessed 21 July 2023; and

partially or wholly involved in the death according to three categories: pharmaceutical drugs, illegal drugs and alcohol. While 74.1% of all overdose deaths in 2020 were caused by a combination of prescription medicine, prohibited substances and/or alcohol, what is remarkable is that around 75% were caused by pharmaceuticals alone or in combination with the above.[9] When the statistics are further expanded, the main prescription medicines that contributed to the deaths involved in average across each year were benzodiazepines (54.5%), opioids (41.3%), antidepressants (34.9%) and antipsychotics (21.1%).[10]

This chapter explores the idea that pharmaceutical corporations invest in the continuity of life to the point where they allow individuals to perish. It discusses the increase in overdose deaths due to prescription medicine in Australia over the past decade and considers the role that corporations perform in facilitating these economies of overdose deaths. The chapter argues that a fundamental aim of pharmaceutical corporations – known as 'big pharma' – is the expansion of drug consumption. However, inextricable from and inherent in the consumption of prescription medicine are adverse effects that may cause pain and suffering, or even may result in death. In other words, while managing chronic conditions, easing pain and suffering, and curing infections are core to the mission of pharmaceutical corporations, the commercial practices of developing, manufacturing and marketing drugs are always already entangled with an economisation of life and death. We categorise the way that pharmaceutical corporations facilitate economies of overdose deaths in the 21st century as the 'banality of evil' insofar as it is part of the ordinary or everyday course of doing business in an industry that frames life and death according to economic terms.[11] Consequently, we suggest that big pharma normalises a wilful neglect or lack of care for human life by engaging in calculative practices that allow individuals to perish in the pursuit of developing, manufacturing and marketing prescription medicines.[12]

Michael McGowan, 'He was gone: fentanyl and the opioid deaths destroying Australian families', *The Guardian Australia*, 13 May 2018, https://www.theguardian.com/science/2018/may/13/he-was-gone-fentanyl-and-the-opioid-deaths-destroying-australian-families accessed 21 July 2023.

9 Ibid. at 9–10.

10 Ibid. at 11.

11 The term 'banality of evil' is taken from Hannah Arendt's description of the Nazi government in World War II in Hannah Arendt, *Eichmann in Jerusalem: A Report on the Banality of Evil* (first published 1963, The Viking Press 1964).

12 On wilful neglect and lack of care as both definitions of evil, see Penny Crofts, 'Three Recent Royal Commissions: The Failure to Prevent Harms and Attributions of Organisational Liability' (2020) 42(4) *Sydney Law Review* 395.

Regulating Prescription Medicines

Purdue Pharma, and the Sackler family who were its principal owners, have been at the centre of the opioid crisis since the 1990s. The company synthesised a new kind of slow-release form of Oxycodone, named OxyContin, in 1995. OxyContin contains ingredients known in biomedicine for their addictive potential. However, Purdue Pharma suggested that if used properly for managing chronic pain, OxyContin is unlikely to result in adverse health effects, including injury or death.[13] The company argued that it cannot be held responsible for the 'misuse', 'abuse' or 'overuse' of the drug. What has been revealed, though, over the past couple of decades through investigative journalism is that Purdue and its key personnel developed a marketing strategy for persuading and inducing medical practitioners to (over)prescribe OxyContin for pain management, misrepresented how OxyContin worked and its potentialities for addiction, and denied the existence of reports that it was being (ab)used as a recreational drug.[14] Since then, Purdue Pharma and the Sackler family, who bought the company in 1952 and oversaw the development of OxyContin, have been defendants in multiple lawsuits, including class-actions, which led to Purdue's bankruptcy proceedings in 2022. As Patrick Radden Keefe writes for *The New Yorker*,

> [m]any pharmaceutical companies had a hand in creating the opioid crisis, an ongoing public-health emergency in which as many as half a million Americans have lost their lives. But Purdue, which is owned by the Sackler family, played a special role because it was the first to set out, in the nineteen-nineties, to persuade the American medical establishment that strong opioids should be much more widely prescribed—and that physicians' longstanding fears about the addictive nature of such drugs were overblown. With the launch of OxyContin, in 1995, Purdue unleashed an unprecedented marketing blitz, pushing the use of powerful opioids for a huge range of ailments and asserting that its product led to addiction in "fewer than one percent" of patients.[15]

In Australia, the *National Drug Strategy 2017–2026* focuses almost entirely on how to implement harm minimisation strategies in relation to the

13 Patrick Radden Keefe, 'The Family That Built an Empire of Pain', *The New Yorker*, 23 October 2017, https://www.newyorker.com/magazine/2017/10/30/the-family-that-built-an-empire-of-pain accessed 21 July 2023.

14 Barry Meier, 'Origins of an Epidemic: Purdue Pharma Knew Its Opioids Were Widely Abused', *The New York Times*, 30 May 2018.

15 Patrick Radden Keefe, 'The Sackler Family's Plan to Keep Its Billions', *The New Yorker*, 4 October 2020, https://www.newyorker.com/news/news-desk/the-sackler-familys-plan-to-keep-its-billions accessed 21 July 2023.

consumption of illegal drugs, alcohol and tobacco. There is little mention of how prescription medicine may cause injury or death, and there is no discussion of how pharmaceutical corporations could be held responsible for allowing individuals to perish through the design of a drug, its marketing strategy or its (lack of) accessibility. Indeed, the strategy features one short paragraph on legal drugs, such as opioids, benzodiazepines and analgesics, yet its focus still remains on the 'non-medical use' or rather 'abuse' of pharmaceuticals.[16] Despite this lack of attention, the Australian government has more recently recognised the role of patients in 'doctor-shopping' for prescriptions, the role of practitioners in 'prescription-shopping' and the role of pharmaceutical corporations in facilitating, encouraging and profiting from over-prescriptions. In response to these issues, the Australian government introduced SafeScript, a mandatory 'real-time prescription monitoring system prior to prescribing or dispensing a medicine monitored through the system'.[17] Since April 2020, practitioners and pharmacists across Australia must check what a patient has consumed in the past in order to reduce 'pharmaceutical drug related issues that cause significant harm, including prescription shopping, sub-optimal coordination of care between clinicians, drug dispensing errors, and drug prescribing that is clearly inconsistent with good clinical practice'.[18]

The continuing debacle of OxyContin is part of a far-reaching global problem of overdose deaths caused by prescription medicine. Opioids, whether alone or in combination with other drugs or alcohol, are undoubtedly the key contributor of overdose deaths, but so too are benzodiazepines, antidepressants, antipsychotics and analgesics. Paracetamol, in particular, has been highlighted in recent coronial investigations as a primary contributor to overdose deaths, and there have been proposals to improve control of the sale of paracetamol and ibuprofen by pharmacies in Australia. A 2022 review commissioned by the Australian Therapeutic Goods Administration has attributed 50 lives lost yearly to paracetamol overdose, with adolescents and young adults, particularly females, among the most impacted.[19] The review

16 Department of Health, Commonwealth of Australia, *National Drug Strategy 2017–2026* (2017) 33.

17 Ibid. at 20. See also, *National Real Time Prescription Monitoring (RTPM)*, 21 April 2022, https://www.health.gov.au/our-work/national-real-time-prescription-monitoring-rtpm accessed 21 July 2023.

18 Ibid.

19 Therapeutic Goods Administration, *Independent Expert Report on the Risks of Intentional Self-Poisoning with Paracetamol* (Department of Health and Aged Care 2022) https://www.tga.gov.au/resources/publication/publications/independent-expert-panel-report accessed 21 July 2023. See further, Mary Ward, 'Sale of paracetamol under scrutiny amid concern about overdoses in teens', *The Age*, 15 September 2022, https://www.theage.com.au/national/sale-of-paracetamol-under-scrutiny-amid-concern-about-overdoses-in-teens-20220915-p5bi9e.html accessed 21 July 2023.

made a series of recommendations, including reducing the number of tablets available per box, given that ibuprofen and paracetamol are available over the counter in large quantities, and they can be bought in combination form, and limiting the number of boxes that can be purchased by an individual consumer to reduce 'stockpiling'.[20] Our interest in discussing this example, to which we return to below, in this chapter is that it shows how one of the most common pharmaceuticals, such as paracetamol, while different from opioids, is nonetheless embroiled in (self-)injury and overdose deaths.[21]

The marketing tactics of pharmaceutical corporations in the United States are well-documented and frequently rebuked.[22] Certainly, the regulatory environment in Australia is different. But while the 'opioid crisis' and reach of Purdue Pharma may not be as acute in other countries, questions arise about the broader role of pharmaceutical corporations in facilitating economies of overdose deaths in the dispensing of prescription medicines. In the following sections, we theorise the role of pharmaceutical corporations in contributing to the uses and misuses of opioids, benzodiazepines and analgesics. Rather than simply concluding that Purdue and their ilk are exceptional, nefarious and immoral, whether due to facilitating, encouraging and inciting an opioid crisis through aggressive marketing, financial inducements and misleading advertisements, we first find inspiration from critical drug studies which, for example, seek to trouble dichotomies of legality and illegality, normality and pathology, use and abuse, and good and bad drugs.[23] We then conceptualise the way that pharmaceutical corporations create drugs where adverse effects are inextricable from and inherent in the technology itself,[24] and lastly examine how the practice of developing, manufacturing and marketing drugs is always already entangled with an economisation of life and death. We thus argue that big pharma normalises a wilful neglect or lack of care for human life by engaging in calculative practices that allow individuals to perish in the pursuit of dispensing prescription medicines.

20 Note that combinations of paracetamol and codeine, and ibuprofen and codeine are already only available with a prescription.

21 For an insightful critique of the meaning of 'non-medical use' of painkillers, see George C. Dertadian, *A Fine Line: Painkillers and Pleasure in the Age of Anxiety* (Palgrave Macmillan 2019).

22 Kalman Applbaum, 'Pharmaceutical Marketing and the Invention of the Medical Consumer' (2006) 3(4) *PLoS Med* e189; Susan Chimonas et al., 'Show Us the Money: Lessons in Transparency from State Pharmaceutical Marketing Disclosure Laws' (2010) 45(1) *Health Services Review* 98.

23 See, for example, Suzanne Fraser, David Moore and Helen Keane, *Habits: Remaking Addiction* (Palgrave Macmillan 2014) and Kane Race, *Pleasure Consuming Medicine: The Queer Politics of Drugs* (Duke University Press 2009).

24 Jacinthe Flore et al., 'Unravelling subjectivity, embodied experience and (taking) psychotropic medication' (2019) 230 *Social Science & Medicine* 66.

The Banality of Adverse Effects

Distinctions between an intended and a side effect are central to how pharmaceutical drugs are framed and marketed, and how they are talked about in medical spaces and everyday contexts. When trying a new drug, it is common for individuals to identify therapeutic effects and distinguish them from side effects that are typically inconvenient, disruptive and sometimes cause pain or suffering. Likewise, prescribers of drugs will usually describe what a drug does and explain its side effects as a distinct 'other'. It is less common for prescribers to explain to individuals and patients the processes of *how* a drug works, its mechanisms of action and the organs it affects, either because this is unknown or unclear, or because it is considered unnecessary knowledge for 'laypeople'. Nonetheless, the duality of how drugs are described reveals the ambiguities of drugs as (potentially) curative or beneficial and problematic or damaging.

If we take the example of paracetamol – which is sold under a range of well-known brand names – and enter this search in a respected Australian health information website, the results note that paracetamol can be taken for 'mild to moderate pain' related to backache, headache, migraine, as well as for 'fever'.[25] Paracetamol can also be combined with additional pain killers, such as ibuprofen, codeine or the opioid-based dihydrocodeine. Dosage and frequency are contingent upon age and severity of pain; however, the website warns that paracetamol can 'damage your liver, which may be irreversible and fatal', and that it should not be consumed if one has 'liver problems, kidney problems, problems with alcohol'.[26] Noted 'side effects' include 'allergic reaction, blood disorders, liver and kidney damage'.[27] In addition, it is observed that 'the way [paracetamol] works to reduce pain and fever is not fully understood. Paracetamol begins to ease pain and lower a high temperature about 30 minutes after a dose is taken'.[28]

It is worth highlighting that this slipperiness between what is intended and what is a side effect spans all drugs whether available over the counter or with a prescription. For example, psychotropic medications that may 'calm' the mind, or cytotoxic drugs that aim to kill or slow the growth of cancerous cells, can cause a range of complex (sometimes harmful) embodied changes and emotional distress.[29] Despite the language used by pharmaceutical

25 *Health Direct Australia* (last review January 2023) https://www.healthdirect.gov.au/paracetamol accessed 21 July 2023.

26 Ibid.

27 Ibid.

28 Ibid.

29 Flore et al. (n 24); Joanna Moncrieff, *The Myth of the Chemical Cure: A Critique of Psychiatric Drug Treatment* (Palgrave Macmillan 2009); Jodie Rosenberg, Phillis N. Butow and Joanna M. Shaw, 'The untold story of late effects: A qualitative analysis of breast cancer survivors' emotional responses to late effects' (2022) 30 *Supportive Care in Cancer* 177.

corporations and more broadly in the medical profession, the intended and side effects distinction is in fact slippery and unsettled. The case of how paracetamol is described on a health information website demonstrates uncertainty, ambiguity, as well as the 'reach' of drugs once they break down and traverse inside bodies. Hence, pain in one's back might be the target, but paracetamol's effects extend within the liver, kidneys and other organs. In doing so, the drug embroils other organs (and bodily substances, such as blood) while targeting pain somewhere else.[30] Circulating also is the uncertainty of *how* paracetamol works. Its mechanism is 'not fully understood', but what is known here are its possible benefits, as well as its status as a medication in circulation 'for more than 50 years'.[31]

The work of drugs is not an either/or proposition. Despite how the medical profession and pharmaceutical corporations may talk about and indeed market them, their effects are instead experienced *simultaneously* as part of the wide-ranging functioning of drugs.[32] Importantly, this is inherent in the technology of the drug itself. Their multiple actions or effects are integral to how drugs are manufactured, even as certain marketing tactics may attempt to obscure or minimise them. In the circulation of drugs in everyday life, these effects are not easily distinguished and might be better conceptualised as *countervailing forces*. In conceiving of the effects of drugs as 'countervailing', rather than distinguishing between intended and side effects, we aim to trouble the work of drugs in the body, law and society, and draw attention to the banality of their forces. Instead of approaching the effects of drugs as a range of forces of 'equal' import, we interpret the countervailing work of prescription medicines as more nuanced, unsettled and steeped in the quotidian development, manufacturing and marketing of pharmaceuticals. This also serves to point to the entanglements of drugs and trouble the primary/beneficial and secondary/side dyad. Far from fixed objects in a box, drugs, from prescription medicines to the most mundane ones purchased over the counter, and their effects are deeply enmeshed in how pharmaceutical corporations facilitate economies of life and death.[33]

Pharmaceutical Economies of Death

In *Death: New Trajectories of Law*, Marc Trabsky examines how legal institutions reify the economic value of death in the 21st century. The book examines the economisation of legal definitions of death, legal technologies

30 See Elizabeth A. Wilson, *Gut Feminism* (Duke University Press 2015).

31 *Health Direct Australia* (last review January 2023) https://www.healthdirect.gov.au/paracetamol accessed 21 July 2023.

32 Fraser, Moore and Keane (n 23).

33 Suzanne Fraser and Kate Seear, *Making Disease, Making Citizens: The Politics of Hepatitis C* (Routledge 2011).

for registering a death and technologies for recycling cadaveric tissue.[34] Its conceptual framework builds upon Michel Foucault's theory of governmentality and Wendy Brown's critique of neoliberalism. Foucault asserts that the concept of 'economy' is central to understanding how arrangements of governmentality emerge in the 18th and 19th centuries, while Brown conceives of economisation as a 'neoliberal rationality' that has subjugated all spheres of life to economic discourse in the 21st century. In *Death*, Trabsky applies both concepts to analyse how the logic of economisation is inextricable from the governance of death, and how legal institutions have not only witnessed but actively participated in reifying the economic value of death in the world. In the remainder of this chapter, we expand the idea of the economisation of death by exploring how pharmaceutical corporations frame the countervailing forces of drugs within the economic discourse of cost–benefit calculations. These calculative practices normalise a wilful neglect or lack of care for human life in the pursuit of developing, manufacturing and marketing prescription medicine.

'Governmentality' is a term that Foucault coins to describe an analytics of bio-power that emerged in Western societies in the 18th and 19th centuries. It involves a range of political technologies that discipline bodies (*anatomo-politics*) and control populations (*bio-politics*), that is, technologies that intervene at the level of the individual, populations and life itself. Governmentality, as an 'ensemble formed by the institutions, procedures, analyses and reflections, the calculations and tactics that allow the exercise of this very specific albeit complex form of power', targets the management of life and death, regulating the rhythms of the former and monitoring fluctuations in the latter.[35] Oriented towards optimising, fostering and inciting life, the technologies of governmentality entail compiling statistics on the health of the population: morbidity and criminality, wealth and scarcity, and birth and death rates. Too much death in a population is pathological, as Trabsky writes of discourses of 'excess mortality', but so too is a below-average death rate.[36] In 'The Political Technology of Individuals', Foucault mobilises the concept of *thanato-politics* to emphasise how technologies for governing life are always already immanent with technologies for managing death.[37]

34 Marc Trabsky, *Death: New Trajectories of Law* (Routledge 2023).

35 Michel Foucault, 'Governmentality' in Graham Burchell, Colin Gordon and Peter Miller (eds), *The Foucault Effect: Studies in Governmentality* (The University of Chicago Press 1991) 102.

36 Trabsky (n 34) 44.

37 Michel Foucault, 'The Political Technology of Individuals' in Luther H Martin, Huck Gutman and Patrick H Hutton (eds), *Technologies of the Self: A Seminar with Michel Foucault* (University of Massachusetts Press 1988) 160.

Foucault's lectures on 'Governmentality' introduce the idea that 'economy' was central to the emergence of bio-power and the problem of the government of populations in the 18th century. He writes that

> [t]he word 'economy', which in the sixteenth century signified a form of government, comes in the eighteenth century to designate a level of reality, a field of intervention through a series of complex processes that I regard as absolutely fundamental to our history.[38]

Foucault considers the question of how to introduce, facilitate and manage an economy as key to the transformation from sovereign power to bio-power in the West. Indeed, for Jean-Jacques Rousseau,

> [t]o govern a state will therefore mean to apply economy, to set up an economy at the level of the entire state, which means exercising towards its inhabitants, and the wealth and behaviour of each and all, a form of surveillance and control as attentive of that of the head of a family over his household and his goods.[39]

This is concomitant with the decentralisation of power in the state and the dispersal of political technologies throughout different segments of society in the 18th to 20th centuries, which remains 'an indispensable element in the development of capitalism':

> The adjustment of the accumulation of men to that of capital, the joining of the growth of human groups to the expansion of productive forces and the differential allocation of profit were made possible in part by the exercise of bio-power in its many forms and modes of application.[40]

The transformation from sovereign power to bio-power thus cemented the idea that each state has an economy that requires governmental intervention to incite, control and invest in law. While technologies of governmentality are ostensibly oriented towards disciplining bodies and controlling populations, they are as concerned with managing the ordinary fluctuations in birth and death rates, and with recognising the economic value in both its growth and decay. In other words, governmentality and its political technologies reify the notion that 'economic rationality' is essential to the optimisation of life and the governance of death.

38 Foucault (n 35) 93.
39 Ibid. 92.
40 Michel Foucault, *The History of Sexuality, Volume 1: The Will to Knowledge*, tr. Robert Hurley (Penguin Books 1998) 140–141.

The application of economic thought into all domains of life and death, whether that may be human activities that are already conceived of as predominantly economic, or others that may have never been thought of before through this conceptual abstraction, would be for Foucault emblematic of neoliberalism in the 20th century.[41] Wendy Brown expands upon Foucault's writings on the figure of *homo oeconomicus*, that is, the ideal of the economically rational human being, and applies it to understand the specific arrangements of neoliberalism in the 21rst century. Brown notes that '[w] idespread economization of heretofore noneconomic domains, activities, and subjects does not necessarily denote the marketization or monetization of them'.[42] The difference between neoliberalism and capitalism, then, is how the former extends techniques of economisation into all spheres of life without necessarily monetising human activity. Neoliberalism is irreducible to the accumulation of capital, the creation of a free market or the privatisation of public goods. Instead, it is a 'governing rationality' that frames and measures every aspect of life and death by 'economic terms and metrics'.[43] What this ultimately denotes is that a condition of possibility of contemporary life is a historically specific form of economic rationality, which extols, for example, human beings to privilege future benefits over immediate gains, transform themselves into human capital, and optimise the economic value of death.

If neoliberal rationality has become a distinctive form of governance in the 21st century, it is because it constructs persons and states on the model of corporate firms and self-investing, future-oriented entrepreneurs, who participate in an economy of human capital by competing against each other. Economisation is a model for the conduct of government, as well as a model for the government of the self, where persons, states and firms transform society into a market, and themselves into market actors. The *homo oeconomicus* that Foucault introduces in his lectures on biopolitics – and who, as he notes, appears in the writings of philosopher John Stuart Mill – becomes a market actor that 'takes its shape [everywhere] as human capital seeking to strengthen its competitive positioning and appreciate its value, rather than as a figure of exchange or interests'.[44] In *Undoing the Demos*, Brown also builds upon Koray Çaliskan and Michel Callon's performative concept of economisation to describe 'behaviours, organizations, institutions and, more

41 Michel Foucault, *The Birth of Biopolitics: Lectures at the College de France 1978–1979*, tr Graham Burchell (Picador 2008) 323. The following three paragraphs have been taken from Trabsky (n 34) 25–27.

42 Wendy Brown, *Undoing the Demos: Neoliberalism's Stealth Revolution* (Zone Books 2015) 31–32.

43 Ibid. 10.

44 Ibid. 33.

generally, the objects in a particular society ... as "economic"'.[45] Brown deploys this term to account for how *homo oeconomicus* as an ideal state of being extends into areas of life that were once thought of as not exclusively or primarily economic.

Fatmir Haskaj's analysis of the necro-economy seeks to account for how death has become a source of economic value due to 'neoliberalism's tendency to marketize all aspects of human activity'.[46] Indebted to Achille Mbembe's *Necro-politics*, Haskaj focuses on how killings due to war, genocide, poverty, starvation and global warming create necro-economies. Yet the problem with conceptualising death as a negative of bio-politics is that it misses how death, whether sudden or expected, unnatural or ordinary, violent or accidental, is normalised as *allowable* by the state. Necro-economy is not exclusive of bio-power, and death is not the negation of a politics of life, because the institutional routinisation of mortality, and the political technologies that take care of those deaths, are immanent to techniques of economisation. In one sense, necro-economics could describe an arrangement of bio-power, but only if as Warren Montag writes, death is conceived of as a condition of possibility of life. That is to say, if one examines the market and the state as entities that call for, make demands of and allow for death in an economic rationalisation of life. In this schema of necro-economics, we suggest it is possible to frame the figure of *homo oeconomicus* as one 'who with impunity may be allowed to die, slowly or quickly, in the name of the rationality and equilibrium of the market'.[47]

The opioid crisis in the United States has been conceptualised by scholars and journalists through the schema of necro-politics, which frames pharmaceutical corporations as killers and governments as bystanders or accomplices.[48] However, the labour of drugs in the body, how they journey into and are absorbed by organs, constitute countervailing forces – an enmeshment of 'intended' and 'side' effects that cannot be fully detached. We suggest that these countervailing forces, which are inherent in the technology of drugs, should be contextualised within the conceptual framework of economisation. The entanglement of intended and side effects is the result of an eco-

45 Koray Çaliskan and Michel Callon, 'Economization, Part 1: Shifting Attention from the Economy Towards Processes of Economization' (2009) 38(3) *Economy and Society* 369, 370.

46 Fatmir Haskaj, 'From Biopower to Necroeconomies: Neoliberalism, Biopower and Death Economies' (2018) 44(10) *Philosophy and Social Criticism* 1148, 1149.

47 Warren Montag, 'Necro-economics: Adam Smith and Death in the Life of the Universal' (2005) 134 *Radical Philosophy* 7, 17.

48 See, for example, Eve Darian-Smith, 'Dying for the Economy: Disposable People and Economies of Death in the Global North' (2021) 10(1) *State Crime Journal* 61. While they don't explicitly use the conceptual framework of necro-politics, Anne Case and Angus Deaton portray pharmaceutical corporations as 'killers' in *Deaths of Despair and the Future of Capitalism* (Princeton University Press 2021) 129.

nomic rationality of life, where both health and morbidity, living and dying are made sense of by pharmaceutical corporations through economic discourse. The processes of researching, trialling, manufacturing, marketing and dispensing drugs are interwoven with techniques for optimising the health of consumers but also techniques for allowing individuals to perish, where death can be rendered economically valuable in itself.

Hence, we contend that the schema of necro-politics is unable to properly account for how pharmaceutical corporations ordinarily allow individuals to perish due to the countervailing forces of prescription medicine. Likewise, necro-politics does not accurately explain how governments, particularly through delegated authorities such as the US Food and Drug Administration, actively participate in letting individuals die, by framing countervailing forces as either 'rare' adverse effects or the misuse or abuse of a drug by 'irresponsible' consumers. Corporations are conducting multiple cost–benefit calculations in the development, manufacturing, marketing and dispensing of drugs that involve manipulating fluctuations in mortality rates and shaping the conditions that can increase or decrease overdose deaths. In deciding whether to hold pharmaceutical corporations responsible for causing overdose deaths or shaming individuals for the misuse or abuse of their consumption, state institutions are also reifying the economic value of death in the world.

Conclusions

It is all too tempting then to cast big pharma as 'evil corporations' that prey on individuals with a propensity towards misusing and abusing drug consumption. Instead, this chapter describes the work of pharmaceutical corporations as ordinarily *letting* individuals die by economising their life and death in the development, manufacture and marketing of prescription medicines. This perhaps exemplifies the 'banality' of evil that Hannah Arendt speaks of in *Eichmann in Jerusalem*. An 'evil' that is not extraordinary or exceptional, but rather, integral to how capitalism functions, which James Martel discusses previously in this edited collection. In allowing individuals to perish through the (over-)consumption of drugs, big pharma engages in an ordinary process of framing life and death according to economic terms, whether that may consist of calculating the costs and benefits of manufacturing, marketing or dispensing a particular drug or participating in decision-making about whether to embed known adverse effects in the medicine itself. We have been living alongside analgesics and synthetic opioids for over a century. There is nothing new about how pharmaceutical corporations economise death in the development, manufacturing and marketing of prescription medicines that directly or indirectly cause overdose deaths. However, what we are discovering is that legal institutions can be complicit in or hold corporations responsible for *banally* or *ordinarily*, in the course of doing business, allowing individuals to die.

Chapter 6

The Corporate Evil of Unsafe Products

Strict Liability, Negligence and the Expressive Force of the Law

Hui Chia and Jeannie Marie Paterson

Introduction

The iconic science fiction film *Alien* tells the story of a parasitic alien that implants itself in the body of its host, whom it later graphically kills by erupting from their chest. Towards the end of the film the main characters discover that their desperate fight for survival against the alien was actually part of the business plan of their employer corporation, who was seeking to acquire the alien for research purposes. The corporation's priority was to bring the alien back for analysis. All other considerations were secondary; the crew expendable. *Alien* ends with the potential for redress, with the sole survivor, Ripley, hurtling towards Earth accompanied by the ship's cat.

The evil corporation that prioritises scientific discovery over human life, only to have that discovery escape and wreak havoc, is a familiar theme of the sci-fi horror genre. In this narrative, although the manifest evil appears to come from the alien, it is gradually revealed that the 'mind' behind the carnage is a corporation. The alien is merely acting to survive or reproduce; the real evil lies in the corporation prepared to squander human lives to further its own ends.[1] However, from a purely economic perspective, the corporation's behaviour is rational. There are many humans and only one intriguing alien that could potentially lead to far-reaching scientific discoveries. A cost–benefit analysis might suggest that the alien is a more valuable asset to the company than the lives of a few, replaceable employees.

Films like *Alien* have a real-life parallel in pharmaceutical companies, which have released, and continued to produce dangerous products in pursuit of profits, resulting in extensive human suffering.[2] But in these scenarios, there may be no heroic resolution, and certainly not by a brave woman and her cat. Indeed, real-life defective products may prove more horrific than

1 Penny Crofts, 'Aliens: Legal Conceptions of the Corporate Invasion' (2022) 34 *Law & Literature* 387.

2 See, e.g., Casey Cep, 'Johnson & Johnson and a new war on consumer protection' *New Yorker* (New York, 19 September 2022).

DOI: 10.4324/9781003402534-9

fiction, with the corporations involved more evil, and even more dedicated to maximising profit in disregard of the suffering this causes.

Consider a corporation selling a product that it has failed adequately to test, neglects the anatomical differences arising from its use on women, ignores potentially dire outcomes, misrepresents its certification in Europe and fails to warn consumers, surgeons and hospitals of the emerging side effects, which in any event it has failed to monitor over the long term. Surely this scenario is too evil to be plausible? In fact, this horror is real. Product liability litigation in countries including the United States, United Kingdom and Australia over the use of a synthetic pelvic mesh reveals how a poorly tested and monitored product implanted in women's bodies caused horrific ongoing injuries, literally re-emerging from their bodies in gruesome forms.[3] This is the moral equivalent of the company in *Alien* sending in its crew to retrieve the alien, despite the warning sent from those who had previously encountered the alien, but here there are no survivors, human or animal.

Ethicon, which manufactured the pelvic mesh, may not have set out to cause the harms that arose. But the litany of its failings makes that point irrelevant. This was no mere oversight that only became apparent with the benefit of scientific hindsight. Ethicon was arguably consumed by the pursuit of profit and indifferent to the consequences of its actions. Philosophical accounts of evil are not limited to actions where harm was maliciously intended; accounts of evil include 'banal and thoughtless self-interest'.[4] Russell explains that 'banal' in this context does not mean that the evil action itself is ordinary or excusable, rather that the motivations behind the evil action are common and unremarkable motivations.[5]

The law's response to 'banal' evil is unexpectedly muted. Crofts has argued that the harms caused by corporate wrongdoing are so extreme as to be horrific, but 'the inability of the criminal legal system to respond to corporate wrongs communicates that these harms are a cost of doing business rather than blameworthy wrongs'.[6] The focus of this chapter is civil liability, and its response to unsafe products. We suggest that strict product liability, as commonly understood, likewise risks reducing liability to a cost–benefit analysis.[7] We ponder therefore whether negligence, with its intuitive and compelling theme of corrective justice, provides more expressive and therefore impactful

3 See Michelle Llamas, 'Transvaginal Mesh Lawsuits' (*drugwatch*, 11 November 2022) https://www.drugwatch.com/transvaginal-mesh/lawsuits/ accessed 17 April 2023.

4 Luke Russell, *Evil: A Philosophical Investigation* (Oxford University Press 2014) 70.

5 Ibid. p. 74.

6 Penny Crofts, 'The Horror of Corporate Harms' (2022) 38 *Australian Journal of Corporate Law* 23, 24.

7 See also Cristina Carmody Tilley, 'Just Strict Liability' (2022) 43(6) *Cardozo Law Review* 2317–2384.

response to normative wrong that is exhibited in this kind of thoughtless, careless conduct.

Product liability regimes arose in response to public outrage at injuries caused by unsafe products, where it was difficult to prove that the manufacturer had been negligent.[8] The solution was strict liability, removing the requirement for plaintiffs to prove fault by the manufacturer. The aim of strict product liability regimes was to ease the burden on plaintiffs seeking to bring a case against product manufacturers, by directly requiring manufacturers to internalise the costs of harm from unsafe products, albeit with a defence for unforeseen risks. The theory is that the risk of such liability provides a financial incentive to corporations to make their products safer, and where this cannot be done, or is too expensive, to either absorb or pass on the cost of compensation to those who are injured.[9]

A (not inevitable) consequence of removing the element of fault is that product liability analysis is typically silent on the wrongfulness of the manufacturer's behaviour.[10] We argue that it may not be enough for the law to function as a financial deterrent because if the only motivation for obeying the law is a financial incentive, then the truly horrible realisation sinks in: it makes sense for corporations to be evil. It makes sense to treat human suffering and loss of life as budget items that can be outweighed by increased profits if a finding of legal liability means nothing more than a financial cost to the corporation.

Negligence, by contrast is premised on coherent normative principles of fault and interpersonal responsibility. Compensation for victims and financial deterrence to product manufacturers are appropriately vital aims of the law, but this should not come at the sacrifice of weakening the expressive function of a finding of fault.

Tort is arguably an expressive institution, and a finding of fault sends the message that the defendant wronged the plaintiff.[11] As Hershovitz has argued, 'sometimes we need to say, clearly and loudly, this defendant wronged that plaintiff, and our saying so can be significant quite apart from any material consequences that follow'.[12] Hershovitz also discusses the expressive function of compensation, that the award of damages expresses to the defendant

8 See generally Mauro Bussani, Anthony Sebok and Marta Infantino, 'Common Law and Civil Law Perspectives on Tort Law' (Oxford University Press 2022) ch VIII (on products liability).

9 See e.g., the classic rationale for strict product liability in *Escola v Coca Cola Bottling Co* 24 Cal 2d 453 (Cal 1944), 5441 (Traynor J.).

10 John C.P. Goldberg and Benjamin Zipursky, 'The Strict Liability in Fault and the Fault in Strict Liability' (2016) 85 *Fordham Law Review* 743, 771–778; Tony Honoré, 'Responsibility and Luck: The Moral Basis of Strict Liability' (1988) 104 *Law Quarterly Review* 530, 539.

11 Scott Hershovitz, 'Treating Wrongs as Wrongs: An Expressive Argument for Tort Law', (2017) 10 *Journal of Tort Law* DOI:10.1515/jtl-2017-0004

12 Ibid. p. 4.

'This is your fault – the disability, the disfigurement, the pain and suffering'.[13] Apart from the practical utility of the money for the plaintiff, the award of compensatory damages sends the message that the defendant was wrong to treat the plaintiff in this way. The expressive function of the law is particularly justified in the context of corporations.[14] Unlike the punishment of natural persons, where the expressive value of the law must be weighed against the rights of a person, a corporation cannot suffer.[15] Thus, there is a stronger justification for the expressive value of corporate liability compared to liability for natural persons.

Following this line of argument, we suggest that negligence provides a more normatively compelling response to harmful products than strict product liability. The expressive force of this condemnation – that the conduct was negligent – communicates that this conduct is reprehensible and will not be tolerated.[16] For everyone who feels outraged at the conduct of pharmaceutical companies in showing scant care for people, and especially for women's bodies, we want the law to provide compensation for the harms incurred and to declare loud and clear 'This was wrong'.

The Origins and Aims of 'Strict' Product Liability

The origins of strict product liability began with every parent's worst nightmare: the devastating news that their newborn baby has severe impairments that will impact the child for the rest of its life.

In 1957, the drug thalidomide was approved in most countries, with the exception of the United States, as a sedative, painkiller and for treatment of morning sickness in pregnant women.[17] From 1957 to 1961, 10,000 children in 46 countries were born with serious congenital deformities, most of them being phocomelia, the absence of limbs, due to the teratogenic effect of thalidomide on developing foetuses.[18] During trials of thalidomide, no testing was performed on pregnant animals to check if the drug would have any harmful effect on the developing foetus,[19] and the drug was not promptly recalled even when the concerns became evident.

13 Ibid. p. 23.
14 Gregory Gilchrist, 'The Expressive Cost of Corporate Immunity', (2012) 64 *Hastings Law Journal* 1.
15 Ibid. pp. 55–56.
16 Cf, in the context of criminal law, Grant Lamond 'What is a crime?' (2007) 27(4) *OJLS* 609, 610.
17 PJ Lachmann, 'The penumbra of thalidomide, the litigation culture and the licensing of pharmaceuticals', (2012) 105 *QJM* 1179.
18 Ibid.
19 Ibid.

The tragic consequences of thalidomide brought about far-reaching change, both in the scientific and legal spheres. In medicine, there was increased research and advances made in the study of causes of birth defects.[20] More stringent testing standards and regulations for medical drugs emerged. In the legal sphere, public outcry from thalidomide became a catalyst for demanding greater liability of product manufacturers for harms caused by their products.[21] Whilst there were fears that negligence would be difficult to prove, the liability of the manufacturer of thalidomide was never actually determined in court as manufacturers and victims settled out of court.[22] Over the next two decades, the emotive significance of thalidomide fuelled support for the eventual implementation of strict liability regimes for product manufacturers for personal injury or death caused by their products.[23]

In the United Kingdom, the Royal Commission on Civil Liability and Compensation for Personal Injury (Pearson Commission) was established in 1973, largely to address concerns about personal injury following thalidomide.[24] The Pearson Commission Report[25] was in favour of a tort of strict liability.[26] The reasons for favouring strict liability were: to be in harmony with the European trend towards strict liability, and to extend to all consumers the benefits enjoyed by a purchaser under contract, based on the economic rationale that the manufacturer is the best placed insurer.[27] Regarding the financial impact of strict liability on producers, the Commission stated that it would be impossible to predict the cost of strict liability accurately but concluded the chapter on product liability by reasoning that this would be accounted for by increased product prices.[28]

In 1977, the Strasbourg Convention on Products Liability in regard to Personal Injury and Death introduced the concept of 'defect' as the basis for strict liability of a product.[29] The committee rejected fault as the legal

20 A Bernstein, 'Formed by thalidomide: Mass torts as a false cure for toxic exposure' (1997) 97 *Columbia Law Rev* 2153, 2156.

21 Chanapa Tantibanchachai, 'US Regulatory Response to Thalidomide (1950–2000)', *The Embryo Project Encyclopedia* (2014) https://embryo.asu.edu/handle/10776/7733 date accessed 17 April 2023.

22 Bernstein (n 20), 2158–2159.

23 Ibid. 2158–2161.

24 H.C. Deb 17 November 1978, vol. 958, cols 771–876.

25 *Royal Commission on Civil Liability and Compensation for Personal Injury* (Report, 1978) Vol. I (Pearson Report).

26 Pearson Report (n 25), 262, paras 1230–1236.

27 Ibid. 262–263. Similar themes informed US products liability law: see further Bussani, Sebok and Infantino (n 8) ch. VIII (on product liability).

28 Ibid. 273–274, para. 1278.

29 Council of Europe, *Explanatory Report to the European Convention on Products Liability in regard to Personal Injury and Death* (ETS 91, 1977) para. 13–15 (Strasbourg Convention Explanatory Report).

basis for liability, reasoning that fault 'no longer constituted a satisfactory basis for the system of products' liability in an era of mass-production, where technical developments, advertising and sales methods had created special risks, which the consumer could not be expected to accept'.[30] The committee considered that, 'as insurance made it possible to spread risk over a large number of products, producers' liability, even for development risks, should not be a serious obstacle to planning and putting into circulation new and useful products'.[31]

The 1985 EU Directive on Liability for Defective Products[32] adopted the central concept of 'defect' as the basis of product liability. The preamble declares that 'liability without fault on the part of the producer is the sole means of adequately solving the problem, peculiar to our age of increasing technicality, of a fair apportionment of the risks inherent in modern technological production'.[33] The preamble also states that 'a fair apportionment of risk between the injured person and the producer implies that the producer should be able to free himself from liability if he furnishes proof as to the existence of certain exonerating circumstances'.[34]

One of these exonerating circumstances was the inclusion of the state-of-the-art defence, that a producer will not be liable for a defect that was not discoverable with the state of scientific knowledge at the time.[35] This is a notable departure from the recommendations of both the Pearson Commission and the Strasbourg Convention, which were against the inclusion of such a defence because it reintroduced the element of fault.[36] In likely recognition of the controversial nature of this defence, the EU Directive gave member states the option to not include the state-of-the-art defence in their domestic ratification of the Directive.[37]

The EU Directive would greatly influence an international trend towards strict liability of product manufacturers for defective products, including in Australia.[38] Part 3–5, Div 1 of the Australian Consumer Law (ACL)[39] contains a statutory product liability law under which consumers who suffer loss or damage because of defects in a manufacturer's goods may recover that loss

30 Strasbourg Convention Explanatory Report (n 29), para. 10.
31 Ibid. para. 41.
32 Council Directive 85/374/EEC of 25 July 1985 on the approximation of the laws, regulations and administrative provisions of the member states concerning liability for defective products [1985] OJ L 210/29 (EU Directive 1985).
33 EU Directive 1985, Preamble.
34 Ibid.
35 Ibid. Article 7(e).
36 Strasbourg Convention Explanatory Report (n 29), para. 40.
37 EU Directive 1985, Preamble.
38 David Harland, 'The Influence of European Law on Product Liability in Australia', (1995) 17 *Sydney Law Review* 336, 338–339, 341.
39 *Competition and Consumer Act 2010* (Cth), sch. 2.

or damage from the manufacturer.[40] The ACL also contains a 'state of the art' defence under which manufacturers can avoid liability if they prove that the defect in their product could not have been discovered given the state of scientific and technical knowledge at the time the goods were supplied.[41]

Ethicon: Addressing the Evil of Defective Products

Product liability cases, by definition, concern corporations releasing unsafe and dangerous products. One of the recent, high profile, and horrific, cases in Australia, as elsewhere, concerned pelvic mesh, provided by Ethicon companies (together 'Ethicon'), which were all members of the Johnson & Johnson group. The case was a representative action by Kathryn Gill, Diane Dawson and Ann Sanders. The products in question were tension-free vaginal tape for the treatment of urinary stress incontinence, and pelvic mesh for the treatment of pelvic organ prolapse. It was established at trial that these products carried risks of serious injury, including chronic inflammatory reactions, extrusion or erosion of the mesh into surrounding organs, infection, chronic pain and other side effects.[42] Each of the applicants suffered severe and ongoing complications after surgery implanting the devices.

Medical devices sold in Australia must be approved by the Therapeutic Goods Administration (TGA) for inclusion on the Australian Register of Therapeutic Goods (ARTG).[43] In this case, the respondents relied on a 'CE' mark on the devices. A CE mark on a medical device represents that the product conforms to the requirements of the applicable European directive and is an indication that the product may lawfully be sold in all member states of the European Union.[44] At the time the products were included on the ARTG, where products carried a CE mark, the TGA did not conduct any independent assessment of the safety or efficacy of the products and did not require the manufacturer to demonstrate that independent pre-market testing of safety and efficacy of the products had been carried out.[45]

As subsequently found by the trial judge, Katzmann J. in *Gill v. Ethicon Sàrl (No 5)*,[46] this reliance on the CE mark was unjustified as Ethicon 'did not in fact have adequate clinical evidence' to affix the CE mark to its products.[47] Katzmann J. held Ethicon liable for contraventions of the product safety regime in Section 138 of the ACL because the mesh products were supplied

40 Ibid. sch. 2 s. 138.
41 Ibid. sch. 2 s. 142(c).
42 *Gill v. Ethicon Sàrl (No. 5)* [2019] FCA 1905 [2560]–[3035].
43 *Therapeutic Goods Act 1989* (Cth) pt 4–11 div. 3.
44 *Gill v. Ethicon Sàrl (No.5)* [2019] FCA 1905 [1392].
45 Ibid. [1391].
46 Ibid.
47 Ibid. [1480].

with a safety defect, being not as safe as consumers were entitled to expect.[48] Katzmann J. rejected the statutory defence pleaded by Ethicon that the state of scientific or technical knowledge at the time the devices were supplied was not such as to enable the defects to be discovered. Ethicon admitted during the trial to being aware of those risks before any of the devices were supplied.[49]

Katzmann J. also found that the respondents were liable in negligence.[50] Ethicon had breached its duty of care to the plaintiffs by failing to undertake any, or any adequate, clinical or other evaluation of the devices before releasing them in Australia. The evidence showed that the devices were brought to market with 'unseemly haste' and with a lack of attention to the safety of the women who would use the devices.[51] Ethicon, moreover, failed to conduct any, or any adequate, evaluation of safety and effectiveness of the devices after their release in Australia.[52]

Katzmann J. awarded damages to the applicants together of more than A$2 million and issued an injunction to prevent the respondents from supplying, promoting and distributing the devices without a revised warning in Australia.[53] An appeal was dismissed, and the first-instance findings upheld.[54] The High Court of Australia refused a special leave application brought by Ethicon and Johnson & Johnson.[55]

Notably, for our purposes, the findings in product liability and in negligence were similar. Strict liability did not actually provide an advantage for the plaintiff compared to negligence in this case. This was because the elements of the strict liability action – specifically the existence of a safety defect and a state-of-the-art defence – entail similar reasoning to establishing negligence, a point we return to below.[56]

The Safety Calculus

In considering the role of strict liability and negligence in responding to defective products, we need to start with the idea of safety. Safety is not an absolute concept. Goods can be more or less safe. All surgery carries some risk and patients may be taken to understand that. Often the risk is dealt with by disclosure of the potential harms, to assist the patient in deciding whether a medical procedure is suitably safe or effective for them. In deciding whether a

48 Ibid. [3458], [3500].
49 Ibid. [3513].
50 Ibid. [3879]–[3884].
51 Ibid. [3764].
52 Ibid. [3826].
53 *Ethicon Sàrl v. Gill* [2021] FCAFC 29 [3].
54 Ibid. [928].
55 Transcript of Proceedings, *Ethicon Sàrl v. Gill* [2021] HCATrans 187.
56 See text pp. 103–104 below.

product has a safety defect, product liability law applies a similar calculus to negligence, namely that manufacturers should be held liable where the cost to avoid the harm (e.g., cost to make a product safer), is less than the cost of the harm (i.e., compensation to victims and the number of victims). However, this outward similarity belies a fundamental difference between the normative justification for the safety calculus in strict liability and negligence, and hence an important difference in their expressive value.

Justifications for Strict Product Liability

How does product liability justify why a manufacturer should have to pay compensation? Let us recall the main rationales for strict product liability that were proposed in the 1970s by the Pearson Commission and Strasbourg Convention:

- That fault should not be the basis for manufacturer liability, due to the modern context of mass production.
- That liability should be based on an objective standard of the level of safety that the community is entitled to expect.
- The manufacturer is the party best placed to respond to the risk of defective products, by improving safety and by arranging insurance to cover the harms that do eventuate.
- The financial impact of strict liability on manufacturers will not curb innovation because manufacturers can pass on this cost to consumers by increasing their product prices to account for the cost of greater care/taking insurance.
- It is justifiable for consumers as a whole to pay for the cost of compensating injuries that result from a product.[57]

This reasoning is consistent with the law and economics school deterrence theory of tort, including product liability.[58]

Calabresi argued in 1961 that liability for personal injuries should be determined according to efficient resource allocation, instead of fault being the basis of liability.[59] He argued that manufacturers should be liable for

57 See Pearson Report (n 25) and Strasbourg Convention Explanatory Report (n 29).

58 On the debate in the United States between tort law as premised on the lowest cost avoider approach to preventing harm and the recognition of wrongs see Catherine Sharkey 'Modern Tort Law: Preventing Harms, Not Recognizing Wrongs' (2021) 134 *Harv L Rev.* 1423, discussing John Goldberg and Benjamin Zipursky, *Recognizing Wrongs* (Harvard University Press 2020).

59 Guido Calabresi, 'Some Thoughts on Risk Distribution and the Law of Torts' (1961) 70 *Yale Law Journal* 499, 500. Also generally Guido Calabresi, *The Cost of Accidents* (Yale University Press 1970).

harm caused by their product, where the cost of taking precautions to avoid that harm was less than the cost of the harm, with consideration of the probability that harm would occur.[60] Liability thus imposes on the manufacturer a financial incentive to take as much precaution in making the product safe, up until the cost of precaution is greater than the cost of the harm. As we have seen, this thinking was key in informing strict product liability regimes.

The Normative Coherence of Negligence

What about the justification for why manufacturers are liable to pay compensation under negligence? Negligence declares that manufacturers have a duty to take reasonable care of their consumers, and that all consumers have a right to not be injured. The corrective justice approach posits that negligence expresses a moral responsibility for the relational wrong when a person such as a customer is carelessly harmed by the manufacturer's lack of care.[61] Corrective justice views the positions between the parties before the transaction has occurred as being equal, the defendant's negligent act wrongly transfers resources from the plaintiff to themselves, thereby providing the moral justification for tort law to restore the plaintiff to their initial position.

One question that has presented as a challenge for the moral conception of negligence has been the negligence calculus, exemplified in the famous Learned Hand formula.[62] The formula defines negligence as being where the burden of precautions is less than the harm multiplied by the probability of the harm. The formula can be interpreted to be based upon economic or utilitarian grounds, rather than moral grounds. Ernest Weinrib refutes the economic interpretation of the Learned Hand formula and argues that the calculus is consistent with a Kantian conception of negligence.[63]

Weinrib argues that the Hand formula can be understood as a two-stage hypothetical:[64]

> First, we consider the hypothetical where the defendant is occupying both his own position and the position of the plaintiff. In such a scenario, the defendant would decide whether or not he should take a precaution, based on the calculus of the burden to himself of that precaution versus the cost of the harm to himself, factoring in the probability of that harm occurring.

60 Guido Calabresi and Jon T. Hirschoff, 'Towards a Test for Strict Liability in Torts' (1972) 81 *Yale Law Journal* 1055.
61 Allan Beever, 'Corrective Justice and Personal Responsibility in Tort Law' (2008) 28 *Oxford Journal of Legal Studies* 475, 476–478.
62 Judge Learned Hand in *United States v. Carroll Towing Co.*, 159 F2d 169 (2d Cir. 1947).
63 Ernest J. Weinrib, 'Toward a Moral Theory of Negligence Law' (1983) 2 *Law and Philosophy* 37.
64 Ibid. 51–53.

> Second, if the defendant would have taken the precaution to protect himself against the harm, then the Kantian principle of the impermissibility of self-preference demands that he should have taken that precaution to protect the plaintiff. The imposition of tort liability is thus based upon the moral justification that the defendant has acted to prefer himself over another person, which is a wrong that the law aims to correct.

In embodying principles consistent with Kantian ethics, negligence carries considerable moral resonance in the societies in which it operates. Law is often considered in terms of its coercive capacity, forcing people to behave in particular ways. But it is also possible that law works to support desirable social norms that benefit individuals and society.[65] Cooter refers to 'expressive law' which promotes cooperation and reduces the need for coercive intervention.[66] This is of course an instrumental use of negligence, contrasting with the deontological moral premise of corrective justice. But corrective justice theorists such as Wienrib, and also civil recourse theorists such as Goldberg and Zipursky, see tort laws recognition of relational wrongs as expressive of a just society that holds defendants responsible for their wrongs to others.[67]

Incentives to Care about People

Turning now to consider the expressive value that flows from the justifications for strict liability and negligence, we examine what incentives either form of liability gives to manufacturers to care about people. One of the justifications for strict liability was that it would not harm manufacturers, because they could pass on the costs of insuring against harm to consumers. Hence, strict liability patently does not create a financial incentive for manufacturers to care more about the safety of their consumers, if financial liability is passed on to consumers. The point can be made that this would also be true of negligence. If a product manufacturer was found liable in negligence, the manufacturer could equally pass on the costs of damages to consumers through raising its product prices. Therefore, from the perspective of deterring unsafe products, on a practical level there may be no difference as to how financial liability is applied, whether through strict liability or negligence. But what that means is that the expressive value or normative justification of a finding of liability is even more important, because any financial disincentive will have a limited effect when the product manufacturer can simply pass on this

65 Andrew Robertson, 'On the Function of the Law of Negligence' (2013) 33(1) *Oxford Journal of Legal Studies* 31.

66 Robert Cooter, 'Expressive Law and Economics' (1988) 27 *Journal of Legal Studies* 585, 596.

67 Also Goldberg and Zipursky (n 58) esp. p. 123.

cost to its consumers. If financial disincentives do not have adequate power to deter corporations from selling unsafe products, then it matters even more what a finding of liability means as a normative statement.

A finding of negligence is a clear statement that the manufacturer failed to take adequate care to make their product safe, that the manufacturer did not behave as they should have. A finding of strict liability, if one applies the lowest-cost insurer approach, does not make any statement about the manufacturer's behaviour being wrongful. The finding merely states that the product caused harm to some customers, and so the manufacturer will have to spread the costs associated with that harm amongst all its customers.

If we compare the expressive values of these two statements, the responsibility of the manufacturer whose product causes injury has been reduced from the violation of a social norm to an effective insurer. This might have been considered a desirable trade-off due to fears that plaintiffs would struggle to prove negligence. But this trade-off underappreciates the importance of the expressive value of a finding of fault, or wrong-doing, in the harm that is caused, and, as we shall see, overestimates the advantage provided by the version of products liability in place in Australia, in adopting the EU model. When legal liability is reduced to being only a financial disincentive, this has the perverse impact of encouraging the corporate indifference that makes it more likely plaintiffs will be injured by unsafe products in the first place – corporations seeing people as nothing but a number of dollars to be made.

One might argue that making the level of compensation payable in product liability cases greater would increase the financial disincentive to the point that manufacturers would decide not to sell the product at all. But it is difficult to use compensation for deterrence.[68] Perhaps product liability should be supplemented with a general safety obligation,[69] which increases the costs of unsafe products by imposing criminal or civil penalties for contraventions. Even this response, however, which is aimed solely at deterrence,[70] requires some way of judging the extent to which the corporation was culpable. In awarding civil penalties, there is a proportionality between the culpability of the corporation that produces harm and the penalty award.[71] Thus, such liability piggybacks most successfully off a fault-based compensatory regime.

68 See Elise Bant and Jeannie Paterson, 'Should specifically deterrent or punitive remedies be made available to victims of misleading conduct under the Australian Consumer Law?' (2019) 25 *Torts Law Journal* 99; Elise Bant and Jeannie Paterson, 'Effecting Deterrence though Proportionate Punishment: An Assessment of Statutory and General Law Principles' in Elise Bant and others (eds), *Punishment and Private Law* (Hart Publishing 2021) 255–286.

69 CAANZ, *Australian Consumer Law Review: Final Report* (Commonwealth of Australia 2017) 33.

70 *Australian Building and Construction Commissioner v Pattinson* [2022] HCA 13.

71 Jeannie Paterson and Elise Bant, 'Intuitive Synthesis and Fidelity to Purpose?: Judicial Interpretation of the Discretionary Power to award Civil Penalties under the Australian

A Moral Account of Strict Liability?

Whilst the lowest-cost insurer rationale was used to justify the introduction of strict product liability regimes, it is open for us to contemplate whether the resultant strict liability regimes can be interpreted in a way that expresses the same values as negligence about how a manufacturer ought to behave. Goldberg and Zipursky have argued that 'strict' product liability involves a normative wrong, namely injuring another through the sale of a dangerously defective product.[72] Additionally, the formulation of the strict product liability regime under the EU model at least invokes this kind of more morally redolent inquiry. This is because the inquiry into a 'safety defect' and 'state-of-the-art' defence may be similar to assessing the reasonable standard of care.[73]

In *Ethicon,* Katzmann J.'s judgement seems to have incorporated the concept of the reasonable manufacturer into strict liability, by interpreting the level of safety that people are entitled to expect as being set by the standard of a reasonably prudent manufacturer:

> Persons generally are entitled to expect manufacturers of an implantable medical device, particularly one designed to remain in the body permanently, to err on the side of caution. Certainly that is how a reasonably prudent manufacturer would behave [74]

The Full Court did not explicitly adopt Katzmann J.'s reasoning of whether the actions of Ethicon were consistent with expectations of how a reasonably prudent manufacturer would behave. Nevertheless, the Full Court agreed with Katzmann J.'s finding[75] that 'persons generally are entitled to expect that the manufacturer would provide … information about known and foreseeable risks'.[76] It seems that courts, when deciding strict liability, end up relying, directly or indirectly, upon concepts of foreseeability and what the reasonable person would expect, when applying the 'defect' test of whether a product has the level of safety that people are entitled to expect.

This reintroduction of the reasonable standard of care imports the evidentiary burden that plaintiffs would have had under negligence into strict

Consumer Law' in Prue Vines and Scott Donald (eds) *Statutory Interpretation in Private Law* (Federation Press, Leichhardt 2019).

72 Goldberg and Zipursky (n 10), 771–778, argue that 'strict' product liability involves the wrong of injuring another through the sale of a dangerously defective product.

73 Bussani, Sebok and Infantino (n 8) ch. VIII 242 (on products liability, discussing the EU approach), and also noting in the US strict liability applies only to manufacturing defects not instructional or design defects (at 228).

74 *Gill v. Ethicon Sàrl (No. 5)* [2019] FCA 1905 [3345]. See also [3368], [3376].

75 Ibid. [3376].

76 *Ethicon Sàrl v. Gill* [2021] FCAFC 29 [650], [651].

liability. The trade-off discussed earlier, that strict liability loses the expressive value of a finding of fault by the manufacturer, but justified on the basis that it is easier for plaintiffs to obtain compensation, is an even worse trade-off if strict liability reintroduces the evidentiary burdens of negligence but without the expressive value.

The state-of-the-art defence is another example of elements of negligence being reintroduced into strict liability. It effectively relieves the manufacturer where it could not have foreseen the issue giving rise to harm. Unlike negligence, the burden is on the defendant to raise the defence. But in other respects, it is unclear how the inclusion of the state-of-the-art defence should be interpreted as modifying the best-placed insurer justifications for strict product liability. The defence further makes it difficult to construct a clear moral account of strict liability. It is certainly much more elusive and ambiguous compared to the strong moral account of negligence.

Being Evil Is Profitable

The lack of a clear moral account means that strict liability is only relying on financial deterrence. This means that for strict product liability to have its desired effect, we must assume that from a financial standpoint, it makes financial sense to do the right thing and make products safe. The *Ethicon* case demonstrates that, actually, it makes financial sense to be evil in the sense of willingly risking and/or causing widespread harms. As Russell has described, evil is not confined to accounts of malice, but includes accounts of evil which are 'banal and thoughtless self-interest'.[77]

There are four, overlapping, strategies available to product manufacturers to reduce the financial cost of potential compensation for product harms:

1. Take greater care of people by making the product safer.
2. Insure against the costs of harm and pass on the costs to consumers, increasing product prices to pay for compensation.
3. Neglect developing scientific knowledge about potential safety risks, to improve the chances of relying on the state-of-the-art defence.
4. Assume products for disadvantaged groups can be less safe – groups like women and low-income earners will cost less to compensate, so there is less financial incentive to make their products safe.

In theorising about the consequences of strict product liability, we should not assume that the first response is the most likely response from product manufacturers. Making products safer is a very expensive exercise for manufacturers and the return on investment for discovering new safety risks is

77 Luke Russell, *Evil: A Philosophical Investigation* (Oxford University Press 2014) 70.

difficult to demonstrate. Additionally, in the context of medical products, where the defect causes injury to only a minority of users, the financial risk of compensating a minority is negligible, especially if there is more profit to be made from the majority.

Strategy 2, as discussed previously, is openly recognised as being an aim of strict product liability regimes, that product manufacturers will not be negatively impacted by the imposition of strict liability because they can pass on the costs of the risk of having to compensate injured individuals to consumers generally. The larger a corporate manufacturer and the more diverse the range of products it has, the greater the corporation's ability to self-insure by diluting the costs of compensation.

Strategies 3 and 4 are not intended consequences of strict product liability but, as we examine in the Ethicon case, we see that these strategies may be the logical consequence of legal liability amounting to nothing more than a financial cost.

Ethicon targeted its mesh products at women, despite the fact that this specific use of the mesh was not what the product was originally designed for, and there was scant research into understanding the particular risks of this new use for women. The development of the Ethicon devices began with the development of the synthetic material, Prolene, in the 1960s for use as a surgical suture.[78] In the late 1990s, Ethicon developed Prolene Soft mesh, a knitted mesh constructed from the suture material for use to repair hernias generally. Shortly after, Ethicon developed Gynemesh PS which was to be used to repair hernias specifically of female pelvic organs.[79]

Ethicon repurposed the mesh for use in the treatment of pelvic organ prolapse, despite the lack of knowledge of specific biomechanics of the female pelvis, or obtaining additional regulatory approvals.[80] Justice Katzmann noted the fact that research regarding the safety risks of using the mesh for female pelvic organ prolapse was conducted years *after* the launch and worldwide marketing of the product, as a 'damning indictment' that Ethicon prioritised profits over women's safety.[81] Ethicon brought the mesh to market with 'unseemly haste' in an attempt to beat their competitors to the newly emerging market for prolapse repair products.[82] Katzmann J. observed that given the limited investigations conducted, Ethicon's belief in the safety of the product was 'little more than a leap of faith',[83] with many of the existing

78 *Gill v. Ethicon Sàrl (No.5)* [2019] FCA 1905 [39].
79 Ibid. [135]–[137].
80 Ibid. [3714].
81 Ibid. [3715].
82 Ibid. [3764].
83 Ibid. [3730].

studies 'of poor quality with small patient numbers and non-standard outcome measures'.[84]

We can further consider the Ethicon case against the backdrop of other unsafe medical devices and products that exclusively affect women. In the United States since 2000, of the more than 100 medical-related product liability multi-district litigation cases, only four were products that exclusively affected men, whilst 22 exclusively affected women.[85] As the *New Yorker* report on another unsafe product targeted at women, Johnson & Johnson talcum powder, comments 'There's this sense that it's O.K. to experiment on women's bodies in real-time'.[86] That is exactly what Ethicon did, marketing worldwide a product that was in fact an experiment, with almost no clinical evidence as to the safety and effectiveness of the product. Worse still, this outcome might be seen as rational when we think about product liability as being only a financial disincentive. Women as a group earn less income than men and therefore cost less to compensate.

Ethicon's cavalier attitude towards the safety risks for women was particularly reprehensible given that the mesh was designed to be implanted permanently. The mesh was designed with pores that would provoke an inflammatory response in the body, causing scar tissue to form in and around the pores of the mesh.[87] This enables the mesh to adhere to the vaginal tissue, for the aim of strengthening the tissue to correct the prolapse.[88] By design, the woman's tissues would grow into all the pores of the mesh, making it permanently part of her body and making the potential harms irreversible. This also meant that the mesh had long-term consequences which should have informed the kind of studies conducted, including over the longer term.[89]

Finally, we reflect on the fact that not only was Ethicon's sale of the mesh product an experiment on women's bodies, it was an experiment on women's sexual wellbeing. Even before the launch of the mesh products, Ethicon was aware that the products carried risks of severe and lifelong complications to women's sexual organs, with devastating consequences to women's self-esteem and sexual wellbeing. As discussed in *Ethicon:*

> The literature merely states for example that the mesh erosion rate is for instance 10 per cent after mesh implant surgery. It does not state that those who suffer erosion are often sexually active young women who are unable to have intercourse because of a repulsive vaginal discharge, bleeding and

84 Ibid. [3733].

85 Casey Cep, 'Johnson & Johnson and a new war on consumer protection' *New Yorker* (New York, 19 September 2022).

86 Ibid.

87 *Gill v. Ethicon Sàrl (No. 5)* [2019] FCA 1905 [345].

88 Ibid. [341].

89 Ibid. [346].

chronic pain on sitting, standing or movement and that this may not be easily corrected.[90]

The willingness of Ethicon to gamble with women's bodies and sexual well-being was exceptionally vile. If we applied the cheapest cost-avoider rationale, that Ethicon was the best placed to assess what is the cost of making the product safer, versus the cost of compensating these women for their injuries – unable to have intercourse, walk or sit normally for the rest of their lives, how much should that cost be estimated at? Maybe the cost of compensation is $2 per mesh sold? Surely only an evil, or perhaps economically rational, corporation would conclude – 'That's Ok, the cost of harm is less than the profits'.

Conclusion

The corporate evil represented in *Aliens* may not be as dramatic as the alien who informs the title of the movie, as well as its sequels.[91] So too in real life, harmful pharmaceutical products continue to cause untold suffering, while the corporate manufacturers continue, or regroup. Compensation, if payable, may be seen as a cost of doing business, with human lives treated no differently than any other business expense. The strict liability regime for harms caused by pharmaceutical products, whilst well-intentioned in its aim to lower barriers to compensation, may have the perverse effect of encouraging the callous cost–benefit analysis that causes corporations to sell unsafe products in the first place.

These kinds of products do not injure by accident. The cheapest cost-avoider rationale that underpins strict product liability regimes, that corporations should make their product safer only if that makes financial sense compared to the cost of compensation, is deeply misguided because, through one lens, it makes perfect financial sense to be evil, if we adopt a definition of evil as causing widespread harms. The Ethicon products did not injure by accident. The harm was the consequence of poor testing and an unwillingness to withdraw a profitable product from the market, even after it was revealed to be unsafe. Furthermore, whilst in theory strict product liability removes the requirement of fault, it actually reintroduces the element of fault through the state-of-the-art defence. Strict product liability thus reinstates the barriers to compensation that plaintiffs would have under negligence, but without the expressive value of a finding of fault.

The strength of negligence is in its affirmation of the moral principles that people have a right not to be wrongfully injured, and that people have a

90 *Gill v. Ethicon Sàrl (No. 5)* [2019] FCA 1905 [3232].
91 Crofts (n 1).

responsibility to take reasonable care of others. In preferencing strict liability in responding to harmful pharmaceutical products, we undervalue the loss of the expressive force of negligence in condemning transgressions of these principles. The economic rationale commits the very evil that strict liability was supposed to prevent – the emergent risks of pain and suffering by another human being means nothing if offset by profits. This motif underlies *Alien*, and is sadly worse in real life.

Chapter 7

Data Brokers

Trading on Trust

Olivia Dixon

Introduction

Smartphones have become ubiquitous because of the value they provide to us as individuals. More than nine out of every ten Australians own a smartphone,[1] including 46% of children aged 6 to 13.[2] Providing connectivity, entertainment and efficiency, the average Australian has over 100 applications on their smartphone.[3] Yet unbeknownst to many users, these apps have a dark side. 'Data brokers' harvest sensitive personal information from these apps, without informed consent, as free raw data that is then aggregated and traded for profit. Disturbingly, the volume of this data economy is staggering. A report[4] by Justin Sherman, a cyber-fellow at Duke's Sanford School of Public Policy, found that one broker advertised over '7000 attributes'[5] on each individual while another claimed 'the ability to reach over 2.5 billion consumers'.[6] This information can include real-time location data, spending habits, demographic information and political affiliations. While some of these products may be characterised as beneficial or benign to society,[7] the

1 Deloitte Access Economics, 'Mobile Nation 2019: The 5G Future' (2020).

2 Australian Communications and Media Authority, 'Kids and Mobiles: How Australian Children are Using Mobile Phones' (December 2020).

3 Wave Digital, '2020 App Usage Snapshot: Australians. We Really, Really Love Our Apps' (4 June 2020).

4 Jason Sherman, 'Data Brokers and Sensitive Data on US Individuals' (Durham: Duke University Sanford School of Public Policy, August 2021).

5 Epsilon, 'More Than Just a [FirstName]' ('Our proprietary insights include 200+ million consumer profiles, 7,000+ attributes and millions of cross-device IDs, forming the most accurate identity matches and deepest real-time consumer profiles ever assembled'), https://us.epsilon.com/power-of-me.

6 Acxiom Global Solutions, 'Global Data Navigator' ('Coverage in 62 countries and growing and the ability to reach over 2.5 billion consumers'), https://www.acxiom.com/wp-content/uploads/2018/03/Fact_Sheet_Global_Data_Navigator.pdf.

7 For example, risk mitigation products to help prevent fraud, marketing products to allow consumers to more easily find and enjoy the products and services that they need and prefer or an epidemiologist wanting to track the spread of infectious diseases in a population.

DOI: 10.4324/9781003402534-10

potential effect of on-selling an individual's real-time location data is much more nefarious.

Regardless of jurisdiction, the movement of every individual's smartphone is being logged and tracked by data brokers such as Venntel, X-Mode, SafeGraph, Cuebiq and LocationSmart, all of which collect real-time location via GPS and apps that the user has downloaded.[8] Some apps partner with data brokers directly via embedding software development kits (SDKs) in the app,[9] while others share location data in the process of serving behaviourally targeted ads via real-time bidding. Common apps that use SDKs include weather apps, navigation apps, exercise monitoring apps, 'family apps' like Life360 and augmented reality games like PokemonGo.[10] While many apps require location-based services to be turned on in order to function, such as navigation and mapping apps or ride-sharing apps like Uber, the data that are ultimately collected has the potential to be exploited. Although the companies involved in this US $16 billion industry[11] claim that only aggregated and anonymised data is sold, numerous investigations[12] have shown that is inaccurate. Furthermore, researchers have found that even with anonymised datasets, an individual can be identified through location data with as few as four data points.[13] This sensitive personal data can reveal where individuals live and work, who they associate with, and where they worship, protest and seek medical care. The collateral consequences of publicly exposing such data can be lifechanging. This chapter argues that by prioritising profit over privacy, security and physical safety concerns, data brokers are the epitome of corporate evil, demonstrating a calculated indifference to values that we as a society cherish.[14] The 'Harvesters of Sensitive Personal Data' section describes data brokers, how they obtain and profit from sensitive personal information and the scale of the industry. The 'Vulnerabilities and Exploitation in the Data Broker Industry' section sets out examples of individual exploitation in the data broker industry. The 'Specific Vulnerabilities

8 Charlies Levinson, 'Through Apps, Not Warrants: "Locate X" Allows Federal Law Enforcement to Track Phones', *Protocol* (5 March 2020).

9 Sara Morrison, 'The Hidden Trackers in Your Phone, Explained', *Vox* (8 July 2020).

10 Josh Hafner, 'While You Track Pokémon, Pokémon Go Tracks You', *USA Today* (11 July 2016).

11 Grand View Research, 'Location Intelligence Market Size, Share & Trends Analysis Report By Application (Sales and Marketing Optimization, Remote Monitoring), By Service, By Vertical, By Region, And Segment Forecasts, 2022–2030' (Report ID: GVR-2-68038-401-7).

12 Jennifer Valentino-Devries, Natasha Singer, Michael H. Keller and Aaron Krolik, 'Your Apps Know Where You've Been, and Can't Keep a Secret' *New York Times* (10 December 2018).

13 Yves-Alexandre de Montjoye, César A. Hodalgo, Michel Verleysen and Vincent D. Blondel, 'Unique in the Crowd: The Privacy Bounds of Human Mobility', *Nature* (25 March 2013).

14 Penny Crofts in chapter 8 of this volume.

in Commercialising Geolocation Data' section sets out risks in commercialising location data. The 'Conclusion' section concludes.

Harvesters of Sensitive Personal Data

Data brokers[15] are part of the broader 'surveillance capitalism'[16] infrastructure that harvests and on-sells personal data profiles from hundreds of millions of people, often without their explicit knowledge or informed consent. Traditionally used to populate a consumer profile, these companies collect personal data from a variety of online and offline sources, including social media, public records, rewards and loyalty programmes and other commercial sources or companies. A defining characteristic of this sector is that data brokers transact and exchange data with each other.[17] While each data broker source may provide only a few data points about an individual's activities, data brokers can aggregate these data elements together to form a more detailed composite of that person's life. Data brokers gather data on race, ethnicity, religion, gender, sexual orientation and income level; major life events such as pregnancy and divorce; medical information such as drug prescriptions and mental illness; real-time smartphone location; details on an individual's family members and friends; where they like to travel, what they search online, what doctor's office they visit and which political figures and organisations they support. Often, these companies will use algorithms to 'infer' additional data about these individuals. The information is then aggregated, analysed and packaged into stereotype-based datasets for sale, generally without informed consent. Examples of such datasets include 'viewership-gay', 'pro-choice', 'Rural and Barely Making it', 'Asian Achievers', 'working class', 'seeking medical care', 'tough times'.[18] Some specialised data brokers only process very narrow categories of personal data, while others process and combine many different categories and sources of personal data. While each data source may be anonymised or 'de-identified',

15 Although no actors self-identify as 'data brokers'. Some industry terms include: 'Data Provider' (Facebook Partners; Google Ad Words Partners), 'Database Marketer' (LUMA), 'Identity Resolution & People-Based Marketing' (Axciom), 'Marketing Analytics' (Environics Analytics), 'Data-as-a-Service (DaaS) provider' (Oracle Data Cloud) and 'Global risk information provider' (Transunion).

16 See, e.g., Shoshana Zuboff, *The Age of Surveillance Capitalism: The Fight for a Human Future at the New Frontier of Power* (Profile Books, 15 October 2019).

17 US Federal Trade Commission. (2014) *Data Brokers: A Call for Transparency and Accountability*. Report, Federal Trade Commission, Washington, DC.

18 US Federal Trade Commission, 'A Look at What ISPs Know About You: Examining the Privacy Practices of Six Major Internet Service Providers' (21 October 2021), 22; US Senate Committee on Commerce, Science and Transportation, 'A Review of the Data Broker Industry: Collection, Use, and Sale of Consumer Data for Marketing Purposes' (Washington DC: Senate Committee on Commerce, Science and Transportation, 18 December 2013), ii.

when aggregated an individual becomes capable of identification. Such information is particularly useful for advertisers looking to target advertisements at consumers and predict their behaviour.

Certain data brokers specialise in real-time location tracking, which occurs through publishers embedding third-party software into their smartphone apps, including SDKs. SDKs are usually provided to app developers for free in exchange for the information they can collect from them, or a percentage of the ads that they can sell through them.[19] An SDK is essentially a package of tools that helps an app function in some particular manner. For example, software for taking credit card payments or sending instant messages. Because they're so useful and easy to use, SDKs are embedded in thousands of apps. Facebook, Google and Amazon, for example, have SDKs that allow smaller apps to connect to bigger companies' ad platforms or help provide web traffic analytics or payment infrastructure.[20] As noted by the *New York Times*, 'SDKs are not, by nature, nefarious. But their prevalence can turn almost any application, no matter how mundane, into a data harvester'.[21] For example, apps such as Tinder, Grindr and Pregnancy+ were found to be transmitting sensitive personal information back to Facebook through the SDK it provides to third-party app developers.[22] This data included 'the IP address of the device that used the app, the type of device, time of use, and a user-specific Advertising ID, which allows Facebook to identify and link third-party app information to the people using those apps'.[23]

Most companies that produce these SDKs argue that the data they collect are anonymised, that users must opt into their collection and that privacy policies keep users informed about how their data is used. However, de-identified or anonymised data can quite easily be re-identified and are never truly anonymous. For example, data broker Anomaly Six (A6) uses a simple technique called 'geofencing' to track devices at specific locations.[24] Geofencing involves creating a virtual perimeter around a location and applying a specific treatment or ruleset to devices within the perimeter that have location-based services turned on.[25] Users need only find a location

19 Sara Morrison, 'The Hidden Trackers in Your Phone, Explained', *Vox* (8 July 2020).

20 Charlie Warzel, 'The Loophole that Turns Your Apps into Spies', *The New York Times* (24 September 2019).

21 Ibid.

22 Miriam Ruhenstroth, 'How Facebook Knows Which Apps You Use – And Why This Matters', *Mobilsicher* (13 December 2018).

23 Charlie Warzel, 'Apps Are Revealing Your Private Information to Facebook and You Probably Don't Know It', *Buzzfeed News* (20 December 2018).

24 See Sam Biddle and Jack Poulson, 'American Phone Tracking Firm Demo'd Surveillance Powers by Spying on CIA and NSA', *The Intercept* (22 April 2022).

25 Ibid.

of interest on a map of the Earth and draw a box around it. A6 then fills that boundary with dots denoting smartphones that passed through that area. Clicking a dot will provide users with lines representing the device's, and its owner's, movements around a neighbourhood, city or the entire world.[26] Through their use of geofencing A6 claims it was even able to identify potential US Central Intelligence Agency and National Security Agency officials by drawing boundaries around their respective headquarters, seeing devices that visited both locations, and subsequently tracking them across the world, everywhere from the Middle East all the way back to their individual homes.[27] Unless a user has significant technical expertise, it is virtually impossible to identify if such third-party SDKs are present in an app meaning that in the vast majority of instances, individuals are being covertly tracked.

Vulnerabilities and Exploitation in the Data Broker Industry

From the perspective of governments and corporations, there are compelling arguments in favour of the commercial availability of individual real-time location data. For governments, raw data could provide key insights for transportation studies, government planners and healthcare. For example, UNICEF has a data-sharing partnership with Cuebiq to use aggregated smartphone location data to study epidemics and natural disasters.[28] For companies, seeing the complete 'consumer purchase arc', from an individual initially viewing an advertisement to ultimately purchasing a product, provides a wealth of marketing insight into what individuals want, what they purchased and what motivated them purchase it. By combining data analysis with behavioural psychology, some data brokers profess to be capable of predicting what an individual wants before they know it themselves.[29] This leveraging of behavioural psychology in combination with predictive algorithms has given rise to what is referred to as 'data-driven persuasion'.[30]

26 Ibid.

27 Ibid.

28 Businesswire, 'Cuebiq's Data for Good Program Provides UNICEF with High-Precision Human Mobility Data for Real-Time Response to Humanitarian Needs' (10 September, 2019), https://www.businesswire.com/news/home/20190910005037/en/Cuebiq%E2%80%99s-Data-Good-Program-UNICEF-High-Precision-Human

29 See, e.g., David Gal, 'Predicting Consumers' Choices in the Age of the Internet, AI, and Almost Perfect Tracking: Some Things Change, the Key Challenges Do Not' (2021) 4(1) *Consumer Psychology Review* 135.

30 Wolfie Christl, 'How Companies Use Personal Data Against People', *Cracked Labs*, Working Paper (October 2017), 29.

Yet for individuals, there are potentially life-changing risks and vulnerabilities embedded in exposing sensitive personal data. A 2010 BBC poll found that 79% of people in 26 countries considered internet access to be a fundamental human right.[31] Six years later, in 2016, the United Nations Human Rights Council adopted specific language on the importance of internet access.[32] Most people find it difficult to withdraw from internet usage, and many speculate whether it is even possible.[33] Individuals rely on the internet for daily logistics, social interaction, work, education, healthcare, access to products and services and much more. Data brokers exploit these same channels to extract an individual's personal information and experiences to sell. Withdrawing from the internet entirely is unrealistic in the 'information age', leaving users with no option but to accept whatever collateral consequences may attach.

The potential ramifications of harvesting and selling location data are not hypothetical. In 1999, Amy Boyer was murdered by a stalker, Liam Youens, who purchased her date of birth, social security number, home and job addresses from data broker Docusearch.com, with no questions asked.[34] Had Docusearch searched 'Amy Boyer Liam Youens' online they would likely have found Youens's website documenting his intent to murder Boyer. In 2020, Vice Media's Motherboard reported that X-Mode (now Outlogic) was collecting data from Muslim prayer apps and selling it to US defence and military contractors.[35] The *Wall Street Journal* reported in 2020 that Venntel was selling location data to US federal agencies for immigration enforcement.[36] Also in 2021, Mobilewalla boasted of its ability to track Black Lives Matter protesters' smartphones, and despite such data supposedly being anonymised, the company claimed it could identify protesters' age, gender and race.[37] In 2021, Monsignor Jeffrey Burrill, an administrator for the US Conference of Catholic Bishops, resigned after a newspaper bought smartphone and geolocation data that showed his activity on

31 BBC, 'Internet Access "a Human Right"', *BBC News* (8 March 2010).

32 'The Promotion, Protection and Enjoyment of Human Rights on the Internet' (United Nations Human Rights Council, 27 June 2016).

33 See, e.g., Cecilia Cheng and Angel Yee-lam Li, 'Internet Addiction Prevalence and Quality of (Real) Life: A Meta-Analysis of 31 Nations Across Seven World Regions', 17(12) *Cyberpsychology, Behavior and Social Networking* (December 2014), 755.

34 See generally, Raphael Cohen-Almagor, 'The Murder of Amy Boyer' in *Confronting the Internet's Dark Side: Moral and Social Responsibility on the Free Highway* (Cambridge University Press, 2015).

35 Joseph Cox, 'More Muslim Apps Worked with X-Mode, Which Sold Data to Military Contractors', *Motherboard* (29 January 2021).

36 Byron Tau, 'Federal Agencies Use Cellphone Location Data for Immigration Enforcement', *The Wall Street Journal* (7 February 2020).

37 Caroline Haskins, 'Almost 17,000 Protesters Had No Idea A Tech Company Was Tracing Their Location', *BuzzFeed News* (26 June 2020).

LGBTQ+ social app Grindr and tracked him to gay bars.[38] In early 2022, following the leaked draft US Supreme Court decision in *Dobbs v. Jackson Women's Health Organization*,[39] which overturned *Roe v. Wade*[40] and the US constitutional right to an abortion, SafeGraph was caught selling location information on Planned Parenthood visitors, where they came from and where they went.[41]

As these examples demonstrate, tracking an individual's location can create serious privacy, security and physical safety concerns, for both individuals and businesses. At a micro level, the sale of such data may expose domestic violence victims, law enforcement officers, prosecutors, public officials or other individuals to the risk of stigma, harassment, stalking, discrimination, job loss, doxxing and even physical violence. At a macro level, this data could be bought through shell companies or stolen via hacking.[42] It could then be used to inform counterintelligence operations or identify and target persons of interest in the community.[43] Yet, the strong financial incentives to sell such data, coupled with principles-based rather than prescriptive regulation,[44] gives amoral data brokers every reason to continue selling, including to those who may use it for harm. Privacy laws purportedly protect individuals against such corporate surveillance,[45] but data brokers cannot be challenged until they are discovered. Through increasingly sophisticated tracking technology, they continue to collect and share personal information in ways that most people do not understand and would not allow.

Data brokers legitimise collecting personal information, in perpetuity, pursuant to the ostensible one-time 'consent' that they obtain from users when

38 The Pillar, 'Pillar Investigates: USCCB Gen Sec Burrill Resigns After Sexual Misconduct Allegations', *The Pillar* (20 July 2021).

39 597 U.S. 215 (2022).

40 410 U.S. 113 (1973). See also *Planned Parenthood of Southeastern Pa. v. Casey*, 505 U.S. 833 (1992).

41 Joseph Cox, 'Data Broker is Selling Location Data of People Who Visit Abortion Clinics' *Motherboard* (4 May 2022).

42 In October 2015, for example, the successful hack of international data broker Experian exposed the personal information of 15 million US customers, including social security and passport numbers.

43 For example, in 2019 hackers working for the Chinese government allegedly targeted location data for people moving throughout Asia by breaking into telecom networks: Jack Stubbs, 'China Hacked Asian Telcos to Spy on Uighur Travelers: Sources', *Reuters* (5 September 2019).

44 See generally Julia Black, Martyn Hopper and Christa Band, 'Making a Success of Principles-Based Regulation', *Law and Financial Markets Review* (May 2007), 191.

45 The discussion of privacy law is beyond the scope of this chapter. However, see generally, Katharine Kemp, 'Australia's Forgotten Privacy Principle: Why Common "Enrichment" of Customer Data for Profiling and Targeting is Unlawful', *UNSW Research Paper* (20 September 2022); Ratul Das Chaudhury and Chongwoo Choe 'Digital Privacy: GDPR and Its Lessons for Australia' (2023) 56(2) *The Australian Economic Review* 204.

they originally download an app. Generally, to be valid, consent must be voluntary, informed, specific, current and given by a person with capacity.[46] Yet most smartphone apps use 'bundled consent', requesting consent to a wide range of collections, uses and disclosures. A digital platforms report from the Australian Competition and Consumer Commission (ACCC) found that such a practice undermines the voluntary and specific nature of any consent.[47] The quandary is that with advances in technology, networked devices and online services have become essential to navigating daily life. Yet with limited time to review lengthy privacy policies for each of their devices, applications, websites or services (let alone the periodic updates to them) users have little choice but to accept whatever terms and conditions that these companies offer. The Consumer Policy Research Centre found that only 6% of consumers surveyed reported they had read all the privacy policies or terms of use for all the products they signed up to.[48] A further study found that to read the privacy policies of the apps that we use, it would take us about 30 days per year.[49] Furthermore, these privacy policies are generally so complex and legalistic that they are reportedly not even comprehensible to the average person.[50] Consider the end-user licence agreement to Apple's iTunes Store. On an iPhone, the text of this agreement often extends to more than 50 screens. Even if an individual is aware that they are being tracked and is astute enough to read the privacy policy of the app, the third parties that receive that individual's personal data are generally not named. If they are, the individual then has to read the third-party privacy policy to understand how their data is being used. In turn, these third parties may be sharing the data with their own third parties. It is practically impossible for an individual to have even a basic overview of what and where their personal data might be transmitted, or how it is used, even from a single app. The system behind even the most basic transaction could include hundreds of third parties, that all have their own purposes and policies. If individuals do not have meaningful access to what data is being collected or how it is being used, they cannot make informed decisions about the costs and benefits of using an app. If companies were clearer about how they were

46 Generally, in the context of privacy law, consent may be an exception to a general prohibition against personal information being handled in a particular way, or it may otherwise provide authority to handle personal information in a particular way.

47 See ACCC, *Digital Platforms Inquiry – Final Report* (June 2019), 378.

48 Consumer Policy Research Centre, *Consumer Data and the Digital Economy: Emerging Issues in Data Collection, Use and Sharing* (May 2018), 31.

49 Aleecia M. McDonald and Lorrie Faith Cranor, 'The Cost of Reading Privacy Policies' (2008) 4(3) *I/S: A Journal of Law and Policy for the Information Society* 543.

50 Daniel J. Solove, 'Introduction: Privacy Self-Management and the Consent Dilemma' (2013) 126 *Harv. L. Rev.* 1879, 1885; Aleecia M. McDonald and Lorrie Faith Cranor, 'The Cost of Reading Privacy Policies', (2008) 4 *I/S J. of L. & Pol'y for Info. Society* 543; Irene Pollach, 'What's Wrong with Online Privacy Policies?' (2007) 50 *Comm's ACM* 103.

using an individual's personal information, would anyone agree to share it? Any purported 'consent' is covert and artificial, being nothing more than the one-time acceptance of a pop-up. Data brokers are effectively hijacking an individual's decision rights as to privacy.

Data brokers further justify their business model based on the notion that only anonymised, 'de-identified' or aggregated data is sold, which it is claimed cannot identify particular individuals. This factor is pivotal to the regulation of data brokers in general. The purported use of 'de-identified' data is sufficient to relegate data usage outside the scope of the vast majority of the provisions of the *Privacy Act 1988* (Cth) (Privacy Act) and the *Australian Privacy Principles* (APPs) contained in the Privacy Act. However, in practice, data brokers often use 'pseudonymous identifiers', which are unique numbers assigned to a device or an individual.[51] As noted by the *New York Times* special report *One Nation Tracked*, 'connecting a ping to a person was as easy as combining home and work locations with public information. A seemingly random set of movements turned into a clear individual pattern after we added just one other piece of information'.[52] With respect to real-time location data, de-identification and anonymity is a myth.

Specific Vulnerabilities in Commercialising Geolocation Data

The harvesting of sensitive personal information affects the power dynamic between the company collecting the data and the user, affording the company greater power to direct or disrupt the behaviour of the individual. A 2018 study showed that sharing location data made 75–80% of respondents feel 'stressed, nervous or vulnerable, triggering fears of burglaries, spying, stalkers and digital or physical harm'.[53] Furthermore, '84% of consumers do not trust laws or regulations to ensure that there is no misuse of location data'.[54] There are inevitably practices or relationships that users might want to withhold from friends, family, employers or the government. For others, like survivors of abuse or other vulnerable members of society, the risks of sharing

51 Forbrukerrådet, 'Out of Control: How Consumers Are Exploited by the Online Advertising Industry' (14 January 2020), 25. For an overview of the different types of smartphone identifiers, see Bennett Cyphers and Gennie Gebhart, 'Behind the One-Way Mirror: A Deep Dive Into the Technology of Corporate Surveillance', *Electronic Frontier Foundation* (2 December 2019).

52 Stuart A. Thompson and Charlie Warzel, 'Twelve Million Phones, One Dataset, Zero Privacy', *New York Times* (19 December 2019), https://www.nytimes.com/interactive/2019/12/19/opinion/location-tracking-cell-phone.html.

53 HERE Technologies 'Privacy and Location Data: Global Consumer Study March 2018' (March 2018), 5.

54 Ibid.

location data could be substantial and life-changing. This section highlights three examples of collateral consequences in commercialising location data, including price discrimination, physical safety concerns and purpose creep.

Price Discrimination

Knowing where a user lives, works and spends their time may facilitate price discrimination[55] through inferences based on demographics. For example, a ProPublica investigation revealed that 'The Princeton Review' was charging different prices for its online SAT tutoring course in different postcodes. In some postcodes, the course cost US$6,600; in others that same course was offered for as much as US$8,400.[56] Charging different prices to different geographic regions is regulated in Europe, but is not in the United States or Australia. Geolocation data therefore resulted in inadvertent discrimination. ProPublica found that Asian-Americans were nearly twice as likely to be charged a higher price by The Princeton Review than non-Asian-Americans. The authors provided the following example:

> consider the difference between two ZIP codes with similar incomes in Texas. In Houston's ZIP code 77072, with a relatively large Asian population, the Princeton Review course was offered for $7,200. While in Dallas' ZIP code 75203, with almost no Asians, the course was offered for $6,600. And in heavily Asian, low-income Queens ZIP code 11355, the course was offered for $8,400.

If the price of a product or service differs on an individual level, it also becomes impossible for individuals to assess and compare offers.

Physical Safety

Members of vulnerable communities may not be aware that their data is widely collected, aggregated and sold to whomever is buying, for example LGBTQ+ individuals using dating apps and sharing their GPS location, sexual preferences and sexual health status.[57] For other groups, such as survivors

55 Adam Tanner, 'Different Customers, Different Prices, Thanks to Big Data', *Forbes* (26 March 2014), https://www.forbes.com/sites/adamtanner/2014/03/26/different-customers-different-prices-thanks-to-big-data/?sh=59485fd45730.

56 Julie Angwin, Surya Mattu and Jeff Larson, 'The Tiger Mom Tax: Asians Are Nearly Twice as Likely to Get a Higher Price from Princeton Review' (1 September 2015), https://www.propublica.org/article/asians-nearly-twice-as-likely-to-get-higher-price-from-princeton-review.

57 Chris Stokel-Walker, 'Facebook's Ad Data May Put Millions of Gay People at Risk', New Scientist (24 August 2019), https://www.newscientist.com/article/2214309-facebooks-ad-data-may-put-millions-of-gay-people-at-risk/.

of domestic violence, the release of personal information, such as a home address, could be life-threatening. In her testimony to the US Congress, the World Privacy Forum's Pam Dixon reported[58] finding data brokers selling lists of rape victims,[59] addresses of domestic violence shelters,[60] sufferers of genetic diseases,[61] HIV/AIDS sufferers,[62] sufferers of addiction[63] and more. In particular, users of the dating app Grindr have been located and targeted in one of the 69 countries[64] where homosexuality is a criminal offence.[65] A report *Digital Crime Scenes,*[66] found that police forces in Tunisia, Egypt and Lebanon are increasingly relying on digital tools to identify, entrap and prosecute LGBTQ+ people.

Publicly traded on the Australian Securities Exchange, popular family app Life360 is used by approximately 33 million people worldwide and has been marketed as 'the leading digital safety brand for families'. Life360's app allows the user to see the precise, real-time location of friends or family members, including the speed at which they are driving and the battery level on their devices. Marketed as a safety app, Life360 is popular among parents who want to track and supervise their children. For the app to function, it asks for the broadest location permissions possible. Many apps that use location data allow users to grant access only while it's in use. As Life360 is for tracking whereabouts in real time, the app asks for location data at all times – and does not function unless that permission is turned on. A disclaimer appears in smaller print at the bottom of the permissions screen: 'Your location data may be shared with Partners for the purposes of crash detection, research, analytics, attribution and tailored advertising'. Life360 discloses in the fine print of its privacy policy that it sells the data it gleans from app users:

> **De-Identified Information:** We may also share your information with third parties in a form that does not reasonably identify you directly.

58 Pam Dixon, 'Congressional Testimony: What Information Do Data Brokers Have on Consumers?' *US Senate Committee on Commerce, Science and Transportation* (18 December 2013).
59 MEDbase 200.
60 Firstmark.
61 MEDbase 200.
62 MEDbase 200.
63 Exact Data.
64 Daniele Paletta, 'State-Sponsored Homophobia: Global Legislation Overview Update'(15 December 2020), https://ilga.org/ilga-world-releases-state-sponsored-homophobia-December-2020-update.
65 Matt Payton, 'Egyptian Police Are Using Grindr to Find and Arrest LGBT People', *The Independent* (27 August 2016).
66 Afsaneh Rigot, 'Digital Crime Scenes: The Role of Digital Evidence in the Persecution of LGBTQ People in Egypt, Lebanon and Tunisia', *Berkman Klein Center for Internet & Society at Harvard University* (7 March 2022).

> These third parties may use the de-identified information for any purpose.[67]

Users can opt out of location data sales from the Life360 app through the privacy and security settings. While Life360 has announced that it will stop sales of precise location data to the dozen or so[68] data brokers that it had previously been working with,[69] no law actually prohibits them from doing so. The company reported that revenue from selling location data for the years ended 31 December 2021 and 2020 was US$18.7 million and $16.0 million, respectively.[70]

Purpose Creep

Although an app may claim that it is collecting data for a particular purpose, it will often use the data collected for an entirely unrelated purpose. For example, The Weather Channel app's parent company was found analysing users' location data for hedge funds, according to a lawsuit filed in Los Angeles.[71] In 2019, an Indian fintech company was found to use data collected from mobile apps as part of its credit scoring system.[72] In that case, consumers who had downloaded a music app to their phones were having their contact lists, user IDs and GPS coordinates harvested by the fintech company, which in turn used this as part of its system to help lenders decide whether to approve loan applications. In the lead up to the 2020 US elections, the Trump re-election campaign was reportedly using the services of a data company that uses data from data brokers to influence voters.[73] The company itself admitted that this data includes location data and behavioural data, which was harvested from smartphone apps:

67 Life 360, 'Full Privacy Policy' (4 November 2022), https://support.life360.com/hc/en-us/articles/360043228154-Full-Privacy-Policy.

68 John Keegan and Alfred Ng, 'The Popular Family Safety App Life360 Is Selling Precise Location Data on Its Tens of Millions of Users', *The Markup* (6 December 2021).

69 Life360, 'December 2021 Quarterly Activities Report and Appendix 4C', ASX Announcement (27 January 2022). Life360 announced it will now sell only precise location data to Arity and 'aggregated' location data to PlacerAI.

70 Life360, *Annual Report 2021*, 46.

71 Jennifer Valentino DeVries and Natasha Singer, 'Los Angeles Accuses Weather Channel App of Covertly Mining User Data', *New York Times* (3 January 2019), https://int.nyt.com/data/documenthelper/554-l-a-weather-app-location/8980fd9af72915412e31/optimized/full.pdf.

72 Gopal Sathe, 'How Sai Baba Was Made To Spy on Your Phone For Credit Ratings', *Huffington Post* (8 July 2019).

73 Lee Fang, 'The Trump Campaign is Deploying Phone Location Tracking Technology', *The Intercept* (12 December 2019).

> While voter files are extremely valuable, some campaign managers are beginning to realize that each voter's smartphone is the ultimate voter file. Mobile data can tell them everything from the device operating system (iOS or Android) to what other apps are on the device, what Wi-Fi networks the device joins and much more. And that doesn't even cover the information it's possible to infer, such as gender, age, lifestyle preferences and so on.
>
> Knowing who's in their voter file, campaign managers can use mobile data and mobile advertising to identify and engage voters who give off similar digital signals to their identified supporters. In the cutthroat world of politics, campaign marketers now have access to more power and precision than they've ever had.[74]

More locally, in *Facebook Inc v. Australian Information Commissioner*,[75] the Australian Information Commissioner alleged that the personal information of Australian Facebook users was disclosed to the *This is Your Digital Life* app for a purpose other than the purpose for which the information was collected, in breach of the Privacy Act.[76] The information was exposed to the risk of being disclosed to Cambridge Analytica and used for political profiling purposes, and to other third parties.[77]

Conclusion

Allowing unrestricted data harvesting by data brokers raises significant concerns regarding privacy, security and consumer consent. Recent surveys conducted by the ACCC[78] and the Consumer Policy Research Centre[79] indicate that a large majority of users perceive the monitoring of their offline location and the sharing of their location data with third parties as a violation of their personal information. However, the intricate and lengthy privacy policies implemented by these companies often go unnoticed by users, amplifying the information asymmetry and leading users to mistakenly believe that these policies are intended to safeguard their privacy.[80] In reality, these policies pri-

74 Emily Reynolds 'Before the Gold Rush: A New Way to Reach Voters', *Phunware* (30 November 2017).

75 [2022] FCAFC 9.

76 In breach of Australian Privacy Principle 6.

77 In breach of Australian Privacy Principle 11.

78 86% of digital platforms users surveyed considered the monitoring of offline location and movement without the user's consent to be a misuse of their data: Roy Morgan Research, *Consumer Views and Behaviours on Digital Platforms* (November 2018), 21.

79 71% of consumers surveyed were uncomfortable with their location data being shared with third parties: The Consumer Policy Research Centre, *Submission to the ACCC Digital Platforms Inquiry* (April 2018), 5.

80 See, e.g., Roy Morgan Research, *Consumer Views and Behaviours on Digital Platforms* (November 2018), 6, 31; The Consumer Policy Research Centre, *Submission to the ACCC Digital Platforms Inquiry* (April 2018), 5.

marily delineate the permissions granted to companies, nudging users to provide consent for the collection and dissemination of their sensitive personal information when it is not in their interest to do so.[81] Once this data are in circulation, they become vulnerable to misuse, with limited or no options for retrieval or control. In the absence of meaningful regulatory reform, data brokers will continue to prioritise profit over safeguarding user privacy, security and physical safety concerns. Such calculated indifference to the societal values that we cherish is the epitome of corporate evil.

81 See Patricia A Norberg, Daniel R Horne and David A. Horne, 'The Privacy Paradox: Personal Information Disclosure Intentions versus Behaviours' (2007) 41(1) *The Journal of Consumer Affairs* 100.

Part 3

A Mechanics of Corporate Harms

Chapter 8

Evil Corporations in Horror Fiction

Penny Crofts

Introduction

Criminal law and moral philosophy have had difficulties in grappling with corporations as moral and/or legal agents due to an anthropocentric bias. In contrast, evil corporations are such a staple of horror fiction that they can be portrayed with shorthand gestures. This chapter articulates common tropes of evil corporations in horror fiction to tease out how and why corporations can be wicked, and considers these portrayals in light of criminal and philosophical conceptions of culpability. This analysis is vital, given the relative absence of criminal culpability attributed to the organisations that cause a proliferation of harms. It is as though it is difficult to even imagine imposing criminal liability. One barrier to imposing criminal liability is that the criminal legal system has great difficulty in conceptualising corporations as responsible moral agents, capable of good or evil. This is in part due to the construction of criminal legal doctrine around the classic legal subject – the responsible human being.[1] Attempts to slot the corporation into these pre-existing categories have proven difficult – particularly in terms of the so-called fault elements or *mens rea*. How do we establish what the corporation knows and/or intends? It has been difficult to conceptualise corporations as having subjective fault, let alone proving it, and thus challenging to establish that a corporation is blameworthy. This has manifested in a tendency to write off harms caused by large corporations as failures, tragedies or accidents – language similar to that used in response to natural disasters – as though there were no responsible agent.

In light of our increasing dependence on large organisations and their capacity to inflict widespread harms we urgently need a legal account of

1 Ngaire Naffine, 'Our Legal Lives as Men, Women and Persons' (2004) 24 *Legal Studies* 621. Criminal law has been constructed around the responsible human being, however, see Grear, who has argued that corporations may well be the quintessential liberal legal subject. Anna Grear, 'Deconstructing Anthropos: A Critical Legal Reflection on "Anthropocentric" Law and Anthropocene "Humanity"' (2015) 26 *Law and Critique* 225.

DOI: 10.4324/9781003402534-12

corporations as moral agents that are capable of good and evil. Although criminal law is primarily concerned with the bad, rather than the wicked,[2] philosophies of evil (or wickedness) provide a rich resource to analyse whether corporations can be blameworthy in their own right, or only through the agents or members acting for them. I am using the word 'evil' in the narrow sense as 'the worst possible term of opprobrium imaginable'.[3] As with classic criminal legal doctrine, philosophical accounts of evil tend to be anthropocentric. For example, in his entry to *Stanford Encyclopedia of Philosophy* on the concept of evil, Calder states 'if only human beings are moral agents, then only human beings can perform evil actions'.[4] Even theorists that focus on organisational or systemic wrongs such as the Holocaust, tend to theorise about how individuals come to do evil in group settings – that is, they provide situational accounts of evil but remain anthropocentric.[5]

Traditional responses and conceptualisations by criminal law and philosophy do not adequately respond to the challenge of corporate harms. In contrast to criminal law and philosophies of wickedness, evil corporations are a popular trope in horror fiction.[6] There is a broad literature on the precise definition of horror, which for the purposes of analysis I do not need to resolve.[7] Instead, I adopt a broad definition of genre, that is, that horror fiction has the intention to arouse horror. This chapter analyses the attributes of evil corporations in horror fiction as a way to disrupt the mental block in criminal law and philosophy against conceiving of corporations as moral agents. There are all too many examples of corporate malfeasance in real life – but these have difficulties of proof and various ambiguities. In contrast, corporations in horror fiction are almost always unambiguously evil. They are so common in horror fiction that shorthand gestures are used to construct corporations as evil. In this chapter I analyse these gestures to think through when and how corporations are portrayed as evil to provide a foundation for thinking through philosophical and criminal accounts of corporate culpability.

This approach is part of the project of cultural legal studies that identifies how texts of popular culture (here, horror fiction) and legal constructions (corporate

2 Wickedness may exceed the categories of criminal law, see, e.g., Penny Crofts, 'Monstrous Wickedness and the Judgment of Knight' (2012) 21 *Griffith Law Review* 72.

3 M.G. Singer, 'The Concept of Evil' (2004) 79 *Philosophy* 185, 185.

4 Todd Calder, 'The Concept of Evil' in Edward Zalta (ed.), *The Stanford Encyclopedia of Philosophy* (Winter, 2016) https://plato.stanford.edu/archives/win2016/entries/concept-evil/.

5 Hannah Arendt, *Eichmann in Jerusalem: A Report on the Banality of Evil* (Penguin 1994); Stanley Milgram, *Obedience to Authority* (Harper and Row 1974).

6 https://movieweb.com/evil-fictional-corporations-in-movies/

7 Clive Bloom, 'Horror Fiction: In Search of a Definition' in David Punter (ed.), *A New Companion to the Gothic* (John Wiley & Sons, Incorporated 2012) http://ebookcentral.proquest.com/lib/uts/detail.action?docID=843409 accessed 20 November 2020; Noel Carroll, *The Philosophy of Horror or Paradoxes of the Heart* (Routledge 1990).

criminal law theory) intertwine in our expectations, constructions and perceptions of law. It has the advantage of rendering strange standard approaches and the application of corporate criminal law and philosophies of wickedness.[8] Analysing the attributes of fictional evil corporations provides a way to think about law differently and how law might be different. This is particularly important because despite long-term recognition of the failure of the criminal legal system to adequately conceptualise and respond to corporate harms, nothing much has changed.[9] This chapter turns a critical eye to conventional understandings and theories concerning evil, aiming to improve our concepts of evil and in turn inform criminal legal conceptions of corporate responsibility. We need a more nuanced account and lexicon of evil that adequately responds to and conceptualises the characteristics of corporate wrongdoing.

Prior to commencing analysis, it should be noted that a commonality in fiction and real life is that in terms of harms done by large organisations it does not really matter (particularly to victims) whether the large organisation is a corporation according to specific legal requirements or an NGO, a government organisation, privatised or not for profit. In horror fiction, these differences are not dwelled upon or necessarily clarified. At law, corporations have a specific narrow meaning, which large organisations such as the Catholic Church have drawn upon to evade liability. This chapter avoids technical legal definitions of the corporation and includes large organisations in the analysis to elucidate the capacity for systemic harms.

The 'Proliferation of Harms' section highlights that causing harm is a central means by which corporations are established as evil in horror. The 'Qualitative Modes of Wickedness' section analyses qualitative conceptions of evil – including analysis of how the audience knows, or assumes to know, what the corporation is intending or wanting, and whether these intentions or motives are evil. The chapter concludes with the argument that the central characteristic of evil corporations in horror fiction is that they have a calculated indifference to values that we as a society cherish, reminiscent of early legal conceptions of malice, and this can and should be conceived of as culpable in criminal law and philosophy.

Proliferation of Harms

A central way in which corporations are established as evil in horror fiction is through causing harm to epic numbers of people and the environment.[10]

8 Cassandra Sharp and Marett Leiboff (eds), *Cultural Legal Studies: Law's Popular Cultures and the Metamorphosis of Law* (Routledge 2016).

9 For example, research and reform recommendations from the 1980s continue to be relevant. See e.g., Brent Fisse and John Braithwaite, *Corporations, Crime and Accountability* (Cambridge University Press 1993).

10 For in-depth analysis, see Penny Crofts, 'The Horror of Corporate Harms' (2022) 38 *Australian Journal of Corporate Law* 23.

Anxieties and fears about corporations causing harm have been represented in horror for decades. For example, in the 1973 classic film, *Soylent Green*,[11] rations manufacturer Soylent Corporation deals with the overpopulation problem by making food out of people. This theme in horror fiction of causing harm to establish corporations as evil is consistent with philosophies of wickedness, most of which have harm as a central element of their definitions. For example, in his summary of philosophies of wickedness, Calder argues that harm is an 'essential component of evil'.[12] There are two aspects to this concept of harm – quantity and type of harm.[13] Theorists like Kekes combine the two, arguing that harms of evil must be serious and excessive.[14] Other theorists emphasise the quality of the harm. For example, Claudia Card argues that wickedness involves 'intolerable harms',[15] that is, harm that makes life not worth living from the point of view of the victim, including severe physical or mental suffering, and deprivations. The philosopher Luke Russell does not require magnitude, but rather the type of harm inflicted, asserting that actions are 'evil if and only if it is a wrong that is extremely harmful for at least one individual victim'.[16] Harms caused by corporations in horror fiction meet both magnitude and quality requirements. For example, evil corporations like Umbrella Corporation in the *Resident Evil* franchise and the unnamed laboratory in *28 Days Later* start zombie apocalypses, which cause harm to almost the entire human population *and* these infections are regarded by characters as a fate worse than death. They would rather die than be infected.

Moral philosophers devote a great deal of time to articulating harms caused by individuals, including by fictional characters, but there is a resounding silence about harms caused by corporations – unless they can point to a particular individual or individuals in the corporation who are identified as agents. Corporate harms in real life satisfy the requirements of magnitude and nastiness articulated as central to philosophical accounts of wickedness.[17] Corporations cause a proliferation of harms that radically exceed what an individual can inflict.[18] Given the proliferation of (nasty) harms caused by corporations, the quantitative model of wickedness is particularly apposite for corporations. Accordingly, the lack of philosophical

11 (1973) Richard Fleischer MGM.
12 Calder (n 4).
13 Singer (n 4); L Russell, 'Is Evil Qualitatively Distinct from Ordinary Wrongdoing?' (2007) 85 *Australasian Journal of Philosophy* 659.
14 John Kekes, *The Roots of Evil* (Cornell University Press 2005) 1–3.
15 Claudia Card, *The Atrocity Paradigm: A Theory of Evil* (Oxford University Press 2002) 16.
16 Luke Russell, *Being Evil: A Philosophical Perspective* (OUP 2020) 86–87.
17 Crofts, (n 10).
18 Steve Tombs, 'What to Do with the Harmful Corporation? The Case for a Non-Penal Real Utopia' [2016] *Justice, Power and Resistance* 193.

discourse linking corporate harms with moral responsibility is stark. It is as though corporations cannot be conceived of as responsible agents and the harms that they cause are comparable to natural disasters. The difference is that corporations are structured as responsible legal agents and as such, we need models of wickedness that adequately encapsulate corporate accountability.[19] Likewise, in criminal law, harmful consequences are a classic justification for criminalisation.[20] However, as I have argued elsewhere in more detail, the magnitude of corporate harms may preclude criminalisation – they are too big, too bad, too nasty for current criminal law categories.[21] It is horrific and perverse to exclude these harms from our accounts of culpability. We need a plausible, pragmatic response to corporate harms in philosophies of wickedness and criminal law in order to conceptualise corporate harms as wrong and criminal.

Qualitative Modes of Wickedness

There are many theories of wickedness that require some kind of qualitative difference from badness due to 'an extra quality of evil that is completely absent in the performance of ordinary wrongs'.[22] These theories put motive, intention and/or affect at the centre of the accounts of wickedness. This approach is partially consistent with claims of criminal law privileging subjective culpability in attributions of blameworthiness – expressed in the classic maxim of *actus non facit reum nisi mens sit rea* – that is, that a person shall not be held liable for an act unless the act was done with a guilty mind.[23] Although subjective culpability is much touted, there are a great many exceptions, including negligence, strict and absolute liability – many of which have been developed and/or applied to corporations.[24] Nonetheless, this claim to privileged subjective culpability has proven an obstacle to prosecuting corporations. There are two difficulties that I will consider in turn below by teasing out portrayals of evil corporations in horror fiction. Firstly, the emphasis upon subjective culpability requires ascertaining what the corporation thought, intended or wanted. Second, this then leads to a bigger question, whether the categories of culpability in criminal law and philosophies of wickedness are appropriate for a nuanced account of corporate blameworthiness.

19 Chris Chapple, *The Moral Responsibilities of Companies* (Palgrave MacMillan 2014).

20 George Fletcher, *Rethinking Criminal Law* (Little Brown 1978); John Stuart Mill, *On Liberty* (Penguin 1859); Joel Feinberg, *Harmless Wrongdoing – The Moral Limits of the Criminal Law* (Oxford UP 1988).

21 Crofts, (n 10).

22 H Steiner, 'Calibrating Evil' (2002) 85 *The Monist* 183, 184.

23 *Fowler v. Padget* (1978) 101 ER 1103.

24 Celia Wells, 'Swatting the Subjectivist Bug' [1982] *Criminal Law Review*.

Attributing Intention to the Corporation

Although corporations are legal subjects, there have been difficulties at law in attributing mental states to corporations.[25] At common law, the dominant model of attribution is that of identification theory, whereby the prosecution must identify the directing mind of the corporation (usually senior executives such as Board members) and then prove what members of the directing mind knew and intended and when.[26] There is long-term academic and judicial recognition that the larger a corporation, the more difficult it is to identify the directing mind.[27] A major difficulty of the directing mind doctrine is 'determining who the directing mind is and whether she controls what the organisation does'.[28] In contrast, the United States has adopted vicarious liability, whereby a corporation is responsible for any wrongs committed by an employee of the corporation in the course of their duties.[29] This approach bypasses the problem of identifying a directing mind but generates its own problem – of over-criminalising corporations by holding them responsible for rogue employees, and under-criminalising by failing to recognise the corporateness of corporate wrongdoing. Identification theory and vicarious liability are both nominalist – in that they focus on individuals or members of the corporation to attribute fault.

Horror fiction uses various techniques to portray the intentions of organisations. A common approach is for a character to be portrayed as the embodiment or 'face' of the organisation and this character is shown to make villainous decisions that contribute to the corporation causing harms. This approach is consistent with nominalism, particularly when the 'face' is the CEO of the organisation. For example, in *Poltergeist*, that person is the owner/operator, Teague, who knowingly chose not to remove the corpses from the cemetery but built on top of them.[30] Likewise, in *The Fifth Element*, Jean-Baptiste Zorg as CEO, is the face and name of massive weapons manufacturing firm, Zorg Industries.[31] Many films portray CEOs as the face of the organisation – meeting the legal requirements of directing mind doctrine.

25 Eric W. Orts, *Business Persons: A Legal Theory of the Firm* (Oxford 2013).

26 *Tesco Supermarkets Ltd v. Nattrass* (1971) 2 All ER 127.

27 For examples of judicial criticisms of identification theory, see Lord Hoffman, Privy Council in *Meridian Global Funds Management Asia Limited v. Securities Commission* [1995] 3 All ER 918; Justice Estey, *Canadian Dredge & Dock Co v. R* [1985] 1 SCR 662 at 693.

28 Liz Campbell, 'Corporate Liability and the Criminalisation of Failure' (2018) 12 *Law and Financial Markets Review* 57. 58.

29 Joshua D. Greenberg and Ellen C. Brotman, 'Strict Vicarious Criminal Liability for Corporations and Corporate Executives: Stretching the Boundaries of Criminalization' (2014) 51 *American Criminal Law Review* 79.

30 1982, Tobe Hooper, MGM.

31 1997, Luc Besson, Gaumont.

Any motives, intentions or knowledge that these CEOs have is the knowledge and intention of the(ir) corporation.

Frequently the 'face' of the corporation would not be regarded at law as the 'directing mind'. For example, in *Stranger Things* (Season One), the senior research scientist, Doctor Brenner, is clearly the face of the organisation.[32] He is front and centre of the bulk of breaches of law by the laboratory. Likewise, in *Aliens*, the sleazy middle-manager Burke is the 'face' of the corporation for the audience and the crew.[33] He greets Ripley saying: 'I'm Burke. Carter Burke. I work for the company, but other than that I'm an okay guy'. Burke ordered colonists to investigate the alien and then encourages Ripley to go back to the alien planet, intending to profit from the alien by creating a biological weapon. In both these fictions, what would be legally recognised as the 'directing mind' of the corporation is never on screen or referred to. Other employees regard Burke and Brenner as leaders and their authority as representatives of the corporation are not questioned. Although in *Aliens* there is some dissent, employees follow company processes and hierarchies. Senior management is presumably behind Brenner and Burke, but the audience never see them or hear about them. This is arguably a fairly realistic portrayal of how large corporations work – most employees never meet members of the Board and senior executives. How then do we know what the corporation intends?

Criminal law and philosophy (on the rare occasions when they consider corporate or organisational liability), become mired in debates as to whether a corporate mind exists and how we can work out what the corporation wants. In contrast, in horror fiction, it is not difficult for the audience to work out what the corporation wants – corporate intention is manifested through the actions, omissions and choices of the company. This is in accordance with various theoretical proposals by legal theorists. For example, Peter French argued that the Corporate Internal Decision Structure provided a means of identifying decisions and choices of the corporation,[34] and Elise Bant's theory of system of intentionality argues that a corporation's systems, policies and processes manifest its intentions.[35] Lisa Siraganian has drawn upon Elizabeth Anscombe's arguments about intention to argue that:

> Where and how the group or corporate mind exists (is "thingified" in the world) is not the relevant concern, although it tends to be where most discussions of collective intention become stuck to this day. Instead, the question is whether there might be an answer to the question "why?"

32 2016, Duffer Brothers, 21 Laps Entertainment.

33 1986, James Cameron, 20th Century Studios.

34 Peter French, *Corporate Ethics* (Harcourt 1995); Peter French, 'Integrity, Intentions, and Corporations' (1996) *American Business Law Journal* 141.

35 E. Bant, 'Systems Intentionality: Theory and Practice', Chapter 14 of this volume.

> that could explain a corporation's action—whoever happens to offer that expression.[36]

In *Poltergeist* the question 'why?' was asked after skeletal corpses attacked his wife in the hole for the swimming pool, and coffins and rotting corpses erupt throughout the neighbourhood. Steven confronts his boss, Teague:

> "You son of a bitch! You moved the cemetery, but you left the bodies, didn't you? You son of a bitch, you left the bodies, you only moved the headstones! You only moved the headstones! Why? Why?"

In *Poltergeist*, Teague does not answer this question directly, but it is clear to the audience that the corporation did not move the bodies because it was cheaper to leave them there. Likewise, in *Stranger Things* and *Aliens*, it is assumed that Burke and Brenner are not rogue employees but are acting in accordance with the intentions of the organisation. This does not preclude individual responsibility but does assume and demonstrate organisational motives and approach.

Intentions and Motives of Evil Corporations

In horror fiction, even in the absence of Board meetings and clear articulation of motives, audience members are able to discern the intentions and motives of corporations – and these can be interrogated as to whether they are wicked in qualitative accounts of wickedness.

A classic model of wickedness is that of pure evil, that is, evil for its own sake.[37] The focus here is on the intention of the perpetrator to harm another.[38] Theorists like Steiner argue that the perpetrator's pleasure is what transforms ordinary wrongs into evil,[39] arguing that 'evil acts are wrong acts that are pleasurable for their doer'.[40] Given that the horror genre specifically dwells in transgression and evil, we might expect the portrayal of corporations as pure evil. For example, slasher movies portray perpetrators whose only reason to kill seems to be because they are evil, such as serial killer Michael Myers in the *Halloween* franchise. But corporations tend not to be portrayed as pure evil in horror or science fiction. There are different explanations for this. Arguably, corporations cannot take pleasure in inflicting harm because they lack emotional capacity. Although their CEOs might express some sadistic

36 Lisa Siraganian, *Modernism and the Meaning of Corporate Persons* (Oxford 2020) 119.

37 Phillip Cole, *The Myth of Evil* (Edinburgh University Press Ltd 2006).

38 Todd Calder, 'Is Evil Just Very Wrong?' (2013) 163 *Philosophical Studies* 177.

39 Steiner (n 22) 183. See also, C. Fred Alford, 'Hitler's Willing Executioners: What Does "willing" Mean?' (1997) 26 *Theory and Society* 732; Arne Johan Vetlesen, *Evil and Human Agency* (Cambridge University Press 2005) 105.

40 Steiner (n 22) 189.

pleasure in harming others unnecessarily, or sadness if they miss an opportunity to harm (such as the CEO Zorg in *Fifth Element*), I cannot think of corporations inflicting harm for no other reason than for pure evil in horror fiction. More significantly, it reinforces that corporations are agents with the capacity to reason and that members, particularly shareholders, require corporations to act with reason, even if those reasons are not good reasons.

Rather than pure evil, horror fiction uniformly depicts evil corporations inflicting harms for instrumental reasons, that is, to achieve particular goals. For example, Zorg in *The Fifth Element*,[41] is a greedy and cruel Earth industrialist who freely chooses to work for the central, unseen antagonist, the Great Evil. His involvement is motivated by his belief that life is an inevitable result of destruction. Although this belief is horrible, his complicity with the Great Evil is not pure evil, as it is not suffering for its own sake, but for life. A very common motivation of evil corporations is the pursuit of profit. In the series *Ragnarok*, Jutul Corporation chooses not to correctly store toxic waste because it would be unnecessarily expensive.[42] In many horror fictions, it is never articulated that the corporation is avaricious, this is simply portrayed in their choices and actions. The corporation basically values profit over people, a common complaint regarding corporations. Accordingly, despite horror fiction being a genre of imagination and frequently the supernatural, the portrayal of *why* corporations cause harm is realistic, expressing cultural anxieties about corporations. These aims may not be good aims, but they are comprehensible. This comprehensibility of motive is a plot requirement. If the motives, reasons and actions do not make sense, then the plot makes no sense. These motives and reasons can then be analysed through theories of wickedness to consider whether the corporation is evil or not.

Horror fiction evaluates motives when portraying corporate malfeasance. In some horror fiction, a member of the corporation may be motivated by a desire to save someone from mortal illness – usually wife or a child (e.g., *Resident Evil*). This kind of motive is portrayed as understandable but still wrongheaded in light of the end results. Unleashing a virus that kills most of the world in the quest to save a loved one may be understandable but is still wrong. It is particularly wrong if CEOs or employees are risking others to save their own lives.[43] The pursuit of profit is understandable but represented as wicked because it is not regarded as a good enough goal for the suffering that it causes. Philosophy and criminal law accept that harming someone may not always be a bad thing (for example, performing surgery), but doing so for bad reasons is. There are various ways of thinking through unworthy goals or reasons. Morton argues that evil people are uninhibited by barriers

41 1997, Luc Besson, Gaumont Buena Vista International.
42 2020, Mogens Hagedorn, Netflix.
43 2012, Ridley Scott, 20th Century Studios.

against considering harming or humiliating others that should be there.[44] Garrard has likewise explored the idea of particularly despicable motivation structures.[45] Calder argues that we can evaluate a goal compared to what is sacrificed or that certain things can and should never be justified to be used as means.[46] Midgley would argue that some motives are completely understandable but it is the lack of balance, the monomania of it and the failure to take into account other values that is wicked. Midgley uses Eichmann as an example of someone who wanted to be good at his job. Even though this is completely understandable and ordinary, his failure to be concerned about or value human life was wicked.[47] Although criminal law claims not to be interested in motive it does impact upon choices to investigate, prosecute, jury findings and sentencing.[48] Horror fiction portrays comprehensible motives by corporations which are not good enough to justify the harms that they cause.

Calculated Indifference or Malice

The most common attribute of evil corporations in horror fiction is that of calculated indifference – where corporations are depicted as indifferent to the harms that they are causing. Moral philosophers have explored the idea of calculated indifference in various ways in relation to individuals, and this can be extended to the portrayal of evil corporations. There is dispute amongst theorists as to whether this indifference should be framed as emotional or cognitive. For example, Vetlesen asserted that

> the capacity [Eichmann] failed to exercise is emotional rather than intellectual or cognitive; it is the capacity to develop *empathy* with other human beings, to take an emotional interest in the 'human' import of the situation in which persons affected by his actions found themselves.[49]

Likewise, Haybron has argued that evil people lack motives or sentiments of moral worth, they almost always lack empathy and concern for others and are not motivated to help people or do what is right.[50] But Arendt would

44 Adam Morton, *On Evil* (Routledge 2004) 57; Mordekhai Thomas, *Vessels of Evil: American Slavery and the Holocaust* (Temple University Press 1993) 77.

45 Eve Garrard, 'The Nature of Evil' (1998) 1 *Philosophical Explorations: An International Journal for the Philosophy of Mind and Action* 43.

46 Calder (n 38).

47 Mary Midgley, *Wickedness: A Philosophical Essay* (Routledge 2001).

48 Guyora Binder, 'The Rhetoric of Motive and Intent' (2002) 6 *Buffalo Criminal Law Review* 1. E.g., analysis of jury findings on motives and euthanasia. Alan Norrie, 'Legal Form and Moral Judgment: The Problem of Euthanasia' (2010) 5 *University of Warwick Legal Studies Research Paper* 1.

49 Arne Johan Vetlesen, *Perception, Empathy and Judgment: An Inquiry into the Precondition of Moral Performance* (Pennsylvania State University 1994) 105.

50 Daniel Haybron, 'Consistency of Character and the Character of Evil' in Daniel Haybron (ed.), *Earth's Abominations: Philosophical Studies of Evil* (Rodopi 2002).

argue that emotions can prove and have proven fickle and prefers thinking – self-examination and accountability, critically scrutinising our actions and interactions.[51] In her analysis of Eichmann, Arendt asserted that he was not monstrous (which would have been comforting), but rather that he suffered from 'sheer thoughtlessness'. Svendsen calls it 'stupid evil'.[52] However, corporations are not stupid – rather they choose ignorance and lack of care. It is here that the calculated aspect of indifference arises. Corporations prefer not to know or think about risks associated with undertakings. Corporations are on sufficient notice as to the risks of their activities, have ample resources and legal advice to ensure knowledge of those risks, but despite this, they choose not to concern themselves with harms. This is an active preference, not stupidity.

This assertion of ignorance is common by corporations in real life, where they claim that they did not realise a product was harmful, such as tobacco, asbestos, thalidomide, oxycontin. Can and should we hold corporations responsible for ignorance? In criminal law, ignorance by a corporation of the harms it has caused can make it difficult to identify *mens rea* and thus attribute blameworthiness. In fact, as Chia and Paterson argue in this volume, law may actively discourage corporations from investigating too closely the risks associated with new products.[53] In contrast, horror fiction represents this ignorance as culpable in different ways.

Horror fiction depicts corporations that do not know about harms that they cause because they do not want to know or do not care enough to find out – and this refusal to be aware of harms is depicted as blameworthy. For example, in *Stranger Things*, the laboratory makes it very difficult for the public to communicate any concerns about environmental contamination and missing children, disregards them when they do make contact and tries to make it as difficult as possible for police to investigate. In *Ragnarok*, the Jutul Corporation puts up fences and locks the area in which the toxic waste is stored to ensure that no one will find it. It stops thinking about the waste until a student finds it as a consequence of global warming. The Jutul Corporation expresses ignorance that the waste was dangerous when they stored it (even though it is labelled toxic) and that it had forgotten about it. Despite this ignorance, both the laboratory in *Stranger Things* and the Jutul Corporation are depicted as responsible for creating a dangerous situation and for choosing ignorance. This is in accordance with philosophical accounts of ignorance. For example, Aristotle argued that ignorance is only a legitimate excuse for causing unjustified harm when we are not responsible

51 Valerie Hartouni, *Visualizing Atrocity: Arendt, Evil, and the Optics of Thoughtlessness* (New York University Press 2012) 74
52 Lars Svendsen, *A Philosophy of Evil* (Dalkey 2010).
53 Chia and Peterson in chapter 6 of this volume.

for that ignorance.[54] Examples of culpable ignorance include self-deception, failure to make inquiries, ignoring evidence – all of which could be subsumed into the legal and philosophical category of wilful blindness.[55] Corporations construct firewalls in order to avoid awareness of harms caused.[56] These arguments of culpable ignorance are applicable to corporations because they are recognised as sites of risk for specific harms – they have been given legal notice of those risks with duties imposed. Moreover, corporations have resources available to know about those risks and respond.

Horror fiction depicts situations where corporations may not have known that they were causing harm (although this is a generous reading of many cases of corporate harms), but how they react when they find out is culpable. Corporations in horror tend to deny harms – that the harms have occurred, that they are responsible or that there is anything that they can do about them.[57] The denial can be taken as an indication of culpable intention by the corporation at the time of causing harm and/or the denial can be a wrong in and of itself. This is particularly the case if harms continue while the corporation refuses to admit responsibility and fails to prevent the harms. For example, in *Ragnarok*, when the toxicity of the waste becomes apparent, rather than warning the community and advising them to stop drinking the water, the company kills any witnesses. In the meantime, the public and environment continue to be harmed by the waste. When the toxic waste becomes public knowledge, the Jutul Corporation is charged with failure to properly store toxic materials. The series suggests that at the time when it originally stored the waste the company knew that it was dangerous but did not care. This reaction of denial is an all too common response by corporations, when harms that they have caused become apparent, either within the corporation or more commonly to the general public, is denial.[58] Horror fiction tends to portray this denial as dangerous and culpable.

The failure to think about (potential) harms expresses and is associated with indifference or lack of care. The moral philosopher Nussbaum asserts that what we think about reflects what we care about.[59] In horror films, corporations are depicted as failing to care about the human being as human.[60] This lack of care is manifested in horror by the treatment of people, particularly employees. Workers are frequently portrayed as expendable, as a way

54 Aristotle, *The Nicomachean Ethics* (J. Thomson tr., Penguin 2004) Bk III.

55 David Jones, *Moral Responsibility in the Holocaust: A Study in the Ethics of Character* (Rowman & Littlefield 1999) 82.

56 See Lisa Siraganian in chapter 10 of this volume.

57 Stanley Cohen, *States of Denial: Knowing about Atrocities and Suffering* (Polity 2001).

58 Ibid.

59 Martha Nussbaum, *Upheavals of Thought: The Intelligence of Emotions* (Cambridge University Press 2001).

60 Hannah Arendt, *Responsibility and Judgment* (Jerome Kohn ed., Shocken 2005).

of establishing the ruthlessness of the evil corporation. For example, in *The Fifth Element*, Zorg is utterly ruthless in his treatment of employees. He's advised to fire employees at his weapons manufacturing company because of potential trouble with the economy. He suggests firing a million employees and glares at the manager when he suggests that 500,000 would be enough. Zorg kills Mangalore mercenaries (contract workers) with a bomb for failing to deliver. Likewise, in *Stranger Things*, the first scene depicts the death of a lab worker at work. There is no mourning or risk assessment about how this happened or how to prevent it. The same work continues in the same way. Work conditions in evil organisations tend to be very poor – even CEOs are dispensable and replaceable.

Harms to employees in horror may be direct and intentional, but there is another type of harm which epitomises calculated indifference – where humans are killed due to lack of care by the corporation. For example, in the film *Alien*, Weyland Yutani is the quintessential (fictional) evil corporation, explicitly willing to sacrifice humans in the quest for profit. In *Alien*, the company intentionally gives the crew no notice and inadequate weapons because they do not want the crew to defeat the alien. This is a classic form of positive evil – intentional, duplicitous, devious wrongdoing, with the explicit calculated intention to sacrifice the crew. However, Weyland Yutani in *Aliens* is arguably worse and more realistic. Although the crew is provided with inadequate and malfunctioning equipment, there is no explicit intention to sacrifice the colonists or crew. The poor equipment is just a manifestation of the profit logic of the corporation. The marines are so used to working with malfunctioning equipment that when a character is told his camera is not working he whacks himself on the head to fix it. In *Aliens*, the malfunctioning equipment is a product of cost-cutting, rather than any nefarious motive. Both motives have the same root cause, that is, the regard and treatment of humans as expendable in the rapacious quest for profit. But in *Aliens* the reason is more realistic and insidious – due to calculated indifference. The deaths of employees are simply collateral damage.[61]

The horror genre explores the question of whether or not corporations are designed not to care – after all – they have no souls.[62] Theorists such as Milgram have explored how social conditions can lead ordinary people to perform evil actions and highlighted how the distance of perpetrators from victims can increase the infliction of harms.[63] Arte Vetlesen has argued that

61 Penny Crofts, 'Aliens: Legal Conceptions of the Corporate Invasion' (2022) 34 *Law and Literature* 387.

62 John Coffee Jr, 'No Soul to Damn: No Body to Kick: An Unscandalised Inquiry into the Problem of Corporate Punishment' (1980) 79 *Michigan Law Review* 386.

63 Milgram (n 5).

proximity 'possesses the power to call the bluff of dehumanization'.[64] In the horror genre, corporations are instantly recognisable workplaces. They are frequently represented with impersonal, uncomfortable working environments – cement or glass, bunkers without windows, open plan, sterile – that are not welcoming to humans (there are very rare exceptions where evil corporations ostensibly offer comfortable work environments). The workplace design expresses that humans are cogs in the machine, replaceable, and the focus is on profit. Most corporations are contained in a building that is isolated from the outside world – thus many of the harms inflicted by the corporation are literally external. For example, in *Cabin in the Woods* and *Stranger Things*, the corporation is situated in a bunker – expressing and imposing the distance between the actions of the corporation and the harmful consequences. This portrayal of systemic harms to human beings (and the environment) as collateral damage is consistent with the purpose for which corporations are created – the maximisation of profits for its owners (the shareholders). Legal principles operate to enshrine the central purpose of the corporation – profit – and to protect investors and executives from losses. In the present day, incorporation almost always bestows limited liability for owners and shareholders, that is, the protection from risk. Investors can only lose the capital that they choose to invest. The effect of this legally enshrined irresponsibility has led the legal theorist Bakan to argue that corporations are externalising machines.[65] Accounting practices privilege certain costs and benefits and exclude others, which means that harms (like those to people and the environment) are externalised by the corporation and there is accordingly no requirement to protect against them. This externalisation is manifested in horror fiction by the material buildings of the corporation, as well as the motives and actions.

How then, can we best encapsulate the blameworthiness of corporations that inflict harms with calculated indifference? The model of criminal culpability has as its pinnacle the concept of intentional wrongdoing. But corporations, even evil corporations in the horror genre, do not set out to harm humans as their primary aim – they just do not care. The harms caused by corporations (in horror and real life) are generally unintended except in the sense that in the intended pursuit of maximising profits (or survival and expansion) above all else, people die because proper responsibility has not been taken. Are there ways to capture this as wrong because it is so quintessential to corporate malfeasance? This issue was explored by the criminologist Reiman, who argues that intentionality tends to assume an individual sentience; so what of a corporate employer that does not positively intend

64 Vetlesen (n 49) 120.

65 Joel Bakan, *The Corporation: The Pathological Pursuit of Profit and Power* (Simon and Schuster 2004).

harm, but rather fails to maintain and invest in safety? Take the mining executive who:

> wanted to harm to no-one in particular, but he knew his acts were likely to harm someone-and *once someone is harmed, the victim is someone in particular*. There is no moral basis for treating one-on-one harm as criminal and indirect harm as merely regulatory (original emphases).[66]

In horror films, this calculated indifference is integral to why corporations are evil, and ought to be treated as culpable by the criminal justice system. Reiman argues that corporate offenders may well be more culpable than individual offenders of intentional, one-on-one harm because corporate offenders represent a generalised threat to others, whilst individual offenders tend to harm someone specific.

This idea of a generalised threat as wrongful was expressed in early common law conceptions of malice.[67] Malice was integral to differentiating felonious homicide, which was a capital offence, expressed in Latin in various permutations such as *malitia*, *malitia praecogitata* or *malitia purpense* – from non-felonious slayings, which were those committed with an absence of malice, *ex malitia praecogitata* or *non per malitiam* (or *feloniam*) *ex cogitatam*. In early common law, malice went beyond our contemporary emphasis on intentional wrongdoing to a broader conception of wickedness. The treatise writer Foster's definition of malice is particularly lovely and significant for corporate wrongs:

> Hath been attended by such circumstances as carry in them the plain indications of a heart regardless of social duty and fatally bent upon mischief.[68]

Integral to Foster's definition is an element of social duty and obedience. This definition of malice emphasised not only the moral and spiritual dimension of the common law of homicide but also its social and political dimension. The common law of crimes enforced the royal peace, a monopoly on the authorisation of public violence: 'the jealousy with which the law watcheth over the publick tranquility (a laudable jealousy it is)'.[69] All felonies were also trespasses, manifest breaches of the 'public tranquillity'. Felonies were literally disorderly; they were breaches of the sovereign's order. Many corporate

66 Jeffrey Reiman, *The Rich Get Richer and the Poor Get Prison: Ideology, Class and Criminal Justice* (Allyn and Bacon 2003) 67–70.

67 Penny Crofts, *Wickedness and Crime: Laws of Homicide and Malice* (Routledge 2013).

68 Michael Foster, *A Report of Some Proceedings on the Commission of Oyer and Terminer and Goal Delivery for the Trial of the rebels in the Year 1746 in the County of Surry, and of Other Crown Cases. To which are added discourses upon a few branches of the Crown Law* (London 1762/1982), p. 257.

69 Ibid. p. 320.

law theorists have stressed the idea of corporations operating only as a consequence of a social licence – arguing that if they do not work towards the public good, then this licence can and should be revoked.[70] Historic malice captures the idea of generalised risk-taking, such as throwing a boulder over a wall without looking if someone was there would be a slaying with malice; and the idea of social duty and care. The difference is that horror fiction portrays the systemic massive harms that corporations can inflict when accompanied by a heart regardless of social duty.

Conclusion

Evil corporations in horror fiction are disturbingly prolific, recognisable and realistic, to the extent that, unlike most monsters in horror, evil corporations are so generic that they need no origin story. It is indeed hard to think of any virtuous corporations in horror fiction. Horror fiction seems to answer in the affirmative that corporations are inherently bad – after all, they are soulless.[71] Whilst the harms caused may be supernatural (such as zombie viruses), the motives of evil corporations are all too comprehensible, banal and routine. In the pursuit of motives such as profit, evil corporations in horror treat harms as collateral damage, a form of calculated indifference to values that we as a society hold dear. The horror genre expresses our anxieties that corporations pose a generalised threat – an idea that could perhaps be best expressed through medieval malice – and the idea that corporations will not be held to account for these harms. This generalised threat is facilitated and required through the legal structures of the corporation and our failure to hold corporations responsible. We know that in real life, not all corporations are evil – however criminal law and moral philosophy need to think about corporations as moral agents that can be attributed blameworthiness for calculated indifference or malice to the massive harms that they cause. As such, we can and should rewrite what we expect from corporations.

70 Julia Dreosti, Bimaya De Silva and Katie Walsh, 'A Civil Solution to the Social Licence to Operate and Directors' Duties Condundrum in Australia' (2021) 38 *Company and Securities Law Journal* 404; Pamela Hanrahan, 'Corporate Governance, Financial Institutions and the "Social Licence"' (2016) 10 *Law and Financial Markets Review* 123.

71 Coffee Jr (n 62).

Chapter 9

Corporate Office, Corporate Irresponsibility and the Constitutive Vicariousness of Corporate Power

Timothy D. Peters[1]

Introduction

A fundamental aspect of modern criminal law is the responsible individual. In its key distinctions between intent and action, *mens rea* and *actus reus*, criminal law presupposes an intentional, acting individual that can be held morally and legally culpable for their actions. As has been well canvassed, the challenge of corporate criminal responsibility is how to deal with the individualised focus of criminal law when it comes to corporate entities. Nominalist approaches see the corporation only as a shorthand name for the collection of individuals and criminal responsibility can only be that of the individual, which may then be attributed to the corporation notionally or vicariously. Realist approaches, on the other hand, recognise that corporations have an independent existence separate to their members and that they can be culpable for criminal activity at an organisational level. The tension between these two positions highlights the way in which the corporation itself functions as a mediating device *between* the individual and collective action.

This chapter examines this mediating notion of the corporation by developing a theory of 'corporate office' that looks to the way in which the corporation 'exists' through the effectiveness of the acts performed on its behalf. It argues that the exercise of corporate power is constitutively vicarious – that is, always exercised on behalf of another – and, therefore, never fully reducible or attributable to a particular agent or actor. This constitutive vicariousness gives rise to a structural irresponsibility at the core of the corporate

1 This research is funded by the Australian Government through the Australian Research Council Australian Discovery Early Career Researcher Award (project number DE200100881), examining 'New Approaches to Corporate Legality: Beyond Neoliberal Governance'. Thanks to Penny Crofts for the invitation to be part of this collection, and to all the participants in the 'Evil Corporations' workshop for the stimulating discussion and feedback. All errors are my own.

DOI: 10.4324/9781003402534-13

form, which attempts to impose responsibility come up against. In particular, corporate criminal responsibility is an attempt to reconnect the mechanism of responsibility that the paradigm of corporate office – the constitutive vicariousness of corporate power – disconnects.

The chapter proceeds with four substantive sections. The first section takes up Scott Veitch's work on law's irresponsibility, focusing on the way in which legal constructions of roles and role responsibility function *both* as a 'technology of responsibility' *and* as producing irresponsibility. The second section turns to the way in which corporate law, despite its focus on responsibility and accountability, is constitutive of irresponsibility – not in terms of breaches of the law but the adherence to corporate legality that gives rise to mass harm and suffering. A particular instance of this is found in the nature of role responsibility and the constraints it places upon corporate officers. In the third section, this material on legal role responsibility and the corporate officer is situated in relation to the theorisation of office – both as a mode of responsibility, articulating the rights and obligations of the person fulfilling the office, as well as a mode of irresponsibility, separating the individual from the effectiveness of their actions. This theorisation understands the nature of the corporation and corporate power as something that is constitutively vicarious – always performed by someone who is acting on behalf of another – and, whilst performed by the individual, not reducible to the individual. The fourth section uses this theorisation of office – and the constitutive vicariousness of corporate power – to think about corporate criminal responsibility. It considers whether the imposition of criminal responsibility on the corporation renders inoperative the paradigm of corporate office *or* whether its underlying vision of the 'good' corporation is, in fact, an extension of it. The conclusion briefly considers a turn from the imposition of responsibility to a recognition of a more fundamental notion of corporate obligation.

Technologies of Responsibility: Legal Roles and Irresponsibility

In his book, *Law and Irresponsibility: On the Legitimation of Human Suffering*, Scott Veitch argues that whilst 'law and legal institutions can, and do, hold actors responsible for harmful acts … these same institutions can, and do, contribute to the organisation of irresponsibility that legitimates … suffering.'[2] He highlights the asymmetry that exists between the large-scale production of suffering and the generation of responsibility: 'the greater the

2 Scott Veitch, *Law and Irresponsibility: On the Legitimation of Human Suffering* (Routledge 2007) 1.

suffering caused, the less responsibility can be established for it'.[3] Rather than accounting for such suffering as an 'excess', exceeding the capacity of the law to deal with it,[4] what is *more* at stake is the way in which the law functions to both legitimate suffering and 'disavow' responsibility for it.[5] Focusing not on illegal but legal activities that cause massive harms, Veitch analyses three social structures complicit in the disavowal of responsibility: the division of labour and role responsibility; processes of individualisation; and the transference of responsibilities between social systems (in particular between the political and the economic).[6] Whilst each of these is applicable in relation to the harm or suffering that corporations cause, I will focus here on the first – role responsibility.

Drawing upon the work of Max Weber, Stanley Milgram and Zygmunt Bauman, Veitch highlights the way in which the bureaucratic nature of the modern organisation of society involves a 'dehumanisation' process whereby the 'individual becomes merely the *conduit* for larger processes and definitions *over which* he or she has little, or no control'.[7] In contrast to the vision of humans as autonomous, self-willing agencies engaging in self-defined activities, modern society is made up of a range of roles, tasks and offices. These roles (from the factory worker to the minister of state) and their responsibilities are generally not established by the agent themselves but by the institution that they are part of.[8] It is in the performance of these roles that the individual's actions and responsibilities come to be defined: 'official roles or tasks simultaneously connect responsibility with technical capability for a circumscribed range of activity – that is, they limit responsibility to roles – and thus disconnect alternative value bases of accountability or agency'.[9] The result is a '*separation* between intention and consequence' which 'is firmly entrenched through a limitation of responsibility only to the defined task at hand'.[10]

In this fashion, the fulfilling of the responsibilities of one's role *also* becomes a form of non-responsibility through that very fulfilment:

> under the various roles that the individual occupies and over which he or she has little or no defining capacity, the actor's *lack* of responsibility applies not only to distant consequences, but *even to his or her own*

3 Ibid. 2.
4 On corporate criminal responsibility as 'excess', see Penny Crofts, 'The Horror of Corporate Harms' (2022) 38 *Australian Journal of Corporate Law* 23.
5 Veitch, (n 2) 2.
6 Ibid. 41.
7 Ibid. 44. Emphasis in original.
8 Ibid. 48.
9 Ibid. 43.
10 Ibid. 44. Emphasis in original.

> actions in that role. Under such conditions, the actor, "no longer sees himself as the efficient cause of *his own* actions", this having been subsumed under and attributed to the role itself.[11]

This produces an 'agentic state' which, as Milgram notes, involves 'a fragmentation of the total human act; no one man decides to carry out the evil act and is confronted with its consequences. The person who assumes full responsibility for the act has evaporated.'[12] It is in this way that Veitch argues that 'responsibility practices' can be used as a '*technology*' or a 'normative device' that organises 'how role responsibilities are parcelled out, and ... the terms of their function and limits'.[13] The effect of this 'technology' of responsibility is that 'acting responsible' means acting in accordance with the obligations of the 'task, office or status' and it is 'irresponsible not so to act'.[14] The failure to fulfil the obligations of one's role may lead to censure in relation to the role, but '[b]eyond the defined role is a realm of non-responsibility'.[15]

Law has a privileged position in the constituting of roles and responsibility because legal categories themselves 'define forms of acting that simply *are* constitutive of role responsibility'.[16] A prime example is the corporation that, through separate legal personality and limited liability, involves the creation and structuring of particular rights, responsibilities and authority. Veitch takes the limitation of liability for corporate shareholders as exemplary of the way '[l]egal role responsibilities ... provid[e] ways in which legal actors can understand and use that role to nullify or distance themselves from the causing of harms'.[17] This is because, as Veitch notes,

> the legal rights of a shareholder in a corporation will not be deemed to make him or her responsible for the outcomes of the management decisions of the corporation, nor for activities that the corporation carries out that cause extensive, although legally authorised, harms such as deforestation, sweatshop labour, etc.[18]

11 Ibid. 45. Emphasis in original. Quoting Stanley Milgram, *Obedience to Authority* (Harper and Row 1974) xii.
12 Milgram, (n 11) 11; Veitch, (n 2) 45.
13 Veitch, (n 2) 48. Emphasis in original.
14 Ibid.
15 Ibid.
16 Ibid. 74. Emphasis in original.
17 Ibid. 79.
18 Ibid. 78–79. For a defence of the separation of the shareholder from the corporation, see James D. Nelson, 'The Separation of Ownership and Conscience' (2023) 48 *The Journal of Corporate Law* 577.

Veitch's analysis aligns, therefore, with a broader critical literature on the corporation that highlights the way in which structures that are promoted as providing economic and social benefit are also constitutive of significant harms and irresponsibility.[19]

'Evil Corporations' and Corporate Irresponsibility

Veitch's argument about law's involvement in the co-constitution of responsibility and irresponsibility and, in particular, the way the legal categorisation of roles involves both a demarcation of responsibility and its disavowal, is crucial to a consideration of both the involvement of corporations in the commission of harms and the ability to hold them responsible. This is because the legal mechanisms of responsibility and accountability are constitutive of the corporation and the positive benefits it provides to society, whilst also giving rise to the topic of this collection: 'evil corporations'. The question that arises, however, is whether 'evil corporations' – those that cause enormous harms – are an excess or aberration, functioning in breach of the law and, therefore, need to be held to account, or whether they are simply instances of corporate law 'working'. That is, do corporations sometimes *become* evil because of the actions and greed of particular individuals, poor systems of control, lack of compliance and an over-exuberant seeking of profits, or are corporations, as Gerry Spence argued, 'inherently evil'?[20] This question, though potentially more mutedly framed, has been raised by the literature on corporate irresponsibility that has responded to the plethora of corporate scandals – economic and financial, environmental and social – over the past three decades. Whilst recognising particular failures of policies, oversight and systems of control, this literature raises larger questions of potential inherent or structural issues in relation to the corporation. These include critiques of the nature of corporate personhood, limited liability, shareholder primacy, the drive for shareholder wealth maximisation and profit or more broadly the aggregation of wealth and power that corporations enable.

Over 20 years ago, American jurist Lawrence Mitchell, in his book *Corporate Irresponsibility: America's Newest Export*, located the drivers for corporate irresponsibility in the combination of the corporate social norm of shareholder wealth maximisation and the form of role morality that functions in relation to the corporation – particularly in regards to directors and managers, but which is then also passed down to other employees and

19 See, for example, Joel Bakan, *The New Corporation: How "Good" Corporations are Bad for Democracy* (Vintage Books 2020).

20 Gerry Spence, *From Freedom to Slavery* (1993) 71. Quoted in Douglas Litowitz, 'Are Corporations Evil?' (2004) 58 *University of Miami Law Review* 811, 812.

agents.[21] Whilst, like Veitch, he highlights the insulation of the shareholder from responsibility through limited liability as part of the structure of corporate irresponsibility, he also identifies two other constraints built into the corporation: 'the combination of law and structure that narrowly constrains the corporation in the ends it is permitted to pursue' (primarily profit); and 'the limited and morally stunted role that corporate actors (directors, officers and stockholders) are required to play in directing the corporation to achieve this goal'.[22] These constraints inhibit 'the freedom of the corporation and its directors to act in the manner they think most consistent with the behaviour of a full moral person.'[23] Whilst directors have a large discretion in terms of how they pursue the 'best interests of the corporation', this is only a contingent morality because the freedom they have is only to achieve the ends of the corporation – defined as maximising shareholder profit. For Mitchell, this framework propels corporate irresponsibility because '[t]he corporation that behaves ethically and responsibly is a corporation that incurs greater costs than corporations that choose to comply only with the minimal requirements of law'.[24] Even if an ethical reputation generates greater revenues, some of this will be offset by the greater costs involved.[25]

Mitchell highlights the way in which this framework is built on forms of role morality – 'the rules of behaviour and social expectations we have of people who perform specific functions in the course of performing those functions.'[26] He notes that society has constructed a range of roles, 'each of which has its expected norms of behaviour'[27] and that '[b]ecause we have agreed to create the roles, the norms of behaviour that go with them provide an adequate moral defence for those who are acting within them'.[28] Such roles are diverse, including both 'doctors, clergy, parents, policemen, spouses, and friends' as well as 'mafia bosses, drug kingpins, prostitutes, and terrorists'.[29] Mitchell distinguishes between the first set as 'socially desirable' requiring a 'set of rules that define them in order to fulfil their function'[30] and the second, 'socially undesirable' set, where 'the rules that define them and constrain them are illegitimate (and generally illegal)'.[31]

21 Lawrence E. Mitchell, *Corporate Irresponsibility: America's Newest Export* (Yale University Press 2001).
22 Ibid. 66.
23 Ibid. 68.
24 Ibid. 70.
25 See also Bakan, *The New Corporation*.
26 Mitchell, (n 21) 76.
27 Ibid. 77.
28 Ibid.
29 Ibid.
30 Ibid 77–78.
31 Ibid.

Given this categorisation, Mitchell asks whether the role of a corporate director falls within the first or second set. He questions the social legitimacy of corporations, given that: they are artificial persons 'whose sole objective is to maximize stockholder wealth'; and corporate law presumes, or even encourages, the self-interested actions of its constituents.[32] The legitimacy of the role of a corporate director is, therefore, *also* questionable. Given they are called to act on behalf of an organisation whose purpose is to maximise shareholder value, rather than contribute to society, '[h]ow can we reasonably expect responsible, accountable, and moral behaviour from the enterprise in which this takes place? We have already structured and constrained its morality'.[33]

This argument resonates with the renewed debates over whether corporations should have a broader purpose than simply shareholder wealth maximisation. Alongside increasing interest in social enterprise and benefit corporations, which involve an explicit incorporation of social purposes, strong industry statements of the importance of delivering value for all corporate stakeholders including customers, employees, suppliers, communities, as well as long-term value for shareholders, are being made.[34] Furthermore, projects such as the British Academy's 'The Future of the Corporation', led by Colin Mayer, argue that corporations should be legally required to set out their social purpose and have mechanisms in place to measure and ensure the corporation's accountability to that purpose.[35] In particular, Mayer argues that profit should not be the goal of the corporation but rather its product.[36]

From these perspectives, the problem with defining the corporation's purpose as the maximisation of shareholder wealth is that it 'not only gives managers, stockholders, and workers the excuse to behave badly, but also encourages them to do so'.[37] Otherwise upstanding, ordinary and ethical individuals are required, when acting as a director or manager of a corporation, to take on the 'personality or role of stockholder price maximiser to the

32 Ibid. 78, 81–82.

33 Ibid. 94.

34 Business Roundtable Business Roundtable, 'Statement on the Purpose of a Corporation' 2019) https://s3.amazonaws.com/brt.org/BRT-StatementonthePurposeofaCorporationwithSignaturesApril2022.pdf accessed 11 April 2024; Larry Fink Larry Fink, 'A Sense of Purpose' (*BlackRock*, 2018) https://www.blackrock.com/corporate/investor-relations/2018-larry-fink-ceo-letter accessed 11 April 2024; Klaus Schwab, 'Davos Manifesto 2020: The Universal Purpose of a Company in the Fourth Industrial Revolution' (*World Econ Forum*, 9 December 2019) https://www.weforum.org/agenda/2019/12/davos-manifesto-2020-the-universal-purpose-of-a-company-in-the-fourth-industrial-revolution/ accessed 11 April 2024.

35 The British Academy, 'Reforming Business for the 21st Century: A Framework for the Future of the Corporation' (2018); Colin Mayer, *Prosperity: Better Business Makes the Greater Good* (Oxford University Press 2018).

36 Mayer, n 35. The British Academy, 'Reforming Business for the 21st Century' 8.

37 Mitchell, (n 21) 97.

exclusion of all others' – a role that would ordinarily be considered pathological.[38] Furthermore, directors are then protected in performing this role and absolved of 'responsibility and accountability for their actions' by being permitted to reduce the 'corporation's costs of production by shifting them outside the corporation onto those most vulnerable, the workers, the environment, the consumers, and the community'.[39] Given this is the case, solutions that attempt to align director and shareholder interests by, for example, structuring remuneration packages around shareholder value metrics do not make the corporation more responsible but more irresponsible. Instead, for Mitchell, the solution is to sever the tie or connection between shareholders and directors and management through, for example, removing the ability for shareholders to vote in directors or, at the very least, extending their terms to reduce a focus on short-term metrics. The focus of directors and management could, then, be on a broader social purpose rather than purely shareholder wealth maximisation. Mayer also recommends measures that insulate management from the pressures of short-term shareholder wealth maximisation.[40]

Whilst critical, these approaches still acknowledge and recognise the economic benefits and efficiencies that the corporation produces.[41] As such, proposals to adjust the purpose of the corporation and to whom the board is responsible sustain the underlying *form* of the corporation. This can be seen, in particular, in relation to Mitchell's concern over the way in which role morality produces unethical behaviour but his solution is *not* to address the form of role morality itself, but rather to address the purpose for which it is deployed. In doing so, the underlying structure remains: directors' roles remain constituted by a form of vicariousness in that they exercise powers that are not their own but on behalf of others (whether understood as the corporation or shareholders). Arguments around corporate purpose do not address, therefore, what can be referred to as the constitutive vicariousness of corporate power – vicarious, because the agents exercising corporate power do so on behalf of another and not themselves, and constitutive because the corporate form itself is premised on this vicarious exercise of power.

Corporate Office and the Constitutive Vicariousness of (Corporate) Power

At one level, the claim that corporations can only perform actions through others would appear banal.[42] At the same time, it is only by holding in

38 Ibid. 98; Joel Bakan, *The Corporation: The Pathological Pursuit of Profit and Power* (Simon & Schuster 2004).

39 Mitchell, (n 21) 81.

40 See Mayer, (n 21) 120–22, 59–65.

41 For a critical discussion, see Nelson, 'The Separation of Ownership and Conscience'.

42 *Meridian Global Funds Management Asia Ltd v. Securities Commission* [1995] 3 All ER 918 at 923 per Lord Hoffman.

mind the constitutive vicariousness of corporate power that an appropriate consideration of the mechanisms of addressing corporate irresponsibility can be gained. This is a point made by Douglas Litowitz in his piece 'Are Corporations Evil?', where he argues that it is not the legal form of the corporation that is the issue,[43] but rather what happens when organisations reach a certain scale:

> When a business attains a certain size, the entity itself takes on a kind of transcendental force, converting everyone into mere role players to serve the higher purposes of the institutional empire. Massive size is also correlated with bureaucracy and an advanced division of labor, which ensure that managers remain far removed from the effects of their actions. All of the wrongdoing is mediated through endless layers of agents and advisors, with the result that no single person caused the problem and therefore no one individual is responsible.[44]

For Litowitz, these institutions (which are not limited to corporations) give rise to a 'disturbing paradox' that parallels, but then takes further, Mitchell's concern with the role morality of directors. This is because the 'agents of the corporation feel compelled to engage in morally objectionable conduct to serve the corporation, yet the "corporation" doesn't really exist apart from its agents'.[45] The paradox is that the corporation is made up of 'a vicious circle of endless agents trying to further the interest of an invisible principal.'[46] For Litowitz, this 'borders on idolatry, creating an artificial entity and then claiming that the entity has commanded one to act in a certain way'.[47]

Litowitz draws, as Veitch does, on both Hannah Arendt's notion of the 'banality of evil' and Milgram's concept of the 'agentic state' – the submission of an individual to a form of authority where they no longer see themselves as responsible for their own actions but rather the instrument of another.[48] For Litowitz, corporate scandals are 'part of a larger problem of agency within totalizing institutions (whether in corporate form or not)' and the idea of the 'agentic state' resonates with 'corporate law because agency is the cell form of business organisation'.[49] Such a claim aligns, at one level, with the articulation of the 'core' task of corporate governance as addressing 'agency

43 Litowitz, (n 20) 812.
44 Ibid. 815.
45 Ibid. 834.
46 Ibid.
47 Ibid.
48 ibid. 836–841.
49 Ibid. 839.

costs' that arise from the 'separation of ownership and control'.[50] However, as David Westbrook has pointed out, accounts of the corporation based purely on the modern law of agency – and, in particular, the notion that such agency relations are grounded in contract – fail because they do not recognise the social form of the corporation itself, which is premised on delegations and hierarchies of authority.[51] This can be seen in the sense that the premise of 'agency costs' is that an agent may *not* act in the interests of the corporation – emphasising the distinctiveness of the action of agents from the actions of their principals.[52] At the same time, the notion of 'corporate action' performed by an agent – and the concept of the 'agentic state' whereby the agent is *not* exercising their own power, but that of another – emphasises a connection or unity between the agent and the corporation. Litowitz's articulation of the corporation as a form of idolatry – a 'vicious circle of endless agents trying to further the interests of an invisible principle'[53] – highlights the constitutive vicariousness of corporate power. The source or origin of corporate power functions through a continuous deferral whereby agents are acting on behalf of the corporation, but the authorising of those agents *by* the corporation is, itself, performed by other agents.[54]

This understanding of the vicarious extension of power can be placed within a longer genealogy of thinking about the effectiveness of human actions as separate from the subjective intention of the actor performing them. Italian philosopher Giorgio Agamben traces such a genealogy in terms of the paradigm of 'office' that sought to develop 'a praxis that would be absolutely and wholly effective'.[55] He sees the key location of this development in the translation by the Church fathers of the Greek and Roman sources on office in their attempt to articulate the effectiveness of Christian 'liturgy' performed by the priest. The notion of priestly praxis – in which, in carrying out the liturgical ritual of the Eucharist, the priest acts as an 'animate instrument' of Christ and whose actions are independent 'of the qualities of the subject who officiates it' – provides, Agamben argues, a paradigm of human action that has constituted 'for the secular culture of the West a pervasive and constant pole of attraction'.[56] It is here, therefore, that we find the theological develop-

50 Michael Jensen and William Meckling, 'Theory of the Firm: Managerial Behavior, Agency Costs and Ownership Structure (1976) 3 *Journal of Financial Economics*; Adolf A. Berle and Gardner C. Means, *The Modern Corporation and Private Property* (Comerce Clearing House 1932).

51 David A Westbrook, 'A Shallow Harbor and a Cold Horizon: The Deceptive Promise of Modern Agency Law for the Theory of the Firm' (2012) 35 *Seattle University Law Review*.

52 Ibid. 1387–1388.

53 Litowitz, (n 20) 834.

54 See Westbrook, (n 51) 1384–1388.

55 Giorgio Agamben, *Opus Dei: An Archaeology of Duty* (Stanford University Press 2013) xii.

56 Ibid. xii, 22–28.

ment of the structural paradigm of role responsibility that interests Veitch, Mitchell and Litowitz.

Whilst emphasising the notion of 'priestly praxis', Agamben begins his consideration of 'office' with Cicero's *De Officiis* – a treatise 'on what is respectable and appropriate to do according to the circumstances, above all taking account of the agent's social condition'.[57] Cicero uses the term *officium* not to refer to what we would understand as duty (as modern translations of the term render it) but rather to define the actions of a subject according to their status and situation. Cicero writes: 'no phase of life, whether public or private, whether in business or in the home, whether one is working on what concerns oneself alone or dealing with another, can be without *officio*.'[58] Demonstrating the broad use of the term, Agamben quotes Roman authors who describe the *officium* of the prostitute as opposed to that of the matron and, in a negative sense, the 'office of the rascal'.[59] Agamben concludes, therefore, that

> *officium* is what causes an individual to comport himself in a consistent way – as a prostitute if one is a prostitute, as a rascal if one is a rascal, but also as a consul if one is a consul and, later, as a bishop if one is a bishop.[60]

This understanding, therefore, calls into question Mitchell's distinction between social roles that are 'legitimate' and 'illegitimate' because, instead of an office being about what is 'good' or 'bad', it is a particular paradigm of social expectation and obligations that constitute and govern the way a person of that office is to behave. This would also, therefore, call into question Mitchell's critique of the morality of the role of a corporate director over and above other roles, for the very notion of 'role morality' is one that paradigmatically defines what behaviour *is* moral or appropriate – from prostitute to consul, bishop to corporate director.

We can therefore see a link between the critique of role morality, Agamben's genealogy of office and the broader literature on the ethics of office. Conal Condren, for example, in his study of early modern England outlines the way in which the vocabulary of office carries with it both 'a positive register of rights, liberties, duty, rule and service to the office' as well as a 'negative register imputing neglect, oppression, licence and tyranny' in relation to a failure to appropriately carry out the office.[61] These were explicitly articulated in an

57 Ibid. 67.

58 Ibid. 69–70; Quoting Cicero, *On Duties* (Cambridge University Press 1991).

59 Ibid. 70.

60 Ibid. 72.

61 Conal Condren, 'The *Persona* of the Philosopher and the Rhetorics of Office in Early Modern England' in Conal Condren, Stephen Gaukroger and Ian Hunter (eds), *The Philosopher in Early Modern Europe: The Nature of a Contested Identity* (Cambridge

'oath of office', where an individual would commit themselves to undertaking and performing their obligations of office. Taking this up, Susan Watson has recently traced the modern duties of corporate directors back to the oaths that governors and committees of the chartered trading corporations swore, which included 'faithfully to perform their said Office'.[62] With the re-chartering of the East India Company in 1657, the oath included a commitment 'to be faithfull and true', to 'favour and affect' the 'good estate of the adventurers' and to 'maintaine and preserve' the 'priviledges graunted unto them'.[63] In contrast to accounts that see directors as trustees for shareholders, Watson makes the case that the notion of trust referred to in the early cases of directors' duties was an expectation of trustworthiness in the exercise of office originally articulated in these oaths.[64] This encompassed *both* a sense of public responsibility *and* a responsibility to shareholders whose interests they were to protect.[65] As Condren highlights – and Watson demonstrates in relation to the role of directors – the vocabulary of office institutes a certain expectation about what fulfils the official's good behaviour and what is a failure or abuse of office.[66]

At the same time, whilst the ethics of office articulate the appropriate use of office, Agamben's genealogy highlights the way in which acts of office have a mode of effectiveness that stands independent from the moral qualities of those performing them. This demonstrates the way in which role responsibility can function, as Veitch argues, as a mechanism of *irresponsibility* because the fulfilment of an office renders inoperative the attribution of moral responsibility to the individual. For Agamben, this is most rigorously developed in terms of the 'priestly praxis' found in the theological doctrine of the effectiveness of the sacraments. Here, the role of the priest in performing the Eucharist distinguishes between the *opus operatum*, which refers to the effectiveness or 'effective reality' of the act itself, and the *opus operans* or *opus operantis*, which refers to the action as carried out by the agent and is 'qualified by his moral and physical dispositions.'[67] The liturgical praxis of the Church is, according to Agamben, defined by 'the independence of the objective effectiveness and validity of the sacrament from the subject who concretely administers it.'[68] In recognising the institutional validity of such

University Press 2006) 67; see also Conal Condren, *Argument and Authority in Early Modern England: The Presupposition of Oaths and Offices* (Cambridge University Press 2006).

62 Susan Watson, *The Making of the Modern Company* (Hart 2022) 85.

63 Ibid. 86.

64 Ibid. 92–94.

65 Ibid. 93, 95–96. *The Charitable Corporation v Sutton* (1742) 2 Atk 400, 26 ER 642 per Lord Harwicke at 644.

66 See Condren, (n 61) 6. Watson, (n 62) 82–87.

67 Agamben, (n 55) 21.

68 Ibid.

acts, what becomes determinative is no longer the right intention of the agent but only the *function* that his or her actions carry out. The personal content of the action of the priest is emptied out and he becomes an 'animate instrument', to use St Thomas Aquinas's term, an 'instrumental cause' of a mystery that transcends him, whilst exercising an action that is still in some sense his own.[69] The result is a 'paradoxical ethical paradigm' whereby the connection between the subject and his action is broken and reconstituted on another level: 'an act that consists entirely in its irreducible effectiveness and whose effects are nonetheless not truly imputable to the subject who brings them into being'.[70]

The paradigm of office, therefore, separates an agent from his or her action and, in doing so, leaves open the question of responsibility for such an action. As Nicholas Heron has set out, power here is constitutively vicarious because it is 'irreducible to the nature of the one who exercises it'.[71] At the same time, because the exercise of this power is 'always on behalf of another, yet only to the extent that it is for the sake of another again', it is rendered ethically indeterminate – it 'is essentially unlocalizable and hence constitutively irresponsible'.[72] Given the modern corporation is premised on this form of agentic and official power, attempts to locate the responsibility for corporate actions always come up against the constitutive irresponsibility of official action performed on behalf of the corporation.

Corporate Criminal Responsibility: Limiting or Extending the Paradigm of Office

If, as has been argued above, the exercise of corporate power is constitutively vicarious then the debates over corporate criminal responsibility involve an attempt to reconnect the mechanisms of responsibility that the paradigm of office disconnects. A key consideration is whether criminal culpability arises only from individuals or whether there can be *corporate* criminal actions and, in the context of the latter, what level of liability should apply to the corporation, the individuals directly involved and those responsible for its oversight. Mechanisms of corporate criminal responsibility are generally progressed through the characterisation of certain acts, intentions or states of mind of individuals as being, in some fashion, those of the corporation and for which the corporation should be held responsible and liable. Traditionally the focus has been on the individual, with corporate

69 Ibid. 21, 25.

70 Ibid. 82.

71 Nicholas Heron, *Liturgical Power: Between Economic and Political Theology* (Fordham University Press 2018) 12.

72 Ibid. 10.

responsibility only being attributed in a 'derivative' fashion from individual actions. More recent approaches focus on the corporation as an independent organisation and legal person, which can be independently held criminally liable for corporate acts. A risk of organisational approaches is that, in emphasising the corporate nature of criminal acts, the fact that all corporate acts are performed by individuals that have some degree of responsibility for them is not sufficiently recognised. At the same time, emphasising individual liability may fail to recognise the way in which the nature of acts performed by an individual in an official capacity – in relation to, or on behalf of, the corporation for whom they act – are not the same as actions performed by an individual on their own account. The significance of the theory of corporate office is that it provides a way of thinking the nature of corporate activity as co-constituted between the actions of individuals and the corporate roles that they perform. That is, whilst individuals perform corporate actions they do not do so on their own account but as 'animate instruments' exercising a power that is recognised as independently effective, having been performed on behalf of, and authorised by, another (the corporation).

In this context, the question is whether forms of corporate responsibility and fault are able to address and render inoperative the constitutive vicariousness and irresponsibility of corporate power or whether they function as an extension or continuation of the paradigm of official power upon which the corporation functions. At first glance, derivative approaches to corporate attribution would seem to be most closely aligned to the paradigm of office. This is because they involve an assessment of whether or not the particular individual was engaged in 'official' action. Models of attribution based on agency and vicarious liability look to hold the corporation liable for all actions of directors, managers, employees and agents performed within the scope of their authority and, at least in part, for the benefit of the corporation.[73] This approach retains a sense of individual responsibility because both the action and intent are performed by the individual, but because of their official status, the corporation is deemed to be liable. Criminal law principles struggle with this approach because it appears to hold a legal person criminally liable for an action they did not, themselves, commit.[74] At the same time, the hierarchical nature of agency law would highlight the responsibility of the corporation for acts taken by individuals they have placed in a position of authority.[75]

73 See Australian Law Reform Commission, 'Corporate Criminal Responsibility' (2020) [4.50]–[4.57].

74 Ibid. 457; Ross Grantham, 'Attributing Responsibility to Corporate Entities: A Doctrinal Approach' (2001) 19 *Company & Securities Law Journal* 13, 171–172.

75 See Westbrook (n 51).

In contrast to vicarious liability, Commonwealth jurisdictions have developed theories of identification and the 'directing mind and will'.[76] This approach, whilst also derivative of the individual, is articulated as a form of direct liability in which the conduct and state of mind of certain high level individuals are held to be the embodiment of the corporation.[77] More recent judicial approaches have sought to focus less on determining who was, in general, the 'directing mind and will' of the corporation but rather 'whose act (or knowledge, or state of mind) was [for a particular purpose] intended to count as the act etc of the company?'[78] In both instances certain individuals are held not to be acting on behalf of, but *as*, the corporation. The performance of an 'official' act is not attributed to the individual but to the corporation for which they act as an 'animate instrument'. This raises two questions. First, if the individual is acting as the corporation then is it logically inconsistent to hold them personally liable as well? This is because their act, whilst performed by themselves as an individual, is *not* an act on their own account but, by definition, an act of the corporation.[79] Such is a legal accounting of Milgram's 'agentic state', whereby the individual is no longer the 'efficient cause' of their actions but rather an 'instrumental cause', exercising authority on behalf of the corporation. Second, identification approaches to corporate attribution are more applicable to smaller corporations where the connection between a 'directing mind and will' and the actual performance of the criminal acts is more easily demonstrated. In larger corporations, the diffusion of authority, knowledge and intent – and their distribution across multiple officers, employees and agents – makes it difficult to identify a 'directing mind and will' as having been the one engaged in a specific criminal action.[80] Such highlights the way in which the approach of identification theory, whilst attempting to specifically attribute corporate responsibility *to* the corporation, becomes, in effect, a mechanism of what Veitch would refer to as the 'disappearing' of responsibility. The corporation will only be held liable if the corporate act can be attributed to a 'directing mind and will' and, in other circumstances, only the individual (if anyone

76 Australian Law Reform Commission, 'Corporate Criminal Responsibility' [4.58]–[4.72]; Grantham, (n 74).

77 *Lennard's Carrying Co. Ltd v. Asiatic Petroleum Co. Ltd* [1915] AC 705; *Tesco Supermarkets Ltd v. Nattrass* [1972] AC 153.

78 *Meridian Global Funds Management Asia Ltd v. Securities Commission* [1995] 3 All ER 918 at 924 per Lord Hoffman.

79 See Grantham, (n 74) 178–180. As Grantham notes, for policy reasons this does not necessarily mean limiting the criminal liability of the individuals involved. In Australia, the principle of accessorial liability has been used to hold individuals liable as accessories to the corporate acts that they, themselves, performed: *Hamilton v. Whitehead* (1988) 166 CLR 121.

80 Australian Law Reform Commission, (n 76) [4.68]–[4.69], [9.149]–[9.57].

at all) will be liable, ignoring the official capacity in which the actions were performed.

Organisational approaches to corporate fault, by contrast, hold the corporation responsible for acts that are understood as corporate rather than individual. 'By their very nature', as the Australian Law Reform Commission has noted, 'a corporation's decisions, omissions, acts, and behaviours are generally the accumulation of states of mind and conduct of multiple people'.[81] Recognising the way in which corporate fault functions across multiple individuals, relations and systems within the corporation is necessary to prevent 'a corporation from deliberately structuring its business in such a way to avoid criminal responsibility by ensuring that conduct and intention are diffuse'.[82] Corporations should be held criminally liable for the failure to have in place appropriate policies, procedures and systems of control, as well as the failure to respond appropriately to the commission of offences by corporate officers and employees.[83] Culpability is, therefore, not based on the combined criminal intent and conduct of an individual acting in official capacity, but based on the structures of the corporation that (explicitly or implicitly) authorise, permit or encourage criminal conduct.[84] The creation of an environment that produces forms of role morality, which encourage criminal or negligent behaviour, a culture of non-compliance or that encourages criminogenic behaviour is considered evidence of corporate criminal intent.[85] Such approaches, therefore, address the individual irresponsibility of the 'agentic state' by ensuring responsibility at the level of the corporation. At the same time, regimes of individual liability – for both those involved directly in the corporate criminal acts and, at times, directors and senior managers who have failed in their oversight of the corporation – function alongside corporate liability, in a recognition of individual involvement, even if in an official or agentic capacity.[86]

Models of organisational blameworthiness, therefore, provide a way of holding corporations responsible for criminal acts that recognises the nature of the constitutive vicariousness of corporate power. They envision, and are premised on, a perfection of the paradigm of official power – the recognition that the criminal conduct performed by an individual can be separated from the criminal intent attributed either to other corporate actors or the (lack of) policies, procedures and systems of control. The effectiveness of the individual's action (the performance of the criminal act) is separated from

81 Ibid. [6.42].

82 Ibid.

83 For discussion of these approaches, see ibid. [4.4]–[4.19], [4.73]–[4.79].

84 Ibid. Ch. 6.

85 Ibid. [4.4]–[4.15], [6.95]–[6.120].

86 Ibid. Ch. 9.

their intention (the criminal intention being found elsewhere). The ethically indeterminate status of the corporate officer or actor as 'animate instrument' is addressed by imposing responsibility at the level of the corporation. The paradigm of organisational blameworthiness, therefore, parallels the arguments around the purpose of the corporation. Just as the calls for corporations to engage in a more social purpose do not seek to address the underlying structures of the corporation and the role morality of corporate officers, but simply puts them to different ends, organisational blameworthiness does not render inoperative the constitutive vicariousness of corporate power but rather functions as an extension of it.

This is most clearly seen when we consider the underlying vision of the 'good' corporation that models of organisational blameworthiness encompass. Such approaches involve a defence of having in place appropriate policies and procedures with the aim of incentivising or encouraging a more compliant corporation that will, therefore, reduce the likelihood of corporate criminality. However, the strong policies, procedures and systems of control, hierarchical forms of decision-making and clear delegations of corporate authority that such a vision encourages are the *same* structures that Veitch, Milgram, Mitchell and Litowitz critique as *producing* forms of role morality that sees personal responsibility being fulfilled in the adherence to the requirements of the role or the compliance with policy. That is, the very paradigm of corporate responsibility achieved through a compliance culture and robust policies and procedures involves a 'disappearance' of responsibility – it being limited to compliance with those policies and procedures. What is left out is the way in which a compliance culture involves a *limit* to responsibility for harms that corporations cause in the world which may, and do, extend beyond actions that are criminal or in contravention of the law. The more fundamental question is not addressed: whether the evil that corporations do and the harms that they cause are a result of breaching the law (for which they should be punished) or whether it is the deployment of the mechanisms of corporate legality and responsibility themselves that 'fram[e] out other worlds' where those harms are felt.[87]

Conclusion: From Responsibility to Obligation

The theory of corporate office that I have sketched here highlights the way in which the exercise of corporate power is constitutively vicarious and, as such, involves a particular rendition of responsibility as the fulfilment of authorised activity. An individual's personal responsibility is separated from the ultimate effects of the actions taken, emphasising instead the fulfilment

87 Lilian Moncrieff, 'On the company's bounded sense of social obligation' in Daniel Matthews and Scott Veitch (eds), *Law, Obligation and Community* (Routledge 2018) 79.

of the duties and requirements of the role or office to be performed. Whilst methods of corporate criminal responsibility that focus on organisational blameworthiness seek to hold the corporation responsible, they do so by promoting a perfected form of bureaucratic authority – a 'compliant' corporation – that *reduces* responsibility. This is because it emphasises the processes that corporations are already effective at – the redefining of the complexity of the world and the multiple relations and affective ties that make up both the social substrata of the corporation and its connections to the world in terms of the corporation's own 'sense of right'.[88] The responsibility of the corporation thus comes in a form of limit – the need to have certain policies and systems in place in order *not* to be held liable for a criminal act – rather than a recognition of the harms (whether legally defined or not) that the corporation produces.

What is needed, therefore, are not only mechanisms that hold corporations responsible for the criminal acts that they engage in but new lines of accountability that encourage corporations to recognise their boundedness and obligations as a result of being part of the world and the harms they cause. This requires a recognition of the underlying affective relationships that form the basis of corporate activity and to use these to ground a form of corporate *obligation* rather than responsibility. Obligation, in this sense, is seen as something primary within which social and legal relations are always-already founded, rather than something that is to be imposed *upon* the corporation after the fact.[89] This would require a rendering inoperative of the effectiveness of corporate actions that separate them from the individual performing them and a redefining of corporate and collective action as one that is obligated to each other, to community and to a corporate being together in the world. It is only in thinking corporate office in such a trajectory that we might be able to more fundamentally address the evil that corporations do.

88 Ibid. 79.

89 See, in general, Daniel Matthews and Scott Veitch, *Law, Obligation, Community* (Routledge 2018).

Chapter 10

Blindness without a Will

The Dilemma of Corporate Collective Knowledge and Intention in *Succession*

Lisa Siraganian

You Can Steer Clear of the Whole Death Pit

In the fourth episode of HBO's *Succession* (2018), Tom Wambsgans (Matthew Macfadyen), the opportunistic new head of Waystar RoyCo's Parks and Cruises division, learns a disturbing secret – one whose history, future revelation and management are key to why the series is so compelling. Apparently, there has been an 'unofficial policy' (and a deliberate, decades-long cover-up) of brazen acts of corporate misconduct, including unreported assaults, rapes and murders.[1] A fictionalised account of the infighting in a family-run public corporation, the award-winning, hit television satirical dramedy is loosely based on Rupert Murdoch's news and television empire. Ageing media magnate Logan Roy torments his disappointing adult children, who battle for the CEO-throne and their father's love as in *King Lear*.

In this scene, Bill Lockhart (Mark Blum), the retiring head of the Parks and Cruises division, dispatches information to Tom through a set of legalistic procedures. Bill turns off the Wi-Fi so his computer cannot connect to the internet, and prints out a document with various names and code numbers, including the contact information of an outsider used 'as a firewall to deal with the blowback from the NDAs' (*Succession,* S1:E4). Tom is baffled, his hackles raised by Bill's obvious, premeditated and elaborate liability shielding from any possible incriminating connection. Whether creating and printing out a document carrying no trace of its maker, forcing victims to sign non-disclosure agreements or hiring third-person legal intermediaries, these and other calculated actions already indicate a number of people vigilantly manoeuvring to protect themselves and the firm from legal liability. When Tom asks what exactly he is being asked to safeguard, Bill clarifies the stakes: 'You have two viable options. I can tell you everything, and that's fine. Or I can not tell you, and ... you wouldn't know, and then you can steer clear of the whole death pit. And that would be fine too' (S1:E4). Tom does not

1 'Sad Sack Wasp Trap', S1:E4, *Succession* [2018], HBOTimeWarner.

DOI: 10.4324/9781003402534-14

yet understand that Bill is offering him a future chance to perform an act of calculated ignorance – otherwise known as *wilful blindness*, the deliberate disregard of criminal activity to protect himself from learning more about the bad actions occurring in the corporation. Tom could file away the anonymous document with the relevant names and numbers and do nothing else, remaining 'blind' to the suspected bad actions at the corporation, goings-on that he is sharp enough to presume are illicit.

The legal doctrine of wilful blindness (also termed wilful ignorance) is traditionally understood to apply 'whenever a person becomes suspicious of criminal conduct, yet deliberately chooses to remain ignorant by failing to make further inquiries'.[2] To ease findings of *corporate* wilful blindness, some courts have also developed a second, related doctrine of 'collective knowledge' (or 'collective scienter'), which 'imputes to a corporation the aggregate constructive knowledge of all or some of its employees for the purpose of creating the necessary guilty intent, or scienter, for the corporation'.[3] Tom's dilemma in *Succession* neatly dramatises an act of wilful blindness of criminal activity in a corporation, but his situation also illustrates the difficulty of simply knowing these crimes collectively or corporately, as these doctrines seek to prove.

This chapter focuses on the legal and theoretical problems raised by Tom's situation to explore, more broadly, what *Succession* apprehends about the corporation's way of collectively knowing and intending. A real-life portrait of the contemporary corporate person emerges – not just the fictional Waystar, but of a corporation imbricated in the lives of a vile, obscene, yet very human extended family. In the process, *Succession* suggests various reasons why the prevailing model of corporate knowledge and intention, relying on a corporate decision and organisational structure – what corporate ethicist Peter French calls the CID, or Corporate Internal Decision, Structure – fails to capture how corporations know and act on that knowledge.[4] Corporate agents might act 'wilfully blind', and corporations might not be aware (either wilfully or not) of all the actions of their agents. But attempting to identify a deliberate instance of corporate wilful blindness ends up exposing constitutive and severe incapacities of the corporate form – deficiencies of reflection and will, of knowledge and insight, and of normative deliberation in a social realm. Courts and legal scholars are still struggling to make corporate crime doctrines, like wilful blindness and collective knowledge, function the way they were intended to; *Succession* suggests why that struggle will continue.[5]

2 'Willful blindness doctrine', 1 *White Collar Crime* § 3:11 (2nd ed.), July 2018 Update.

3 Blake Weiner, Kimberly Austin, John Lapin, Mary McCullough, 'Corporate Criminal Liability', (2018) 55 *Am. Crim. LR* 961, 970.

4 Peter A. French, 'Integrity, Intentions, and Corporations', (1996) 34 *Am Bus LJ* 141, 151.

5 Some of the problems I identify have been discussed by other legal scholars. See Mihailis E. Diamantis, 'Corporate Criminal Minds', (2016) 91 *Notre Dame LR* 2049, 2049–2050.

Maybe It's Probably Something That You Don't Want to Know

At any given time, does anyone really know what is going on at Waystar? Doubts are planted in *Succession*'s very first scene. Before we know that Logan is the foulmouthed, ruthless creator and exorbitantly wealthy head of the company, before he has a haemorrhagic stroke, we watch an old man stumble in the dim light, unseeing, mumbling 'Where am I?', and urinating on the carpet in a room that is not a bathroom. We begin, then (as in *Lear*), with serious questions about this corporate king's senility, health, and general mental state – questions about what he knows and what he can see and do – reservations that wax and wane as the series continues and he struggles to recover. 'Who's in charge right now?' asks Stewy Hosseini (Arian Moayed), a private equity financier, several episodes later, upon glimpsing a disheveled Logan shuffling around corporate headquarters; around the same time Stewy raises this question Logan is again urinating – purposefully? disorientedly? vengefully? absently? – on the carpet of his son Kendall's office. By the episode's end, the ill Logan, detecting that he is about to be retired, manages to snatch back the CEO throne from Kendall. But the question of authority is one that many people in the firm, and many investing in it (and later, investigating it), are also asking.

Combining Logan's 'Where am I?' and Stewy's 'Who's in charge?' gives us one of the series' key questions: does (or can) anyone consistently, cogently represent what we might call the corporate will or mind of this operation? Although in one obvious sense Waystar's will and corporate mind seem to emanate from Logan, in another sense any determinable corporate mind is in real doubt, starting from the series' first scene. This uncertainty about Logan's mindful presence or absence at the company helm will also be crucial to how the series explores the problem of corporate crime and responsibility. For while Logan's status as uncertain corporate mind is a crisis for the fictional Waystar, in a larger sense this situation is the *norm* for any corporate entity. And, to gesture ahead for a moment, an intermittent absence of a will, the indeterminacy of a mindful presence (variably and symbolically represented by the person of Logan in *Succession*), could undermine the prospect of positing something like corporate blindness or corporate ignorance in the first place.

In the US context, one of the foundational rulings on these particular corporate crime doctrines was *United States v. Bank of New England* (1st Cir 1987). In that appellate decision, the Prudential Branch of the Bank of New England failed to file the required Currency Transaction Reports (CTRs) within 15 days of James McDonough, a regular customer (as well as gambler and bookmaker) withdrawing more than $10,000 – on 31 separate occasions. Because McDonough combined multiple cheques, each one less than $10,000, and presented them simultaneously to a single bank teller, who then, in a single action, handed him a wad of cash equal to more than

$10,000, the government argued that the CTRs should have been filed; the bank contended that 'the evidence did not suffice to show that it wilfully failed to file CTRs on McDonough's transactions'.[6] The trial court found for the government, arguing that the bank (like Waystar, with its 'unofficial policy' of misconduct) knew well enough that illegality was going on.

Upholding the trial court's verdict, the First Circuit observed that criminal liability requires a finding that the bank '"willfully" violates' the CTR filling requirement, and a finding of 'willfulness' also requires proof that the defendant knew of the reporting requirements and specifically intended not to fulfil their obligations. The court acknowledged that the process of discovering 'willfulness' is not necessarily obvious when a commercial institution like a bank is involved. Aggregating collective knowledge of various agents might be necessary to prove this element of the crime. But, argued the court, such a step is defensible following fundamental agency principles of respondeat superior:

> The acts of a corporation are, after all, simply the acts of all of its employees operating within the scope of their employment. The law on corporate criminal liability reflects this ... Similarly, the knowledge obtained by corporate employees acting within the scope of their employment is imputed to the corporation.[7]

Note that, in issuing this verdict, the First Circuit invoked an implicit theory of the hierarchical corporation as (merely) the sum of its agential parts.[8] Large corporations must 'compartmentalize knowledge' in order to function, 'subdividing the elements of specific duties and operations into smaller components'.[9] That structural reality requires combining all of those component parts together to add up to what the corporation knows about any given operation, whether or not employees in one department know what the employees in another are up to. Citing to an earlier case, the court affirmed that '[A] corporation cannot plead innocence by asserting that the information obtained by several employees was not acquired by any one individual who then would have comprehended its full import'.[10] Culpability, like information, can be sought, found, and combined in different ways. In this case, the court examined multiple kinds of substantiation to find the

6 *United States v. Bank of New Eng., N.A.*, 821 F.2d 844, 847 (1st Cir. 1987).

7 *Bank of New Eng.*, at 856.

8 The summation of employee conduct has become the received account of the collective corporate knowledge doctrine. See Martin J. Weinstein and Patricia Bennett Ball, 'Criminal Law's Greatest Mystery Thriller: Corporate Guilt Through Collective Knowledge', (1994) 29 *New Eng. LR* 65, 67.

9 *Bank of New Eng.*, at 856.

10 Ibid. citing to *T.I.M.E.–D.C.*, at 738.

Bank's 'wilfulness': the evidence included internal memos, the Prudential branch's official bank manual, the instructions on the back of CTR forms, and reported conversations between a bank auditor and the head tellers of the Prudential branch.

For the *Bank of New England* court, the crucial point is that although corporate knowledge and wilfulness come in many different guises and might be spread out between many people and departments, the characteristics of knowledge and wilfulness can nonetheless exist in a constructive, composite form. *Bank of New England* is not the only US case to work through the doctrines of corporate wilful blindness and collective knowledge, but it is one of the most significant and high profile in part because it examines how the two doctrines might work in concert to successfully find corporations liable for criminal acts.[11] Whether or not they are truly standalone doctrines in the corporate context (a debatable point), the collective knowledge rule is at least 'a logical corollary to the doctrine of willful blindness'.[12] They combine to prove, most basically, as Alexander Sarch writes, that 'if an employee deliberately blocks himself from acquiring salient knowledge during his employment with a corporation, the missing knowledge can be imputed to him, and from there, to the corporation'.[13] And, as the Seventh Circuit explained in a decision after *Bank of New England*, it is not only the supervisors' knowledge that counts: '[c]orporations "know" what their employees who are responsible for an aspect of the business know. ... what's so special, for this purpose, about supervisors?'[14]

Carefully portraying Tom's unfolding dilemma, Episode 4 initially seems to offer a clear-cut case of wilful blindness and collective knowledge in action, fulfilling the requirements that the *Bank of New England* court (as well as Sarch and other legal scholars) have laid out. Consider when Tom, after reading through enough of the hidden documents to realise how bad the crimes and cover-up are, decides to divulge what he has learnt to Logan's second eldest son Kendall Roy (Jeremy Strong), who is Tom's boss as well as acting CEO:

TOM: There's something that you don't know about, and maybe it's probably something that you *don't* want to know about. And, uh--

11 *New York Cent. & H.R.R. Co. v. U.S.*, 212 U.S. 481, 495–496 (1909) began to work out a rationale and method for finding corporate specific intent for crimes, and in the process, invoked a metaphor of wilful blindness.

12 Thomas A. Hagemann and Joseph Grinstein argue that the two doctrines are doing the same work: 'The Mythology of Aggregate Corporate Knowledge: A Deconstruction' (1997) 65 *Geo. Wash. LR* 210, 245–256.

13 Alexander Sarch, *Criminally Ignorant: Why the Law Pretends We Know What We Don't* (OUP 2019) 232.

14 *United States v. Ladish Malting Co.*, 135 F.3d 484, 492–493 (7th Cir. 1998).

KENDALL: [interrupting] You know what my dad always said? He'd say he loved all his employees, but he particularly loved the guys who ate the shit for him and he never even knew it.

TOM: Got it. Got it. Excuse me while I get myself a knife and a fork and some hollandaise. (S1:E4)

This conversation represents the archetypal scenario that the legal doctrines are meant to capture. Interrupting Tom from making a disclosure, Kendall, literally standing in his C-suite office, deliberately 'blocks himself from acquiring salient knowledge' that appears to be both important and damaging.[15] Tom calls it 'something that you *don't* want to know about', a truth that Kendall acknowledges by characterising the potential disclosure as 'shit' and praising the self-sacrificing employees whose devious actions his father 'never even knew' about. Kendall wants Tom, a relatively minor executive, to take the brunt of potential legal exposure, and for that risk Tom is implied special 'love' in future. The wilful blindness and collective knowledge doctrines infer, however, that even if Tom gobbles up the sauce-covered shit, Kendall and the corporation, by extension, have not exculpated themselves. Adding up what Bill disclosed to Tom (or the incriminating documents released to Tom's safe-keeping), and what Tom is thwarted from disclosing to Kendall, shows that corporate collective knowledge existed. The missing knowledge could be imputed to acting CEO Kendall – who attempts to wilfully blind himself from it – and from there to the corporation.

So far, so good: Waystar's criminal liability could be found. But courts and legal commentators have objected that the collective knowledge doctrine has potential problems, and *Succession* teases out some of these complications – and adds a few more – while using the very language of 'knowledge' to do so. Although the US Supreme Court has let the decision stand, other federal appellate courts generally have declined to follow *Bank of New England*; a quick WestLaw search reveals only a handful of cases that track its reasoning on collective knowledge, and more recent cases have not.[16] Reasons why are readily apparent. Simply adding up knowledge might not accurately model knowledge and action in a corporate structure, leading to assigning corporate liability too far in the hierarchy or not far enough (a form of scapegoating). Questions about corporate intention, action, state of mind and the

15 Sarch, (n 13) 232.

16 US decisions upholding *Bank of New England*'s collective knowledge doctrine include *United States v. Farm & Home Sav. Ass'n*, 932 F.2d 1256, 1259 (8th Cir. 1991) and *United States v. Penagaricano-Soler*, 911 F.2d 833, 843 (1st Cir. 1990). US decisions rejecting or revising the collective knowledge doctrine include: *Nordstrom, Inc. v. Chubb & Son, Inc.*, 54 F.3d 1424, 1435 (9th Cir. 1995); *Southland Sec. Corp. v. INSpire Ins. Solutions*, Inc., 365 F.3d 353, 366 (5th Cir. 2004); and *Makor Issues & Rts., Ltd. v. Tellabs Inc.*, 513 F.3d 702, 707 (7th Cir. 2008), among others.

problem of how to attribute them to the corporation, frequently arise.[17] The difficulty courts face when finding and proving factual answers to these questions, and resolving the 'epistemological conundrum[s]' that arise along the way, clearly suggests why it might be easier to look for *individual* culprits with single human minds rather than searching for 'corporate intent'.[18] That method could seem a better way to avoid the dangerous mismatch between a potential *mens rea* and *actus reus*.[19]

Some legal commentators are in agreement with this trend, noting that trying to find legal corporate intent is not possible because corporations do not have actual mental states, and thus courts must problematically rely on a legal fiction or construction. Anthony Ragozino argues that aggregating various agents' or employees' mental states 'into one corporate state of mind', might make the *mens rea* requirement for corporate criminal liability easier to satisfy, but 'it does so by sacrificing fairness for conviction'.[20] A better approach would be to 'encourage[e] corporations to adopt corporate compliance programs and impose a special duty upon corporate superiors' instead of trying to postulate a fictive 'corporate mens rea'.[21] But corporate compliance programmes are not exactly a panacea. A number of high-profile companies were lauded for their good corporate citizenship and corporate compliance programmes *before* massive frauds and crimes were uncovered, notes William Laufer. This was precisely the scenario in the Enron scandal. 'Without liability rules that fairly and justifiably construct blame', regulations might instead incentivise 'corporations to dissimulate in artful, gamelike ways', covering up crimes or shifting blame to the lower middle management running the corporate compliance programme.[22] A corporate *mens rea* might be avoided, in that case, but finding a lower middle manager's *mens rea* might not be a just result.

Along with Laufer, other legal scholars are exploring promising ways to contend with these issues. Tackling the problem of characterising corporate knowledge either too narrowly or too broadly, Mihailis Diamantis deploys organisational science to develop a theory of 'functional corporate

17 Patricia S. Abril and Ann Morales Olazábal, 'The Locus of Corporate Scienter', 2006 *Colum. Bus. LR* [2006] 81, 84–85.

18 I discuss the longer legal, philosophical and cultural history of this debate in Lisa Siraganian, *Modernism and the Meaning of Corporate Persons* (OUP 2020).

19 See Ann Foerschler, 'Comment, Corporate Criminal Intent: Toward a Better Understanding of Corporate Misconduct', 7 *Cal. LR* [1990] 1287, 1296–1297.

20 Anthony Ragozino, 'Replacing the Collective Knowledge Doctrine with A Better Theory for Establishing Corporate Mens Rea: The Duty Stratification Approach', 24 *Sw. U. LR* [1995] 423, 425–426.

21 Ibid, 428.

22 William Laufer, *Corporate Bodies and Guilty Minds: The Failure of Corporate Criminal Liability* (University of Chicago Press 2006) 102–103.

knowledge', a kind of corporate epistemology that would be 'normatively defensible'.[23] Sarch, arguing that the current corporate wilful blindness doctrine 'does not go far enough' proposes an 'Iterated Reckless Ignorance Principle' to help supplement it.[24] Working within the Australian legal framework, Elise Bant notes that precisely because individuals within a corporation are 'motivated by collective aims and coordinated through group rules of recognition', an alternative model of liability would work better, one of '"systems intentionality" in which the corporate mind is manifested through its corporate systems, policies, and patterns of behavior'.[25]

Of value in all of these proposals is their insight that collective corporate knowing has too often been assumed easy to tally up and apportion out, when that is rarely the case at all. The next section teases out how *Succession* makes this point in its own way – but also suggests why even these new strategies are likely to run into problems in practice. Whatever *actual* collective corporate knowledge and wilful blindness is, the series suggests, it cannot possibly only amount to the adding up of individual agents' small pool of knowledge and decision-making. But neither can it be simply captured in a corporation's organisational chart, systems and policies, for reasons we will explore. Instead, it invariably entails an interactive, deliberately communicative and intersubjective process of people knowing, convincing and coercing one another. Such collective corporate knowledge and wilful blindness will almost certainly entail individuals craftily shielding themselves from potentially criminal disclosures, as Kendall does with Tom, and as Bill offers Tom. Most problematically, collective corporate knowledge and wilful blindness will also involve responding to corporate happenings that are characterised as viruses or natural accidents – happenings that cannot, or will not, be characterised as intentional or purposeful at all.

This May Not Be the Best Situation

From the start, *Succession* was pitched as a 'sort of King Lear meets the media industrial complex'.[26] For public figures (like Murdoch and Logan) or sovereigns (like Lear), their private lives are inextricably woven into their public personas. Like Lear in his kingdom of Britain, these contemporary royals – Logan, his children, their extended family members, and the attendant corporate counsels – lord over a public world as proximate strangers to one another, always first checking how their manoeuvres are reflected in the

23 Mihailis E. Diamantis, 'Functional Corporate Knowledge', 61 *Wm. & Mary LR* [2019] 319, 330.

24 Sarch, (n 13) 176.

25 Elise Bant, 'Culpable Corporate Minds', 48 *U.W. Aus. LR* [2021] 352, 358, 354-55.

26 Interview with Jeremy Strong, quoted in James Andrew Miller, *Tinder Box: HBO's Ruthless Pursuit of New Frontiers* (Henry Holt 2021) 862.

company stock price or on Twitter. 'That's how much people don't like me', Kendall complains, holding up a graph of the corporation's plunging stock price after he takes over ('Lifeboats' S1:E3).

Succession understands being *of* the corporation as being fashioned and evaluated by the public at virtually every moment of your life, even during an intimate conversation with your family. All interactions are assumed to be business negotiations, and the series delights in moments when manoeuvring swerves from the business-political to the private-filial. One such moment occurs at the end of the pilot episode, when Logan and three of his adult offspring are negotiating a revision of the family legal trust (on board a private helicopter, of course). 'Officially the deadline has passed', Logan pressures them, looking at his watch, playing a little hardball, 'So … what do you say, kids?' (S1:E1). Rather than sharing opinions, the 'kids' have been taught to provide only tactical positions during a deal and so, demurs Shiv, 'our position is this doesn't quite work for us. At present'. Roman backs her up: 'It's not sufficiently attractive as a proposition'. When Logan balks and starts mumbling incoherently, Roman and Shiv initially and quite rationally assume that his erratic behaviour is a familiar bargaining strategy: 'Dad, it's just a first position', Roman whines, but Logan is barely conscious, slumped over, haemorrhaging.

Because these familial relationships are *always* potentially public and political, they are also instrumentalised, fake and typically lead to psychological suffering. Running this corporation requires treating one's fellow executives (and executives-in-training), whether higher up or lower on the organisational chart, as expendable tools to be manipulated, and on whom literalised 'knowledge' (i.e., evidence of culpability) can be physically shifted. Instead of trying to talk, one employee (Bill) will print out a document and hand it to someone else (Tom). Tom takes it as the coercion was intended: a piece of evidence to be blame-shifted. And while *Succession*'s focus is on Waystar, no other corporation or executive is portrayed as operating any differently.[27]

Physically passing on evidence (to clean one's hands of it) is how 'knowing' works at Waystar, and, subsequently, the series relies on *literalised* metaphors of viral contagion, ingestion and degradation to depict such corporate knowledge. Consider another scene from Episode 4. After Kendall rebuffs the attempted criminal disclosure, Tom, gutted and desperate, calls in his underling, Greg (Nicholas Braun), Logan's ludicrously awkward and conniving grand-nephew. 'It seems I have been exposed to a virus', Tom intones portentously; 'it's a deadly virus and now … [nervously laughing] now I'm fucked, forever!' He feels compelled to speak to someone, but talking to

27 The other corporations we see represented in the first season (media brand Vaulter, purchased by Waystar, and the unnamed rival media conglomerate owned by Sandy Furness and financed by Stewy Hosseini) also function antisocially and fraudulently.

anyone would 'effectively kill' them. He then hands Greg 'the death pit' folder and, with a terrifically menacing '[y]ou're *family*', forces a reluctant Greg to read it. Tom describes the 'unofficial company policy' to avoid reporting crimes ('theft, sexual assault, rape, murder') on-board the company's cruises, and reveals evidence that the systemic criminal activity and cover-ups went straight to the top of the division:

TOM: Everyone we could, we paid off, we hushed up. But there are emails, there's correspondence – it's ready to blow. It's a fucking time bomb.
GREG: So ... what are you gonna do?
TOM: I don't know! I don't know! Because anyone I ask for advice, I make complicit. If you know about this stuff, you should tell. But you can't because you're gonna spread the virus.
GREG: So, [pause] I have the virus, don't I? (S1:E4)

Greg does indeed have the virus – because Tom cruelly infected him with it. Now they both carry the burden of possessing criminal knowledge that they should divulge. Tom contemplates holding a press conference, hoping that transparency will relieve him of his guilt. Greg decides to warn Gerri, Waystar's chief corporate counsel, about Tom's plans, calculating that an act of corporate loyalty (and personal treachery) might earn him special favours – which it does. In a moment like this one, *Succession* identifies and depicts something like an externalised, collective wickedness virus spreading throughout a corporation, regardless of the corporate social culture (that is, the corporate ethos) that may be helping it proliferate.[28]

Their language of viral contagion implies both intimacy and domination. Although Tom wants to talk with Greg, he really needs to pass on something – detailed criminal collective knowledge – that will bind Greg to him. And Greg realises, from the beginning of this conversation, that Tom's need to divulge is a deliberately performative speech act, which is both threatening and desperate. Listening to the disclosure renders his underling complicit in the cover-up, such that Tom will no longer have to agonise alone with the affliction and liability of the crimes and the anxiety it creates. Unlike Bill, who in handing him the files at least offers to stay mum about the incriminating details, giving Tom a pretence to wilful blindness, Tom repeats Bill's gesture more brutally while naming it for what it is: a career death sentence. In it together (sometimes homoerotically), their lives now intertwined, Tom and Greg are infected with the deadly virus/time bomb that is corporate criminal knowledge.

Importantly, both men experience acquiring this information not as enabling them to act, or helping them develop the company's future actions,

28 Pamela H. Bucy, 'Corporate Ethos: A Standard for Imposing Corporate Criminal Liability', (1991) 75 *Minn LR* 1095, 1099.

which is to say, not as a kind of practical reasoning that helps corporate agents reach a desired end for the corporation. Rather, both see themselves as undergoing a damaging external event: a tragic act of fate has *happened* to them, severely undermining whatever agency they imagined they once had. That is one reason why their conversation takes on a strangely alienated, sardonic and panicked tone: this is conversation not as an act of learning, sharing and knowing, but as an experience of watching destructive knowledge oozing towards them from afar. An impending disaster looks like it will eventually reverberate on them like 'a fucking time bomb', whose effect Tom rightly sums up: 'now I'm fucked, forever!' What lends both irony and a certain pathos to their situation are their relative positions: formally, they are not marked as tragic protagonists but as mocked and frequently preposterous characters (Greg even has a jaunty musical theme setting him apart from the Roy family's more classical one). Diegetically, within the social world of Waystar, they suffer lowly positions both within and outside the family. The Roy family repeatedly chooses to imperil them; Logan surely promoted the eager Tom to head Parks because its corporate crimes needed a fall guy and his future son-in-law was manipulable. If anything, imagining themselves as tragically marked might help Tom and Greg avoid the humiliating recognition that their supposed intimates view them as almost entirely expendable.[29]

We might put this a slightly different way to say that, for Tom and Greg, learning real truths about Waystar, in the way that they do, leads to a very dangerous set of thoughts: that they do not feel like agents of the corporation but like tormented subjects menaced by unavoidable evil forces that they have no option but to accept. Such a fatalistic response to an act of knowing is a real hazard that tends to feed on itself. Fatalism, as Mary Midgley describes it, is

> the superstitious acceptance of unnecessary evil, based on a false belief in human impotence to do anything about it. As a practice, it means taking no steps to cure that evil. As a temper, it is the tendency to take up false beliefs in order to excuse inaction.[30]

Suffice it to say that Tom and Greg, and many other Waystar employees, display evidence of such fatalism both as a practice and temper.

I bring up this fatalism because Tom's defeatist response also tells us something about how corporate intention is conceptualised, since neither man – corporate agents both – sees the corporation's past acts as something they must internalise as their own, or even as acts they are in some distant way responsible for. Rather, they envision the scandals at Cruises as of

29 I am grateful to Alecia Simmonds' insight on this point.
30 Mary Midgley, *Wickedness: A Philosophical Essay* (Routledge 1984) 96.

that 'particular class of dangers which are not powers vested in humans, but which can be released by human action', as anthropologist Mary Douglas theorises about pollution.[31] While people can pollute intentionally, she notes, intention is not a requirement for pollution to have destructive effects. Tom and Greg react to these threats and events similarly, in the way anyone must respond to bad things that happen beyond their control (extreme weather, a car accident, war, a poisonous gas cloud). But they do not own these viral, pollution-like events; they suffer them. Being of the corporation, as they understand it, entails subjecting oneself to regular toxic exposure that you do not control and can do nothing to avoid.

As liminal corporate players, the two men are particularly susceptible to (and become sources of) perilous contamination. Later, when corporate counsel Gerri confronts Tom about his press conference plans and warns him 'to shut up', she, in effect, articulates his new reality through an allegory:

> *GERRI:* Have you ever heard of the Sin Cake Eater? ... He would come to the funeral and he would eat all the little cakes they laid out on the corpse – he ate up all the sins. And you know what? The Sin Cake Eater was very well paid. And so long as there was another one who came along after *he* died, it all worked out. So, this may not be the best situation, but there are harder jobs, and you get a fuckload of cake. (S1:E4)

Tom's lucrative, earmarked job is to suffer by compartmentalising and internalising bad corporate knowledge, eating up 'all the sins', for which he will be richly rewarded ('very well paid' with 'a fuckload of cake') and protected in the future by someone else who will assume his role 'after *he* died'. Although the position comes with stigma and distress – the shame of 'eating shit' (as Kendall put it earlier), of ingesting a taboo 'cake' to personally incorporate and neutralise the sins of corporate 'corpses' – 'there are harder jobs' in the world.

Most importantly, this situation means that the self-serving actions that Tom and Greg choose in response to the sinful information that they alone are obliged to 'know', are actions that they see, not unreasonably, as responses to their fate in the system, rather than as actions that extend or further purposeful crimes. In other words, because so many other people in the corporation really *do* know enough about the crimes and cover-ups, but for only these two has fate marked them out as 'sin cake eaters', they find it permissible to act in different ways, following different dictates, and working to better their relative positions in this system. Greg insinuates himself with

31 Mary Douglas, *Purity and Danger: An Analysis of Concept of Pollution and Taboo* (Routledge 2003) 140.

Gerri and then Kendall, while Tom eventually aligns himself with Logan against Shiv and Kendall.

Power-plays, deceptive performative speech acts, lying, shaming and all sorts of other interpersonal betrayals are the patterns in which collective corporate knowledge and intention function. We might reasonably judge and denounce all of these corrupt characters, requiring that each of them, individually, *should* be acting far more nobly and courageously than they do, however unjust their personal situations. They should indeed. But they do not – and they fail to act better while being coerced into accepting incriminating evidence, and treated instrumentally by their family, and exposed resignedly to viral corporate pollution, and shamed and stigmatised. All of which tells us that, according to *Succession*, failing to act better under these conditions is *precisely* how corporate wilfulness and knowledge work. This is the corporate structure in action, for better but, clearly, usually for worse.

What I am trying to emphasise here is how these men's experience of learning about, and contributing to, a corporate criminal conspiracy reveals something essential about how collective knowledge and wilfulness in a corporation (and likely in many other contemporary institutions) functions. There is complex and reflexive psychological, social and political drama – not merely knowledge to be added up or aggregated – in these interactions between Bill, Tom, Kendall, Greg and Gerri, and the reason the series is so compelling is that these corporate dynamics are not unique to prestige streaming television but are entirely common and familiar to us. These characters' motives and patterns of thought, ones incorporating distancing, projection and fatalism, their ways of engaging, ignoring and tormenting one another, are part of what makes knowledge and wilfulness either blind to itself or collectively seen. These motives cannot be severed from the corporation any more than they can be severed from any one of us. At the very least, *Succession* insists, collective knowledge and wilfulness must be more than just the operations, or the cumulative additions, of individuals or of a functioning system. Rather, collective knowledge and wilfulness must be working in the sometimes duplicitous, coercive and self-blinded, occasionally enlightened way any kind of human knowing and acting happens, which is to say, as part of our culture as it is now, following our patterns of thought, feeling and interpersonal drama.

Chapter 11

Corporate Misuse of Legal Professional Privilege

Concealing and Constituting Crimes

Liz Campbell

Introduction

Detecting and then gathering sufficient evidence to pursue corporate wrongdoing is tricky.[1] Whether we prefer the criminal or civil law as a means of regulating and penalising corporate crime,[2] and whether we regard corporate liability as deriving from the conduct and state of mind of individuals or as reflecting the fault of the corporation itself,[3] corporate blameworthiness is evidenced by and proved through the entity's records and reports. So, documented information is key both to guarding against and responding to corporate crime adequately.

Regulators such as the Australian Securities and Investments Commission (ASIC), the Australian Competition & Consumer Commission (ACCC), the Australian Taxation Office (ATO) and the Australian Transaction Reports and Analysis Centre (AUSTRAC) have coercive investigatory powers which enable them to obtain information from individuals and legal entities. Moreover, obligations are imposed on certain corporations to report and retain certain information and suspicions, such as in anti-money laundering law.[4] That said, such powers and duties generally are subject to claims of legal professional privilege (LPP, a.k.a. client legal privilege), which keep certain documents and communications confidential. This means that corporations have a powerful and distinctive capacity to control information in a practical sense, both as a consequence of its sheer volume, as well as in the reliance on legal privilege, often to the delay and detriment of any public enforcement action.[5]

1 Eugene F. Soltes, 'The Frequency of Corporate Misconduct: Public Enforcement versus Private Reality' (2019) 26 *Journal of Financial Crime* 923.
2 Australian Law Reform Commission, *Corporate Criminal Responsibility* (Report 136), 2020, 13.
3 Jonathan Clough, 'Bridging the Theoretical Gap: The Search for a Realist Model of Corporate Criminal Liability' (2007) *Criminal Law Forum* 267.
4 Anti-Money Laundering and Counter-Terrorism Financing Act 2006 (Cth).
5 See Elise Bant in chapter 14 of this volume for a consideration of the opacity of corporate systems and the mechanisms that enable bureaucratic evil.

DOI: 10.4324/9781003402534-15

This chapter draws on two contemporary Australian case studies, of PricewaterhouseCoopers Australia and the Star Casino, to contend with the following questions:

1. How is LPP being used by corporates and regulators?
2. Can this misuse conceal and/or constitute criminal behaviour?

These two case studies exemplify how the misuse of privilege can stymie public enforcement actions. They highlight the central role of lawyers in this dynamic, and indicate how law reform is needed.

While LPP can seem technical and somewhat arcane, in fact it is a central dimension of the state's ability to enforce its laws against corporate crime. The core problem I am focusing on here is its capacity to get in the way of the state investigating and prosecuting corporations for wrongdoing.

The chapter is structured as follows. The 'A Brief Outline of Legal Privilege' section provides an outline of LPP; the 'Concerns about Privilege' section flags some key concerns before the 'Case Studies' section turns to two case studies. The final section sets out themes for discussion and concludes by considering some possible avenues for reform.

A Brief Outline of Legal Privilege

Legal professional privilege limits the disclosure of information or documents which would reveal communications between a client and their lawyer where those communications were made for the dominant purpose of giving or obtaining legal advice or services, or in preparation for 'actual or anticipated' (not merely possible) legal proceedings.[6] This might be in relation to a transaction; an investigation, be that internal or otherwise; prospective civil or criminal proceedings; in the course of preparing for a royal commission, etc. Crucially, the privilege belongs to the client rather than the lawyer, and so is characterised as 'client legal privilege' in the Uniform Evidence Acts.

Recognition of the privilege is seen as crucial to the rule of law.[7] The privilege may be regarded in an instrumental as well as in a deontological sense, that is, in enabling frank disclosure which is of practical benefit to the administration of justice and in respect of compliance with the law as well as in safeguarding and constituting rights of the individual against state power. LPP 'exists to serve the public interest in the administration of justice

6 *Baker v. Campbell* [1983] HCA 39; *Esso* (n 12) [35]; *Mitsubishi Electric Australia Pty Ltd v Victorian Workcover Authority* (2002) 4 VR 332.

7 Justice Mark Weinberg, 'Some Recent Developments in Corporate Regulation – ASIC from a Judicial Perspective', paper presented to the *Monash University Law School Commercial CPD Seminar* (Melbourne, 16 October 2013) 11.

by encouraging full and frank disclosure by clients to their lawyers',[8] and is of 'great importance to the protection and preservation of the rights, dignity and freedom of the ordinary citizen under the law'.[9]

In limited instances, communications between a client and a third party such as an accountant may be privileged, provided the dominant purpose was for the client to be provided legal advice.[10] This might include, say, a situation where the accountant prepared notes for counsel for the purpose of obtaining legal advice for a client or in respect of litigation. Moreover, LPP protects communications with in-house counsel, as long as that legal advisor is consulted in a professional capacity and the communications are confidential and arise from the lawyer/client relationship.[11] It also applies to multidisciplinary practices where both legal practitioners and non-legal practitioners are involved in the work, though this will be fact specific.[12]

LPP is not absolute; it may be waived, and more rarely abrogated. LPP may be waived by the client, either expressly, or impliedly through acting in a way inconsistent with confidentiality of the communications.[13] One way to secure the confidentiality of a document is by express agreement which sets out the basis upon which disclosure is made and the generally very strict limitations upon its further use.[14] In terms of abrogation, while some statutes empower agencies to require persons to reveal privileged communications, the material is not admissible in proceedings against the person.[15] Section 206 of the Proceeds of Crime Act 2002 (Cth) overrides the privilege for the

8 *Esso Australia Resources Ltd v. Commissioner of Taxation of the Commonwealth of Australia* [1999] HCA 67 [35].

9 *Attorney-General (NT) v. Maurice* [1986] HCA 80.

10 *Pratt Holdings Pty Ltd v. Commissioner of Taxation* (2004) 136 FCR 357, where the High Court of Australia considered whether LPP extends to documents prepared by a firm of accountants for the client.

11 *Waterford v. The Commonwealth* (1986–1987) 163 CLR 54 (Deane J. at 79–82; Dawson J. at 96). There is some circularity here: communications are regarded as confidential because privilege attaches to them, and vice versa.

12 See further *Commissioner of Taxation v. PricewaterhouseCoopers* [2022] FCA 278 in the 'Case Studies' section.

13 *Attorney-General (NT) v. Maurice* [1986] HCA 80; *Mann v. Carnell* (1999) 201 CLR 1. In *TerraCom Ltd v. Australian Securities and Investments Commission* [2022] FCA 208, the Federal Court considered whether a waiver of legal professional privilege over part of a privileged investigation report would result in privilege being waived over the entirety of the report. The Court found that a company waived LPP attaching to a report prepared by PwC, by means of letters to shareholders and an Australian Securities Exchange (ASX) announcement which conveyed the proposed conclusion of the report's subject matter.

14 'Legal professional privilege and the government' *Legal Briefing* 30 June 2021 https://www.ags.gov.au/sites/default/files/2021-07/lb117-legal-professional-privilege.pdf (accessed 11/4/2024)

15 e.g., Ombudsman Act 1976 (Cth) and the Law Enforcement Integrity Commissioner Act 2006 (Cth). See ALRC '*Traditional Rights and Freedoms – Encroachments by Commonwealth Laws*' (Report 129, 2015) 12.5.

purpose of production orders issued under Section 202, but this is not admissible in proceedings against a natural person.[16] The privilege may be denied to a communication that is made for the purpose of frustrating the processes of the law, even where no crime or fraud is contemplated.[17] Furthermore, a party cannot rely on LPP where there is evidence of illegality or improper purpose,[18] such as involvement in fraud or other misconduct.

Australia's national corporate regulator, the Australia Securities and Investments Commission (ASIC), has clear policies on LPP and its waiver. ASIC's investigation and enforcement information sheets confirm that the recipient of an ASIC compulsory notice is not required to waive LPP, but may do so:[19]

> ASIC believes there can be a public benefit in accepting privileged documents (or documents claimed to be privileged) ... as it may assist in the effective and efficient conclusion of ASIC's investigation and determination of consequential steps (which might include no further regulatory action). It may also assist the parties to identify efficiently, and with precision, the critical issues to be addressed in an investigation. It will often be in the public interest for ASIC, in seeking to perform its regulatory functions, to have access to LPP material and it will often not be detrimental to the privilege holder for this to occur.[20]

Likewise, the Australian Competition and Consumer Commission (the chief competition regulator, ACCC) encourages but does not require the production of privileged communications.[21]

Concerns about Privilege

The crux of the issue is that big corporations are misusing or overusing privilege to avoid or obstruct investigations, litigation and prosecution. Corporations use LPP to control information, which obstructs enforcement efforts, and also then dictates the media narrative and public discourse on corporate wrongdoing. The Australian Federal Police says that 'blanket LPP

16 S 206.
17 *Attorney-General (NT) v. Kearney* (1985) 158 CLR 500 [17].
18 *R v. Bell; ex parte Lees* [1980] HCA 26.
19 ASIC 'Claims of legal professional privilege' Information Sheet 165, December 2012 at https://download.asic.gov.au/media/1339100/infosheet-165-legal-professional-privilege.pdf and INFO 145 at https://asic.gov.au/about-asic/asic-investigations-and-enforcement/asic-s-compulsory-information-gathering-powers/. See Tom Middleton, 'The Role of Lawyers in the Context of ASIC's Investigative and Enforcement Powers' (2010) 28 *Companies & Securities Law Journal* 107, 119–120.
20 Ibid. section 5.
21 Australian Competition & Consumer Commission, *ACCC Cooperation Policy for Enforcement Matters* (31 July 2002) 2 https://www.accc.gov.au/publications/accc-cooperation-policy-for-enforcement-matters.

claims can make it very difficult to obtain admissible evidence to support prosecutions' and that the resolution of claims can take a 'significant period of time',[22] and the Australian Taxation Office has indicated that '[r]eckless LPP claims over non-privileged documents unduly hinder ATO investigations and lead to extended disputes about information gathering, instead of focussing on the resolution of the substantive issue'.[23] While the number of spurious or false claims of LPP is unknown, the perception is that the situation is far from ideal. By mid-2019, it seems that 24 multinational companies responded to ATO audits with blanket claims, constituting one in five large audits.[24]

Of course, the privilege is not just of use to private for-profit entities. ASIC has sought, successfully, to uphold claims of privilege over its own documents.[25]

Nonetheless, regulators and agencies are now more proactive in confronting and disputing claims of LPP, with the Australian Tax Office described as 'bellicose',[26] while ASIC has announced that it is prepared to take court action to resolve 'inappropriate' claims.[27] Both ASIC and ATO have taken legal action pushing back against claims of privilege, which in doing so have delineated the scope of LPP and of their powers.[28] In *Carlton United Breweries Australia Holding Pty Ltd v. Federal Commissioner of Taxation,* the Federal Court of Australia decided that ATO's statutory powers extend to seeking particulars of LPP claims, where Carlton United Breweries sought to use the privilege to withhold information during a tax audit.[29] In *Whitebox Trading Pty Ltd v. Whitebox Trading Pty Ltd*, ASIC sought successfully to adduce in

22 Attorney General's Department, *Cross-agency Submission No 32 to Senate Standing Committee on Economics*, Inquiry into Foreign Bribery, 2015, 13. For a comparable UK position see Stuart Alford, 'Enforcing the UK Bribery Act – The UK Serious Fraud Office's Perspective', *Serious Fraud Office Speeches at the Anti-Corruption in Oil & Gas Conference 2014*, 17 November 2014.

23 ATO 'ATO provides certainty on Legal Professional Privilege Claims' 22 June 2022 https://www.ato.gov.au/Media-centre/Media-releases/ATO-provides-certainty-on-Legal-Professional-Privilege-claims/

24 Tom McIlroy, 'Legal privilege claims in 20 per cent of ATO multinational cases', *Australian Financial Review*, 26 June 2019.

25 *Bolton v. ASIC* [2018] AATA 4640; *ASIC v. Harold Mitchell & Anor* [2019] FCA 1484. See Adam Murphy, 'Check your privilege: The foundation of legal professional privilege within the Commonwealth Director of Public Prosecutions' (2021) 45(3) *Criminal Law Journal* 153.

26 Eu-Jin Teo, 'Under pressure'?: Section 39 of the legal profession uniform law and the federal commissioner of taxation' (2022) 37 *Australian Tax Forum* 273.

27 ASIC 'AMP and Clayton Utz surrender in ASIC court battle over failure to produce documents' 11 March 2019 https://asic.gov.au/about-asic/news-centre/find-a-media-release/2019-releases/19-052mr-amp-and-clayton-utz-surrender-in-asic-court-battle-over-failure-to-produce-documents/>.

28 See Glencore, Carlton, PwC.

29 *Carlton United Breweries Australia Holding Pty Ltd v. Federal Commissioner of Taxation* [2021] FCA 43.

evidence at the hearing otherwise privileged documents acquired through its compulsory information-gathering powers.[30]

Expansive and questionable claims of privilege obscure the nature of corporate behaviour and block enforcement actions. This stalling tactic can lead to very protracted processes in ascertaining the appropriate scope of the claim, as the reasons for claims of privilege are not always apparent. Such challenges through litigation might result in disclosure, whether partial or total.

We will see from the case studies below that strategic, wholesale claims for LPP are not uncommon and have the effect of frustrating public enforcement actions against corporations. Moreover, both understanding and using LPP is predicated on the involvement of lawyers. Indeed, it has been suggested that the availability of LPP provides a competitive advantage for lawyers or benefit for clients vis-à-vis accountants.[31] Thus lawyers play a central role here.

Case Studies

This section now considers two case studies, that of PricewaterhouseCoopers Australia (PwC) and the Star Casino. PricewaterhouseCoopers Australia used LPP to obstruct an Australian Tax Office audit of its client, a Brazilian multinational company with Australian subsidiaries.[32] The Star scenario concerned the reliance on LPP by in-house counsel to prevent disclosure of internal reports to the Australian Transaction Reports and Analysis Centre (AUSTRAC – the Australian government financial intelligence agency responsible for monitoring financial transactions), in the context of recurrent and seemingly endemic issues of money laundering in its and other casinos.[33]

PricewaterhouseCoopers Australia

Here, in essence, PwC intentionally set out to manipulate LPP – as shown by staff emails – and the Federal Court judge was very dubious about these practices.

30 *Whitebox Trading Pty Ltd v Whitebox Trading Pty Ltd* [2017] FCA 324.

31 Katie Walsh, 'Lawyers fight to deny accountants legal privilege', *Australian Financial Review*, 15 August 2011; Ed Tadros, 'Hayne commission leads Norton Rose into risk consulting', *Australian Financial Review*, 9 November 2018. The ALRC recommended that LPP should accrue in relation to tax advice also: Australian Law Reform Commission, *Client Legal Privilege and Federal Investigatory Bodies* (Discussion paper 73, 2007) [Proposal 6-3].

32 *Commissioner of Taxation v. PricewaterhouseCoopers & ors* [2022] FCA 278.

33 State of New South Wales, *Review of The Star Pty Ltd, Report of the Inquiry under Section 143 of the* Casino Control Act 1992 *(NSW)* (31 August 2022) Vols 1 and 2.

A Brazilian multinational company called JBS SA owned a number of Australian companies including Flora Green Pty Ltd and JBS Holdco Australia Pty Ltd. PwC was providing taxation and other services to JBS Australia Group. PwC was doing this as a multidisciplinary practice, meaning that both PwC lawyers and staff who were not lawyers provided advice. The Australian Commissioner of Taxation commenced an audit of Flora Green and issued notices to produce documents to someone called Glenn Russell, a partner of PwC, as well as the company Flora Green. PwC claimed privilege on behalf of Flora Green over approximately 44,000 documents. The Tax Commissioner disputed the claims of privilege over approximately 15,500 of these.

It's worth noting two emails referred to in the judgement. One Australian legal practitioner (ALP) in PwC Australia sent an email to two of her colleagues, one of whom was a lawyer also, the other was not:

Stefen and Glenn,

> Can you please sign off the below documents in DMS for JBS? **Glenn I have included you in order to claim privilege** and as you are project partner for stamp duty purposes.
>
> Kind regards
>
> Jess[34]

A cognate observation was noted in another email from Glenn Russell:

> *As a generally [sic] rule JBS like to have Australian tax advice prepared as a legal service* ***so that the work is covered by Legal Professional Privilege*** *in Australia. We have always been able to accommodate this through ensuring that we set up the engagement in the correct way at the outset.*[35]
>
> (Emphasis added to both quotes in the judgement.)

The Tax Commissioner asked the Federal Court to decide whether the form of the engagements between PwC Australia and JBS, and the services provided, established a relationship of lawyer and client which would be sufficient to ground a claim for LPP. He also asked whether the documents in dispute were made for the dominant purpose of giving or obtaining legal advice from PwC lawyers – this determines whether the documents are privileged or not.

The Federal Court held that the form of the engagements established a relationship of lawyer and client sufficient to ground privilege claims, and that the services were provided under a relationship of lawyer/client, meaning the documents could be privileged.

34 *Commissioner of Taxation v. PricewaterhouseCoopers* [2022] FCA 278 [118].
35 Ibid. [122].

Moshinsky J. stated: '[w]hether or not the Documents in Dispute are privileged is to be determined by reference to whether, as to each particular document, it constitutes or records a communication made for the dominant purpose of giving or obtaining legal advice'.[36] To be able to judge this, the Court carried out a documentary analysis of a sample of 116 documents (rather than the tens of thousands of documents implicated) to ascertain if they were made for the dominant purpose of giving or obtaining legal advice. While many of the sample documents were subject to legal professional privilege, the majority were not.

Moshinsky J. was heavily critical of 'non-legal advice being "routed"' through Glenn Russell 'in order to obtain the protection of legal professional privilege'.[37]

The implications of this Federal Court decision for both corporations and enforcement agencies are significant. While ATO was vindicated in challenging the privilege claims, the court also confirmed that work done by multidisciplinary practices attracts LPP in some instances. In practice, this may influence who is providing advice to a client, with multidisciplinary practices continuing to use lawyers strategically.

Another salient dimension of this case study is that PwC requested an undertaking from ATO that it would not recommend prosecution of the firm or its staff for claiming privilege falsely if PwC lost. (Failure to comply with an ATO order to produce documents, including falsely claiming LPP, is a criminal offence.[38]) PwC's request was refused initially;[39] then after lengthy discussions ATO agreed that it was prepared to 'give comfort' to PwC that it would not prosecute.[40] It seems that ATO agreed in order to access information, and perhaps to keep PwC onside. It is so difficult to access information about corporations that a regulator will forgo a chance to prosecute in order to get that material. This is a notable illustration of the negotiation that is commonplace in corporate regulation.

The Star

The second and even more unsavoury example is that of Star. Star is the corporation that holds the casino licence in New South Wales (NSW), and

36 Ibid. [205].

37 Ibid. [611]; [624]; [726] and [739].

38 Taxation Administration Act 1953, s8C on Failure to comply with requirements under taxation law. Also see Australian Securities and Investments Commission Act 2001, DIV 7 on offences.

39 'ATO won't promise not to prosecute PwC for tax offences', *Lawyerly*, 3 February 2021.

40 'ATO prepared to rule out prosecuting PwC for tax offences after privilege fight', *Lawyerly*, 16 April 2021.

the ultimate holding company is Star Entertainment.[41] On 10 October 2021, 'the television programme *60 minutes* broadcast an episode which made a number of very serious allegations about conduct of The Star Entities',[42] mirroring allegations made in 2019 against Crown Resorts regarding the enabling of money laundering.[43] Then the allegations were developed further by newspapers such as *The Sydney Morning Herald* and *The Age*.[44] An independent Chartered Accounting firm was engaged to provide an expert report regarding anti-money laundering and counter-terrorism financing (AML/CTF) issues relevant to Star.[45] A public hearing was held from mid-March to late-May 2022.[46]

Star was required by law to disclose certain matters, and was acting contrary to legal duties. Star breached money laundering law in different ways, in failing in its legal duty to disclose as well as deploying privilege strategically. It's worth recounting some of these facts, to illustrate the nature and extent of the wrongdoing withheld from enforcement agencies.

In addition, Star's largest 'junket' customer, the tour operator Suncity, was connected to organised crime. In 2017, Star offered a private and exclusive gaming room to Suncity, where cash dealings involving the exchange of chips/gaming plaques for cash were observed in CCTV footage in 2018, potentially contravening the *Anti-Money Laundering and Counter-Terrorism Financing Act 2006* (Cth).[47] In 2019, Star came to know about the report on Suncity's ongoing connections with triads and Suncity's facilitation of organised crime.[48] Regardless, The Star knowingly continued cooperating with Suncity and did not disclose this to the Independent Liquor and Gaming Authority.[49]

Star enabled certain processes to avoid Chinese capital flight laws, and breached its agreements with its bank. From July 2013 to March 2020, patrons could swipe China UnionPay (CUP) debit cards at the hotel of Star to fund gambling at The Star Casino, to disguise the use of CUP cards for gambling as hotel expenses.[50] Star's board believed that UnionPay (the proponent of the CUP card scheme) prohibited the use of CUP cards to fund gambling and that potentially it breached the Merchant Agreement Star had with

41 State of New South Wales, *Review of The Star Pty Ltd, Report of the Inquiry under Section 143 of the* Casino Control Act 1992 *(NSW)* (31 August 2022) ('*Report*') Vol. 1, 2[1].
42 Ibid. Vol. 1, 130[4].
43 Ibid. 55 onwards.
44 Ibid. 130[5].
45 Ibid. 131[13].
46 Ibid. 135[40].
47 Ibid. 6[26]–6[36]. See also ch. 13.
48 Ibid. 9[42]–[43].
49 Ibid. 9[42], 10[44]–11[51].
50 Ibid. 3[6]–[7]. See also ch. 5.

NAB (the supplier of the merchant terminals), but did not disclose the use of the cards in this way to the Independent Liquor and Gaming Authority.[51] Star made several misleading statements to both NAB and UnionPay.[52] Star Management was aware that this process was to circumvent Chinese capital flight laws. The value of the transactions was A$908 million.[53]

Beyond these examples, one of the ways that Star was able to continue to enable money laundering or to fail to stop money laundering was through claiming privilege.

Star Entertainment has two 'reporting entities' within its designated business group for the purposes of the AML/CTF legislation, and had a joint AML/CTF Programme which covered each of them. There is an obligation under the AML/CTF Act to have some of the joint AML/CTF Programme audited independently.[54] KPMG was engaged on 27 November 2017 to conduct an audit of Star Entertainment's AML/CTF Programme and in May 2018, KPMG provided drafts of its reports to senior Star Entertainment executives to confirm for factual accuracy.

KPMG's final reports made a series of findings about serious shortcomings in Star Entertainment's AML/CTF Programme, including that people could walk into the casinos with hundreds of thousands of dollars in cash but not be assessed as higher risk for that reason alone; that the AML/CTF Programme (contrary to its name) did not consider terrorism financing at all; and that there was no documented money laundering or terrorism financing risk assessment or risk assessment methodology in relation to junkets. The reports also noted that there were inadequate AML/CTF resources.[55] KPMG found that Star Entertainment had a manual transaction monitoring process which was inconsistently applied across the casino properties.[56]

Star Entertainment (through its subsidiary Star) resisted producing the KPMG report to AUSTRAC (the Australian government financial intelligence agency responsible for monitoring financial transactions) for 16 months in the face of at least four separate written requests from AUSTRAC to do so.[57] Star had asserted legal privilege in two of its responses,[58] which was then disputed by AUSTRAC on two occasions. Finally, Star 'relented' and provided a copy, noting that 'The Star does not intend to waive legal professional privilege in relation to the report'.[59]

51 Ibid. 3[8].
52 Ibid. 5[16]–6[25]. See also ch. 5.
53 Ibid. 3[6]
54 Ibid. [86–87].
55 Ibid. [88].
56 Ibid. Vol. 2. 254 [21].
57 Ibid. 267 [91].
58 Ibid. 267 [92–95].
59 Ibid. 267 [95].

The Inquiry found that the KPMG reports were 'clearly not privileged', as they were not prepared for the dominant purpose of Star Entertainment or Star being provided with legal advice or legal services relating to an actual or anticipated proceeding.[60] Rather, the dominant purpose of KPMG's engagement was to perform an independent review of Star Entertainment's AML/CTF Programme.[61] Having found that the privilege claim over the KPMG reports was 'clearly incorrect' and the dominant purpose test 'clearly not satisfied', the Inquiry turned to the evidence of Ms Martin, then the Group General Counsel and Company Secretary, and the head of the Legal Department of Star Entertainment.[62] She had stated in evidence that she did not make a claim for privilege over the KPMG reports which she considered to be inappropriate at the time. Accepting this, the Inquiry found that she 'had an unsatisfactory understanding of the law relating to legal professional privilege'.[63] Similarly, Andrew Power, Star's former general counsel 'admitted to having a practice of marking documents "privileged" without turning his mind to whether there was a proper basis to do so'.[64]

This is a restrained and generous interpretation of the situation and of the lawyers' role. This was a cynical and strategic use of privilege to obstruct any efforts to investigate Star's wrongdoing, which was sophisticated, ongoing and very lucrative. As the Inquiry noted, Star should have provided AUSTRAC with the KPMG reports immediately after receiving AUSTRAC's initial request. The consequence of Star's privilege claim was that the KPMG reports were wrongly withheld from AUSTRAC over a period of 16 months while Star Entertainment took steps to address the problems identified by KPMG without any proper regulatory scrutiny.[65]

Despite a lot of rhetoric and ostensible action, Star continues to operate. The Inquiry recommended that the Independent Liquor and Gaming Authority take steps to require Star Casino to provide the report of any independent review of its AML/CTF Programme to the Authority within 14 days of the issue of the report.[66] Then on 13 September 2022, the NSW Independent Casino Commission issued a notice to Star to explain why its licence should not be revoked. Star responded that the Commission should allow it to continue to operate the casino under strict supervision.[67] On 17

60 Ibid. 265 [82].
61 Ibid. 265 [83].
62 Ibid. 266 [90].
63 Ibid. 266 [90].
64 Ibid. Vol. 1. 20 [99].
65 Ibid. Vol. 2. 268 [103].
66 Ibid. 268 [115].
67 *Disciplinary Action and Appointment of Casino Manager by NSW Independent Casino Commission* (ASX announcement, 17 October 2022) 6 https://company-announcements.afr.com/asx/sgr/fb7aff5b-4dcc-11ed-ae65-b2a7466ef4a4.pdf.

October 2022, the NSW Independent Casino Commission issued a notice to suspend Star's licence indefinitely and a pecuniary penalty of A$100m.[68] Star engaged international law firm Allen & Overy LLP as the Independent Monitor for its remediation programme and released the first report in October 2022.[69] The AUSTRAC also commenced civil penalty proceedings in the Federal Court against the Star Entities for alleged serious and systemic non-compliance with anti-money laundering and counter-terrorism financing laws.[70]

While the licence was suspended, Star continues to operate. The Commission appointed a new manager of the Sydney casino for a period of 90 days, and this has been extended to January 2024.[71] On that basis, The Star Sydney casino remains open, and it is anticipated that staff will be unaffected.[72]

Notably, the Chief Commissioner stated that 'We found them [Star] very adversarial during the whole of the inquiry ... Their mindset wasn't anywhere near cooperative in terms of getting the job done'.[73] That said, Star chairman's subsequent apology and commitment to reforms in a letter to shareholders were regarded as crucial. 'Had Star not published this letter, it is very likely that there would be a different outcome announced here today', the Chief Commissioner said.[74] This is a remarkably conciliatory response to a calculated communication by Star.

Star used LPP strategically and in a manipulative way to continue bad practices in laundering money as well as facilitating others' criminality. It remains in business.

Discussion and Concluding Remarks

These two case studies indicate how privilege is used, both by external legal/multidisciplinary firms as well as in-house counsel, to thwart attempted public enforcement actions. A few key themes emerge here, around the empirical state of affairs, the centrality of lawyers; the practical matter of resources; and the case for reform.

68 Ibid. 7.

69 *First Independent Monitor Report* (ASX announcement, 24 October 2022) https://www.asx.com.au/asxpdf/20221024/pdf/45gn0nzlfrgcwt.pdf.

70 'AUSTRAC commences proceedings in the Federal Court against Star Entertainment Group entities', 30 November 2022.

71 The Star 'Extension of term of manager of the Sydney Star Casino' 16 December 2022 https://www.starentertainmentgroup.com.au/wp-content/uploads/2022/12/16-December-2022-ASX-Announcement-Extension-of-term-of-Manager-of-The-Star-Sydney-casino.pdf

72 Ibid. p. 1.

73 Elouise Fowler, 'Star gambles on after Sydney casino licence suspended', *Australian Financial Review*, 17 October 2022

74 Ibid.

First, it is unclear how representative these case studies are. Are they aberrations or reflective of a more embedded problem? And beyond this, how and by whom is privilege misused in relation to actions against corporates? (When) Is this deployment of LPP a conscious and strategic choice by certain actors, or an unreflective and unquestioned dimension of information management within corporations? Pursuing these empirical questions further in the contemporary Australian context is my next project.[75]

Second, what *is* evident, regardless of the absence of other data, is the centrality and influence of lawyers: the NSW Independent Casino Commissioner said Star's general counsel and her deputy were 'very heavily implicated' in the problematic conduct.[76] Despite this, there was no study of evil/culpability or even of intention/motive in the Star Inquiry. While this might be viewed as a benign interpretation of wrongdoing by lawyers, an 'unsatisfactory understanding' of the law might be as damning a description as we could expect in this context. Moreover, ASIC has commenced civil penalty proceedings in the Federal Court against 11 current and former directors and officers of The Star Entertainment Group, including the Group General Counsel, for alleged breaches of their duties under Section 180 of the Corporations Act.[77] While it is unclear whether any complaints have been lodged with NSW Legal Services Commissioner, the bar is set very high for professional misconduct.

It is important to note that lawyers often are key enablers of money laundering and other economic crimes.[78] Despite the avenue open to ASIC as in Star, it is noteworthy that in Australia lawyers do not fall within the scope of the AML/CTF regime and so are not required to make suspicious activity reports regarding suspected money laundering.[79] While this has been

75 For existing work see Vincent Alexander, 'The Corporate Attorney-Client Privilege: A Study of the Participants' (1989) 63 *St John's Law Review* 191; Geoffrey R Stone, 'Above the Law: Research Methods, Ethics and Law of Privilege' (University of Chicago Public Law & Legal Theory Working Paper No 21, 2002) 2; Petter Gottschalk, *Financial Crime and Knowledge Workers: An Empirical Study of Defense Lawyers and White-Collar Criminals* (Palgrave, 2014).

76 Hannah Wootton and Michael Pelly, 'Star casino report tightens screws on legal privilege claims', *Australian Financial Review*, 15 September 2022.

77 ASIC 'ASIC launches proceedings against 11 current and former Star Entertainment directors and officers' 13 December 2022 https://asic.gov.au/about-asic/news-centre/find-a-media-release/2022-releases/22-351mr-asic-launches-proceedings-against-11-current-and-former-star-entertainment-directors-and-officers/ 13 December 2022.

78 Katie Benson, *Lawyers and the proceeds of crime: the facilitation of money laundering and its control* (Routledge 2020); Michael Levi, *Lawyers, their AML regulation and suspicious transaction reporting*, Report for the Cullen Commission, British Columbia (2020).

79 Attorney-General's Department, *Report on the Statutory Review of the Anti-Money Laundering and Counter Terrorism Financing Act 2006 and Associated Rules and Regulations* (April 2016) https://www.ag.gov.au/Consultations/Documents/StatutoryReviewAnti-MoneylaunderingAndCounter TerrorismFinancingActCth200/report-on-the-statutory-review-of-the-anti-money-laundering.pdf. Attorney-General's Department, *Legal practitioners and*

criticised,[80] and consultation is ongoing,[81] the Law Council of Australia described certain obligations of reporting entities under the AML/CTF Act as inherently 'incompatible with LPP'.[82] This has sought to be addressed in jurisdictions, such as Canada and New Zealand, by tailoring requirements which apply to lawyers. Despite scepticism about the value of suspicious activity reports in general,[83] and the 'technical' quality of reports by lawyers in particular,[84] at least it might put lawyers on notice as to their duties and the risks inherent in certain spaces.

Third, in a practical sense, the risk appetite of regulators to challenging privilege claims and attitude of commissioners is central. This is also a matter of resources.

Finally, in responding to this issue, there is the possibility of abrogation of LPP, or more radically, its removal from corporations. There is a precedent in limiting the privilege against self-incrimination from corporations. In *Environment Protection Authority v. Caltex Refining Co Pty*, the High Court of Australia held by a 4:3 majority that an incorporated company is not entitled to the privilege against self-incrimination.[85] In contrast to the dominant interpretation regarding LPP, McHugh J. in *Caltex* spoke of 'the harm to the administration of justice which would result from allowing corporations to claim the privilege [against self-incrimination]'.[86] I argue that LPP is analogous to the privilege against self-incrimination, and so its abolition in relation to certain offences should be considered. There is precedent in relation to specific corporations[87] as well as certain types of crime, so this is not an outlandish suggestion.

conveyancers: a model for regulation under Australia's anti-money laundering and counter-terrorism financing regime (November 2016) 2 https:I/www.ag.gov.au/Consultations /Documents/AM L-CTF/Iega1-practitioners-model-for-reguIation.pdf 19. Karin Svedberg Helgesson and Ulrika Mörth, 'Client privilege, compliance and the rule of law: Swedish lawyers and money laundering prevention' (2018) 69 *Crime Law Soc Change* 227.

80 Financial Action Taskforce, *Australia, Mutual Evaluation Report* (2015).

81 AUSTRAC submission to *The Adequacy of Australia's Anti-Money Laundering and Counter-Terrorism Financing Regime* Submission 33 https://www.aph.gov.au/Parliamentary_Business/Committees/Senate/Legal_and_Constitutional_Affairs/AUSTRAC/Submissions

82 *The adequacy and efficacy of Australia's anti-money laundering and counter-terrorism financing (AML/CTF) regime* https://www.aph.gov.au/Parliamentary_Business/Committees/Senate/Legal_and_Constitutional_Affairs/AUSTRAC/Submissions, Submission 30, 23.

83 Benson (n 78).

84 Law Commission, *Anti-Money Laundering: the SARs Regime* (Consultation Paper No 236) (2018) 5.7–5.8.

85 *Environment Protection Authority v. Caltex Refining Co. Pty* (1993) 178 CLR 477; [1993] HCA 74.

86 Ibid. [36].

87 See James Hardie, and POCA. See further Liz Campbell, 'Legal Professional Privilege and Corporate Wrongdoing', (2023) 44 *Adelaide Law Review* 339.

While the conventional understanding in the justice system is of the might of the state pitted against an impecunious defendant, the resources of corporations confound traditional protections regarding the burden of proof and so on.[88] Restraining the use of LPP in this instance would be an appropriate limitation on corporate power.

88 Michael Levi, 'Lawyers as Money Laundering Enablers? An Evolving and Contentious Relationship' (2022) 23(2) *Global Crime* 126, 136.

Part 4

Future Approaches

Chapter 12

The Monster Within

Representing Corporate Evil

*Mihailis E. Diamantis**

> *How can anyone be frightened*
> *by what they know does not exist?*[1]

Introduction

Long ago, a mad stroke of human genius animated an artificial person. This technological marvel now navigates the world, seemingly of its own accord and with calculating intelligence. It has the power of two, of 20, of 20,000 men, yet it obsessively fixates on a singular purpose. Humans who stand in its way do not last long. It inspires awe, and sometimes also terror.

The ambitions behind the modern business corporation were innocent enough.[2] It was the gradual work of centuries, not a single electric flash. Each innovation incrementally built the corporation's power with unforeseen consequences. Originally, it was conceived as a very limited entity, permitted solely to undertake ambitious, predefined public projects.[3] Over the decades, courts and legislatures dropped restraint after restraint and shaped corporations increasingly in our image. Corporate purposes came to encompass any legitimate private enterprise creators could conjure.[4] Lawmakers released the shackles of the *ultra vires* doctrine, which had prevented corporations from

* Many thanks to Jacob Schiller for his research assistance on a range of exotic topics, and to Penny Crofts and W. Robert Thomas for valuable comments on earlier drafts.

1 From: *The Philosophy of Horror: Or, Paradoxes of the Heart* p. 8, First Edition by Noel Carroll, Copyright 1990 by Routledge. Reproduced by permission of Taylor & Francis Group.

2 The history, law and enforcement priorities I discuss throughout this paper reflect the US experience with corporate crime. Some of the motivations and proposals may, for that reason, seem insular. However, I hope that there are some resonances for readers from other jurisdictions.

3 Mark M. Hager, 'Bodies Politic: The Progressive History of Organizational "Real Entity" Theory' (1989) 50 *U. Pitt. L. Rev.* 575, 594–595; 'Constructive Notice of the Charter of a Corporation' (1913) 26 *Harv. L. Rev.* 531, 541.

4 Elizabeth Pollman, 'The History and Revival of the Corporate Purpose Clause' (2021) 99 *Tex. L. Rev.* 1423.

DOI: 10.4324/9781003402534-17

acting contrary to their charter purpose.[5] Looking uneasily at what they had created, lawmakers would then tried to subdue it.[6] But this completed the cabalistic summoning ritual, breathing the life of full legal responsibility into corporations.[7] Like any Faustian bargain, even this well-intentioned sorcery backfired. The responsibilities of legal personhood brought with them the rights of legal personhood.[8] Corporations, having both, now overcome us in the courtroom as well as in the marketplace.

Our weightiest tool of corporate control – corporate criminal law – has been stuck in a century-long rut. It comes saddled with an anaemic conception of its own purpose – the vaguely consequentialist mandate to prevent crime.[9] It has at its disposal only a paucity of punitive tools – monetary fines and toothless mandates to reform.[10] Both are demonstrably ineffective. Corporate fines are neither large enough (the requisite fine would exceed the assets corporations have available) nor targeted enough (shareholders hold the purse, but managers exercise control) to incentivise good behavior.[11] Reform mandates fails because we do not yet know how to fix corporations.[12] Recidivism rates are high.[13] Vaunted successes soon turn bad.[14] And

5 Hager (n 3) 594–595.

6 *N.Y. Cent. & Hudson River R.R. Co. v United States* (1909) 212 US 481, 494–495. *See generally* W. Robert Thomas, 'How and Why Corporations Became (and Remain) Persons Under the Criminal Law' (2017) 45 *Fla. St. U.L. Rev.* 479.

7 Dictionary Act, 1 USC § 1 (2018) (defining 'person').

8 *See, e.g.*, *Burwell v. Hobby Lobby Stores, Inc.* (2014) 573 US 682 (holding that corporations have the constitutional right of free exercise of religion).

9 Legally speaking, corporate crime has diverse aims, 'Corporate Crime: Regulating Corporate Behavior Through Criminal Sanctions' (1979) 92 *Harv. L. Rev.* 1227, 1231, but scholars and legal actors usually ignore goals like incapacitation and retribution. *See* W. Robert Thomas, 'Incapacitating Corporate Criminals' (2019) 72 *Vand. L. Rev.* 905 (arguing that scholars improperly overlook incapacitative goals in corporate criminal law); Sam Buell, 'Retiring Corporate Retribution' (2020) 83 *L. & Contemp. Probs.* 25.

10 Mihailis E. Diamantis and William R. Thomas, 'But We Haven't Got Corporate Criminal Law' (2022) 47 J. Corp. L. 191; 18B AM. JUR. 2d Corporations § 1826.

11 Mihailis E. Diamantis, 'Clockwork Corporations' (2018) 103 *Iowa L. Rev.* 507. Empirical economics shows that higher corporate fines do not increase deterrence. Cindy R. Alexander & Mark A. Cohen, 'The Causes of Corporate Crime: An Economic Perspective' in Anthony S. Barkow and Rachel E. Barkow (eds), *Prosecutors in the Boardroom: Using Criminal Law to Regulate Corporate Conduct* (2011) 24.

12 Mihailis E. Diamantis, 'An Academic Perspective' in Anthony S. Barkow, Neil M. Barofsky and Thomas J. Perelli (eds), *The Guide to Monitorships* (3d. ed., Glov. Investigations Rev., 2020) 79 (arguing in favour of corporate rehabilitation, but acknowledging the limits of current knowledge about how to do it).

13 Edwin H. Sutherland, *White Collar Crime* (1949) 218.

14 For example, in 2008, after Siemens pleaded guilty to public corruption charges and underwent several mandatory reforms, the DOJ proudly declared that the company set a 'high standard for multi-national companies to follow'. Department's Sentencing Memorandum at 1, *United States v. Siemens Aktiengesellschaft*, No. 1:08-cr-00367-RJL (D.D.C. 12 December 2008),

the list of provably rehabilitated corporations does not exist. Consequently, we find ourselves in a world where corporations run amok. White-collar crime inflicts 20 times more economic damage each year than all other crime combined.[15] We respond by crossing our fingers and throwing the same economic fetish at them.

Corporate criminal law is long overdue for a rebranding of both its mandate and its method.[16] Even as the incidence and effect of corporate crime grows, the public sense of urgency remains curiously mute. One might wonder whether the purely economic narrative of corporate crime and punishment is to blame. Authorities rarely have trouble fomenting public reaction to human criminals – drug dealers, kidnappers and serial killers – whose aggregate effect pales by comparison. But the sort of economic analysis prosecutors use to diagnose and describe corporate misconduct has a tendency to psychologically crowd out moral concern.[17] It drains public agitation for reform and dulls authorities' imagination for how to intervene. Corporate criminal law needs more ideas.

Other scholars have already proposed horror as a fertile framework for reconceptualising the nature of corporate transgression. For nearly a century, the story of corporate law has elicited comparisons to tales of laboratory terror like Frankenstein.[18] These narratives follow the arc of human hubris through a common three-step horror trope: (1) man creates man, (2) man becomes monster and (3) man destroys man. As a creation story, the analogy to corporate history is apt. But it offers little guidance to prosecutors and policymakers for reform. The moral of its story – do not meddle in God's creative domain[19] – comes too late. Our fate is

---

https://www.justice.gov/sites/default/files/criminal-fraud/legacy/2013/05/02/12-12-08siemensvenez-sent.pdf. Five years later, Siemens' filings with the SEC noted it was under new investigation for public corruption in at least 14 other countries. Siemens Aktiengesellschaft Form 20-F Annual Report at 40–42 (27 November 2013), https://www.siemens.com/investor/pool/en/investor_relations/financial_publications/sec_filings/2013/20_f.pdf.

15 *See* Julie O'Sullivan, 'The Indefensible White-Collar Ecosystem' (2022) 47 *J. Corp. L.* 1044 (comparing the cost of white collar crimes to other types of crime).

16 W. Robert Thomas and Mihailis E. Diamantis, 'Branding Corporate Crime' [forthcoming 2024] 92 *Fordham L. Rev.*

17 This may be why corporations also use a morally neutral narrative framework of 'interpretive denial', which characterises misconduct in terms of 'administrative mistakes' or 'systems errors'. Elise Bant, chapter 14 in this volume.

18 *See, e.g.*, Louis K. Liggett Co. v. Lee (1933) 288 US 517, 567 (discussing 'the Frankenstein monster which states have created by their corporation laws'). *cf.* Michael McKenna, 'Collective Responsibility and an Agent Meaning Theory' (2006) 30 *Midwest Studs. Phil.* 16, 31–32 (considering whether corporations are more akin to Godzilla or to Frankenstein's monster).

19 Mary Wollstonecraft Shelly, *Frankenstein* (1818) ('Learn from me, if not by my precepts, at least by my example, how dangerous is the acquirement of knowledge, and how much

already bound up with our economic Frankenstein. Once underway, the story typically careens toward mutual destruction.[20] We might hope for more.

Recent work on horror and corporate law has taken a more productive turn. Penny Crofts drew on the movie *Aliens* to lay bare the 'legal failure of imagination in conceptualizing and attributing corporate responsibility'.[21] This chapter continues and extends that work, with an even more granular and pragmatic purpose. It argues that authorities' public portrayal of corporate crime as predominantly an economic issue is self-undermining because it fails to provoke the emotional exigency that could provoke public mobilization for change. Horror offers a set of tropes, vocabulary and rhetorical modes for fomenting a sense of urgency, even toward atypical malefactors. From horror, corporate prosecutors might excavate the tools needed to convey the high moral stakes of corporate crime.

This chapter proceeds in three steps. The 'The Official Rhetoric of Corporate Crime' section elaborates how the current economic language and thinking within corporate criminal law undermines corporate criminal justice. The default rhetorical and evaluative framework that most enforcers and scholars adopt is poorly calibrated to the gravity and threat of corporate offence. It therefore fails to validate victims of corporate crime or to stimulate sustained public outrage. These expressive shortcomings have tangible effects. The public becomes passive, frequently harmed by corporate misconduct but unmotivated to rally for necessary reform. Additionally, there is good reason to think that corporations would behave better if the true moral valence of their offences were not consistently shrouded in a sterilising economic mantle.

The 'Can Corporations Be Evil?' section proposes that prosecutors need to learn how to develop a rhetoric of corporate evil. Evil is a morally evocative concept that primes listeners for action. Yet three common attributes of corporate criminals seem incongruous with portraying them as evil. (1) Corporations lack the familiar hallmarks of corporate agency, like consciousness and will. (2) Corporate crime is often perpetrated by a just few employees within a larger corporate structure. (3) Corporate offenders often create positive social and economic goods, like paying jobs and valuable consumer services. These rhetorical obstacles can disarm moralised discourse, leaving a vacuum that economic analysis is poised to fill.

---

happier that man is who believes his native town to be his world, than he who aspires to become greater than his nature will allow'.).

20 Ibid. ('He is dead who called me into being; and when I shall be no more, the very remembrance of us both will speedily vanish'.).

21 Penny Crofts, 'Aliens: Legal Conceptions of the Corporation Invasion' (2022) 34 *L. & Lit.* 387.

The 'Inspiration from Horror' section argues that prosecutors should turn to horror film and literature for inspiration. One of the defining traits of horror is that it presents antagonists as odious, frightening and condemnable. Different subgenres of horror feature nemeses that exhibit the same three attributes which, in the corporate context, seem to be rhetorical impediments. Through horror, prosecutors could learn to reshape how the public, and how corporations themselves, perceive corporate crime. Prosecutors might think of themselves as the producers of a true-to-life horror pageant and us as their audience. Horror films offer methods that, suitably adapted, could be up to the task.

The Official Rhetoric of Corporate Crime

An alien anthropologist determined to study corporate criminal law would be hard pressed to find it. Criminal law, on most accounts, is supposed to single out various shades of evil – reprehensible conduct that violates our most basic social understandings and values. But in the world of corporate misconduct, the line between civil and criminal has blurred almost to the point of disappearing.[22] Many commentators have rightfully lamented the criminalisation of civil law – vague statutes that allow aggressive prosecutors to formally charge many civil violations as criminal offences.[23] But the opposite trend is also well underway in corporate law – the civilization of criminal law. This section describes the mechanisms that drain corporate criminal law of its indignant bite and the tangible effects of that rhetorical shift.

Enforcers Use Sanitised Economic Language

Corporate prosecutors have scrubbed their job of its combative ugliness and reduced it to a largely transactional affair. They rarely (2% of the time) try corporate suspects in open court, where the full measure of the offence would be on display.[24] The vast majority of corporate convictions are plea deals, negotiated beforehand and finalised in short measure before a rubber-stamp judge. For the largest corporate criminals that commit the most serious wrongs, prosecutors have an even more sanitised process.[25] By concluding civil pretrial diversion agreements, prosecutors help the worst corporate

22 Diamantis and Thomas, (n 10).

23 Julie Rose O'Sullivan, *The Federal Criminal 'Code' is a Disgrace: Obstruction Statutes as Case Study*, (2006) 96 *J. Crim. L. & Criminology* 643.

24 Diamantis and Thomas (n 10) 198–199.

25 Cindy R. Alexander and Mark A. Cohen, 'The Evolution of Corporate Criminal Settlements: An Empirical Perspective on Non-Prosecution, Deferred Prosecution, and Plea Agreements' (2015) 52 *Am. Crim. L. Rev.* 537.

offenders avoid prosecution entirely in exchange for promises of reform and a monetary exchange.[26]

Even though they are reminiscent of civil contracts, pretrial diversion agreements still give prosecutors an opportunity to publicly portray how reprehensible corporate misconduct can be. It is an opportunity that prosecutors unwaveringly squander. They reuse a tried three-part template for these agreements: a stipulated statement of facts, a monetary penalty and terms for mandatory reform. Each part disappoints. The statements of facts are case studies in sterile chronology. Corporate suspects, their attorneys and their PR teams vet every line ahead of time, erasing any tinge of judgement or evaluation. In most cases, even the words 'guilt' and 'admit' are conspicuously absent.[27] Observers hoping that the monetary penalty portion of the agreements would pick up some of the retributive slack are unfailingly disappointed. Half of all pretrial diversion agreements impose no fine at all.[28] Of those that do, the fine is routinely below the lower threshold of the federal sentencing guidelines range,[29] on average a paltry 0.04% of market capitalisation[30] and <1% of annual corporate revenue.[31] The final section of pretrial diversion agreements imposes usually toothless terms of reform. There are no publicly available records validating that corporations even follow through with their commitments.[32]

Prosecutors often feel forced to use pretrial diversion agreements in order to avoid potentially catastrophic collateral consequence from convicting a corporation. The Arthur Anderson parable still looms large in enforcement

26 Brandon L. Garrett, 'Collaborative Organizational Prosecution' in Anthony S. Barkow and Rachel E. Barkow (eds), *Prosecutors in the Boardroom: Using Criminal Law to Regulate Corporate Conduct* (2011) 154, 157.

27 Pacific Gas & Electric again serves as a telling example. Despite all of its prior criminal history and ongoing criminal investigations causing devastating wildfires, PG&E's most recent prosecution agreement formally acknowledges no wrongdoing. Associated Press, 'The Nation's Largest Utility Agrees To Pay More Than $55 Million for Two Wildfires' *NPR* (12 April 2022) https://www.npr.org/2022/04/12/1092259419/california-wildfires-pacific-gas-electric-55-million.

28 Brandon L. Garrett, *Too Big to Jail: How Prosecutors Compromise with Corporations* (2014) 70.

29 Todd Haugh & Mason McCartney, 'DPA Discounts' (forthcoming) 61 *Am. Crim. L. Rev.*

30 Ibid.

31 Dorothy S. Lund and Natasha Sarin, 'The Cost of Doing Business: Corporate Crime and Punishment Post-Crisis' (Fac. Scholarship at Penn L. 2147, 2020) 36, https://scholarship.law.upenn.edu/faculty_scholarship/2147/.

32 Corporate monitors usually implement the reforms, but the reports they file with the Department of Justice are invariably secret. Kathleen M. Boozang and Simone Handler-Hutchinson, '"Monitoring" Corporate Corruption': 'DOJ's Use of Deferred Prosecution Agreements in Health Care' (2009) 35 *Am. J. L. & Med.* 89.

circles. But it cannot explain why prosecutors refuse to speak more evocatively about corporate crime.[33] Corporate convictions and prosecution agreements are inconsistently communicated through sporadic press releases from the DOJ's Office of Public Affairs. Even when authorities uncover misconduct, official records of it can be hard to come by. The Department of Justice (DOJ) sometimes even keeps pretrial diversion agreements secret[34] and has resisted freedom of information act suits to force their disclosure.[35] Prosecutors talk about corporate crime and punishment in purely transactional terms. Sometimes, it may seem as though they would rather not talk about corporate crime at all.[36]

Language Matters

The sterile language that authorities use to portray corporate crime has consequences, both moral and practical.[37] These consequences vary with the audience in question. There are at least three to consider: victims, corporations themselves and the voting public.

Sanitised language fails to validate victims of corporate crime. It casts them as unfortunate collateral damage of otherwise beneficial profit-generating enterprises.[38] But that representation is out of touch with a more natural moralised perspective.[39] We all have psychological predispositions to see corporations as moral agents and the injuries they cause as wrongs.[40] Authorities

33 William R. Thomas and Mihailis E. Diamantis, 'A Marketing Pitch for Corporate Criminal Law' (2023) 2(1) *Stetson Business Law Review* 1.

34 Boozang and Handler-Hutchinson (n 32) 117–118.

35 Justin Wise, 'DOJ Withholding Public Records in Violation of FOIA, Says Garrett's Collaborator in Duke-UVA Corporate Prosecution Registry' *Duke Law News* (22 November 2021) https://law.duke.edu/news/doj-withholding-public-records-violation-foia-says-garretts-collaborator-duke-uva-corporate/.

36 In this respect, they are not unlike other bystanders whom Penny Crofts has analogised to the townspeople in Stephen King's *IT*. Penny Crofts, 'The Townspeople of Derry in Stephen King's *IT*: Bystanders and Responsibility for Evil' in Whitney May (ed.), *Encountering Pennywise: Critical Perspectives on Stephen King's IT* (University of Mississippi Press 2022).

37 Hui Chia and Jeannie Marie Paterson, 'The Corporate Evil of Unsafe Products' in this volume (p 102) ('If financial disincentives do not have adequate power to deter corporations from selling unsafe products, then it matters even more what a finding of liability means as a normative statement …'). While this chapter focuses on domestic corporate crime, concerns about expressive deficits in corporate criminal law may be even more important in international law. Joanna Kyriakakis, 'Ecocide, Evil and the Corporation' in this volume.

38 Mihailis E. Diamantis, 'What Do We Owe the Victims of Corporate Crime' in Miranda A. Galvin and Williams S. Laufer (eds), *Corporate Crime: The Firm as Victim and Offender* (Routledge, forthcoming 2023).

39 W. Robert Thomas, 'The Conventional Problem with Corporate Sentencing (and One Unconventional Solution)' (2021) 24 *New Crim. L. Rev.* 397, 399–401.

40 Mihailis E. Diamantis, 'Corporate Criminal Minds' (2016) 92 *Notre Dame L. Rev.* 2049, 2077–2080.

communicate a different message when they treat corporate crime in functionally civil law terms.[41] This wrongs victims a second time by sending the message that corporations are above the criminal law, thereby erasing the moral valence of the injuries victims suffer at corporations' hands.[42]

Consider the DOJ's stance toward the 346 people whom Boeing's defective planes killed in 2018–2019.[43] The DOJ pushed through a pretrial diversion agreement that traded a financial pittance in exchange for inoculating Boeing against any charges for wrongful death.[44] In order to block the victims' families from exercising their rights to participate, the DOJ explicitly argued the passengers killed were not 'victims' at all.[45] In the DOJ's view, the injuries they suffered were mere economic consequences of the true injury to the Federal Aviation Administration (which Boeing misled) and the airlines (who bought Boeing jets).

In terms of what prosecutors' rhetoric communicates to corporations themselves, there is good reason to think that formulaic economic messaging enables corporate crime. As criminal law theorists[46] and white-collar crime scholars[47] have argued, criminal law's distinctive mark is to convey that certain behaviour is categorically prohibited. That is why the law reserves the harshest sanctions – jail and (in many countries) execution – for criminals. But when judges and prosecutors equate corporate crime with 'economic misconduct', they characterise the corporate decision to commit crime as a business decision.[48] Judges and prosecutors double down on this impression by imposing

41 Gregory M. Gilchrist, 'The Expressive Cost of Corporate Immunity' (2012) 64 *Hastings L.J.* 1, 51.

42 Mihailis E. Diamantis, 'Invisible Victims' (2021) *Wisc. L. Rev.* 1; William S. Laufer and Robert C. Hughes, 'Justice Undone' (2021) 58 *Am. Crim. L. Rev.* 155.

43 Press Release: Boeing Charged with 737 Max Fraud Conspiracy and Agrees to Pay over $2.5 Billion' https://www.justice.gov/opa/pr/boeing-charged-737-max-fraud-conspiracy-and-agrees-pay-over-25-billion.

44 Niral Chokshi, 'Families of Boeing Crash Victims Say the U.S. Failed to Consult Them' *N.Y. Times* (16 December 2021), https://www.nytimes.com/2021/12/16/business/boeing-crash-victim-families.html; *see* John C. Coffee, 'NoseDive: Boeing and the Corruption of the Deferred Prosecution Agreement' (Harv. L. Sch. Forum on Corp. Gov. 2022) https://corpgov.law.harvard.edu/2022/05/25/nosedive-boeing-and-the-corruption-of-the-deferred-prosecution-agreement/.

45 Michael Laris, 'Those Killed in 737 Max Crashes Aren't "Crime Victims," Justice Says' *Wash. Post* (4 May 2022), https://www.washingtonpost.com/transportation/2022/05/04/boeing-737-max-crime-victims/. A federal judge subsequently reversed the DOJ's determination. Michael Laris, 'Judge Rules DOJ Violated Rights of Boeing Max Victims in Prosecution Deal' *Wash. Post* (21 October 2022), https://www.washingtonpost.com/transportation/2022/10/21/boeing-max-justice-department/.

46 Joel Feinberg, 'The Expressive Function of Punishment' (1965) 49 Philosophy of Law 397.

47 John C. Coffee, 'Does Unlawful Mean "Criminal"?: Reflections on the Disappearing Tort/Crime Distinction in American Law' (1991) 71 *B.U. L. Rev.*

48 John Braithwate, *Crime, Shame and Reintegration* (1989) 141 ('Unfortunately much thinking about corporate crime ... adopts an overly economically rational conception of the

only civil-style penalties on corporate criminals: fines and compliance reform mandates. In practice, these supposedly criminal penalties are often only a fraction of the total civil liability corporations pay to private parties and government regulators for the same breach.[49] This dynamic conveys to corporations that authorities place a price on corporate crime, rather than prohibit it.[50] So, it should be unsurprising when corporate managers, pursuing their mandate to generate shareholder value, also see criminal sanctions as mere costs of doing business – worth it if the potential payout is high enough.[51]

By avoiding forceful and evocative language for corporate crime, authorities abandon criminal law's most powerful tool for stimulating pro-social behaviour. Data shows that criminal penalties can explain only a small fraction of criminal law's impact on people's practical reasoning.[52] People obey the law much more than deterrence economics would predict. What picks up the preventive slack is people's perception of criminal law as a legitimate expression of society's basic norms[53] and a pro-social desire to avoid the stigma and condemnatory impact of being found in violation.[54] This dynamic translates to the corporate context because managers share in the moral and social fate of their corporate employers. Psychologists have shown that corporate officers sympathetically identify with their corporations and internalise the stigmatic effects of corporate shame.[55] When prosecutors and judges refuse to invoke stigmatic language toward corporate criminals, they undermine criminal law's ability to induce corporate leaders to steer corporations on the right path.

Perhaps the biggest casualty of the way prosecutors communicate about corporate crime is its effect on the voting public. In the modern era, we have made very little progress forward combating corporate crime. The basic law

---

corporation; it excessively downplays the corporation's role as a choosing collective agent with organizational policies and values about social responsibility; it downplays the fact that the corporation is constituted of individuals with consciences'.).

49 Garrett (n 28) 70.

50 W. Robert Thomas, 'The Ability and Responsibility of Corporate Law to Improve Criminal Fines' (2017) 78 *Ohio St. L. J*

51 This seems to be exactly what happened in the infamous case of Ford's exploding Pinto car. Mark Dowie, 'Pinto Madness' (*Mother Jones*, September 1977), https://www.motherjones.com/politics/1977/09/pinto-madness/. For a modern cases, see Mark Trabsky and Jacinth Flore, chapter 5 in this volume ([B]ig pharma normalizes willful neglect or lack of care for human life by engaging in calculative practices that allow individuals to perish'.).

52 See Paul H. Robinson & John M. Darley, 'The Utility of Desert' (1997) 91 *Nw. U. L. Rev.* 453, 458.

53 Paul Robinson, *Intuitions of Justice and the Utility of Desert* (2013) 176–188 ('[T]he criminal law's moral credibility is essential to effective crime control …'.).

54 Jennifer Arlen and Lewis A. Kornhauser, 'Battle for Our Souls: A Psychological Justification for Corporate and Individual Liability for Organizational Misconduct' (2022), https://papers.ssrn.com/sol3/papers.cfm?abstract_id=4152960.

55 Samuel W. Buell, 'The Blaming Function of Entity Criminal Liability' (2006) 81 *Ind. L.J.* 473, 525.

for holding corporations criminally liable has not changed since it was first introduced over a century ago.[56] The public has never agitated for reform. Many people do not even know that corporate criminal law exists. When it comes to individual criminals, whom prosecutors know full well how to publicly condemn, the long catalogue of new criminal statutes and penalty enhancements is a testament to the public's sense of (often misplaced) moral urgency. No similar movement has ever built against corporate criminals, though the aggregate toll they exact is much more severe.

Can Corporations Be Evil?

'Evil is *different*. Evil is *distinctive*'.[57] Phillip Cole argues that '[w]e ought to dispose of the concept' because he observes that 'evil' (at least in the sense of monstrous or mythological wickedness that concerns him) has historically been used to oppress marginalised communities.[58] By branding a person as evil, we 'close[] off all possibility of understanding' the richness of personal history and psychology that tend toward evaluative nuance. By contrast to the individuals who were Cole's concern, corporations are hardly marginalised and, as argued above, have benefited from too much evaluative nuance.

'Evil' may be precisely the corrective concept that corporate prosecutors need. It is a powerful trope that could fill the rhetorical void in how they talk about corporate crime. It is a narrative placeholder for 'the antagonist'.[59] When predicated of an entity, it functions as a complete explanation of their transgressions and 'do[es] away with any need to understand their history, their motives, their psychology'.[60] In this way, evil forecloses empathy. We call someone evil when we have given up trying to understand them.[61] That is why it is such a dangerous concept when applied to individuals. 'Evil' thereby simplifies story lines. At the same time, it invites condemnation.[62] '[Evil] is that which opposes us, that which rebels against the authoritative order of things, and by describing others as evil we condemn them as negative, resentful destructive rebels'.[63] That is the sort of story that corporate prosecutors need to become more adept at telling. Corporations do not need our empathy. It would be misplaced on them anyway.

56 William R. Thomas, 'Corporate Criminal Law Is Too Broad—Worse, It's Too Narrow' (2021) 51 *Ariz. St. L.J.* 505.
57 Luke Russell, *Being Evil: A Philosophical Perspective* (2020) 23.
58 Phillip Cole, *The Myth of Evil* (2006) 235.
59 Neil Forsyth, *The Satan Epic* (2003).
60 Cole (n 58) 237.
61 David Pocock, 'Unruly Evil' in David Parkin (ed.) *The Anthropology of Evil* (1985) 49.
62 John Kekes, *Facing Evil* (1990) 7.
63 Cole (n 58) 213.

Can corporations be evil? One might worry that describing them as evil would be a category mistake, like saying that a photograph is sour or a jug of milk is friendly. There may indeed be a mismatch between corporations and the concept of 'pure evil'. Pure evil refers to 'the pursuit of suffering and destruction of others for its own sake'.[64] While one could imagine a purely evil corporation, organised for the sole purpose of suffering and destruction, none probably exist.[65] There is a lot of flexibility in the purposes that regulators will approve for corporate charters, but 'death and demise' is not among them. Even if a purely evil corporation were created, it probably would not last very long; suffering-for-its-own-sake is not a very good business proposition.

Instrumental evil is the more helpful concept in this context. It describes situations 'in which a person does something to harm another in order to reap some further benefit'[66] 'Some evildoers have minds filled with hatred and vengefulness, other evildoers are thinking about meeting their targets at work and trying not to disappoint their bosses'.[67] For corporations, the likeliest goal of instrumental evil is profit. The means of pursuing that goal can qualify as evil if 'the nature and severity of [its] harms'[68] are serious and the corporation nonetheless silences adequate consideration of them.[69] Luke Russell offers the example of a corporate board that nonchalantly boosts profits by approving a pharmaceutical with lethal side effects.[70]

Even if instrumental evil is in the right conceptual vicinity, prosecutors may hesitate to invoke it because it seems so incongruous with the way they presently talk about corporations. Consider three important themes in prosecutorial rhetoric and policy:

> *Corporations Are Not Moral Agents*: There is no philosophical consensus about what makes someone a moral agent, but the most prominent proposals – like free will, intentionality, ethical perspective, responsiveness to moral reasons – are attributes that many people think corporations lack.[71] Whether corporations are mindless machines, complex systems of production, or mere redescriptions of business relationships, they have no point of view, no consciousness, and are at best borderline cases of genuine

64 Ibid. 3.

65 Penny Crofts observes that horror movies do not portray purely evil corporations either. Penny Crofts, chapter 8 in this volume.

66 Colin McGinn, *Ethics, Evil, and Fiction* (1997).

67 Russell (n 57) 77.

68 Claudia Card, *The Atrocity Paradigm: A Theory of Evil*.

69 Eve Garrard, 'The Nature of Evil' (1998) 1 *Phil. Explorations* 43.

70 Russell (n 57) 53–54. Hui Chia and Jeannie Marie Paterson discuss a real-life example in Chapter 6 in this volume.

71 Samuel Buell, 'Retiring Corporate Retribution' (2020) 83 *L. & Contemp. Probs.* 25.

decision making.[72] The wrongs they commit are more often the product of defective oversight, broken culture or deficient compliance than anything like a choice to do wrong. If moral assessment of corporations is unfitting, how could ascriptions of evil possibly stick?[73]

Corporations Are Often Hijacked by Rogues: Most corporate crime is not a programmatic endeavour of the entire organisation. It is usually the product of individual agents seizing opportunities to boost their own agendas (pay, promotion, reputation, etc.), often at the expense of their employers' long-term profitability.[74] Economists refer to this mismatch between institutional and individual incentives as 'agency costs'. Employees who exploit agency costs in this way by subverting corporate oversight and breaking internal corporate policies are so-called 'rogue actors'.[75] Could corporations be truly evil if, from a credible perspective, they are as much victims as they are perpetrators?[76]

Corporations Are Often Also Good: For all the harm they cause, corporations have done much more to advance human wellbeing. Even individual corporations that engage in serious misconduct are often simultaneously important fixtures of an interconnected economy, offering investment, employment and consumer value. The Janus-faced relationship society has to corporate criminals is front-of-mind for prosecutors from the start of an investigation through its resolution.[77] 'Collateral consequences' is the term prosecutors use to refer to the harm that corporate prosecution and punishment causes to the interests of innocent shareholders, employees, creditors and consumers.[78] What sense could there be to designating an entity as evil if we must also acknowledge that it generates good?[79]

72 Developments in the Law, 'Corporate Crime: Regulating Corporate Behavior Through Criminal Sanctions' (1979) 92 *Harv. L. Rev.* 1227, 1241.

73 John Hasnas, 'Ethics and the Problem of White Collar Crime' (2005) 54 *Am. U.L. Rev*

74 Mihailis E. Diamantis, 'The Law's Missing Account of Corporate Character' (2019) 17 *Geo. J. L. & Pub. Pol's* 507, 880. It is worth noting too that sometimes the individuals in corporations are not fully free agents either. Lisa Siraganian, chapter 10 in this volume ('[T]hey do not feel like agents of the corporation but like tormented subjects menaced by unavoidable evil forces that they have no option but to accept'.) 169.

75 Memorandum from Larry D. Thompson, Deputy Attorney Gen., US Dep't of Justice, to Heads of Dep't Components, US Dep't of Justice (20 January 2003), available at http://www.usdoj.gov/dag/cftf/business_organizations.pdf.

76 *US v. Sun-Diamond Growers of California* (1999) 526 US 398.

77 Joel Slawotsky, 'Reining in Recidivist Financial Institutions' (2015) 40 *Del. J. Corp. L.* 280, 297.

78 Miriam H. Baer, 'Organizational Liability and the Tension Between Corporate and Criminal Law' (2010) 19 *J.L. & Policy* 1, 7.

79 Mary Midgley, *Wickedness* (2001), would argue that there is no tension here at all since an entity must be capable of doing good in order to properly qualify as evil.

Prosecutors are not wrong about these attributes of corporations. Indeed, each is an important consideration that prosecutors should bear in mind when thinking about how to respond to corporate misconduct, particularly when developing an appropriate sanction. For example, punishing a corporation too severely can end up doing more harm than good to innocent bystanders.[80] The question, though, is whether there is a rhetorical mode from which prosecutors could portray criminal corporations as evil without losing sight of these metaphysical and economic truths.

Inspiration from Horror

Horror novelists and directors solved the problem facing prosecutors long ago. Horror's mode of presentation temporarily silences our quibbles about metaphysics. Its antagonists are often degenerate, deviant and hybrid examples of moral agency. Yet audiences are all too familiar with the experiences of disgust, urgency, threat and animosity that successful tales of horror evoke. This section offers examples from classic subgenres of horror whose villains exhibit precisely the three attributes that seemed to disqualify corporations from being candidates for evil.

The Nexus between Horror, Evil and Crime

Prosecutors and judges are not just other actors in the public telling of the story of corporate crime – they are the story's producers and directors. At every step of the way, they decide how an investigation unfolds, which corporations to charge, which corporations to sanction and what sanction to impose. Authorities could do worse than looking to cinema for inspiration.

Several film genres offer templates for conveying messages about social threat, but horror warrants particular attention because '[b]oth horror films and criminal law provide sustained meditations on wickedness'.[81] As argued in the previous section, the language of criminal law fails to portray corporate crime as despicable, condemnable or evil. The waffled messaging of present economic thinking on corporate crime conveys a conception of corporate wickedness that is riddled with exceptions and caveats. The case of Google's relationship to its own seemingly straightforward mantra – 'Don't Be Evil' – and its participation in developing warfare drones shows how ambiguous understandings of corporate wrong tend to enable rather than prevent.[82]

80 John Hasnas, 'The Centenary of a Mistake: One Hundred Years of Corporate Criminal Liability' (2009) 46 *Am. Crim. L. Rev.*

81 Penny Crofts, 'Monstrous Bodily Excess in The Exorcist as a Supplement to Law's Accounts of Culpability' (2015) 24 *Griffith L. Rev.* 372, 373.

82 *See generally* Penny Crofts and Honni van Rijswijk, 'Negotiating "Evil": Google, Project Maven and the Corporate Form' (2020) 2(1) *Law, Technology and Humans* 75.

The language, tropes and communicative techniques of horror could set the record straight.

Horror stories and portrayals of evil are intimately connected.[83] Some theorists define evil in terms of horror,[84] or horror in terms of evil.[85] More importantly for present purposes, evil and horror play similar narrative roles. As discussed in the 'The Official Rhetoric of Corporate Crime' section, portraying an entity as evil invites condemnation of it and calls its audience to resistance. The leading philosopher of horror also understands the genre 'in virtue of the emotional effects it is designed to cause in the audience'.[86] By casting even everyday entities (like birds, or perhaps, corporations) 'in an ominous light',[87] horror forces us to question 'the idea of a secure, regular everyday world'.[88] Horror is an 'alerting fiction' that 'ha[s] the power to revive consciousness'.[89] In the hands of corporate prosecutors, it could awaken a sleeping public to the danger of corporate misconduct.

Zombies, Demons and Werewolves

In some respects, corporations should be prime subject matter for horror. The genre emphasises objects or entities that are 'impure', i.e., 'categorically interstitial, categorically contradictory, incomplete, or formless'.[90] That describes pretty well the space that corporations inhabit: 'people' who are not human.[91] Cast in the right light, corporations could disturb and terrify us precisely because they 'cannot be connected with an identifiable physical object and ... elude classification and naming'.[92] What is more, corporations are not inert. They are fictional entities that are nonetheless 'threatening', 'dangerous', seemingly 'unstoppable', i.e., beings of the sort that a good horror story constitutively requires.[93]

Seen in this light, the attributes of corporations that may have disqualified them from being described as evil could fit well into tropes that are fixtures of horror subgenres. There are different schema for categorising

83 Cole (n 58) 97 ('Horror and terror are therefore intertwined in our experiences of evil').
84 Russell (n 58) 31 ('[According to t]he horrifying account of evil action[, a]n action is evil if and only if it causes feelings of horror').
85 Philip Tallon 'The justification of torture-horror' in Thomas Fahy (ed), *The Philosophy of Horror* (2010). ('Horror makes us recognize evils that must, if we know anything about the world at all, be wrong').
86 Carroll (n 1) 8.
87 Philip J. Nickel, 'Horror and the Idea of Everyday Life: On Skeptical Threats in *Psycho* and *The Birds*', in Fahy (n 85) 22.
88 Ibid. 30.
89 Dani Cavallaro, *Gothic Vision: Three Centuries of Horror, Terror, and Fear* (2002) 15.
90 Carroll (n 1) 32.
91 Penny Crofts, 'The Horror of Corporate Harms' (2022) 38 Austl. J. Corp. L. 23.
92 Cavallaro (n 89) 15.
93 Carroll (n 1) 37, 42.

horror movies. The Horror Film Wiki, for example, uses categories that emphasise the type of threat portrayed, like 'Gore and Disturbing', 'Killer' and 'Paranormal'.[94] The Horror Villain Archetypes of GutsNGore focuses more on character attributes of the villain, like 'Strong and Silent', 'Chaotic/ Unhinged' or 'Talkative Wisecracker'. Steve Hutchinson's book *Rivals of Terror 2019: Horror Movie Villains* uses physical attributes to distinguish subtypes from alien to robot.[95]

Below, I take an idiosyncratic approach. I use three recurrent archetypes – zombies, demons and werewolves – as leading examples of three different moral attributes that cut across standard horror categories.[96] As I argue, corporate criminals fit into these categories too. By more consciously classifying corporate criminals as analogues of zombies, demons or werewolves, prosecutors could draw on principles of representation in horror to shape the rhetoric they use.

Zombies, Definitely Not Moral Agents: In a lot of ways, zombies are not unlike corporations. Both are lumbering threats to human existence and also philosophical archetypes of unconscious automata.[97] They inhabit an uncertain space between animate and inanimate. Zombies are just one example of subhuman monster – whether it's aliens, giant sea creatures or an oozing blob – that 'terrorize and kill whatever is in their path and use their strength and size to destroy'.[98] They may be capable of intelligent seeming behaviour, but we are in no position to reason with them. Zombies and other monsters are threats, but their conduct is not, properly speaking, immoral. Yet horror movies have little trouble conveying a sense of evil and urgency to the movie audiences. Directors have developed tools for splitting the difference by portraying a threat that is viscerally evil while not registering a moral valence.

Demons, The Rogues of Horror: In 'demonic possession' films like *Poltergeist* and *The Exorcist*, evil spirits or demons fuse with and partially control their victims. The composite entity inevitably terrorises the people around them, but moral evaluation is complex because the innocent host is driven by an outside antagonist. There is no longer a clean line between

94 'Horror Film Wiki' https://horror.fandom.com/wiki/Horror_Film_Wiki last accessed 23 August 2023.

95 *See also* 'Los Angeles Film School, Subgenres of Horror Explained' https://www.lafilm.edu/blog/subgenres-of-horror-films-explained/ last accessed 23 August 2023.

96 Science fiction could also be a fertile ground to explore. *See* M.K. Ramirez, 'The Science Fiction of Corporate Criminal Liability: Containing the Machine Through the Corporate Death Penalty' (2005) 47 *Ariz. L. Rev.* 333.

97 John Searle, 'Zombies' (Entry for the Stanford Encyclopedia of Philosophy 2003) https://plato.stanford.edu/entries/zombies/ last accessed 23 August 2023.

98 Ibid.

good and bad.[99] This moral circumstance is analogous to the corporation which, through the intercession of a rogue employee, goes on to break the law. Despite the mixed moral status of possessed individuals, horror movies often convey them as an evil threat, an eerie blend of a demonic and human elements.

Werewolves, Which Have Two Faces: Werewolves are examples of what Noel Carrol calls 'fusion figures', in which 'categorically contradictory elements are fused or condensed or superimposed in one unified spatiotemporal being whose identity is homogenous'.[100] Other fusion figures include Dr Jekyll/Mr Hyde and, perhaps, more realistically, Hannibal Lecter (the brutal cannibal, who as an extremely intelligent psychiatrist, gives FBI agents the insights they need to track another serial killer). These figures all have two sides, the human and helpful which attracts empathy, and the monstrous.[101] Films about them force their protagonists and us (the audience) to harbour conflicting attitudes of disgust, fear, admiration and dependence. Prosecutors would do well to learn how to express simultaneously indignation toward corporate criminals and appreciation for the social essential role they may play in customers' and employees' lives.

Each of these three genres gives the lie to the suggestion that the rhetoric of evil must be incompatible with the sort of entity that corporations are.

Now What?

'The horror film ... casts our reliance on the everyday world around us into shadow ... There is a distinctive way that horror fiction and film can bring this threat home to the reader or viewer'.[102] I have argued that horror film manages to accomplish something that still eludes corporate prosecutors – it portrays morally inert, morally ambiguous and morally ambivalent entities as evils that are to be condemned, feared and resisted. But, to get down to brass tacks, what does this mean for corporate prosecutors? Even if they are persuaded that corporations are morally analogous to zombies or werewolves, I haven't exactly offered a concrete action plan.

What prosecutors should take from this chapter is some optimism about the prospect of representing corporate crime in a way that will do justice by its victims and arouse the public's moral ire. Adapting horror tropes to the corporate context will require some ingenuity and nuance. The surface

99 Crofts (n 81).

100 Carroll (n 1) 45.

101 Richard Davis, *The Encyclopedia of Horror* (1981) ('[The werewolf] arouses compassion and pity even amongst his potential victims').

102 Nickel (n 87) 18.

features of horror may not translate directly. I would not recommend that prosecutors invest in fake blood and caution tape to dress up their media appearances. Rather, prosecutors should look to the techniques operating in the background of horror movies for eliciting audience response.

For example, prosecutors might investigate narrative methods by which writers and directors induce antipathy toward fictional entities. Portraying the entity as fearful or threatening is a device familiar from horror stories. Critics distinguish three specific tools: (1) ascribing intentionality to the entity or to someone who controls it, (2) emphasising the dire consequences of the entity's behaviour and (3) focusing on the entity's causal responsibility.[103] As discussed above, prosecutors presently eschew all three when they talk about corporate harms as mere compliance failures. Change would be easy if only prosecutors were willing to talk differently. They could describe corporate misbehaviour in more intentional terms, born of familiar motivations like greed and disregard.[104] They could highlight the harmful consequences of corporate conduct by amplifying victim voices and experiences.[105] And they could prime judgements of causal responsibility by refusing to offer explanations of 'why' corporate misbehaviour occurred until after establishing 'that' it did.[106]

But the place prosecutors should start is in displaying their own indignation, condemnation and disgust with corporate crime.[107] Horror movies don't work just by showing horrifying scenes. Some of the scariest films have very little gore and hint only vaguely at a malicious entity. Horror movies work by modelling the reactions that directors hope to induce. 'The emotional reactions of characters … provide a set of instructions or, rather, examples about the way in which the audience is to respond to the monsters in the fiction'.[108] We know we are supposed to be scared not only because we see something out of place, but because we see a look of dread or hear a blood-curdling scream. If prosecutors want us to see that corporate crime is evil, perhaps they should start acting like it is.

103 Jens Kjeldgaard-Christiansen, 'A Structure of Antipathy: Constructing the Villain in Narrative Film' (2019) https://www.researchgate.net/publication/332536489_A_Structure_of_Antipathy_Constructing_the_Villain_in_Narrative_Film. Penny Crofts excavates tools that horror films use specifically for portraying corporate villains. Penny Crofts, chapter 8 in this volume.

104 *See, e.g.*, Terrence Rafferty, 'The Monster That Morphed Into a Metaphor' *NYT* (2 May 2004). Discussing corporate culture in these terms may do the trick. Vicky Comino, chapter 16 in this volume. Some robust conception of corporate vice might work too. Stephanie Collins, chapter 3 in this volume.

105 Kjeldgaard-Christiansen (n 103).

106 Ibid.

107 William S. Laufer, 'Where Is the Moral Indignation Over Corporate Crime?' in Dominik Brodowski and others (eds), *Regulating Corporate Criminal Liability* (2014) 19.

108 Carroll (n 1) 17–18.

Chapter 13

Corporations as Haunted Entities

Conceptualising Responsibility for Historical Harm

Penny Crofts and Honni van Rijswijk

Introduction

Many contemporary corporations were founded on harmful actions, having profited across time from the dirty work of colonialism and slavery. In deriving their benefit from the initial and ongoing violence, they were often aided by their governments and by law. Corporate and capitalist origins are imbricated with this violence. Ian Baucom argues that the roots of speculative finance and global capitalism can be read in the 18th-century case concerning the slave ship *Zong*, and the practices and institutions that adjudicated and ultimately condoned the violence that occurred upon it.[1] In 1781, on its journey from the Cape Coast to Jamaica, encountering a shortage of provisions as a result of navigational error, the captain of the *Zong*, Captain Luke Collingwood, ordered that 133 African slaves be thrown overboard to their deaths. The subsequent legal case was not a murder trial but an insurance claim for loss of property, as it was common business practice to insure slaves as cargo – the trade in slaves accounted for up to 40% of the cargo insurance premium in the London market of the late 18th century, dominated by Lloyd's of London.[2] Later in court, Captain Collingwood argued that the scarcity of fresh water made his violence necessary, to preserve the remainder of the human cargo, as well as the crew. Further, he expected that the loss would be covered by the ship's insurance policy. Baucom argues that this event is central to understanding not only the specific history of the transatlantic slave trade but the foundations and ethical frameworks of modern capital more widely – not as

1 Ian Baucom, *Specters of the Atlantic: Finance Capital, Slavery and the Philosophy of History* (Duke University Press 2005). Federman conducts a similar analysis of the complicity of railway corporations in their role in the deaths of the Holocaust – Sarah Federman, *Last Train to Auschwitz: The French National Railways and the Journey to Accountability* (University of Wisconsin Press 2022).

2 Guy Faulconbridge, 'Some facts about London's role in insuring the slave trade' (2020) *Insurance Journal* June 19. https://www.insurancejournal.com/news/international/2020/06/19/572859.html viewed 8 April, 2024.

DOI: 10.4324/9781003402534-18

an isolated tragedy but as part of its underlying logic. We would add that it is also essential to understanding law's complicity in conceptualising and responding to corporate violence. Baucom shows that the murders and the trials that followed revealed processes of speculative finance and capital accumulation, processes that continue today. In contemporary life, finance capital is abstracted and this effect has been heightened by technology, but we should never lose sight of the material histories on which they are based – and that law's role in these histories has been unbroken. Slavery sustained the economy and society. The emphasis upon past practices of slavery destabilises stories of capitalism, successful corporations and the legal system. Sven Beckert argues that a 'flurry' of recent work by historians insists that slavery was not incidental to the national economy of the United States or a 'Southern pathology', but rather 'a key part of American capitalism'.[3]

Given the (potential) immortality of corporations, a question that has been increasingly explored by courts, academics and some organisations is the extent to which long-established corporations are responsible for past wrongs, and if so, should they atone? In this chapter, we draw upon the idea of haunting to explore responsibility for past wrongs, specifically, corporate responsibility for slavery. We emphasise the material traces of slavery – not only the harms but also the benefits – that have been disavowed but continue to haunt corporations and the legal system. There is a great deal of academic literature on haunting and hauntology. For example, in the context of settler colonial violence, Amber Dean uses the phrase 'following ghosts' to describe the process of inheriting the past.[4] This practice, she says, is comparable to approaches of Derrida in his work *Spectres of Marx*.[5] Dean argues that:

> Hauntings draw our attention to the social and psychic remainders of injustice, violence, disappearance, trauma, and loss – in other words, to the past's ongoing claims on the present.[6]

This summarises key themes of haunting that we explore in this chapter – the liminality of time; and the repression of past wrongs and injustices that nevertheless return to the present and the future. In this analysis, we are indebted to Avery Gordon's theory of social reality in *Ghostly Matters*.[7] Gordon argues that we should look beyond positivist models to understand

3 Sven Beckert and Seth Rockman (eds.), *Slavery's Capitalism: A New History of American Economic Development*. Philadelphia: University of Pennsylvania Press, 2016.

4 Amber Dean, *Remembering Vancouver's Disappeared Women: Settler Colonialsim and the Difficulty of Inheritance* (University of Toronto Press, 2015).

5 Jacques Derrida, 'Spectres of Marx'. (1994) 205 *New Left Review* 31.

6 Dean (n 4) p. 59.

7 Avery F. Gordon. *Ghostly Matters : Haunting and the Sociological Imagination* (University of Minnesota Press, 2008).

reality; instead, Gordon proposes the concept of haunting, which captures the presence of that which does not appear to be present: 'To study social life one must confront the ghostly aspects of it'.[8] This is a form of knowledge that goes beyond categories of the past and the present, as well as the relation between representation and materiality: haunting is one way in which abusive systems of power make themselves known and their impacts felt in everyday life, especially when they are supposedly over and done with.[9] Incorporating haunting into our knowledge of the corporation, then, produces a means of telling a different story about corporations, the origins of their wealth and how they may have exploited people to enable current and future profitability, as well as what continues to happen. Key to this argument is not just the history, presence and future of the harms and losses caused by slavery – but also the benefits. Whereas haunting in critical and trauma theory has generally been used as a means to represent the pain and suffering of victims and survivors – which is usually difficult to represent due to its overwhelming horror and excess – here we use haunting to switch to the point of view of the agent of harm, the corporation. We consider what it means to think of the corporation as a haunted house, from the perspective of that culpable figure as it has been theorised by horror novels and films.

Haunting draws our attention to what lingers, not only as memory and idea, but in material reality, 'linger[ing] well beyond our individual time, creating that shadowy basis for the production of material life'.[10] For victims and survivors, this materiality incorporates suffering and economic or social deprivations but can think, too, of corporations as being haunted by harms they have committed in the past not just in a metaphorical but in a very literal way – haunted not by pain but by the continuing material benefit of past wrongs to corporations in the present and into the future. The benefit of drawing this connection is to provide both law and the wider culture a way to reimagine corporate responsibility.

We use the haunted house as a conceptual metaphor to explore disruptive forces and the afterlives of slavery, through an analysis of the case that has become known as *In re African-American Slave Descendants Litigation*.[11] Although they failed legally, we believe that these claims provided something valuable to the legal archive: our reading shows that they conceptualise, in legal terms, corporations as being haunted by the benefits they have obtained for the past. We read the case as a story of corporate haunted houses, where the plaintiff's claims put this haunting in legal form by reconfiguring causality

8 Ibid. p. 7.
9 Ibid. p. xvi.
10 Ibid. p. 166.
11 *In re African-American Slave Descendants Litigation* 471 F.3d 754, 762–763 (7th Cir. 2006).

and temporality. Throughout, we explore the question of who or what is haunted – arguing that it is not only the descendants of slavery that are haunted, but also the corporations that profited from slavery, and the legal system in its complicity. The trope of the corporation as haunted house helps us to think through what stays constant across time, haunting disrupting the linearity of time – for victims and for perpetrators. Haunting is one means to force a reckoning with the malignant inheritance of law. We conclude with the question of how can and should we respond to this haunting?

The Corporation as Haunted House

In theorising the corporation as a haunted house, we draw on horror stories that have imbued haunted houses with intentionality, agency and powers. Like corporations, haunted houses are structures that are afforded agency and protections, as well as extraordinary powers. Since the first recorded instance of a haunted house story, the *Epic of Gilgamesh*, in which the hero Enkidu enters a haunted house and is attacked by demons. Writers and filmmakers have claimed and reworked this figure, imbuing the haunted house with agency, will and even evil intent, or for the haunted house to benefit in some way from harms caused – through sadistic enjoyment of its victims' pain or through their presence or even by its power to be left alone to enjoy its own propriety. In his short story, 'The Fall of the House of Usher', Edgar Allan Poe uses the haunted house as a symbol of the decay and horror caused by the Usher family. The narrator describes the house as having 'an atmosphere which had no affinity with the air of heaven, but which had reeked up from the decayed trees, and the gray wall, and the silent tarn'.[12] Shirley Jackson's *The Haunting of Hill House* (1959) features a house that has infamously ill intent, as well as agency and extraordinary powers over its victims. The novel begins: 'Hill House, not sane, stood by itself against its hills, holding darkness within'.[13]

Haunted houses place an emphasis on property and ownership. Many horror films start with families putting everything they own into buying a (surprisingly cheap) property which turns out to be haunted by past wrongs, an exchange that leads them to be indebted to the house (e.g., *The Conjuring* (2013), *Amityville Horror* (2005)). Some fiction explicitly explores the idea of a trade-off – past harms inflicted for the profit of another. For example, the film *Winchester* (2018) connects the profit and wealth of the company Winchester with haunting of the seemingly never-ending mansion by the many people who were killed by Winchester rifles. The Netflix films, *Fear Street Trilogy* (2021), represents the link of past injustices with harms to one

12 Edgar Allan Poe. *The Fall of the House of Usher: and Other Tales and Prose Writings of Edgar Poe* (W. Scott, 1889) 3.

13 Shirley Jackson, *The Haunting of Hill House* (Penguin Publishing 2006) 1.

town and benefits to another – *both* towns are haunted by these past and continuing injustices, one is haunted by benefit and the other by loss. Toni Morrison's novel *Beloved*, which is wholly concerned with representing the trauma of slavery across time and features a ghost who is both figurative and literal, begins with the point of view of an evil house: '124 was spiteful'.[14] However, evil intent is not required for the haunted house to cause harm – haunted houses may also be 'neutral' in their intent while they nevertheless derive benefit. For example, the haunted house in the film *The Others* (2001) is a home to violent and tragic acts that produce possessive ghosts, but the house itself is not the agent of harm, nor does it derive pleasure from that harm in the way that the house in *The Haunting of Hill House* delights in it.

Literary critics have argued that American gothic literature is obsessed with, even driven by, the harms of slavery. In her recent book, *Haunted Property: Slavery and the Gothic*,[15] Ford considers how Gothic novels from the 19th century to the present use tropes such as the haunted house and the ghost, to show 'the horror of a person being considered property':[16] In particular, Ford argues that the Gothic genre reveals the nexus between the American Dream of property ownership and the nightmare of slavery. We want to look at this horror from the other point of view, focusing not on the trauma and horror of the suffering of slaves and their descendants, but on the horror of the unjust benefit to corporate entities that their suffering produced. The figure of 'the haunted house' represents a stable entity within which trauma continues across time. Likewise, although contemporary CEOs of corporations had no personal involvement in past wrongs that occurred centuries ago, their corporations were founded upon and profited from past wrongs such as slavery, colonialism and genocide that also continue across time, into the present and the future. Stories of haunting are intended to arouse horror, an emotion that we feel in response to schema incongruence.[17] The harms and benefits of slavery are schema incongruent – they are incommensurable and incalculable and given how imbricated slavery was and is in systems of capital – it feels horrific and impossible to conceive of how the harms and benefits can be atoned and resolved.

Case Study: In re African-American Slave Descendants Litigation

The case that has become known as *In re African-American Slave Descendants Litigation* began as nine lawsuits filed around the country against American

14 Toni Morrison, *Beloved* (Vintage Books, 2008) 3.

15 Sarah Gilbreath Ford, *Haunted Property: Slavery and the Gothic* (University Press of Mississippi, 2020).

16 Ibid. p. 191.

17 Pamela Marie Taylor and Yukiko Uchida, 'Awe or Horror: Differentiating Two Emotional Responses to Schema Incongruence' (2019) 33 *Cognition and Emotion* 1548.

corporations in different US states. These were consolidated in federal court in the Northern District of Illinois, where the plaintiffs filed a First Consolidated and Amended Complaint on 16 June 2003. In the appeal to this decision, *In re African-American Slave Descendants Litigation,* the US Court of Appeals for the Seventh Circuit considered an action comprising '... class actions on behalf of all Americans descended from slaves", against companies or their successors who had been slaveowners, or who had provided services (such as insurance, finance and transportation) to slaveowners.[18] By way of relief, the claimants demanded an accounting and disgorgement of the profits arising from companies' dealings with slaveowners to the class members. This appeal was the last in a line of class action reparations cases which, since the 1980s, have tried different formulations of claiming at common law. But the plaintiffs' action failed, and the case arguably puts an end to this form of reparations claim at common law.

The plaintiffs include a number of named individuals as well as anonymous plaintiffs, many of whom, it was alleged, had been held as slaves after the period of legal slavery ended. The plaintiffs also filed on behalf of others similarly situated, thereby including in the plaintiff class all the descendants of persons who had been enslaved in the United States. One of the plaintiffs, Deadria Farmer-Paellmann, found evidence that Aetna Insurance had insured the lives of slaves for profit and that predecessors to the financial services institution, JP Morgan Chase, had 'accepted approximately 13,000 enslaved individuals as collateral on loans and took possession of approximately 1,250 enslaved individuals'.[19] The defendants included the following companies: FleetBoston Financial Corporation, CSX Corporation, Aetna Inc., Brown Brothers Harriman, New York Life Insurance Company, Norfolk Southern Corporation, Lehman Brothers, Lloyd's of London, Union Pacific Railroad, JP Morgan Chase Manhattan Bank, Westpoint Stevens Inc., RJ Reynolds Tobacco Company, Brown and Williamson, Liggett Group Inc., Loews Corporation, Canadian National Railway, Southern Mutual Insurance Company and American International Group. The essence of the complaints was that these American corporations had profited from slavery by owning slaves, insuring slaves or lending money to slave-owners, and that those who descended from slaves have civil claims based on the benefits these companies received, including unjust enrichment and conversion, as well as the harms they caused (including conspiracy, intentional infliction of emotional distress and negligent infliction of emotional distress). The plaintiffs

18 *In re African-American Slave Descendants Litigation* 471 F.3d 754, 762–763 (7th Cir. 2006)

19 Nick Mathiason, *British Firms Could Be Sued for Slave Trade*, *The Observer*, 1 July 2007 at 3. Cited in Lolita Buckner Inniss, 'A Critical Legal Rhetoric Approach to *In Re African-American Slave Descendants* Litigation', (2009) 24 *St John's Journal of Legal Commentary* 649, p. 651.

requested a number of forms of relief: an accounting of profits, disgorgement of profits, creation of an 'independent historical Commission' to study defendants' actions, a constructive trust, restitution and compensatory and punitive damages arising out of the defendants' past and continued wrongful conduct relating to slavery.

Trauma theorists argue that trauma exceeds usual practices of representation due to the impossibility of such a direct access to events – by definition, in its vastness and horror, trauma overwhelms our frameworks of meaning, and people are left unable to articulate or narrate their pain. According to Cathy Caruth,

> For history to be a history of trauma means that it is referential precisely to the extent that it is not fully perceived as it occurs; or to put it somewhat differently, that a history can be grasped only in the very inaccessibility of its occurrence."[20]

Unlike the trauma caused by slavery, which is so horrific and vast that it defies representation, the haunting of corporations can be represented with forensic precision. It was a genius tactic for the claimants to claim an accounting of profits, and a disgorgement of profits: this would produce spreadsheets that show this haunting of benefit to the corporations, and through forensic accounting this could be calculated to the last cent. In contrast to the difficulty of representing trauma, the culpability of corporations is mundanely apparent.

On 26 January 2004, United States District Court Judge Norgle granted a joint motion to dismiss filed by all defendants, while giving leave for the plaintiffs to refile, which the plaintiffs did on 5 April 2004.[21] On 6 July 2005, Judge Norgle dismissed this Second Amended Consolidated Complaint again, with prejudice. Judge Norgle found that the plaintiffs did not have standing, as the harms suffered were derivative and general injuries, not sufficient to satisfy the injury in fact requirement (at 1052) and, among other arguments, concluded that slave reparation claims were not justiciable in part because 'reparations to former slaves following the Civil War was considered and rejected by the Representative Branches' (1056–1060).

Each of the *In re African-American Slave Descendants Litigation* judgements was decided on different technical grounds, but underlying all of them is an assertion of the impossibility of a successful claim for the historical injuries of slavery because of problems relating to specificity of injury, causality and time. The problem of specificity refers to specificity of damages as well as

20 Cathy Caruth, *Trauma: Explorations in Memory and History* (Duke University Press 1995), 8.

21 *Farmer-Paellman v. FleetBoston Fin Corp* (EDNY 6 April 2004).

the identity of specific plaintiffs and defendants; the difficulty in establishing causal connections refers to the connection between past events and continuing present damage, and problem of the statute of limitations refers to the length of time (over 150 years) since the events of slavery. Some legal critics have argued that none of these arguments is insurmountable from a legal point of view and give examples of cases in which each of these problems has been addressed favourably by the court; the case also produced a significant amount of legal commentary that uses both technical legal frameworks and broader frameworks of ethics and policy to consider the possibility and desirability of reparations claims.[22] In the next section, we consider the courts' unwillingness to enter into consider these legal possibilities and their implications for corporate haunting.

The Harm of Disavowal of Past Harms and Injustice

Haunted houses bear the imprint of past traumas and injustices. In popular culture, the reason why a house is haunted may not be explained or explored – the mansion in *The Haunting of Hill House* has no origin story but is encountered from the start of the story is a malicious entity. But in much of horror fiction, the haunting is explicitly due to transgressions and injustice. The small house in *Beloved* is evil because Sethe, while trying to escape slavery, murdered her baby. In films such as *The Amityville Horror* and *The Conjuring*, characters buy their dream home for a bargain price only to find out that it is haunted by past murder sprees (although this then raises the question of why those original murders occurred). A classic (problematic) trope in horror is to suggest that the house is constructed on sacred indigenous land as an explanation for present hauntings; for example, the Overlook hotel in *The Shining* is built on sacred Native American land. In *Poltergeist*, the Freeling family's home is haunted because it is built on a cemetery and the developer has not moved the bodies. In *Fear Street Trilogy* (2021 Netflix), the entire town of Shadyside is haunted by a deal made hundreds of years ago by the Goode family, so that all the wealth and success flow to the neighbouring town of Sunnydale, while Shadyside suffers economically and from regular massacres. In the words of Nick Freeman, it 'supplies continuity in that it exists in the present as both a historical artefact and a contemporary residence …'.[23] In haunting fiction, the past, present and future coalesce.

22 See for example Charles J. Ogletree, Jr, 'Repairing the Past: New Efforts in the Reparations Debate in America' (2003) 38 *Harv. C.R.-C.L. L. Rev.* 279 and Christina E. Lutz, 'The Death Knell Tolls for Reparations in *In re African-American Slave Descendants Litigation*' (2008) 3 *Seventh Circuit Rev.* 532, at http://www.kentlaw.edu/7cr/v3-2/lutz.pdf.

23 Nicholas Freeman, 'Haunted Houses', in Scott Brewster, Luke Thurston (eds), *The Routledge Handbook to the Ghost Story* (Routledge, 2017).

In *Re African-American Slavery Descendants*, the injustice haunting the plaintiffs, corporations and the legal system is slavery. These harms continue into the present.

> '[t]hey still endure daily indignities from the legacy of slavery, including, but not limited to, racial profiling, racial slurs, and improper and hurtful assumptions regarding their overall status'. FACC ¶ 102. Further, Plaintiff's allege that they 'are also likely to encounter future harm, as they are more likely to have a shorter life expectancy; more likely [to] go to jail; and are more likely to be murdered, than their white counterparts'.[24]

But the court found that the plaintiffs 'fail[ed] to allege any concrete and particular injury-in-fact that they have suffered apart from their race generally'.[25] Further, their claim did not contain allegations 'that any specific conduct of the Defendants was a cause of the continuing injuries of which Plaintiffs complain'; their broad claims were not even alleged 'to be fairly traceable to the challenged action of the defendant, and not the result of the independent action of some third party not before the court'.[26] The court concluded on this point that 'Plaintiffs' allegations of abstract stigmatic injury are not cognizable absent specific allegations of conduct on behalf of the Defendants that has been directed at Plaintiff's or their ancestors'.[27]

In the appeals case of *In re African-American Slave Descendants Litigation*, one of Posner's key objections to the plaintiffs' claims concerns the distinction between the original victims and the descendants. Posner argues:

> There is a fatal disconnect between the victims and the plaintiffs. When a person is wronged he can seek redress, and if he wins, his descendants may benefit, but the wrong to the ancestor is not a wrong to the descendants. For if it were, then (problems of proof to one side) statutes of limitations would be toothless. A person whose ancestor had been wronged a thousand years ago could sue on the ground that it was a continuing wrong and he is one of the victims.[28]

Implicit in Posner's argument is the idea that the damage claimed is limited in time by the lifespan of the 'victims', those who materially suffered directly

24 *In re African-American Slave Descendants Litigation*, MDL No. 1491, Lead Case No. 02 C 7764, 28–30 (N.D. Ill. 2004).

25 Ibid.

26 Lujan, 504 U.S. at 560.

27 Cf. Allen, 468 U.S. at 755–756.

28 *In re African-American Slave Descendants Litigation 471 F.3d 754, 762–763 (7th Cir.2006)* at [15].

under the conditions of slavery. Later in the judgement Posner argues that if in some way claims by these victims have survived which he then asserts is probably impossible anyway – then those plaintiffs who are the victims' descendants can sue as representatives. However, the plaintiffs' connection to the original damage is too remote and so they cannot sue in their own right. There are two factors here – the failure to acknowledge sustained harms and the refusal to acknowledge that whilst original slaves might have died, the perpetrators, corporations, have continued on and thrived. If the remedy of forensic accounting had been granted, however, it is arguable that a direct and continuing connection across time could in fact be proved.

Courts adjudicating reparations cases have also consistently held that plaintiffs are not entitled to sue because so much time has passed since the events of slavery, far exceeding the time permitted under statutes of limitations. However, the statute of limitations is an arbitrary creation; further, even within the terms of the principle, it is open to these courts to disregard the statute of limitations using the principle of equitable tolling, which recognises that in some situations it is impossible for potential plaintiffs to make a claim.

In *Sandvik v. United States*, the court formulated the principle as follows:

> equitable tolling is appropriate when a movant untimely files because of extraordinary circumstances that are both beyond his control and unavoidable even with diligence.[29]

In the context of litigation for damages arising out of the Holocaust, the statute of limitations was again tolled over many years in *Bodner v. Banque Paribas* because of 'extraordinary circumstances,' the court stating:

> [o]ne example of an 'extraordinary circumstance' meriting equitable tolling may be where plaintiffs can show that it would have been impossible for a reasonably prudent person to learn or discover critical facts underlying their claim.[30]

In applying equitable tolling and disregarding the statute of limitations, the court recognises the specific, material realities in which the claim is made, including the historical context of the claim. And yet, the history of slavery and what followed do not count as 'extraordinary circumstances' in the Slave Descendants case: no consideration is given to the collective wrongdoing during slavery, nor to the effects of slavery and racism from 1865 onwards. During the Reconstruction period following the official end of slavery, and

29 *Sandvik v. United States 177 F.3d 1269, 1271 (11th Cir. 1999)* at 1271.
30 *Bodner v. Banque Paribas, 114 F. Supp. 2d (EDNY 2000)* at 135.

into the 20th century, racism operated systematically, both outside the law's boundaries – through practices such as lynching – but also as a matter of law, through cases such as *Plessy v. Ferguson*, which upheld the constitutionality of racial segregation through the principle that the races were 'separate but equal'. However, Judge Posner refused the availability of equitable tolling in Slave Descendants, arguing:

> ... suits complaining about injuries that occurred more than a century and a half ago have been barred for a long time by the applicable state statutes of limitations. It is true that tolling doctrines can extend the time to sue well beyond the period of limitations—but not to a century and more beyond. Slaves could not sue, and even after the Thirteenth Amendment became effective in 1865 suits such as these, if brought in the South, would not have received a fair hearing. However, some northern courts would have been receptive to such suits, and since the defendants are (and were) northern companies, venue would have been proper in those states. Even in the South, descendants of slaves have had decades of effective access to the courts to seek redress for the wrongs of which they complain. And it's not as if it had been a deep mystery that corporations were involved in the operation of the slave system.[31]

Although Posner admitted that slaves and ex-slaves 'would not have received a fair hearing' in the south, he insisted they could have made claims in the north. But Posner's consideration of the hypothetical case in which a slave or ex-slave might have made a reparations case in the north before the statute of limitations expired ignores material historical conditions, especially the legal reality of the operation of racism in the courts following the official end of slavery.

When Posner states that 'descendants of slaves have had decades of effective access to the courts', he means that technical, formal access to the courts was available to African Americans. However, African Americans had little material access to the courts, and even when claims were made, they failed or were retracted: African Americans have been attempting to make reparations claims to unreceptive courts for a long time, since the post-Civil War demands for 'forty acres and a mule'.[32] But for Posner, the only 'deep mystery' concerning the absence of reparations cases lies with the limited question of the state

31 *In re African-American Slave Descendants Litigation 471 F.3d 754, 762–763 (7th Cir. 2006)* at [24–25].

32 Ariella Gross, 'When is the Time of Slavery? The History of Slavery in Contemporary Legal and Political Argument' (2008) 96 *California Law Review* 283 at 311–312; and Charles Ogletree 'Repairing the Past: New Efforts in the Reparations Debate in America' (2003) 38 *Harvard Civil Rights-Civil Liberties Review* 279 at 286–287.

of knowledge of the plaintiffs, who should have obviously understood that 'corporations were involved with in the operation of the slave system'; rhetorically, this move allows Posner to occlude other possibilities that explain the failure of these cases, such as failures of the legal system itself. The case reveals the incompatibility of two logics, each relying on two different kinds of history: the plaintiff's history is materialist and new historicist, and argues the political and legal impossibility of staging reparations claims until a fairly recent point in time; the court's (and the defendants') is positivist and formal. It might seem tautological that the court's representation of time is legal and formal; and yet, there is no legal necessity requiring the court to rely on such a restricted reading of time, which in turn narrates a particular history. This history is the classical liberal narrative of how things work, a history that denies the materiality and specificity of experience, and the operations of power arising out of race, class and gender. By failing to read legal and extra-legal racism across time as 'extraordinary circumstances'. the court not only excludes reparations for past suffering but also disguises the fact of the law's historical complicity in these exclusions. It would be impossible to disentangle the law's responsibility for racism from cultural responsibility: the effect of racism across time is an effect of both legal and extra-legal practices. However, as a matter of social justice (as well as the arguably more narrow concept of legal justice), it is crucial that the law examines its narrative of the past and becomes aware of its role in narrating a limited history. If legal racism across time is not an extraordinary circumstance, this suggests that it is an ordinary circumstance, of law's making.

The arguments by the plaintiffs reflect the idea of harms as returning and persisting.[33] They are haunted by practices of slavery in the present and in their opportunities for the future. The failure by law to recognise these harms is itself harmful and horrific – mediating and shaping collective memory which constitutes social values, law and language – and alienating the generations of descendants of the enslaved.

Haunting of Corporations and the Legal System

The response of the courts to the reparations claims epitomises why the haunting metaphor is apt. The haunted house is neither historical nor timeless. Haunting disrupts time and undermines the present-ness of the present. Rather than engaging with the ways in which harms were caused in the past, continue in the present and threaten the future, the common law's approach is to draw a line under this 'reprehensible time period' rather than include it in law's jurisdiction. The assertion of the absence of slavery's harms in the

33 Michael Fiddler, Travis Linnemann and Theo Kindynis, 'Ghost Criminology: A Framework for the Discipline's Spectral Turn' (2024) 64 *British Journal of Criminology* 1.

present assists with the erasure of law's complicity with slavery. For example, contemporary stories of law focus on abolition, rather than the past and continuing effects of slavery. Hall has argued that even the history of abolition needs to be reframed or rewritten – pointing to the continuation of practices of slavery after abolition, and that much of abolitionist discourse assumed white superiority, which she argues 'has had powerful echoes into the present'.[34] By disavowing the intergenerational trauma of slavery from law's account, this absence haunts the present by continually needing to be repressed. As is the extent to which corporate and legal identity are tied up with the extent to which this grim past is disavowed and yet forms the foundation of and continuing structures of the present.

The exclusion of harms and benefits belies the extent to which legal practices were and are imbricated in practices of slavery. For example, the problem with the courts' finding that the plaintiffs' claims did not meet the standing requirements because their injuries claimed were too general and not 'particular injury-in-fact' is that these standards of proof are inconsistent with the nature of slavery, where records were destroyed and enslaved people were refused the opportunity to learn to read and write. There is a circularity in these evidentiary arguments that is reminiscent of a classic trope of haunted houses – a character seeks to escape but the hallway gets longer and longer. Escape is within sight but always out of reach. Descendants of slaves cannot meet evidentiary standards of the harms of slavery because of the very conditions and harms of slavery. Instead of the courts acknowledging this historical truth – the impossibility of liberal legal evidentiary demands – they are complicit in occluding historical truth, strengthening the corporation's powers to paper over the past and strengthening, too, the demons that haunt the corporation. The house in *The Haunting of Hill House* has hidden passageways and basements, rooms that appear and manifest differently for different characters; similarly, the court is enabling haunted corporations, empowering them in their illusion that all is what it seems. It also fails to adequately acknowledge the intersection of property and personhood under slavery, both as matters of law and of fact, which in a material way provides a way to connect injury through the generations across time, and also in a material way connects the benefit of slavery to the corporation across time. One of the remedies sought by the plaintiffs, a forensic accounting across time, would make the material benefit of this haunting apparent. The plaintiffs' demand to require an accounting of the benefits of slavery is also a way of recounting slavery – of telling the story as well as accounting for the material benefits of slavery. The relationship of property to personhood both before and after

34 Catherine Hall, 'Doing Reparatory History: Bringing "Race" and Slavery Home' (2018) 60 *Race and Class* 3, 6.

slavery involves the complex intertwining of the material and the immaterial, as well as the spectrality of the race and the ways in which race is also a process of reading, and neither material nor immaterial. This accounting and recounting is not just a rhetorical tactic that forms part of the bundle of reparations tools, but one which reveals and reflects legal, material and historical realities. The potential of the common law is that it combines an interpretation of the past, through precedent, with a creative incorporation of new circumstances. The failure to acknowledge past harms and wrongs, and the way that they continue in the present and threaten the future, is harmful in and of itself. Slavery involved the transformation of personhood into property, the injuries, as well as the benefits, continue in material ways (through the personhood of the descendants of the victims, and through the corporate form of the beneficiaries). This is why the plaintiffs' claims against corporations who historically benefited from slavery to provide an account for the profits of slavery is not just symbolic. If all the benefits and injuries had been recorded during slavery, then there would be a forensic accounting of injury that should survive to the present. There is a direct connection between responsibility and a demand for accounting and recounting the material benefits of slavery – benefits to companies, to the government and to private owners – but the courts need to allow the claim in order to prove this formal standing.

These reparations cases highlight not only historical wrongs, but the extent to which corporations continue to benefit from those wrongs. Recent analysis of slavery and abolition has traced the (forgotten) material benefits of slavery – some of which are officially documented.[35] For example, The Legacies of British Slave-ownership project established by University College London has started to trace the cultural, economic and political benefits of slavery.[36] A core goal of the project is an online Encyclopaedia of British Slave-ownership containing information about every slave-owner in the British Empire at 1833, the time of abolition, as well as all slave-owners, attorneys, mortgagees and legatees identified for the period 1763–1833, mostly individuals.[37] In the United Kingdom, pro-slavers resisted emancipation for as long as possible, and then used their parliamentary power to get the best possible compensation for themselves for the loss of 'their' human property – receiving £20 million (£16 billion in today's money). They then bound freed people to work unpaid for fixed hours for the next four to six years.[38]

35 Nicholas Draper, *The Price of Emancipation: Slave-Ownership, Compensation and British Society at the End of Slavery* (Cambridge University Press 2010).

36 www.ucl.ac.uk/lbs

37 https://www.ucl.ac.uk/lbs/project/details/

38 Hall (n 34).

Conclusion

The historical record shows the nastiness of slavery – the cruelty, torture, terror and horror that was integral to the process of transforming humans into profit. Present-day corporations are produced and haunted by the harms they have caused in the past in a way that is analogous to critics' reading of both material and non-material aspects of Marx: the ways in which capitalism relies on processes of reading as much as it does on tangible goods, or in Thomas Keenan's words, a kind of process that is 'a matter of signification, expression, substitution, and hence something that must be read'.[39] In *Specters of Marx*, Jacques Derrida extended Marx's interrelation of figuration and materiality by his use of the term '*revenant*' or spectre. Both metaphor and thing or something in between the two – the spectre, described by Derrida as a 'proper body without flesh', corresponds in Marx's analysis.[40] Derrida's analysis of the logic of the '*sensuous non-sensuous*' (his formulation of Marx's suggestion that exchange-value is both sensuous and suprasensible).[41]

Popular culture highlights that failing to respond to a haunting is not an adequate response – as the haunting will continue and is likely to worsen. In fiction, haunted houses suffer reputational damage, expelling any new inhabitants and tend to be sold dirt cheap. This reflects the reputational damage and material losses that corporations may experience in the effort to deny or disavow past wrongs.[42] Refusal to acknowledge and address unatoned-for crimes looks like complicity.[43] In *Ghostly Matters*, Gordon argues that to make amends necessitates a process of 'calling up and calling out'.[44] This requires an act of conjuring that 'merges the analytical, the procedural, the imaginative and the effervescent'.[45] Conjuring is an important aspect of dealing with a haunting. This includes, at a minimum, an investigation and then

39 Thomas Keenan, 'The Point Is to (Ex)Change It: Reading *Capital*, Rhetorically', in *Fetishism as Cultural Discourse*, ed. Emily Apter and William Pietz (Ithaca, N.Y.: Cornell Univ. Press, 1993), 174.

40 Jacques Derrida, *Specters of Marx*, trans. Peggy Kamuf (New York: Routledge, 1994), 7. Derrida critiques theories of ontology by elaborating a somewhat playful 'hauntology'. For Derrida, the spectre returns, but from where – the future? the past? It isn't clear, and so the notions of both 'the present' and of presence are unclear. Spivak suggests that Marx argues the social *is* spectral – and that communism is about using the spectrality of the social to benefit all rather than the privileged few. 'In capital's subject', Spivak argues, '[the ghostliness is] poison; for the social subject, medicine' 'Ghostwriting' (1995) 25 *Diacritics* 64, 74.

41 Derrida, (n 40) 150.

42 Federman (n 1).

43 Sarah Federman, 'How Companies Can Address Their Historical Transgressions' [2022] Harvard Business Review 82, 87.

44 Gordon (n 7) 88.

45 Ibid. 22.

acknowledgement of past wrongs. For example, in *Poltergeist*, this means realising and then acknowledging that the house was built on a cemetery. In her role as claimant, Farmer-Paellmann's research in the *Re African-American Slave Descendants* cases led the state of California and other state and municipal jurisdictions to compel other companies to search their records for involvement in slavery and make this information public.[46] But this alone is not enough – although it would be a step in the right direction for corporations and the legal system. In some fiction, such as *Poltergeist* or *The Haunting of Hill House*, the houses are irredeemable and the only resolution to haunting is to (attempt to) burn down or destroy the evil house. *Poltergeist* ends with the house imploding and being sucked down into a sinkhole. This idea of burning down the house is reflected in arguments by Tombs and Whyte that corporations are irredeemable and should be abolished.[47]

We are caught between relationships of debt and inheritance.[48] Thus, stories of haunted houses show a way through via acknowledgement of past wrongs and exorcism. In *The Cruelest Month* by Louise Penny,[49] the Old Hadley House is portrayed as a site of evil, attracting all the wrongs, negative energy and murders in the fictional town of Three Pines. However, the book concludes with the idea that the house can be redeemed with an exorcism, love and attention – so that it becomes a different kind of house. This is an optimistic and future-oriented concept of justice, requiring ethical imagination and hope for a different, unimagined future. Toni Morrison's novel *Beloved* ends with a community coming together to exorcise the evil in the house of 124. What would an exorcism of corporations entail?

Corporations should investigate past wrongs and acknowledge them – providing an historical timeline where they acknowledge involvement in abhorrent practices. They can apologise, fulsomely, for these wrongs – which includes acknowledgement, sincere regret and a promise not the repeat past wrongs.[50] But words without actions are meaningless and the enormity of the past wrongs are incommensurable; some estimates for appropriate slave reparations in the United States total about $14 trillion.[51] Georgetown University provides an example of not a corporation but an institution that is trying to

46 Jason Levy, 'Slavery Disclosure Laws: For Financial Reparations or for "Telling the Truth"?', [2009] *Columbia Bus. L. Rev.* 468, 472–473. Cited in Inniss, (n 19) 651.

47 Steve Tombs and David Whyte, *The Corporate Criminal: Why Corporations Must Be Abolished* (Taylor & Francis 2015).

48 Fiddler, Linnemann and Kindynis (n 33) 5.

49 St Martins Press 2007.

50 Martha Minow, *Facing History after Genocide and Mass Violence: Between Vengeance and Forgiveness* (Beacon Press 1998).

51 Federman (n 43) 89.

lay to rest of past ghosts.[52] In 1838, Georgetown University faced insolvency and sold 272 enslaved people to pay off its debts. In 2016, the university considered what support it could offer the descendants of the slaves, and found that most of them lived in a single town in Louisiana. It funded research to find them and then offered preferential admission and scholarships to university. Georgetown students advocated for even more action and in 2019 voted to add $27 each to their student fees to support the Louisiana community. The institution now works with the community to identify useful investments.[53] In response to the Black Lives Matter movement in 2020, *The Guardian* researched the historical links between its founders and slavery, finding that the journalist John Edward Taylor who founded the Manchester Guardian in 1821, had links with transatlantic slavery, as did nine of the 11 men who loaned Taylor money. In response, *The Guardian* issued an apology and announced a decade-long programme of restorative justice. The fund will be used to support community projects in the areas directly affected by slavery, expand its bursary scheme to create three new places each year for Black prospective journalists in the United Kingdom, United States and Australia, and improve public understanding of transatlantic slavery's history and legacy.[54] Corporations have not come to the table, and neither has the law. While some individuals and institutions are attempting reparation projects, these are framed as projects of generosity and good -faith (a cynical person might say they are even framed as public relations activities). The projects are not based on forensic accounting or true calculations of compensation, and they are not projects arising out of obligation. The benefits and harms of slavery may seem to be immeasurable, inconceivable – beyond any capacity to recompense – and yet we can and should try. Corporations need to do better, and the law should play a much greater role in making sure they do so.

52 https://www.georgetown.edu/slavery/. Other US universities are also tracing their relationship to slavery and attempting recompense, including Brown University (https://slaveryandjustice.brown.edu) and Harvard University (https://legacyofslavery.harvard.edu).

53 Federman (n 43).

54 https://www.theguardian.com/news/2023/mar/28/the-guardian-and-slavery-what-did-the-research-find-and-what-happens-next

Chapter 14

Corporate Evil

A Story of Systems and Silences

*Elise Bant**

Introduction

Corporate evil often wears an impersonal, bureaucratic face. Corporations frequently operate through complex and opaque systems that simultaneously give effect to, yet also deflect attention from, their organisational purposes, values and beliefs. Thus, even very egregious and repeated wrongdoing that benefits a corporation may be framed in terms of an 'administrative error'. Consistently, corporate culpability is frequently framed in terms of organisational 'omissions' and 'deficiencies' rather than in positive terms of blameworthiness and responsibility. Generally, these narratives are facilitated by structural silences: information silos within the organisation that fracture knowledge between individuals or prevent knowledge of misconduct reaching the corporation's formal human 'alter egos'.

The purpose of this chapter is to challenge these narratives, using the corrective lens of 'Systems Intentionality'. This model of corporate blameworthiness proposes that corporations manifest their states of mind through their systems of conduct, policies and practices.[1] It enables us to interrogate,

* This article forms part of my Australian Research Council Future Fellowship project FT190100475: see https://www.uwa.edu.au/schools/research/unravelling-corporate-fraud-re-purposing-ancient-doctrines-for-modern-times. My sincere thanks to Penny Crofts, Jeannie Paterson, Tim Peters and Liz Campbell for their helpful feedback on this chapter, and to Nic Cokis for his research assistance. All remaining infelicities and errors are mine.

1 Elise Bant, 'Culpable Corporate Minds' (2021) 48 *University of Western Australia Law Review* 352; Elise Bant and Jeannie Marie Paterson, 'Systems of Misconduct: Corporate Culpability and Statutory Unconscionability' (2021) 15 *Journal of Equity* 63; Jeannie Marie Paterson, Elise Bant and Henry Cooney, '*Australian Competition and Consumer Commission v. Google*: Deterring Misleading Conduct in Digital Privacy Policies' (2021) 26 *Communications Law* 136; Elise Bant, 'Catching the Corporate Conscience: A New Model of "Systems Intentionality"' [2022] *Lloyds Maritime and Commercial Law Quarterly* 467; Elise Bant, 'Reforming the Laws of Corporate Attribution: "Systems Intentionality" Draft Statutory Provision' (2022) 39 *Company & Securities Law Journal* 259; Elise Bant, 'The

DOI: 10.4324/9781003402534-19

understand and rebut corporate strategies of 'interpretive denial' that seek to cast egregious misconduct in terms of administrative error or inadvertence. On this approach, systems are inherently purposive and reveal corporations' knowledge through their objective design. It follows that omissions and gaps, and structural silences, built into a system may be understood as matters of organisational choice. This has profound consequences for understanding the nature of corporate evil.

The chapter proceeds in the 'Corporate Narratives of Interpretive Denial' section by identifying narratives of interpretive denial that cast corporate blame in terms of bureaucratic 'failings', thereby potentially denuding the misconduct of qualities of positive wickedness. The 'Systems Intentionality' section outlines the model of Systems Intentionality and explains how it challenges such narratives. The 'Counter-Narratives of Corporate (Ir)responsibility' section contains two examples of the very different perspective, or counter-narrative, this model brings to quintessentially bureaucratic evil. The first example concerns the notorious real-life practice of Australian banks charging fees for no services through automated systems. Here, the absence of human hands in the till seemed to frustrate any characterisation of the corporate 'takings' as knowing or deliberate. The second example lies in the heartland of literary fiction, in Franz Kafka's *The Trial*.[2] Here, the object is to demonstrate the radically different, more sinister and purposive characterisation of the depicted Court bureaucracy that becomes possible through the lens of Systems Intentionality. This reading challenges more broadly the standard framing of real-life 'Kafka-esque' organisations in terms of senselessly complex and deficient bureaucratic processes.[3] Rather, these processes

---

Culpable Corporate Mind: Taxonomy and Synthesis' (ch. 1), 'Systems Intentionality: Theory and Practice' (ch. 9), 'Modelling Corporate States of Mind through Systems Intentionality' (ch. 11) and, with Jeannie Marie Paterson 'Automated Mistakes' (ch. 12), all in Elise Bant (ed.), *The Culpable Corporate Mind* (Hart Publishing 2023); Elise Bant and Rebecca Faugno, 'Corporate Culture and Systems Intentionality: Part of the Regulator's Essential Toolkit' (2023) *Journal of Corporate Law Studies* https://doi.org/10.1080/14735970.2023.2292837; Elise Bant, 'Where's WALL-E: Corporate Fraud in the Digital Age' in Hans Tijo and Paul S Davies (eds.) *Fraud and Risk in Commercial Law* (Hart Publishing 2024) (forthcoming); Jodi Gardner et.al. (eds.) Politics, Policy and Private Law: Volume II - Contract and Commercial Law (Hart Publishing 2024) (forthcoming).

2 This assumes that as complex organisations there are, inevitably, structural and behavioural similarities between corporations and other group agents, such as the Court and indeed state actors, which are relevant to ascertaining group mental states, agency and, ultimately, responsibility: see, e.g., Christian List and Philip Pettit, *Group Agency: The Possibility, Design and Status of Corporate Agents* (Oxford University Press 2011) and below at n 4. This does not deny that legal responsibility rules (such as available primary claims and defences) might differ between group types, but asserts that it is possible to identify group mental states through a similar analytical framework.

3 See, e.g., 'Kafkaesque' (*Merriam Webster.com Dictionary*) https://www.merriam-webster.com/dictionary/Kafkaesque accessed 19 March 2023: having a 'nightmarishly complex,

manifest clear organisational values, choices and intentions. The hope is that, taken together, the examples illustrate the utility of Systems Intentionality as a way of unmasking organisational blameworthiness, in all its guises.

Corporate Narratives of Interpretive Denial

The sorts of narratives of denial, the subject of this chapter, which hinge upon impersonal bureaucratic organisational structures, are not, of course, limited to corporations.[4] And they may have a particularly powerful, and dangerous, impact upon important questions concerning the moral and legal accountability of individuals for actions undertaken for their particular collective or community.[5] Thus Hannah Arendt commented that, on some views, it is 'the essence of totalitarian government, and perhaps the nature of every bureaucracy ... to make functionaries and mere cogs in the administrative machinery out of men, and thus to dehumanise them'.[6] As she observed, given that the law demands a guilty mind or intention as a condition of committing a crime, the transformation of individuals into elements in a system is remarkably effective in obscuring the true nature of individual culpability involved.[7]

Arendt was particularly concerned to understand the implications of this conversion for individual responsibility. The following analysis also touches on this important issue. However, its primary concern is to consider the implications of a bureaucratic system, and associated deflective narratives, for the culpability of the organisation that deploys them. In particular, is it necessary to identify an individual repository of fault who represents, or instantiates, the guilty corporate mind? Currently, the law's attribution rules largely support such an approach. The effect, when dealing with corporate bureaucracies, is to find a ready means to frame a story of serious misconduct

bizarre, or illogical quality'; 'Kafkaesque' (*Collins Dictionary*) https://www.collinsdictionary.com/dictionary/english/kafkaesque accessed 19 March 2023: marked by a 'senseless, disorienting, often menacing complexity'.

4 See above (n 2); see also Penny Crofts, 'Strategies of Denial and the Australian Royal Commission into Misconduct in the Banking, Superannuation and Financial Services' (2020) 29 *Griffith Law Review* 21, 23, drawing on Stanley Cohen's analysis applied to State actors, see Stanley Cohen, *States of Denial: Knowing about Atrocities and Suffering* (Polity Press 2001). For an example applying Systems Intentionality to evasive narratives offered by the Commonwealth of Australia, see Elise Bant, 'Submission to Robodebt Royal Commission' (Royal Commission into the Robodebt Scheme, October 2022), available at https://unravellingcorporatefraud.com/publications/law-reform-submissions/ accessed 19 March 2023.

5 See, e.g., Mary Midgley, *Wickedness: A Philosophical Essay* (rev edn, Routledge 2001) ch. 3 generally and, in particular, 51–53 on 'Losing the Individual' to corporate (collective) perspectives.

6 Hannah Arendt, *Eichmann in Jerusalem: A Report on the Banality of Evil* (Penguin 2006) 289.

7 Ibid., 277. See further T. Peters in chapter 9 of this volume.

so as to deflect, diminish and disavow corporate responsibility for egregious misconduct.

Drawing upon Stanley Cohen's taxonomy of denial, Penny Crofts has powerfully explored a range of strategic narratives offered by large Australian corporations to negate and diminish their history of egregious misconduct.[8] This chapter focuses on the identified strategy of 'interpretive denial,'[9] by which corporations accept that they have engaged in (or sometimes been implicated in[10]) some sort of repeated and harmful misconduct, but characterise it in terms of an 'administrative mistake' or 'systems error'. Where blameworthiness is conceded, it is generally framed in terms of omissions and deficiencies, thereby relegating it to the level of organisational negligence or bureaucratic ineptitude.

As Crofts separately notes, this tactic has been hugely successful at disabling conceptions of corporate wickedness dependent on proof of some positive and culpable mental state:

> The positive model is insufficient to cope with the likely causes of harm by large organisations in the 21st century. In many cases of systemic harms, it is the lack of knowledge and care, and/or the failure of policies and procedures, that is culpable.[11]

This deficit narrative is arguably enabled by the law's individualistic attribution rules, which generally require a human locus of fault upon which corporate culpability depends.[12] In large and complex corporations, knowledge, and hence responsibility, is often diffused between individuals, teams and departments.[13] Information silos may prevent free passage of information, ensuring that it is kept below board level or from the nominated 'responsible' officer in the official organisational hierarchy. Silence is golden. A classic example is where unlawful or harmful practices routinely are not reported

8 Crofts, (n 4).

9 Ibid., 30–32. See also V. Comino in chapter 16 of this volume, discussing narratives that seek to recharacterise corporate wrongdoing and its responses.

10 For example, Crown Resorts companies 'facilitating' money laundering by criminal elements outside of the corporation: State of Victoria, *Victorian Royal Commission into Casino Operator and Licence* (Report, October 2021) (VCCOL) Vol. 1, 171–178.

11 Penny Crofts, 'Three Recent Royal Commissions: The Failure to Prevent Harms and Attributions of Organisational Liability' (2020) 42 *Sydney Law Review* 395, 421.

12 See generally, Australian Law Reform Commission, *Corporate Criminal Responsibility* (Report No 136, April 2020) (ALRC Final Report) ch. 4; Law Commission, *Corporate Criminal Liability* (Options Paper, 10 June 2022) ch. 3.

13 Brent Fisse, 'Reconstructing Corporate Criminal Law: Deterrence, Retribution, Fault, and Sanctions' (1983) 56 *Southern California Law Review* 1141, 1189.

'up the line' to the responsible officer.[14] Another is where the corporate hierarchy omits any direct reporting line between an on-ground area of operation and responsible officers.[15] Under conventional attribution principles, these structures and practices ensure that the corporation's 'directing mind and will' remains safely ignorant of the corporation's wrongdoing until (at best) after the event, thereby whitewashing the corporate conscience of prior fault. Conversely, where wrongdoing is exposed, the corporate practice may be to hang an individual scapegoat, caught carrying out the general practice.[16] Further, individual cogs in the organisational wheel may have little idea of how their roles contribute to the corporation's broader business model(s). If they are following established (even if not formal) practice, they may well assume that their conduct is unremarkable. It follows that they may not know to stop, or to report, or to declare their activities to a 'responsible officer'.[17]

Further, corporate processes are increasingly automated. There may be little human contribution to the corporate conduct carried out on a daily basis through these systems. This has led to another related set of exculpatory narratives, again drawing on the language of 'systems errors'. These include the assignment of corporate blame to defective 'legacy systems', or 'off the shelf' algorithms, that are difficult (that is, expensive and/or time-consuming) to correct or replace. Since automated systems are neither human, nor (properly understood) computer 'agents',[18] but mere tools of the corporation, this strategy seems particularly effective in reducing corporate blameworthiness to, at most, a negative model consisting of corporate failure.[19] As there are no human persons involved, there is no hook from which to hang the guilty corporation.

14 State of New South Wales, *Review of The Star Pty Ltd: Inquiry Under Sections 143 and 143A of the Casino Control Act 1992 (NSW)* (Report, 31 August 2022) Vol. 1, 9 [48], 28 [148], 29 [155]–[156], 256 [271]. See also L. Siraganian in chapter 10 of this volume.

15 See, for example, 'Board Review of Cultural Heritage Management' (*Rio Tinto*, 25 August 2020) https://www.riotinto.com/en/news/releases/2020/Rio-Tinto-publishes-board-review-of-cultural-heritage-management accessed 19 March 2023, characterising the 'siloing' of indigenous heritage information within its corporate structure as a 'fatal flaw' and a 'defect in the information management system': at [40]–[41]. cf Elise Bant and Jeannie Marie Paterson, 'Rio Tinto and the Anatomy of Corporate Culpability' (*Pursuit*, 11 September 2020) https://pursuit.unimelb.edu.au/articles/rio-tinto-and-the-anatomy-of-corporate-culpability accessed 19 March 2023.

16 For example, see Sarah Derrington and Samuel Walpole, 'Culpable Ships' in Elise Bant (ed.), *The Culpable Corporate Mind* (Hart Publishing 2023), 358, 371; Bant, 'Catching the Corporate Conscience' (n 1) 494 and V. Comino in chapter 16 of this volume. cf Siraganian (n 14).

17 For example, the casino aggregation practices under consideration in VCCOL (n 10) 83–84 [3.113]–[3.119], 88 [3.164]–[3.167], 174–178 [6.87]–[6.102] and Bant, 'Reforming the Laws of Corporate Attribution' (n 1) 274.

18 Paterson and Bant, 'Automated Mistakes' (n 1) 255, 267–268.

19 *Royal Commission into Misconduct in the Banking, Superannuation and Financial Services Industry* (Final Report, February 2019) (FSRC Final Report) Vol. 1, 139.

As Crofts has separately argued, a 'negative' account of wickedness can capture such forms of misconduct:

> The negative account conceives of evil as privation, something missing, dearth or failure. The negative model of wickedness provides a philosophical foundation for the conception of organisational failure as culpable. Organisations are most likely to inflict systemic harms due to a failure to prevent and a failure to adequately respond to harms. The negative model of culpability provides a means to redefine 'responsibility practices', emphasising that it is this failure to act that has caused the systemic harms, and it precisely this failure that is culpable.[20]

This is an important and powerful insight. It explains how corporate narratives of interpretive denial, which cast misconduct in terms of bureaucratic 'failings' and 'mistakes', can be rebutted to expose a negative form of corporate wickedness. The following sections argue, however, that it is possible to go even further and understand 'deficient' systems in terms of positive mental states.[21] This enables corporate wrongdoing to be characterised, and condemned, in terms of positive wickedness. Omitted processes may not be a matter of forgetfulness or inattention, but an intrinsic aspect of a system's design, necessary to achieve the corporation's true ends. Consistently, information silos and other structural silences may shout the corporation's intentions in ways that cannot be ignored.[22] Through this lens, the exculpatory narratives of interpretive denial are disabled, enabling the full, expressive power of the law's condemnation of positively culpable mental states held by corporations.

Systems Intentionality

For present purposes, it is only necessary to sketch the outlines of the model of 'Systems Intentionality', in order to appreciate the counter-narrative of organisational blameworthiness it offers. In brief, Systems Intentionality proposes that corporations manifest their states of mind through their adopted and deployed systems of conduct, policies and practices. As I have explained elsewhere:

20 Crofts, (n 11) 421–422, drawing on Midgley (n 5).

21 Crofts has more recently also expressed this view: see Penny Crofts, 'Crown Resorts and the Im/moral Corporate Form' in Elise Bant (ed.), *The Culpable Corporate Mind* (Hart Publishing 2023). For implications for 'Failure to Prevent' offences, see Bant, 'Taxonomy and Synthesis' (n 1) 3, 31, 33–34 and Bant and Faugno (n 1).

22 See generally Elise Bant and Jeannie Marie Paterson (eds), *Misleading Silence* (Hart Publishing 2020). Corporate strategies of concealment may be deceptive on this approach: for interesting potential examples in the context of legal professional privilege, see L. Campbell in chapter 11 of this volume.

> A 'system of conduct' is the internal method or organised connection of elements operating to produce the conduct or outcome. It is a plan of procedure, or coherent set of steps that combine in a coordinated way in order to achieve some aim (whether conduct or, additionally, result). A 'practice' involves patterns of behaviour that are habitual or customary in nature. A practice may cross over into a system, where the 'custom' or 'habit' has become an embedded process or method of conduct. Finally, corporate 'policies' partake of the same nature of systems, but can be understood as generally operating at a higher level of generality. These manifest overarching and high-level purposes, beliefs and values. They embody and reveal the overall corporate mindset, which is then instantiated or operationalised through corporate systems at more granular and event- or conduct-specific levels.[23]

The basic idea at the core of this model is extremely simple.[24] Natural persons routinely use systems of conduct to guide their decision-making and, hence, conduct. Common examples are recipes, directions on a map and notations or records. These 'extended mind' supports enable a person to achieve their purpose: to make a cake, find a location or recall how to do something.[25] Similarly, corporations utilise systems of conduct to enable them to achieve their corporate purposes. The trick is that this is the *only* way in which corporations can do so (other than acting entirely randomly and trusting to chance). Corporations lack a natural mind, or memory, so are wholly dependent on systems of conduct to engage purposefully with the real world. It is hence unsurprising that core default rules concerning the role of the board of a company, or the shareholders in general meeting, address the need to create corporate decision-systems to transform the corporation from a passive shell to an operational legal person.

Corporate Mental States

This simple idea offers some powerful insights for understanding the spectrum of corporate mental states. I explore these in detail elsewhere.[26] Here, I merely outline their significance for 'general' intentionality and actual

23 Bant, 'Modelling Corporate States of Mind through Systems Intentionality' (n 1) 231, 245–246. Policies, on this analysis, most closely resemble the Australian concept of 'corporate culture,' perceptively discussed in V. Comino in chapter 16 of this volume. See also Bant and Faugno (n 1).

24 See further Bant, 'Catching the Corporate Conscience' (n 1) 471–477.

25 Mihailis E. Diamantis, 'The Extended Corporate Mind: When Corporations Use AI to Break the Law' (2020) 98 *North Carolina Law Review* 893.

26 See in particular Bant, 'Modelling Corporate States of Mind through Systems Intentionality' (n 1) and Bant and Paterson, 'Systems of Misconduct: Corporate Culpability and Statutory Unconscionability' (n 1); Bant, 'Corporate Mistake' (n 1).

knowledge, as the most basic building blocks for other, more complex mental states and normative conceptions (such as mistake, 'specific' intention, dishonesty and recklessness).

Firstly, the model contends that corporations manifest (that is, reveal and instantiate) their general intentions through their adopted systems of conduct. Systems of conduct are inherently purposive: this is the very nature of a system. An unintended system is a contradiction in terms. Language gives this away: systems are 'plans', 'strategies' or 'methods' of achieving some aim, whether that is conduct (for these purposes, a 'general' intention to act) or, additionally, some specific outcome(s) through that conduct (a 'specific' intention).[27] The starting point for any analysis, therefore, once a system of conduct is identified, is that the corporation has a general intention to engage in that conduct.

This immediately challenges corporate narratives that frame systems of conduct as unintended, accidental or mistaken.[28] It is not impossible for patterns of behaviour, which are themselves neutral as to intention, to mimic systems of conduct.[29] For example, repeated corporate behaviours or outcomes may be purely coincidental. But once patterns of behaviour are determined to reflect, or be the observable consequences of, a *system* of conduct, that conduct is necessarily intended.

It is also possible to deploy a system by mistake (for example, where an employee presses a wrong button, initiating a payment or deduction process). So genuine 'systems errors' are not impossible. However, once a system of conduct is prima facie established, the analytical starting point is that the conduct is intended. The evidential onus then lies on the corporation to substantiate any allegation of mistake or accident (for example, through an employee witness admitting to accidental deployment of the system).[30]

A further consequence of this analysis is that since a system of conduct is, by definition, intended, a corporation will know at least its broad outline and the key features required for it to be deployed. Absent proof of mistake

27 See, e.g., *Australian Competition and Consumer Commission v. EDirect Pty Ltd* [2012] FCA 1045 [91] (Reeves J.) and Bant, 'Systems Intentionality: Theory and Practice' (n 1).

28 Intention and mistake are not necessarily exclusive: mistakes commonly involve 'vitiated' intention, where one of the reasons for action is contrary to the true facts, so intention is undermined but not absent: see further Bant, 'Modelling Corporate States of Mind through Systems Intentionality' (n 1) 232–235 and 248–249. Mistakes of law and fact both count as reasons for relief: by contrast, ignorance of the law is no excuse (or defence) to liability: see generally James Edelman and Elise Bant, *Unjust Enrichment* (Hart Publishing, Oxford 2016) Chapter 8. The sorts of (systems) errors considered here are inherently factual, being mistakes as to the fact of the corporation's intended behaviour, not its (lawful or unlawful) quality.

29 Bant, 'Systems Intentionality: Theory and Practice' (n 1) 189–192.

30 See below at n 41.

or similar, a corporation cannot sleepwalk a system of conduct.[31] This means that the starting point for any inquiry is that corporations know the nature of the conduct in which they are engaged through those systems. That is, corporate knowledge of the key features of a system, and the fact of its operation, is implicit in its successful deployment by the corporation. This applies as much for organically developed practices as it does for systems that operationalise 'on the ground' some higher-level corporate policy.

Again, this significantly challenges corporate narratives that characterise the corporation as ignorant (and therefore innocent) of its conduct conducted through its own systems. On this approach, information barriers that prevent responsible officers from actual knowledge of the corporation's misconduct do not necessarily protect the corporation itself from that knowledge, although the officer's ignorance may (depending on the circumstances) mitigate the officer's liability for breaches of their own duties. Similarly, scapegoating individuals on the grounds that they have been discovered performing the corporation's own practices no longer operates as an effective diversion of organisational blameworthiness.[32] This does not mean, of course, that individuals' responsibility for harmful conduct is automatically excluded: the 'cog in the wheel' excuse is not thereby endorsed.[33] Rather, it means that the individual's responsibility must arise from and reflect their own personal or positional fault.[34] This may be of a quite different order than that of the corporation.

Finally, it will be apparent that the analysis removes another helpful and liability-reducing corporate narrative of deficiency: namely that the corporation's formal policies and processes were entirely ethical and robust but that there was some (relatively innocent or merely careless) failure to embed these 'on the ground'. Rather, any analysis of corporate mindsets must start with the actual, de facto or instantiated system of conduct. Formal corporate policies however remain relevant as a statement of fact, or representation, of the corporate state of mind. It follows that a significant gap between formal policy, or the textbook 'standard operating procedures' of a company, and the reality of its corporate intentions and knowledge as manifested through its daily systems, may constitute a form of misleading or, in some cases, deceptive conduct.[35]

31 FSRC Final Report (n 19) Vol. 1, 157: fees for no services were 'part of an established system and were not matters of accident'.
32 See Bant, 'Catching the Corporate Conscience: A New Model of "Systems Intentionality"' (n 1) 484, 492–95.
33 Arendt (n 6) 289. See further L. Siraganian in chapter 10 of this volume, on the distinctive fault that may attach to individuals embedded within evil corporate practices.
34 See below n 81.
35 See, e.g., *Competition and Consumer Act 2010* (Cth) sch. 2 s 18 (prohibition on misleading or deceptive conduct in trade or commerce); *Magill v. Magill* (2006) 226 CLR 551, 567 (Gleeson CJ), 574 (Gummow, Kirby and Crennan J.J.) (tort of deceit).

Systems of Omissions

We are now in a position to consider the character of corporate structures that exclude or omit key processes. This is necessary if we are to dismantle many corporate strategies of interpretive denial, which frame misconduct in terms of failures to convey information or to correct misconduct, and hence organisational negligence.

As we have seen, systems of conduct necessarily reflect a general corporate intention. Critically, however, understood as integrated steps and processes, systems of conduct will often comprise *both* positive and negative and proactive and reactive, elements.[36] Primary (and seemingly positive) systems (for example, a marketing strategy or fee deduction system) themselves necessarily entail the adoption of certain steps *and* omissions of others. It is the coordinated *set* of processes taken as a whole, framed holistically as a system of conduct at a certain level of generality, which constitute intended conduct.[37] It is, therefore, potentially a(nother) false narrative to frame corporate systems solely in terms of positive conduct, which has separately been affected by unintended or careless omissions or deficiencies. Omissions may form an intrinsic part of a system's overall design.

The insights offered by this analysis for bureaucratic wrongdoing are now explored through two examples.

Counter-Narratives of Corporate (Ir)responsibility

Fees for No Services

The first example was spotlighted in the Australian Royal Commission into Misconduct in the Banking, Superannuation and Financial Services Industry.[38] A number of leading Australian banks[39] extracted 'fees for no services' from customers through automated systems, over extended periods of time. Many such fees were for life insurance charged after the customer had died. Typically, before the Commission, bank executives emphasised the individual honesty and work ethic of their employees and, by extension, the corporation itself. Consistently, they framed the misconduct in terms of administrative mistakes or systems errors, arising from 'legacy' systems which were difficult to change. They were willing to admit to truly

36 Brent Fisse, 'Reactive Corporate Fault' in Elise Bant (ed.), *The Culpable Corporate Mind* (Hart Publishing 2023) 139; Bant, 'Taxonomy and Synthesis' (n 1) 3, 5.

37 See further Bant, 'Systems Intentionality: Theory and Practice' (n 1) 183, 192.

38 FSRC Final Report (n 19) Vol. 1, 139–157, discussed in Bant, 'Catching the Corporate Conscience: A New Model of "Systems Intentionality"' (n 1) 487–490; Bant, 'Culpable Corporate Minds' (n 1) 361–368, 385–387; Crofts, (n 11).

39 Or, more broadly, 'financial service providers'.

remarkable corporate incompetence in these terms rather than suffer the suggestion of dishonesty.[40]

Through Systems Intentionality, however, another analysis is possible. The customers were natural individuals whose circumstances would be prone to change. Corporate knowledge of that fact was patent in the banks' own systems: it was the reason why the customers sought life insurance, after all. Notwithstanding, the banks' automated systems operated as 'set and forget' models, the default setting for which was to 'keep taking fees until manual intervention'. Tellingly, the banks had no, or no functional, manual audit or oversight systems. Consequently, there was no means to correct the consequence that, given clients would die, the authorised fees would inevitably degenerate into unlawful takings.

On the Systems Intentionality approach to such scenarios, the proactive elements of the systems ('takings') are prima facie intentional conduct. There was no apparent error in the deployment of these positive systems.[41] As designed, they kept taking until stopped.[42] Alongside the proactive features sat reactive elements of the systems: the omitted audit and remedial processes. This analysis expands the level of generality at which the 'fees for no services' systems of conduct are conceptualised and assessed to encompass both proactive and reactive components. This is entirely appropriate, given that the systems were designed to roll out over long periods, with respect to many customers, to the substantial benefit of the corporations.[43]

Seen from this integrated perspective, where a professedly expert corporation (such as a leading bank) deploys positive elements of a system that are objectively apt to produce a harmful outcome and omits related audit or remedial processes, this omission can be understood as a matter of corporate choice. The package of conduct is thus revealed as knowing and deliberate. While it is not possible to do more than sketch the barest outline here, such findings may invite further conclusions on the nature of the corporation's culpability. For example, the corporation deploying the system may be considered reckless as to the harms caused by its conduct,[44] in the sense that: (a) it has a general intention to engage in the conduct; (b) it has knowledge of the harmful outcome (unlawful takings) that the conduct is patently apt to produce; and (c) its decision to proceed with the conduct in light of that known

40 FSRC Final Report (n 19) Vol. 1, 139.

41 cf *Australian Securities and Investments Commission v. AMP Financial Planning Proprietary Limited* [2022] FCA 1115 [47] (Moshinsky J., accepting a coding error led to fees for no services. As the judge remarked, this did not explain the highly culpable failures to audit and remedy the operation of the system: [52]–[54].

42 An alternative system default setting manifesting an ethical mindset would be to stop 'taking' until authorisation was confirmed.

43 On the temporal perspective, see Fisse (n 36).

44 On conceptions of recklessness and Systems Intentionality, see Bant, 'Modelling Corporate States of Mind through Systems Intentionality' (n 1) 235–239, 250.

risk is unreasonable. In some cases (depending on the facts), it will be open to conclude that the harmful outcome is specifically intended (in the sense of chosen, rather than desired), so that the system manifests a predatory mindset.[45] This may be so where the harmful outcome is not merely likely, but inevitable, and the corporation continues to deploy the system, without adjustment, in the face of repeated notice of harm.

Each case (and system) must be assessed on its own terms, but this example suggests how defective systems need not, nor should they, be solely understood in terms of organisational negligence. Further, automation does not necessarily diminish corporate culpability as a form of 'computer error'. On the contrary, automation of key processes itself represents a corporate choice. Indeed, the 'default settings' for those systems also manifest corporate choices, often at critical ethical pressure points.[46] Systems Intentionality thus gives us a new vocabulary to develop a powerful counter-narrative that expresses a full spectrum of corporate blameworthiness in such cases.

The Trial

For the second example, I draw on and interpret aspects of Kafka's *The Trial*[47] through the lens of Systems Intentionality. To the extent that this constitutes an addition to the burgeoning body of law and literature analysis of this landmark novel,[48] it is important to be clear about its limited aims. The text[49] is widely recognised as offering an iconic vision of bureaucratic evil: a faceless, impersonal and labyrinthine Court that operates seemingly at random, without apparent rationale, to devastating effect.[50] Thus, at the outset

45 On specific intention, see ibid. 235–239, 246–248.

46 See also Paterson, Bant and Cooney (n 1) on Google's data harvesting default settings; on automation and systems intentionality, see Paterson and Bant, 'Automated Mistakes' (n 1).

47 Roberto Buonamano, 'Kafka and Legal Critique' (2016) 25 *Griffith Law Review* 581, 591: 'The essence of the trial is process, as the semantics of the German title for the novel (*Der Process*) suggest. And as is insinuated throughout the novel, the legal process is inexhaustible'.

48 See Patrick J. Glen, 'The Deconstruction and Reification of Law in Franz Kafka's Before the Law and the Trial' (2007) 17 *Southern California Interdisciplinary Law Journal* 23, 23–26.

49 I have used the translation by Willa and Edwin Muir: Franz Kafka, *The Trial* (Willa Muir and Edwin Muir (trs), Compact Books 1994). cf Roman Altshuler, 'Kafka's "Trial" Gets New Translation' (*The Harvard Crimson*, 9 October 1998) https://www.thecrimson.com/article/1998/10/9/kafkas-trial-gets-new-translation-pithe accessed 19 March 2023, and below at n 51.

50 e.g., Mark Spilka, *Dickens and Kafka: A Mutual Interpretation* (Indiana University Press 1963); Randy Hodson and others, 'Rules Don't Apply: Kafka's Insights on Bureaucracy' (2013) 20 *Organization* 256; Yi Yang, 'Beyond Weber and Kafka: Conceptualizing a Critical Realist Model of Bureaucracy' (2022) 54 *Administration & Society* 500.

of *The Trial*, the accused, K, is arrested for no clear reason.[51] As he tries to navigate the Court's justice system, he initially denounces the 'great organisation' of engaging in 'senseless proceedings' against innocent persons through its corrupt officials and employees.[52] On this reading, the innocent are victims of endemic and unresponsive organisational negligence. However, as the novel and Court processes unfold, Systems Intentionality suggests a more sinister and purposive characterisation, with clear lessons for interrogating real-life bureaucratic mindsets.[53]

In this counter-narrative, Kafka's Court manifests through its web of processes a concerted and malign intention with respect to all those accused. Specifically, the Court knowingly and deliberately inflicts a form of prolonged psychological torture on every accused that results, inevitably,[54] in their death or destruction. While the following analysis focuses on this general intention, the characterisation prompts further, chilling possibilities in the text, which merit brief mention here. Thus, as the outcome for every accused is known and inevitable, it may be that the Court also specifically intends their destruction, as a necessary sacrifice to a greater end.[55] This particularised intention need not require knowledge of specific victims or their characteristics, or an emotional desire for their destruction.[56] The fact that there is 'nothing personal' in K's destruction may only emphasise the brutality of the organisation.[57] Further, the seemingly ad hoc targeting of individuals such as K, together with the inescapable and destructive effect on them of the Court's processes, suggests that the ultimate end or purpose of this intended conduct is a broader coercive and tyrannical social control.[58] From this perspective, the inevitable, dawning realisation of their fate, which must be experienced by all those who stand accused, and are thereby condemned, is one of the most cruel and effective elements of the process. As Arendt observes, in her examination of another

51 Compare the Mitchell translation 'for without having done anything **truly** wrong he was arrested'. The Muir translation omits 'truly'. As discussed by Altshuler (n 49), this critical word may suggest that K has committed some wrong, which he does not recognise or acknowledge. This would be significant for determining the Court's intentions.

52 Kafka (n 49) 54, the Court, its capitalisation emphasising its separate persona.

53 cf Hodson and others (n 50) 259.

54 As the priest explains, 'the proceedings gradually merge into the verdict': Kafka (n 49) at 232; see also Glen (n 48) 62.

55 See preceding section. Certainly, the manifested state of mind would likely satisfy the conception of recklessness outlined earlier.

56 Bant, 'Modelling Corporate States of Mind through Systems Intentionality' (n 1) 250 and *Australian Securities and Investments Commission v. National Exchange Pty Ltd* [2005] FCAFC 226, (2005) 148 FCR 132, 140–41 [33], 142–43 [43], discussed in Bant and Paterson, 'Systems of Misconduct: Corporate Culpability and Statutory Unconscionability' (n 1) 81–82.

57 Compare Arendt (n 6) 26.

58 Suggesting an affinity with Orwell's *1984*.

evil bureaucracy, 'the system which succeeds in destroying its victim before he mounts the scaffold ... is incomparably the best for keeping a whole people in slavery'.[59]

Turning to the text itself, Kafka identifies the critical features of the Court's system, relevant for this analysis, which ensure it operates effectively to destroy the lives of those accused ensnared within it. A key feature is its impenetrable nature: information about the trial process is fractured and dissipated amongst the Court agents and broader legal participants. The system's information silos epitomise the 'diffused responsibility' that we have seen characterises many modern, complex corporations. Consistently, in *The Trial*, none of the Court's members, employees or agents actually understand fully how the system operates. An example is the mere 'difference of opinion' between judge and advocate over whether the proceedings against another accused, Block, have even started.[60] Another is the insight that no judge has access to the Court's final judgements, which are not recorded.[61] It is therefore structurally impossible for K to understand the nature of the charge against him or how best to fight it from those operating within the system. None of these features are accidental or 'senseless', on this interpretation. Rather, they are aspects of the system's 'choice architecture'[62] geared to operate, consistently and in a coordinated way, to the Court's true ends.

On a Systems Intentionality analysis, the fact that the formal procedures of the Court are not how it operates in practice is another, very significant, feature of Kafka's creation. On this interpretive approach, it is necessary to assess objectively the de facto operation of the Court's constituent processes, through which it manifests its true nature and purposes. However, this poses a seemingly hopeless paradox, since even experts on the law are reduced to 'bewilderment'[63] on this subject. Ultimately, it is the Court painter, an outsider, who explains the true nature of the Court's processes to K and so also, from the perspective of Systems Intentionality, allows the reader to undertake an objective assessment of the Court's state of mind. The painter is, by birth and training, a describer and interpreter of the system, who therefore has 'the confidence of the Court'.[64] He is also the sole person to ask K the question 'Are you innocent?'[65] As K comes to understand, that question is irrelevant to, and unanswerable within, the system to which he is subject.

59 Arendt (n 6) 12 (quoting David Rousset).
60 Kafka (n 49) 217.
61 Ibid. 171.
62 Paterson, Bant and Cooney (n 1) 138.
63 Kafka (n 49) 240.
64 Ibid. 163.
65 Ibid. 165. See also Arendt (n 6) 21.

The painter reveals that the Court's formal system is quite distinct from the Court system in practice.[66] Contrary to appearances, no amount of pleading or proof before the judges will persuade them of K's innocence.[67] However, it is 'quite a different matter with one's efforts behind the scenes'.[68] The painter identifies and describes in detail the three forms of acquittal that might, in theory and practice, be obtained: definite, ostensible and indefinite postponement.[69] The painter's long 'experience' of Court practice is that no-one within or outside of the system can assist in getting a definite acquittal. The only factor that may count is the innocence of the accused. Yet there is no means to establish that innocence.[70] 'Legends' of definite acquittals cannot be cited before the Court. Moreover, if a definite acquittal is granted, all Court documents simply vanish from sight and are destroyed.[71] Unfortunately for K, the other, more likely possibilities of ostensible and indefinite postponement only offer the certainty of prolonged psychological torture. Both entail the uncertain and never-ending navigation of labyrinthine, hidden practices of the Court, in the hope of avoiding final sentence. And from final sentence, it seems, there is no appeal to the higher Court.[72] The very existence of this reputed higher Court serves as a final, vicious twist in the process, simultaneously offering apparent due process while denying it as a matter of course.

We have seen previously that, through the lens of Systems Intentionality, this dissonance between the formal representation of an organisation's state of mind (here, that the Court is concerned with K's innocence or guilt, and acquittal is a real possibility) and the reality of its intentions can be understood as a form of misleading or deceptive conduct. This fundamental deception can be understood as a key design feature of the Court's processes, and part of what discloses its malevolent intention. The dawning realisation of the hopelessness of his position is part of K's gradual destruction.[73] Indeed, the omission of any further description of the trial process, before the conclusion of the novel in K's submission to his execution, from this perspective makes perfect sense. The trial could have no real bearing on the end-point of the system, and hence the Court's ultimate purpose. It could only constitute a staging post, or procedural dogleg, providing another psychological wound en route to K's inevitable destruction.

66 Kafka (n 49) 170.
67 Ibid. 166–167.
68 Ibid. 167.
69 Ibid. 169–180.
70 Ibid. 171.
71 Ibid. 176.
72 Ibid. 256.
73 Ibid. 243.

Finally, the critical distinctions drawn by Systems Intentionality between formal and de facto practices also cast a potentially interesting light on the roles and culpabilities of the individual employees and the agents of the Court embedded within its system. We have seen that this is likewise a matter of significant concern for corporate misconduct. An example is the warders' claim that it is 'a tradition that body-linen is the warders' perquisite, it has always been the case'.[74] When they are punished for taking K's clothing, one pleads that he was only following the example of his senior colleague, 'my teacher, for better or worse.'[75] Yet the tradition was, in reality, forbidden, and if disclosed 'punishment is bound to follow'.[76]

This duality need not be inconsistent: an organisation may tacitly permit some wrongdoing, and even encourage it, on the understanding that if the behaviour should ever be revealed that its individual authors will be scapegoated.[77] Hence the warder's whipper explains that the punishment is 'as just as it is inevitable'.[78] K protests that he doesn't 'in the least blame [the warders], it is the organisation that is to blame, the high officials are to blame'.[79] The whipper is unmoved: what K says 'sounds reasonable enough … but I refuse to be bribed. I am here to whip people and whip them I shall.'[80] From the perspective of Systems Intentionality, this statement reflects his loyalty to the organisational ethos and purpose: his personal ethos and rationality is suspended in his role within the Court's system.[81] As explained previously, this does not excuse the whipper from personal or positional responsibility, on the ground that he is a mere cog in the Court's machine. But Systems Intentionality invites further and deeper enquiry into the role and responsibilities of the petty official and officious bureaucrat who contributes to a greater and coordinated system of conduct, which itself manifests organisational intention.[82]

Conclusions

The object of this chapter has been to demonstrate how Systems Intentionality offers a means to construct a principled, analytical counter-narrative of

74 Ibid. 95.
75 Ibid. 97.
76 Ibid. 95.
77 Derrington and Walpole (n 16) 351, 371.
78 Kafka (n 49) 95.
79 Ibid. 97.
80 Ibid.
81 See also the priest's comment at ibid. 244 that he 'belong[s] to the Court'. Compare again with Arendt (n 6): Eichmann's 'extraordinary diligence in advancement' was his abiding motivation: at 287; see also at 22, 25–6, 56–57. On the conundrum of separating and reconciling personal and positional responsibility, see T. Peters in chapter 9 of this volume and, by contrast, Matthew Harding, 'Associations and Moral Responsibility: Some Ground-Clearing' in Elise Bant (ed.), *The Culpable Corporate Mind* (Hart Publishing 2023).
82 See further Bant, 'Submission to Robodebt Royal Commission' (n 4).

corporate strategies of interpretive denial, which commonly cast egregious misconduct in terms of administrative error or inadvertence. It reveals the spectrum of corporate mental states hiding behind the bureaucratic façade, with significant implications for liability doctrines in which defendant states of mind are key requirements.

Chapter 15

Redeeming Corporations

Designing Legal Interventions for Complex Adaptive Systems

*Rebecca Wallis and Simon Bronitt**

Introduction

Baron Edward Thurlow, the English judge and jurist, famously observed in the 18th century that corporations have 'no soul to be damned and no body to be kicked'.[1] This much-cited dictum received a modern spin by Joel Bakan, the Canadian law professor who, in 2004, diagnosed the modern corporation with 'Anti-Social Personality Disorder', a thesis he famously promoted in his book and subsequent award-winning documentaries.[2] According to Bakan's view, the modern corporation is 'a pathological institution, a dangerous possessor of the great power it wields over people and societies'.[3] These two views of modern corporations highlight the ongoing struggle in conceptualising and responding to the 'evil corporation': specifically, should we view corporations, legally speaking, as the sum of their individual human parts, or do they stand apart from their constituent human actors in some way? If they stand apart, how and when can they be held responsible for wrongdoing?[4] This question may seem abstract, but how we frame the question of 'corporate legal personality' impacts upon legal liabilities and

* We also acknowledge the invaluable research assistance provided by Riley Vaughan and offer our thanks to him, and to Penny Crofts for her insightful comments and feedback on this chapter.

1 Baron Thurlow, quoted in J Poynder, Literary Extracts John Hatchard, London, 1844, Vol 1. p 268.

2 Joel Bakan, *The Corporation: The Pathological Pursuit of Profit and Power* (Simon & Schuster, 2004) ('*The Corporation*'); *The Corporation* (Big Picture Media Corporation, 2004) http://www.thecorporation.com/. See also Joel Bakan, *The New Corporation: How 'Good' Corporations Are Bad For Democracy* (Vintage Books, 2020) ('*The New Corporation*').

3 Ibid. 2.

4 This question is explored in detail by Bant in chapter 14 of this volume, and see also Elise Bant, 'Catching the Corporate Conscience: A New Model of "Systems Intentionality"' [2022] *Lloyd's Maritime and Commercial Law Quarterly* 467 ('*Bant No 1*'); Elise Bant, 'Systems Intentionality: Theory and Practice' in Elise Bant (ed.), *The Culpable Corporate Mind* (Bloomsbury Publishing, 2023) 183 ('*Bant No 2*' in '*Culpable Corporate Mind*'); Elise Bant, 'Modelling Corporate States of Mind through Systems Intentionality' in *Culpable Corporate Mind* 231 ('*Bant No 3*')). Similarly, see generally, Chris Chapple, *The Moral Responsibilities of Companies* (Palgrave MacMillan, 2014).

DOI: 10.4324/9781003402534-20

immunities, which in turn influences the range of regulatory tools – civil, criminal and administrative – available to intervene to prevent or respond to corporate misconduct.

We consider that the modern corporation should be viewed neither as anthropomorphic nor unnatural in form. Rather, we propose that the modern corporation should be understood as a 'complex adaptive system'. This perspective frames corporations as comprised of multiple component parts, operating interactively and in patterned but adaptive ways to shape the structure and trajectory of the system as a whole, over time.[5] Importantly, characterising the corporation as a 'complex adaptive system' allows us to draw on developed insights about systems behaviour from other fields, and to apply those insights to understand dimensions of corporate wrongdoing.[6] Applying this conceptualisation, we set out to specifically consider the design of a model of responsive regulation that can provide a coherent frame for the ordering and deployment of existing and innovative legal and regulatory mechanisms, and that may safeguard against the adaptive capacity of corporations to avoid and frustrate regulatory efforts.

The Limits of Corporate Anthropomorphism

The modern corporation has been anthropomorphised.[7] The history of the common law involved the gradual separation of the 'body corporate' from the legal identity and liabilities of the constituent individuals that create, own, govern and serve these entities.[8] The basis for corporate criminal responsibility has varied over time. In the United States, courts extended vicarious liability (*respondeat superior*) to hold corporations liable for the criminal wrongs of their agents/servants.[9] In the latter part of the 20th century, this form of strict liability was rejected, with courts in England assigning

5 See generally, Christian List and Philip Pettit, *Group Agency: The Possibility, Design, and Status of Corporate Agents* (Oxford University Press, 2001); Philip Pettit, 'Group Agency and Supervenience' (2006) 44 *Southern Journal of Philosophy* 85; John Miller and Scott Page, *Complex Adaptive Systems: An Introduction to Computational Models of Social Life* (Princeton University Press, 2007) ch. 1.

6 Ibid. See, generally, Tim Sullivan, 'Embracing Complexity', *Harvard Business Review* (online, September 2011) https://hbr.org/2011/09/embracing-complexity.

7 *Anthropomorphism* is the 'attribution of human personality or characteristics to something non-human, as an animal, object, etc.': *Oxford English Dictionary* (online at 6 September 2023) 'anthropomorphism' (def 1b). Its application, and limitations, are explored in Sally Wheeler, 'The Corporation and the Anthropocene' in L.J. Kotzé (ed.) *Environmental Law and Governance for the Anthropocene* (Hart Publishing, 2017).

8 See, for the origin of corporate personality, *Salomon v. Salomon & Co* [1897] AC 22, 53 (Lord Macnaghten); see Samuel Stoljar, *Groups and Entities: An Inquiry into Corporate Theory* (ANU Press, 1973).

9 Australian Law Reform Commission, *Corporate Criminal Responsibility* (Report No. 136, April 2020), 140–142 [4.50]–[4.57].

corporate responsibility for criminal wrongs to the 'controlling mind' of the corporation: the board of directors or other senior managers, but which hived off corporate civil and criminal liabilities from its shareholders, managers and employees.[10] By the end of the 20th century, the corporation had solidified firmly in the legal imagination as a 'legal person' in this form, and this remains the dominant model in many common law jurisdictions including the United Kingdom and Australia. In the United States, corporate anthropomorphism has extended even further, conferring constitutional rights upon corporations – due process rights, like the privilege against self-incrimination, under the Fifth and Fourteenth Amendments, which includes the privilege against self-incrimination, and free speech rights under the First Amendment.[11]

This model has some serious limitations, as revealed in cases where the board members and senior executives of corporations insulate themselves from knowledge of crimes committed by employees, agents or contractors far removed from the C-suite.[12] This has prompted attempts to articulate and ascribe a more expansive, less anthropomorphic idea of corporate responsibility.[13] For example, federal criminal law in Australia, somewhat uniquely, has sought to plug this gap by imputing corporate criminal responsibility in cases where there is an 'organisational culture' that either approves of, or fails to prevent, the commission of the offences.[14] Such a model attempts to capture and address the aggregated but diffused nature of corporate

10 For the origins of the model, see *Tesco Supermarkets Ltd v. Nattrass* [1972] AC 153, 171 (Lord Reid), 180 (Lord Morris of Borth-y-Gest), 187–188 (Viscount Dilhorne), 190 (Lord Pearson). For its implementation at the Commonwealth level, see *Criminal Code Act 1995* (Cth) sch. 1 s. 12.3 ('*Criminal Code*'). For a discussion more generally, see *Australian Law Reform Commission*, (n 9) [4.58]–[4.72].

11 For a 'primer' on American law governing corporate criminal responsibility, see Miriam H. Baer, 'Corporate Criminal Law Unbounded' in Ronald F. Wright, Kay L. Levine and Russell M. Gold (eds), *The Oxford Handbook of Prosecutors and Prosecution* (Oxford University Press, 2021) 478–479. See also, e.g., *Disney v. DeSantis* (United States District Court for the Northern District of Florida, 4:23-cv-00163, commenced 26 April 2023), where the Disney corporation has sued for an alleged violation of their First Amendment rights. Cf *Environment Protection Authority v Caltex Refining* (1993) 178 CLR 477, 507–508 (Mason C.J. and Toohey J.), where the High Court did not extend the privilege against self-incrimination to corporations.

12 Australian Law Reform Commission, (n 9) 144–145 [4.66]–[4.69], citing Tahnee Woolf, 'The Criminal Code Act 1995 (Cth) — Towards a Realist Vision of Corporate Criminal Liability' (1997) 21 *Criminal Law Journal* 257, 258.

13 Reflected in the work of Bant and others, above n 4.

14 *Criminal Code* (n 10) ss 12.3(2)(c)–(d). The 'organisational culture' provisions of the Criminal Code have never been tested in the Australian courts and are also expressly excluded from application to the financial services industry by *Corporations Act 2001* (Cth) s. 769A. See also, Vicky Comino, Chapter 16 of this volume.

misconduct, which often extends beyond the individual actions and fault of those who comprise the corporation, whether they be directors, board members, employees or shareholders.

The modern law's bifocal view on the attribution of fault – whether grounded in the fault of individual corporate leaders or wider corporate organisational culture – has been met by corporate crisis management responses that will often seek to identify a number of high-profile rogue employees as responsible for any crises, and then address the totality of the issue by making superficial changes to leadership and governance that are advertised as strengthening the integrity of the company's organisational 'culture'. These responses can side-step the need to address the complex systemic drivers within firms, at both individual and organisational behavioural levels, that might determine and dictate the 'natural' rational behaviour of corporations towards particular forms of harmful misconduct.[15] Moreover, responses typically ignore complex systemic drivers that are located outside of the firm itself but which may condition a firm's operation in significant ways.[16]

The remainder of this chapter considers the corporation as a complex adaptive system. This perspective highlights the wrongdoing that may arise within various domains of influence that comprise the architecture of a system, but also considers how complex interactions between these domains can evince emergent properties that may also warrant regulatory identification and response.[17] In addition, it emphasises how such systems can become deeply path-dependent and therefore resistant to change, such that they can adapt quickly to incorporate new regulatory measures in ways that do not interrupt the systemic *status quo*. This has implications, we contend, not

15 For example, John Coffee, 'Crime and the Corporation: Making the Punishment Fit the Crime' (2022) 47(4) *Journal of Corporation Law* 964, identified these drivers as including 'criminogenic' incentive compensation schemes and key performance indicators for executives that encourage corporate leaders to place short-term profitability, extreme cost-saving and undue risk-taking above the long-term interests of shareholders, employees and consumers. He also examines how rarely penalties (both criminal and civil) impact corporate misconduct in the United States, noting that the value of the economic gains dwarfs the penalties imposed: at 970–976.

16 This includes the wider political culture in which the corporation does business, where the payment of bribes to foreign officials may simply be viewed as the 'cost of doing business': see *The King v. Jacobs Group* [2023] HCA 23, [14] (*'Jacobs'*), citing Replacement Explanatory Memorandum, Crimes Legislation Amendment (Serious and Organised Crime) Bill (No 2) 2009 (Cth) 188.

17 We are not alone in advancing the argument that a corporation is more than the sum of its parts. Such a view is fundamental to the work of Bant: see chapter 14 in this volume, and see Bant, *Systems Intentionality* (n 4). The nature of the interactional and emergent properties of a corporation is also well developed in Chapple (n 4). See further List and Pettit (n 5) ch. 3; Pettit (n 5).

only for how criminal responsibility might operate in this system, but for the form of regulatory response and intervention more generally – which is the primary focus of this chapter.[18] In the next section, the key features of complex adaptive systems are introduced and mapped to our understanding of corporate behaviour. From this platform, further consideration is given to the future role of law and regulation in responding more effectively to address corporate misconduct.

The Modern Corporation and Complex Adaptive Systems

Calling for a 'systems' approach to modern corporations is neither novel nor original.[19] Many legal scholars now acknowledge the 'systemic' nature and qualities of corporate misconduct, along with the consequential difficulty that this has for identifying and allocating corporate criminal responsibility. For example, the ability to locate and ascribe responsibility to a corporation has been thoroughly explored in the work of Bant, who considers how systems intentionality can be disclosed by the structure and functioning of the corporate 'system'. Similarly, Chapple also examines the question of a company's moral responsibility from a systems perspective, noting the interactional and emergent properties that can signify the moral capacity of a company.[20]

On the other hand, much less legal scholarship has been directed towards an examination of systems theories as a foundation for illuminating and *responding* to the systemic characteristics of corporate wrongdoing beyond the question of fault attribution alone. Similarly, despite the potential for law and regulation to shape the conditions of system development and to interrupt and redirect system trajectories, specific consideration of the role law plays within a complex system has rarely been a focus of systems theories.[21] A careful dissection of the way a corporation is structured and functions as a 'complex adaptive system' paves the way for more nuanced regulatory design and innovation that can be better tailored to respond to systemic phenomena. There is considerable potential in marrying systems theories to

18 See generally, above n 4. For practical examples, see *Bant No. 2* (n 4) 203–20; *Bant* (n 4) 251–253.

19 List and Pettit (n 5) 5–6; Aleksandra Jordanoska, 'Regulatory Enforcement Against Organizational Insiders: Interactions in the Pursuit of Individual Accountability' (2021) 15(2) *Regulation & Governance* 298, 313; see above n 4.

20 Elise Bant, Chapter 14 of this volume.

21 More has been done in this space with respect to public policy and public administration, which is sometimes analogous to legal regulation: see, e.g., Graham Room, *Complexity, Institutions and Public Policy: Agile Decision Making in a Turbulent World* (Edward Elgar, 2011). Similarly, the work of Chapple highlights the centrality of 'rules' to the operation of a system but leaves room for further examination of how rules (especially in the form of law) might be leveraged as a mechanism for reform: Chapple (n 4) 158–163.

regulatory design in this way, which first requires engagement with some of the key features of systems theories.

Systems theories have been extensively applied within many disciplines of the natural and social sciences.[22] In relation to social psychology, for example, systems theories are often utilised to help explain how a person shapes and is shaped by their environment through a complex set of integrated interactions and relationships. Development systems theory (DST) explains and categorises these interactions into three levels or domains: the micro-level (the individual themselves); the meso-level (the social contexts and relationships that have direct bearing on the individual) and the macro-level (the broader social, institutional and cultural milieux that condition an individual and their immediate social contexts).[23] The DST approach is usually depicted as a set of nested circles, with the individual at the centre and their communities and interactions surrounding them; it aims to identify the structural features of the system and the mechanisms that play out within and across its various levels that help to shape an individual's development over time.[24]

Complex adaptive systems (CAS) theories maintain a similar focus on understanding the structure of a system and the complex network or 'system properties' that emerge from the multiplicity of interactions between individual agents over time, but do not necessarily focus on human development as a core output of this activity. Instead, CAS theories are interested in understanding the behaviour of *the system* itself. In its application to modern corporations, therefore, a CAS-informed approach is less concerned with how systems shape the development of individual actors (e.g., directors, officers or employees of a corporation), and instead invites a more focused examination of the corporation's systemic characteristics and trajectories over time.[25] *Temporality* is an important additional dimension of many systems theories, highlighting how interactions across a system can develop and solidify into certain pathways or trajectories that become increasingly ingrained and difficult to disrupt. Life course criminology, for example, considers how a

22 Urie Bronfenbrenner, 'Environments in Developmental Perspectives: Theoretical and Operational Models' in Sarah L. Friedman and Theodore D. Wachs (eds), *Measuring Environment Across the Life Span: Emerging Methods and Concepts* (American Psychological Association, 1999) 3; Richard M. Lerner and Domini R. Castellino, 'Contemporary Developmental Theory and Adolescence: Developmental Systems and Applied Developmental Science' (2002) 31 *Journal of Adolescent Health* 122.

23 Urie Bronfenbrenner, 'The Ecology of Cognitive Development: Research Models and Fugitive Findings' in Robert H. Wozniak and Kurt W. Fischer (eds), *Development in Context* (Psychology Press, 1st ed., 1993) 3, 15, 20, 24.

24 See, e.g., Lerner and Castellino (n 22) 127.

25 JB Ruhl, 'Law's Complexity: A Primer' (2008) 24 *Georgia State University Law Review* 885, 894; Room (n 28); Esther Thelen and Linda B. Smith, 'Dynamic Systems Theories' in William Damon and Richard M. Lerner (eds), *Handbook of Child Psychology* (John Wiley and Sons, 6th ed., 2006) 258.

person's development is shaped by interactions over time that, in turn, set up life course trajectories that can become less amenable to change or redirection the more embedded they become. This makes it harder to interrupt long-term negative trajectories, but also makes it less likely that positive trajectories can be easily derailed.[26] A life course perspective, therefore, seeks to identify the mechanisms and interactions that occur within a person's developmental system that become key to their trajectories so as to better understand and predict life course pathways and to potentially interrupt and redirect negative trajectories.

Moreover, in addition to examining the architecture of a system and how it functions over time, a CAS approach draws attention to the issue of *complexity* and places emphasis on the *adaptive* nature of complex systems. So, while both DST and CAS theories place emphasis on the individual and the environment and emphasise the way that interactions and feedback between these domains shape development over time (of the individual or the system itself), some additional concepts emerge from CAS theories that are usefully applied to corporations and corporate wrongdoing. In particular, a CAS approach highlights the specific way that complex systems have *emergent* qualities.[27] A system is complex and adaptive because of its non-linear or emergent properties that are 'more than the sum of its parts' and which cannot be ascribed fully to a single interactional relationship alone. Ruhl explains that '[b]ecause emergent properties are the system-wide product of many such local interaction rules, it is not possible to describe emergent properties simply by describing the interaction rules'.[28] In addition, a CAS approach highlights the *stable disequilibrium* of any complex system, where change is a constant feature of the system produced as individual actors constantly shape and reshape their behaviours in response to changes within the system. The complexity inherent within these systems suggests that the way any new initiative will play out within it is inherently *uncertain* and will likely, itself, be consumed into the system architecture. Ruhl concludes that complex adaptive systems:

> ... are not normatively good or bad—we impute those subjective judgements on them—and there is no way to extract the "bad" parts from a system without affecting what remains *unpredictably*. ... Often we do in fact solve the problem the targeted part was causing, but because that part was connected to other parts, some of which we valued as "good," we

26 See, e.g., Terrie Moffitt et al., 'Childhood-onset versus Adolescent-onset Antisocial Conduct Problems in Males: Natural History from Ages 3 to 18 Years' (1996) 8 *Development and Psychopathology* 399.

27 See above n 25.

28 Ibid. 894.

> cannot cut off the feedback through the network that regulating the "bad" part is bound to prompt.[29]

The way that systems adapt to remain stable even though they are subject to this constant process of change is a key insight into the behaviour of corporations.[30] Despite constant change being a feature of CAS, there is a strong tendency towards *path dependence,* which can make some systems surprisingly resilient and resistant to change.[31] The ongoing inscription of patterned behaviours over time creates deep pathways that tend to keep future actions confined to these predictable routes. For this reason, small-scale 'tinkering' is likely to be ineffective, which invites a more nuanced examination of how long-term sustained change might be achieved within such a system. A complex adaptive system can be pushed beyond this state of stable disequilibrium such that a *field change* occurs, where there is a paradigmatic shift in the architecture and therefore functioning of the system. This can be caused by a significant 'knifing off' event but may also be the product of the accumulation of small variations over time that eventually set off a cascading effect within and across the entire system.

These features of CAS can help shape our understanding of how best to intervene to respond to corporate misconduct. Understanding the adaptive capability of the modern corporation helps us to understand why legal and regulatory controls may fail to deter corporate wrongdoing; why corporate compliance remains challenging; and why the aspirations of practitioners, regulators and policymakers to 'shift corporate cultures' remain unfulfilled. Framing corporate wrongdoing as 'systemic' in the sense conveyed by CAS allows for a more skilled dissection to take place to locate and address misconduct. Applying a CAS perspective to the modern corporation encourages regulatory design that focuses attention on the architecture of the system (including an examination of wrongdoing at each level and the interactions occurring within and between them that sustain this) but at the same time considers the system's emergent properties and its long-term trajectory (which demonstrates both path-dependency and resistance to change). In the 'Corporate Misconduct within Complex Adaptive Systems: Reframing Responsive Regulation' section, we will consider how a CAS-informed approach can reframe responsive regulation to incorporate these systemic perspectives, and using the modern corporation as an example, demonstrate how CAS theories assist our understanding of and responses to corporate misconduct across micro-, meso- and macro-levels.

29 Ibid. 907.

30 Chapple (n 4) 64, taking inspiration from Robert Nozick, considers how corporations reflect but also *demand* the stable patterns of individual behaviours.

31 Ruhl (n 25) 895–896.

Corporate Misconduct within Complex Adaptive Systems: Reframing Responsive Regulation

A CAS-informed approach to understanding and responding to corporate misconduct suggests that legal and regulatory responses need to be embedded across multiple levels in different ways. A systems approach is not a 'zero-sum' game of criminalisation versus regulation; punishment versus prevention; fault versus no-fault liability; or individual versus corporate liability. Rather, the systems approach outlined above demands a more nuanced and adaptive approach, which we believe can be used to reframe a model of responsive regulation (RR).[32] RR is often represented by the visual heuristic of an enforcement pyramid, within which the first and predominant focus of regulatory activity is located at the base or foundation of the pyramid: 'persuasion' by prevention and education. In the event of initial non-compliance, the pyramid recommends the taking of more coercive measures, with its sharp but infrequently used apex reserved for punitive measures of 'last resort'. RR provides regulators with a wide and flexible range of options in terms of regulatory responses, allowing them to 'speak softly [while] carry[ing] big sticks'.[33]

The primary focus at the base of the pyramid on 'softer' measures of prevention and education does not mean that the 'crimes of the powerful' should not be targeted for tougher punishment. While rejecting 'zero tolerance' policies generally, regulatory scholars do recognise that exemplary prosecution and punishment of serious white-collar crime may be needed as measures of first rather than last resort.[34] Condoning coercive responses, however, does not legitimate the stigmatic shaming of white-collar criminals but is instead understood as a key mechanism in effective regulation.[35] Ultimately, criminalisation is reserved as a matter of last resort, for compliance failures which are the most serious, in terms of both culpability and harm. The moral

32 John Braithwaite, 'Convergence in Models of Regulatory Strategy' (1990) 2 *Current Issues in Criminal Justice* 59.

33 Ibid. 59. For a range of examples of the pyramid see Peter Mascini, 'Why Was the Enforcement Pyramid so Influential? And What Price Was Paid?' (2013) 7 *Regulation and Governance* 48. These themes are explored in Simon Bronitt, 'Regulatory Bargaining in The Shadows of Preventive Justice: Deferred Prosecution Agreements' in Tamara Tulich et al. (eds), *Regulating Preventive Justice: Principle, Policy and Paradox* (Routledge, 2017) 211.

34 See John Braithwaite and Peter Drahos, 'Zero Tolerance, Naming and Shaming: Is There a Case for It with Crimes of the Powerful' (2002) 35(3) *Australian and New Zealand Journal of Criminology* 269. This model of shame is not stigmatic but restorative: see John Braithwaite, *Crime, Shame and Reintegration* (Cambridge University Press, 1989) 63.

35 Ibid. The risk of impunity for corporate offenders who are considered 'Too Big To Gaol' has also given rise to administrative and statutory schemes governing 'deferred prosecution agreements' in the United States and United Kingdom: see e.g., Bronitt (n 33); Liz Campbell, 'Revisiting and Re-Situating Deferred Prosecution Agreements in Australia: Lessons in England and Wales' (2021) 43(2) *Sydney Law Review* 187.

force of criminal punishment should not be squandered on low-level minor regulatory failures, which would be more appropriately managed through civil and administrative measures.

A CAS-informed approach builds on the innovative 'regulatory mix' of RR, though reconfigures regulatory interventions to accommodate the adaptive and systemic qualities of corporations outlined above. This means that multiple interventions within the enforcement pyramid may occur both simultaneously and systematically, to address different levels of the corporate system and address the interactions between them. Regulators would need to map the vulnerability to wrongdoing within corporations across multiple levels (asking 'where, when, why and how?' questions), and then determine the level and intensity of intervention required within the enforcement pyramid as they apply to *each* dynamic interaction. Moreover, CAS focuses regulatory attention on the emergent properties of the system *as a whole,* seeking to embed regulatory responses that address the adaptive tendencies of the system to capture and neutralise destabilising change. In sum, a CAS-informed approach to corporate wrongdoing requires regulatory responses that are:

- *Tailored to the right level(s) of the system architecture for best effect.* Adopting the foundational principle of RR, this would require the deployment of the punitive options within the regulatory pyramid to the most 'infected' levels of corporate interactions.
- *Designed to affect interactions between levels.* This would require regulatory response to rarely be targeted at just one level, but to instead consider what different and additional responses may be needed elsewhere. For example, a CAS response would employ punitive measures against an individual at the micro-level while simultaneously employing additional preventative and educative measures at the meso- and macro-levels (or vice versa).
- *Responsive to emergent properties.* A CAS approach would be alert to the fact that wrongdoing may be an 'emergent' property of the system that might not be easily attributable to a specific level of the system alone. This would require consideration of the additional measures that may be required to address wrongdoing that is 'more than the sum of its parts'.
- *Tailored to address path dependency and adaptation possibilities.* Finally, a CAS approach would anticipate and address the system's tendency to revert to its 'natural' state beyond any particular regulatory action or event. This might include consideration of how best to effect a *field change* (e.g., through a 'knifing off' event, or by sustained cascading interactions), but must at least consider what follow-up actions or measures are required to ensure that path dependency remains disrupted and new trajectories become embedded.

To explain each of these four aspects in more detail, we provide examples of existing regulatory mechanisms that might be tailored to fit this model at various levels. The chapter then concludes with some final comments about the inherent challenges of regulating corporations as complex adaptive systems, and the limits of law in this context.

Tailoring a Regulatory Response to the Right Level(s) of the System Architecture for Best Effect

Systems theories often structure a system into various levels, commonly distinguishing between the micro-, meso- and macro-levels. Paying attention to the structure and functions of each level is a starting point for understanding the architecture and operation of the system as a whole, as the system-wide interactions are often 'kick-started' and perpetuated by intra-level phenomena. In terms of regulatory response, therefore, identifying and effectively responding to the key drivers and risks for corporate misconduct within each level is a powerful step in addressing systemic wrongdoing. Many existing regulatory and legal mechanisms, including the criminal law, are already 'fit for purpose' to achieve intra-level responses, and could be employed to address this first step as part of a strategic systemic regulatory design. Some examples of intra-level wrongdoing and associated regulatory response are provided here, moving through the micro-, meso- and macro-levels in turn.

(i) Micro-Level Systems: Responding to the Problem of Individual 'Bad Actors'

As noted above, although CAS focuses on system-level phenomena, it does not neglect the important role played by individual actors operating within it. Indeed, the heterogeneity of individuals who comprise the body corporate is a key variable that can have an important effect on the way that any system functions.[36] Individuals within corporations can embody virtuous approaches to compliance, operating as guardians or sentinels that promote a compliant and ethical culture within the corporation.[37] This suggests that a corporate system that attracts, embeds, ignores, promotes or incentivises 'bad actors' or toxic personalities will ultimately be shaped by those persons' interactions with other actors, which will solidify a particular corporate 'culture' and trajectory.[38]

36 List and Pettit (n 5) ch. 9.

37 For an example, see Aleksandra Jordanoska (n 19) 298, in which the author develops an integrated tripartite framework that differentiates between individual-firm, regulator-individual, and regulator-firm interactions to capture the complexity of enforcement proceedings against individuals. See also Sally Simpson et al., 'Corporate Crime Deterrence: A Systematic Review' (2014) 10(1) *Campbell Systematic Reviews* 1, 39.

38 For example, in *Rape Law in Context* (Federation Press, 2018) ch. 9, Patricia Easteal and Simon Bronitt examine the industry-wide use of civil settlements and non-disclosure

The criminal law is often considered the 'go-to' tool at the micro-level, for managing the risk and wrongdoing caused by 'bad actors'. It is suggested that perpetrators and those enablers who conspire, aid and abet 'bad actors' should be held accountable by applying ordinary offences and criminal law doctrines. However, there is little evidence that prosecutions are vigorously – or ever – pursued: the reticence in applying the criminal law to individual wrongdoing within corporations arises for several reasons, not least that white-collar defendants are well-resourced and highly motivated to challenge every step of the criminal investigation and proceedings. This explains why the regulatory focus at the micro-level has often been on applying civil rather than criminal penalties against those individuals responsible for the compliance failures. Apart from civil and criminal action against individuals, there is a wide range of internal policies, procedures and practices that seeks to prevent individual misconduct within a corporation. The type of internal response depends on the underlying misconduct, which spans sexual harassment, abuse and bullying to engaging in unethical or corrupt business practices. Internal compliance processes are typically supported by mandatory training, periodic audits and even the redesign of employee incentive schemes to disincentivise non-compliance. For example, Coffee has suggested that corporate wrongdoing may be minimised by new approaches to remuneration, proposing that corporations: place limits on what can be the excessive incentive remuneration of executives through shares linked to profitability; and widen KPIs to include other indicators of personal achievement (such as customer satisfaction or environmental, social, and governance (ESG) progress).[39]

(ii) Meso-Level Systems: Responding to Bad Corporate 'Cultures'?

Corporate misconduct at the meso-level becomes more complex than the micro-level. At this level, intra-level interactions occur between more complex sets of networked individuals and entities. In a small company, these interactions might be between or across business units or teams, but in larger companies they might comprise complex corporate arrangements such as holding, parent or subsidiary companies which span jurisdictional or even international borders. Different kinds of wrongdoing or harms may arise from these interactions, to which it can be more difficult to attach corporate responsibility, let alone prosecute as crimes.

Moreover, bidirectional interactions between the micro- and meso-levels mean that the structure and functioning of the meso-level can facilitate or amplify the form and nature of misconduct at the micro-level. This can be

agreements in the entertainment industry, in response to individual misconduct that prima facie constituted serious criminal offences.

39 Coffee (n 15) 977–981.

understood as one example of *emergence*, where the wrongdoing is no longer directly attributable to a specific interaction alone.[40] For example, it is sometimes suggested that the individual wrongdoing of senior corporate leaders, while egregious and harmful, sits outside the legitimate core business of the company – in other words, the misconduct is *ultra vires,* standing outside the true scope of their employment or office. This is typically claimed in cases involving cases of sexual abuse or harassment by corporate leaders or in cases involving large-scale deaths or environmental harm. However, this displacement of responsibility is rarely plausible; the nature of an individual's criminality *is* a matter of corporate criminal responsibility when other corporate leaders and senior managers are aware of their behaviours and of the risk of harm, but do nothing, thereby enabling the crimes to continue. This is doubly true in cases where management might seek to 'cover up' individual crimes by, for example, using civil settlements and non-disclosure agreements (NDAs).[41]

At this level, large national or multinational corporations are also apt to become highly adaptive systems, embedding active resistance against regulatory responses into their standard business processes through their proactive management of 'legal risk'.[42] For example, companies may 'hive off' operations to quell the impact of bankruptcies or civil penalties or to ensure that certain groups are insulated from knowledge about the actions of other entities; even if regulatory attention is directed towards one part of the business, other parts can continue to engage in misconduct undisturbed.[43] Corporations might even locate their more 'risky businesses' in jurisdictions with comparatively lax regulatory standards or where enforcement agencies are weak or non-existent.

Legal scholars have grappled with the problem of applying the criminal law to this meso-level and have proposed a range of new legal mechanisms that attempt to respond more effectively to the intra- and inter-level complexity described above.[44] Similarly, recognition of the challenge of mounting prosecutions in some corporate cases of misconduct has given birth to some new regulatory tools: equity fines and deferred prosecution agreements (DPAs) are two examples where enforcement is redirected to changing 'corporate cultures' over time, rather than merely punishing individuals for past wrongs.[45] Moreover, the pathbreaking reforms to corporate criminal

40 Chapple (n 4).

41 See further discussion in Patricia Easteal and Simon Bronitt (n 38) ch. 9.

42 See above n 15.

43 See, e.g., Penny Crofts and Honni van Rijswijk, 'A Case Study of State-Corporate Crime: Crown Resorts' (2023) 35(1) *Current Issues in Criminal Justice* 139.

44 See, e.g., the work of Bant and Comino throughout this volume and elsewhere (above n 4). See also Meredith Edelman, 'Responsive Law and the Problem of Corporate Crime' (2022) 38(1) *Australian Journal of Corporate Law* 46.

45 The use of the 'equity' fine would frame the penalty in terms of a direction by the court to issue shares, to be placed in a trust fund, to compensate those harmed by the corporate

responsibility in the federal *Criminal Code* can be viewed as reform that sought to foreground defective 'corporate culture'.[46] Although those measures in practice have proved difficult to apply, they stand as an innovative attempt to identify the practices and behaviours that sit within this level of corporate blameworthiness, and recognise how such 'culture' may operate to promote and amplify individual wrongdoing at the micro-level. These kinds of regulatory innovations and law reforms are reflections of a more *systemic* understanding of corporate misconduct and the need for an equally sophisticated regulatory response to it.

(iii) Macro-level System: Rethinking Modern Business Ventures and the End of Corporate Empires?

Finally, adopting a macro-level lens reveals how certain types of harmful corporate behaviour – due to interactions with the constraints of existing economic, political, social and systems – can become 'baked into' a particular corporate mission. In the corporate context, this might draw particular attention to the architecture and functioning of capitalism and market economies, in which the mandate of the modern corporation is conceived, in traditional terms, as the unrelenting pursuit of profit-maximisation for shareholders.[47] Examination of how the modern corporation 'fits' within or adapts to changing economic, political and social landscapes, and the identification of interactions of significance at this level, is pivotal to understanding interactions at the meso- and micro-levels. Understanding changes at the macro-level can help to explain why corporations might take a particular form and/or pursue a specific agenda at a particular time and place, acting with wanton disregard for the 'evils' they may cause such as irreversible damage to the environment and cultural heritage.[48] This might permeate to the micro-level as well, helping to illuminate why some 'toxic' senior leaders may be protected by the

misconduct: Coffee (n 15) 981–983. The rationales of DPAs are explored in Simon Bronitt, 'Deferred Prosecution Agreements: Negotiating Punishment Before Conviction?' in Victoria Colvin and Philip Stenning (eds), *The Evolving Role of the Public Prosecutor* (Routledge, 2019) 45

46 The *Criminal Code* extends corporate criminal responsibility to include organisational blameworthiness: *Criminal Code* ss. 12.3(2)(c), (d).

47 Today, 'good' corporations extend their mission to include a wider suite of ESG and CSR objectives. Bakan expresses doubt whether such transformation is genuine, noting that the pathological pursuit of profit remains 'baked into' the corporate operating model: Bakan, *The New Corporation* (n 2) 9–11.

48 See, e.g., the 'Dieselgate' emissions scandal in 2015: Graham Ruddick, 'VW Admits Emissions Scandal was Caused by "Whole Chain" Of Failures', *The Guardian* (online, 10 December 2015) https://www.theguardian.com/business/2015/dec/10/volkswagen-emissions-scandal-systematic-failures-hans-dieter-potsch.

corporation as their 'effectiveness' at the macro-level outweighs their bad behaviour at the micro-level.

Designing regulatory responses that address macro-level influences and interactions is perhaps the most significant challenge faced by law and regulation, and often bleeds into the domain of international relations, political science and political economy.[49] The macro-level perspective reveals the possibility of reimagining global corporations in terms of a new mission, one which extends beyond delivering economic benefits (whether to markets, shareholders or workers) to include protecting human rights, First Nations peoples and the environment. The macro-level can help to explain corporate wrongdoing, but perhaps more importantly, it can prompt regulatory action to be designed to act as a counterforce to the centrifugal power of these macro-level influences. Regulatory action may also be designed as a starting point, or even 'lightning rod', that prompts broader actions within governments and society at the international as well as a domestic level – to address these issues.[50]

Understanding the system as a whole: designing regulation to address the relevant interactions between the levels, and to address emergent properties:

A CAS approach invites an examination of corporate wrongdoing within each level in order to understand the system's architecture and the way that it functions and interacts with other levels of the system. These interactions give rise to a complex system's *emergent* properties. By mapping different levels of the system and beginning to understand the interactions that occur within and across the levels, it is also possible to begin to understand the structure and function of the system *as a whole*. Importantly, this process of dissection allows for regulatory action at any level to be designed with an appreciation of the whole system.

Adopting the CAS approach means that any regulatory response would never solely target one level alone but would instead consider what different and additional responses may be needed elsewhere to disrupt and redirect intra-level interactions. At present, actions may be taken by different agencies and regulators, applying a wide diversity of norms (criminal, civil or administrative) and aiming at different levels of a system, which frequently leads to uncoordinated and ineffective outcomes. Moreover, it is often the case that those most harmed by corporate wrongdoing – innocent shareholders, employees and consumers – are simply 'left out of the bargain', and no

49 For an excellent study, see John Braithwaite and Peter Drahos, *Global Business Regulation* (Cambridge University Press, 2000). See also James Martel, Chapter 1 of this volume.

50 The '#MeToo' movement is an example of how legal action fits into and amplifies broader social concerns and highlights the interactive nature of this kind of legal response. See Stephen Bottomley and Simon Bronitt, *Law in Context* (Federation Press, 5th ed., forthcoming), ch. 4, for further discussion of this movement.

systemic change results despite sometimes sustained, costly and time-consuming regulatory activity. A CAS-informed approach requires coherence in regulatory response, drawing on the full range of criminal, civil and administrative measures and employing these tools in a coordinated manner, not only within a level or to target a specific incident – but across the system.

Tailoring Regulatory Responses to Address Path-Dependency and Adaptation Possibilities

Finally, understanding the features of CAS, such as path-dependency, resistance and resilience, help us to better understand and account for the seeming impunity of corporations, especially their seemingly 'supernatural' ability to regenerate or revert to their 'natural' state following concerted regulatory action taken against them. This adaptive capability of corporations draws attention to the way that legacies of intra- and inter-level interactions *over time* set up pathways or trajectories for corporations that can become deeply embedded, such that they can become difficult to dislodge or redirect.[51] An awareness of the phenomenon of *path-dependency* and the way that this makes a system resistant and resilient to change allows some additional questions to be considered when reframing RR. For example, some examination of the history and duration of the misconduct might be warranted, not only because it might indicate the 'seriousness' of misbehaviour but also because it likely signals the need for powerful and sustained action to counteract the system's tendency to path-dependency which causes behavioural relapse in the future. A CAS framework also directs more critical attention to post-scandal corporate reform, in order to determine whether the restructuring and rebranding is done in good faith, producing systemic and lasting reform, or an insincere, even cynical strategy, to revalue the brand through a thin veneer of 'greenwashing' or integrity initiatives, which do little to transform problematic 'business as usual' practices.[52]

A CAS-informed approach provides considerable scope to continue to develop a more sophisticated understanding of how change can occur (or be induced) within corporations, by asking whether and how any legal or regulatory action might itself provoke the necessary *field change* required to address entrenched patterns and cultures of corporate misconduct. Field changes can fundamentally restructure the architecture and functioning of the system, such that it is no longer recognisable as the same system it was originally.[53] This kind of event can be the product of the cascading effect of

51 Ruhl (n 25) 895–896.

52 Bakan, *The New Corporation* (n 2) 9–11, provides a sceptical view of many of these corporate motives.

53 Ruhl (n 25) 904.

multiple interactions across all levels of the system that eventually put too much pressure on the system's ability to maintain a state of *stable disequilibrium*. Coordinated multi-level regulatory action, sustained for the long-term, may be a potential way to achieve this. Alternatively, field changes may be produced by a major 'knifing off' event, which suddenly and cataclysmically disrupts the system's ability to function as per the status quo. The imposition of significant punitive action may have the potential to act in this way, but any action would need to be strong enough to counteract powerful forces operating particularly at the macro-level. It is important to consider that too significant a 'knifing off' event could even spell the death of modern corporations altogether (at least in their present iterations), which may have unintended consequences for the individual actors, societies and global economies that depend upon them.

Conclusion

Despite ongoing efforts to consider how law can be used to address the systemic problems of corporate misconduct, the current regulatory approaches are a mishmash: veering between calls to prosecute or pursue individual bad actors (the 'rotten apples') on the one hand, and evil corporations with their criminogenic cultures (the 'rotten barrels') on the other hand. This lack of coherence in regulatory terms has produced a smorgasbord of responses: the promotion of new ethical standards (CSR), civil suits and class actions about directors, tougher penalties (both civil and criminal) including equity fines and DPAs. Each of these responses tends to adopt, implicitly if not explicitly, one of the binary models highlighted previously (individual versus corporate; good versus evil; regulation versus deregulation; legal versus ethical norms; civil versus criminal). These binaries limit current regulatory design, which does not effectively account for the systemic complexity of the modern corporation, especially the way that corporations can adapt to and resist regulatory action. This adaptive character leads regulatory and law enforcement agencies to seek and resort to the use of more coercive powers – but periods of tough enforcement are rarely long-lasting and are typically followed by periods of regulatory pragmatism and compromise within the corporate community. Corporations respond adaptively to these cycles, adopting a strategic management approach to 'legal risk' (a compliance environment to be managed and mitigated), which conceals the real systemic causes of corporate misconduct and fails to bring about meaningful change for the future.

The ability of a CAS-informed approach to identify the key aspects of structure and function is its key strength, since it draws attention to the historical, emergent and interactive properties of the modern corporation (as an entity and system) while also keeping in focus the role of individual actors in shaping and re-shaping them over time. This supports the idea of corporate misconduct being 'systemic' which, in turn, must be regulated 'systemically'.

In addition to the identification of the location of corporate misconduct, and its *emergent* characteristics, a CAS approach also explains the current impunity of corporations: path-dependence, resistance and resilience work together to maintain the status quo, subvert attempts to excise wrongdoing and thwart reform efforts.

A CAS-informed approach does not displace the smorgasbord of regulatory responses envisaged by the architects of responsive regulation. Rather, it envisages the non-hierarchical but strategic ordering of those responses, enabling a range of responses across the different tiers of the pyramid, and adding an additional dimension of *time* to ensure that interventions are appropriately sustained. The guide for selection is informed by systems theories – a systemic approach that is cognisant of the micro-, meso- and macro-levels in which corporate misconduct exists. A CAS approach demands greater creativity in regulatory design, underpinned by consideration of how law – from 'soft' law to civil and criminal law measures – might be most strategically employed to shape or respond to interactions and relationships both within and across levels in an integrated way. It also calls for regulatory design that considers, at the macro-level, how the legal system constitutes corporations in the first place, and whether the 'pathological pursuit of profit' for 21st-century corporations continues to remain 'fit for purpose'. Even if calls for macro-level transformations (such as reframing of our global liberal economic order) are naïvely Utopian, a CAS-informed model may assist regulators and lawmakers in recognising the emergent and path-dependent characteristics that produce and sustain misconduct within corporations, so as to determine which future reforms are most likely to be effective.

Chapter 16

'Corporate Culture' is *The* Problem, but Can It Be Regulated?

Vicky Comino

Introduction

Consistent with the theme of this volume, 'Evil Corporations', is the growing realisation by regulators and policymakers worldwide that, regardless of how comprehensive the legal rules and how significant the penalties might be, they 'cannot turn a company whose soul is black into a "good sport" who plays by the rules'.[1] Indeed, the conduct that led to the Global Financial Crisis (GFC) and the succession of corporate and financial scandals post-GFC, both overseas (e.g., rate-rigging in the London Interbank Offered Rate (LIBOR))[2] and in Australia (e.g., by our banks exposed during the course of the public hearings of the recent Royal Commission into Misconduct in the Banking, Superannuation and Financial Services Industry (Hayne Royal Commission)),[3] occurred even though laws and rules were in place that had been created to prevent such wrongdoing.

This begs the question of when global banks manipulated LIBOR or Australian banks engaged in dishonest practices (e.g., charged 'fees-for-no-service', including to the dead)[4] and failed to comply with money laundering laws,[5] did they know that what they were doing amounted to misconduct? In

1 See Ross Grantham, *The Law and Practice of Corporate Governance* (2nd ed.) (LexisNexis, 2022) 486 (citing Royal Commission into Misconduct in the Banking, Superannuation and Financial Services Industry (Interim Report, 2018) Vol. 1, xx, 290 (Hayne Royal Commission Interim Report)).

2 This scandal concerned international banks (e.g., Barclays and UBS) colluding with each other to manipulate global interest rates and make huge profits from trades.

3 The Hayne Royal Commission, presided over by The Hon Kenneth Hayne AC KC, released its interim findings in September 2018: Hayne Royal Commission Interim Report (n 1) and a Final Report in February 2019: Royal Commission into Misconduct in the Banking, Superannuation and Financial Services Industry (Final Report, 2019) Vol. 1 (Hayne Royal Commission Final Report).

4 See further below (n 43).

5 Both the Commonwealth Bank of Australia (CBA) and Westpac Banking Corporation (Westpac) breached anti-money laundering and counter-terrorism financing (AML/CTF) laws, which led to headline cases by Australia's financial intelligence watchdog, the Australian

DOI: 10.4324/9781003402534-21

the case of Australian banks, Commissioner Hayne accepted that it cannot be said that they did not know this.[6] He found that wrongful and unethical conduct took place despite the rules because the 'culture' within these corporations/organisations[7] – one of unrestrained 'greed' and an overly short-termist focus on profit and remuneration systems that rewarded sales above all else, eclipsing regard for the law and for customers – licenced it.[8] The same is arguably true of casino operators, Crown Resorts (Crown) and The Star Entertainment Group (Star), in relation to money laundering,[9] given the link between misconduct and defective culture identified in the series of inquiries held into their 'suitability' to hold casino licences in the various Australian states[10] in which they operate.[11]

'Culture', therefore, is *the* problem or more colourfully put, 'the new black'.[12] As such, it is unsurprising that the resounding message for regulators – especially in the banking and finance sector in the aftermath of the GFC and scandals since – has been to embrace the need to reconceptualise the nature of regulation to not just focus on the regulatory rules, but also

Transaction Reports and Analysis Centre (AUSTRAC), utilising and securing large civil penalties: see *Chief Executive Officer of Australian Transaction Reports and Analysis Centre v. Commonwealth Bank of Australia Ltd* [2018] FCA 930 (*CBA case*) (A$700 million); *Chief Executive Officer of Australian Transaction Reports and Analysis Centre v. Westpac Banking Corporation* [2020] FCA 1538 ($1.3 billion).

6 Hayne Royal Commission Final Report (n 3) 1–2, 333–334.

7 This chapter will use the terms 'corporation' and 'organisation' interchangeably. It will also treat the terms 'corporate culture' and 'organisational culture' as synonymous.

8 Hayne Royal Commission, Interim Report (n 1) Executive summary, xix, 301; Hayne Royal Commission Final Report (n 3) 1–2, 401.

9 *Chief Executive Officer of Australian Transaction Reports and Analysis Centre v. Crown Melbourne Limited and Anor* [2023] FCA 782, resulting in a A$450 million penalty. Recently, civil penalty proceedings were also instigated against the directors of Star for breach of their duties alleging that they failed to give sufficient focus to the risk of money laundering and criminal associations: ASIC, 'ASIC Launches Proceedings Against 11 Current and Former Star Entertainment Directors and Officers' (Media Release 22–351, 13 December 2022).

10 Regulatory control of casinos in Australia takes place under state legislation specific to casinos via a licencing system with state regulators having prime responsibility for regulating casinos.

11 See, e.g., State of NSW, *Inquiry into the Barangaroo Restricted Gaming Facility Granted to Crown Sydney Gaming Pty Limited Pursuant to Section 143 of the Casino Control Act 1992 (NSW)* (Final Report, 1 February 2021, 298 (Bergin Inquiry). In finding that Crown was *not* a 'suitable person' to operate a casino at Barangaroo (Sydney) because of money laundering at existing Crown casinos in Melbourne and Perth, links with organised crime and breaching Chinese laws against gambling, Crown's culture was described as one that avidly pursued profit to the detriment of everything else, including compliance with the law.

12 See Vicky Comino, 'Corporate Culture is the "New Black" – its Possibilities and Limits as a Regulatory Mechanism for Corporations and Financial Institutions' (2020) 44 *University of New South Wales Law Journal* 295.

to tackle the cultural problems *within* corporations themselves to prevent future wrongdoing.[13] Focusing on Australia, this has led to some major regulatory developments, such as our corporate and financial services regulator, the Australian Securities and Investments Commission (ASIC),[14] assigning dedicated staff to the 'Big Four' banks and Australian Mutual Provident (AMP) Limited to monitor their governance and compliance practices in what became known as the Close and Continuous Monitoring Programme (CCM Programme).[15] Significantly, Australia has also been a leader in regulatory innovation in efforts to use 'corporate culture' as a legal mechanism in criminal prosecutions, with a 'culture-based' model for determining corporate intentionality available since the introduction of the *Criminal Code Act 1995* (Cth) (Criminal Code).

Despite the prominence of 'corporate culture' in the Australian regulatory landscape, this chapter will explore whether 'corporate culture' can in fact be used as a regulatory device to encourage compliance in corporations. The chapter first considers whether the inherent vagueness of the expression 'corporate culture' and its definitional elusiveness make it difficult to regulate, or whether the definition of 'corporate culture' found in the Criminal Code (s. 12.3(6)) provides possibilities for using it both as a legal mechanism in criminal prosecutions, and as a regulatory tool. Even though the chapter proceeds to discuss the difficulties which persist in attempts to use 'corporate culture' as a regulatory measure – noting also that regulators are themselves beset by problems, such as falling victim to 'regulatory capture' – it will be argued that it *is* possible for 'corporate culture' to be used as a regulatory device to foster a healthy culture and/or correct the corporate conscience of a formerly wrongdoing corporation. The example given is the apparent success story of the Commonwealth Bank of Australia (CBA).[16]

13 See, e.g., Hector Sants, 'UK Financial Regulation: After the Crisis' (Speech, London, 12 March 2010).

14 The Australian Prudential Regulatory Authority (APRA) is the second 'peak' in financial regulation under our current 'twin peaks' regulatory architecture. It separates responsibility for corporate and market conduct and consumer protection regulation to ASIC from prudential regulation and supervision, the province of APRA.

15 For an assessment of this Programme, which began in October 2018 when the Hayne Royal Commission was still in progress and other culture-focused techniques: see Vicky Comino, '"Culture" Is Key – An Analysis of Culture-focused Techniques and Tools in the Regulation of Corporations and Financial Institutions' (2021) 49 *Australian Business Law Review* 6, 13-5; David Wishart and Ann Wardrop, 'What Can the Banking Royal Commission Achieve: Regulating for Good Corporate Culture?' (2018) 43 *Alternate Law Journal* 81. Note also ASX Corporate Governance Council, *Corporate Governance Principles and Recommendations* (4th edition, February 2019) Principle 3. It recommends that a listed entity should instil a culture of acting 'lawfully, ethically and responsibly'.

16 See discussion below (nn 27–31, 69–75, 78–80).

Vagueness and Definitional Issues: An Obstacle, or Are There Possibilities for the Use of 'Corporate Culture' as a Regulatory Mechanism?

Despite its frequent use, often the first obstacle raised in regulatory conversations about 'culture' is the claim that the 'vague' nature of the concept and definitional issues render it hard to regulate, as well as utilise as a legal tool in criminal prosecutions.[17] There is no single, settled definition of 'culture' or 'corporate culture'. In fact, definitions of these terms differ significantly.[18]

A useful definition suggested by ASIC, endorsing the oft-quoted definition of 'corporate culture' put forward by eminent organisational psychologist, Edgar Schein,[19] is that 'culture' is 'a set of shared values or assumptions'.[20] More useful, however, in the context of attempting to use corporate culture as a regulatory mechanism to deal with flawed cultures within corporations and encourage compliance, ASIC has also described it as 'the internal controls (i.e., policies, rules, courses of conduct, practices or attitudes) within a firm which shape its behaviour and mindset',[21] which is the way 'corporate culture' is defined in the Criminal Code for the purposes of attributing intention to a corporation for criminal liability.[22]

In some previous work, notwithstanding arguments that prosecutorial reluctance for proving corporate criminal liability based on cultural deficiency offered by Part 2.5 of the Criminal Code is due to evidential difficulties associated with proving poor culture,[23] I contended that it is possible to bring legal action and pursue criminal liability under this model.[24] I argued

17 See, e.g., John Colvin and James Argent, 'Corporate and Personal Liability for 'Culture' in Corporations?' (2016) 34 *Company & Securities Law Journal* 30, 36.

18 Ibid.

19 See Edgar Schein, *Organizational Culture and Leadership* (Jossey-Bass, 2010) 18.

20 See John Price, 'Culture, Conduct and the Bottom Line: A Key Aspect of Good Governance is Getting the Culture Right' *The Company Director* (September 2015).

21 Greg Tanzer, 'The Importance of Culture to Improving Conduct within the Financial Industry' (Speech to Thomson Reuters Third Australian Regulatory Summit, Sydney, 27 May 2015) 2.

22 See Criminal Code, s. 12.3(6). It defines 'corporate culture' as 'an attitude, policy, rule, course of conduct or practice existing within the body corporate generally or in the part of the body corporate in which the relevant activities tales place'.

23 See, e.g., Olivia Dixon, 'Corporate Criminal Liability: The Influence of Corporate Culture' in Justin O'Brien and George Gilligan (eds) *Integrity, Risk and Accountability in Capital Markets – Regulating Culture* (Hart Publishing, 2013) 252.

24 Comino, (n 12) 300–301. Significantly, even though the Australian Law Reform Commission (ALRC) in its 2020 review of Australia's corporate criminal regime found that the culture provisions in Part 2.5 were barely used, this model (with minor changes) is one of two options it recommended for attributing criminal responsibility to corporations, with both options incorporating the concept of corporate culture: see ALRC, *Corporate Criminal Responsibility* (Final Report, April 2020) 14 (Recommendation 7).

this because the definition of 'corporate culture' above (in s. 12.3(6) of the Criminal Code) overcomes some of the uncertainty as to what comprises culture by focusing on concrete criteria that may be relied upon as evidence of cultural deficiency – namely, policies, rules and a course of conduct or practices.

Likewise, in seeking to tackle problematic cultures in corporations, those cultures might be evident from written policies and/or rules, though there is the problem of 'decoupling' discussed below, where corporations might and often do have formal written policies and rules in place advocating compliance with the law so that they 'look good on paper', but where the situation on the ground is very different.[25] Accordingly, a course of conduct or a corporation's practices are more likely to demonstrate poor culture.

Bant's concept of 'systems intentionality'[26] seems to reinforce this view as a way of understanding how regulators can and should regulate corporate culture. In her account, the de facto corporate policies are where one finds manifested the corporate values, high-level intentions and beliefs. These prompt conformable decision-making at more granular, daily, on-the-ground levels, where we find working systems and practices that also manifest more particularised corporate mindsets. On this analysis, it should be possible, though admittedly very difficult, to regulate corporate culture. In fact, it would be possible to audit (whether internally or externally) corporate policies and order remedial action to correct the corporate conscience, as I argue below has occurred with CBA.[27] In short, this was made possible by the Australian Prudential Regulation Authority's (APRA) comprehensive 2017–2018 inquiry and report into CBA's governance, culture and accountability (GCA) structures and practices,[28] conducted against a background of scandals at CBA,[29] and the enforceable undertaking (EU)[30] APRA subsequently negotiated from

25 See below, 'Decoupling'.

26 'Systems intentionality' is developed, e.g., in Elise Bant, 'Culpable Corporate Minds' (2021) 48 *University of Western Australia Law Review* 352 and discussed by her in Chapter 14 in this volume.

27 See discussion below (nn 69–75, 78–80).

28 APRA, 'Prudential Inquiry into CBA' (Final Report, 2018) (Prudential Report into CBA).

29 Although the announcement by AUSTRAC in August 2017 that it was bringing proceedings against CBA for money laundering (noted above n 5) triggered APRA's Prudential Inquiry into CBA, it was preceded by several other compliance and conduct issues at CBA (e.g., the mis-selling of margin loans to retail customers to invest in financial products recommended by Storm Financial (2008); use of an outdated definition of heart attack in insurance products sold by Comminsure (2016); and mis-selling of credit card insurance (2013–2018)).

30 EUs provide an explicit measure for regulators to enforce negotiated settlements. Both ASIC and APRA have the power to accept them: see, e.g., s. 18A of the *Banking Act 1959* (Cth) (APRA). Typical terms include undertakings to compensate victims, improve corporate governance and implement new measures to prevent similar breaches occurring in the future.

that bank that established a process to regulate the bank's culture.[31] The key is that the focus cannot be on formal policies, but rather on the instantiated, de facto, real policies and how they are embedded, audited and buttressed through practices throughout the organisation. Commissioner Finkelstein, who oversaw the inquiry into the 'suitability' of Crown to continue to hold a casino licence in Melbourne, comprehended this in his report, which appears to have endorsed 'systems intentionality' and provided some examples of appropriate directive orders, but he also recognised that it is like 'turning the Titanic' as it were. As he noted: '[s]ystemic and sustained change is needed for a culpable corporation to reform its character, as revealed through its systems, policies and processes'.[32]

Problems with 'Corporate Culture'

Nonetheless, some problems remain which present challenges for regulators regarding the use of 'corporate culture' to promote a superior one consistently throughout a formerly wrongdoing organisation or, indeed, a whole industry.

Different Cultures and 'Subcultures'

They include that cultures may, and often will, be different between different corporations and that the organisational culture of an individual corporation is rarely homogeneous, since the emergence of 'subcultures' within individual teams, departments and peer groups is commonplace, particularly within large corporations.[33]

Blurred Lines between 'Criminal' and 'Legitimate' Business Behaviour

Another problem is the indistinct boundaries between 'criminal' and 'normal' business behaviour,[34] with the consequence that wrongdoers (organisations and/or the individuals working for them) and, significantly, the relevant *industry* in which they operate, may regard wrongful conduct as 'legitimate' and fail to appreciate its criminality. A clear illustration is furnished in the

31 See EU, CBA and APRA (30 April 2018), discussed in more detail below (nn 74–75). It is available on the APRA website: https://www.apra.gov.au/sites/default/files/20180430-CBA-EU-Executed.pdf.

32 See State of Victoria, *Royal Commission into Casino Operator and Licence* (Final Report 15 October 2021) 178 (Victorian Royal Commission).

33 See Tanzer (n 21) 5.

34 See Fiona Haines, 'Crime? What Crime? Tales of the Collapse of HIH' in Henry N. Parnell and Gilbert L. Geis (eds) *International Handbook of White-Collar and Corporate Crime* (Springer, 2007) 524, 533.

English case of *R. v. Hayes*.[35] Tom Hayes, a former LIBOR trader, admitted to engaging in rate-rigging between 2006 to 2010 and was convicted.[36] Nevertheless, he pleaded not guilty on the ground that he had not acted dishonestly, arguing that his actions were 'standard market practice'.[37] As Bronitt and Brereton elucidate:

> The routine practice of banks at the time repeatedly attempt[ing] to manipulate and ma[k]e false, misleading or knowingly inaccurate submissions concerning ... global benchmark interest rates demonstrates how deviant behaviours can become entrenched and even encouraged within an industry's culture and operational practices.[38]

'Decoupling'

Yet another problem confronting the use of 'corporate culture' as a regulatory mechanism is a phenomenon known as 'decoupling' in organisational studies. It occurs when there is a mismatch between what is espoused (by leaders and in an organisation's official systems and policies) and its actions and practices.[39] In summary, 'not walking the talk', where there might be pejorative rule-based formal compliance and box-ticking of regulatory requirements by corporations, but missing are substantive compliance and a broader ethical culture of compliance.

The numerous commissions of inquiry into Crown and Star[40] reveal patent evidence of this problem. For instance, commenting on the 'Star's Prevention of Criminal Infiltration', the Bell Inquiry reported that even though:

35 *R v Hayes* [2015] EWCA Crim 1944.

36 He was sentenced to 14 years in prison and although this was reduced on appeal to 11 years, it is still one of the most substantial jail terms for a white-collar defendant in the UK: *R. v. Hayes* [2016] 1 Cr App R (S) 63.

37 See *R. v. Hayes* [2015] EWCA Crim 1944, [8].

38 See Simon Bronitt and Zoe Brereton, Submission to the Attorney-General's Department, 'Combatting bribery of public officials: Proposed amendments to the foreign bribery offence in the Criminal Code Act 1995 (Cth)', *Public Consultation Paper* (April 2017) 4 (citations omitted).

39 See Dionysios D. Dionysiou and Haridimos Tsoukas, 'Understanding the (re)creation of routines from within: A symbolic interactionist approach' (2013) 38 *Academy of Management Review* 181.

40 There were commissions of inquiry into Crown in three states (NSW, Victoria and WA): see, e.g., Bergin Inquiry (n 11). Equally, inquiries into Crown's rival, Star, were commissioned in both NSW and Queensland: see, e.g., State of NSW, *Review of The Star Pty Ltd: Inquiry under Sections 143 and 143A of the Casino Control Act 1992 (NSW)* (Final Report, 31 August 2022) (Bell Inquiry). All these inquiries issued very critical reports and all found that Crown and Star were *not* 'suitable' to hold casino licences. The Bell Inquiry, e.g., found that Star was *not* a 'suitable person' to hold a casino licence in NSW due to money laundering, fraud and criminal infiltration.

> [t]he Star Entities identified a range of controls, procedures and policies that had been implemented by The Star to manage the risk and threat of illegal and undesirable activities at The Star Casino ... [p]olicies, procedures and systems are insufficient of themselves if there is a culture ... of not applying them and permitting high value patrons to gamble without due regard to the risks they pose.[41]

Accordingly, despite regulators focusing on a corporation's practices (not its formal policies) as the key to understanding how they can and should regulate corporate culture discussed earlier, clearly 'decoupling' and corporate unwillingness to 'mend their ways' remain a major difficulty faced by regulators in seeking to deal with problematic cultures in corporations.

Traditional Responses by Corporations to Corporate Scandals and Misconduct

There are also the traditional and plainly inadequate responses to, and in some cases denials of, corporate wrongdoing[42] that we have witnessed routinely by large corporations and their leaders whenever scandals involving them have become public and/or they are confronted with the prospect of further regulation or sanctions, such as criminal prosecution or licence revocation. Foremost among them is the attempt to avoid even long-term, systemic wrongdoing that benefits a corporation being seen as 'criminal', which can involve seeking to recharacterise conduct as 'administrative errors' or 'inadvertence'. This was evident in the way Australian banks at the Hayne Royal Commission sought to deal with the infamous practice of extracting 'fees-for-no-service' through automated systems over lengthy periods.[43]

Other common responses also include another blame-shifting technique, namely, trying to explain away misconduct as 'a few bad apples', rather than 'rotten orchards',[44] 'apologies' and stated commitments to reform programmes

41 Bell Inquiry (n 40) Executive Summary, 22, para. 113, 115.

42 See generally Penny Crofts, 'Strategies of Denial and the Australian Royal Commission into Misconduct in the Banking, Superannuation and Financial Services' (2020) 29 *Griffith Law Review* 21.

43 Although the Hayne Royal Commission Final Report (n 3) 157 rejected that 'fees-for-no-service' were 'matters of accident', this practice met almost exclusively with civil penalty, not criminal, proceedings: see, e.g., *ASIC v. MLC Nominees Pty Ltd* [2020] FCA 1306. Interestingly, the Federal Court's finding in AUSTRAC's case against CBA, which admitted to 23,000 breaches of AML/CTF laws over a three-year period, echoed the sentiments above that the breaches were 'inadvertent: *CBA case* (n 5) [15].

44 'Rotten orchards' denotes corporate misconduct at the systemic level, indicat[ing] that sometimes it is not just the apple, or even the barrel that is rotten, but the system (or significant parts) of the system: see Maurice Punch, 'Rotten Orchards: Pestilence, Police Misconduct and System Failure' (2003) 13 *Policing and Society* 171, 172.

to 'reset' organisational cultures and regain community trust,[45] as well as dismissiveness,[46] lying to regulators[47] and making threats (albeit veiled), as happened with Crown. In a letter to the Victorian Gaming Minister produced as an exhibit to the Victorian Royal Commission, Crown's solicitors stated that if Crown was found unsuitable to hold a casino licence in Melbourne and had an event of default under its debt facilities, '[t]his will impact on Crown's shareholders, employees, unions, trade creditors, patrons, the hotel precinct and the Melbourne tourism industry'.[48] Essentially, this is the idea of 'too big to fail' or 'too big to jail',[49] which notwithstanding the Victorian Royal Commission ultimately finding Crown Melbourne unsuitable as was the case with all the other inquiries into Crown and Star,[50] has seen state gaming regulators and state governments keen to keep them in business.[51]

Another customary response deserving of special attention has been corporations cleaning out their boards, including having the CEO accept responsibility for wrongdoing and resign. Making board changes and replacing the CEO are predicated on the conventional view that 'tone from the top' sets the culture of a corporation.[52] However, while it may seem 'cathartic' to make board changes and replace the CEO, often 'evil' returns in the sense that the culture of the corporation fails to change for the better. This can occur because despite the high-profile scalps, others lower down in the management hierarchy of the organisation at the time of the wrongdoing may be kept on and promoted.[53] Also, cultural improvements (if any) will be short-lived, absent corporations and their new management taking ownership of

45 See, e.g., Ben Butler, 'AUSTRAC Legal Action Against Crown Resorts, Alleging Breach of Finance Laws', *The Guardian*, 1 March 2022, reporting on Crown's statements to this effect.

46 See, e.g., Prudential Report into the CBA (n 28) 4, reporting that a slow, legalistic and dismissive culture characterised many of CBA's dealings with regulators.

47 See, e.g., Michael Janda, 'Banking Royal Commission: AMP Loses Count of How Many Times It Misled ASIC' *ABC News*, 17 April 2018 (online: https://www.abc.net.au/news/2018-04-17/amp-loses-count-of-how-many-times-it-misled-asic/9666612).

48 See Letter to The Honourable Melissa Horne (2 July 2021), Exhibit Reference number EX RCO415, paras 35–40 (accessed on 15 November 2022 at https://www.rccol.vic.gov.au/sites/default/files/2021-07/RC415%20Letter%20from%20ABL%20to%20Minister%20for%20Consumer%20Affairs%20Gaming%20and%20Liquor%2C%202%20July%202021%2C%20tendered%206%20July%202021.pdf

49 See Brandon L. Garrett, *Too Big to Jail – How Prosecutors Compromise with Corporations* (Harvard Uni Press, 2014).

50 As noted above (n 40).

51 See further discussion below (nn 86–87).

52 See also John Braithwaite, 'White Collar Crime' (1985) 11 *Annual Review of Sociology* 1, 17.

53 However, it is not always the case that this scenario is a cause of the culture of an organisation failing to change. A notable example is CBA. Its CEO, Matthew Comyn, who replaced Ian Narev in 2017, was a CBA veteran of 20 years and head of retail banking whose responsibilities included the so-called intelligent deposit machines that were at the centre of

cultural deficits in the first place accompanied by sustained commitment to change at all levels across the organisation.

In this regard, it is interesting to note the following observations made in September 2022 relating to Star. They followed publication of the report of the Bell Inquiry and were made by Philip Crawford (Chief Commissioner of the newly established NSW Independent Casino Commission):[54]

> Despite a series of high-profile resignations during the Bell inquiry, the Commission remained concerned about the 'astounding' level of 'institutional arrogance' at the company … and Star's internal culture.[55]

Crawford continued:

> The Commission wasn't 'getting the vibe' that it [Star] had learnt from its mistakes. There is still an unwillingness to show the right level of transparency.[56]

Such observations suggest that our current approach is ineffectual and that consideration ought to be given to a different approach entirely. Instead of CEOs resigning, perhaps the best course would be if they were forced to stay on as CEO and deal head-on with problems, equipped as they are with invaluable corporate knowledge and so arguably best placed to give companies a real opportunity to change business strategies and cultures of wrongdoing. Similarly, with other executives, replacing them can result in the loss of corporate knowledge so that the same mistakes are repeated.[57]

AUSTRAC's money laundering case against CBA (n 5). This also adds weight to the argument below at (n 57).

54 This Commission was established as part of the NSW Government's response implementing the recommendations of the Bergin Inquiry to address the risks and harms arising from casino operations through increased regulatory oversight. It replaces the former NSW state regulator, the Independent Liquor and Gaming Authority, and commenced operating in September 2022.

55 Reported in Michael McGowan, '"Arrogant" Star found unsuitable to hold a casino licence by independent inquiry' *The Guardian*, 13 September 2022. (online: theguardian.com/australia-news/2022/sep/13/arrogant-star-found-unsuitable-to-hold-casino-licence-by-independent-inquiry)

56 Recent developments concerning Star reinforce these sentiments with a second inquiry into Star Casino Sydney (due to report in May 2024) examining whether it has made the 'deep structural change' needed to be 'suitable' to hold a licence and a second cull of its executive team, including 'clean skin' CEO Robbie Cooke, who was brought in to oversee Star's rehabilitation: see Sarah Gerathy, 'Sydney's Star Casino to Face Second Inquiry After Concerns 'Substantial Shift' Wasn't Achieved', *ABC News*, 19 February 2024 (online: https://www.abc.ned.au/news/2024-02-19/nsw-sydney-star-casino-second-inquiry/103483654).

57 On the latter point: see further Comino, (n 12) 309.

Internal Governance of Organisations Should Be Free from Outside Interference?

Another hurdle encountered in regulatory attempts to deal with problematic cultures within corporations also remains – the claim that they 'should be free to determine how their internal affairs are organised and governed – that they should be internally autonomous'.[58] As I have noted earlier, this claim, which is supported by a key descriptive claim in the debate about what should be done to stop corporations and their employees or agents breaching norms of conduct, namely, that 'organisational culture is impossible to regulate and cannot be prescribed', is a claim that has seemingly hijacked the policy debate, given how often it figures in official reports.[59] This includes in the Hayne Royal Commission Final Report.[60] It stated that:

> Culture cannot be prescribed or legislated. Proper governance, a healthy culture, and accountability are desired outcomes, but they cannot be imposed by rules that say, 'You must …' or 'You may not …'. 'Culture is about behaviours. Behaviours in general are not amenable to legislation or regulation … Sustainable cultures need to arise from, and be embedded in banks' [and other entities] DNA'.[61]

Culture Can Be Assessed and Supervised

Yet, the Final Report did go on to emphasise that '[a]though culture cannot be prescribed or legislated, it *can* be assessed'.[62] Culture can – and *should* – be assessed by organisations themselves (relevantly, financial services entities)[63] since they and their leadership have 'primary' responsibility for their own culture as well as culture remediation when problematic aspects of their culture are identified. Notably, however, the report also recognised the 'important' role for regulators to supervise culture, particularly given the danger that some corporations may be blind to their problematic cultures which are highly likely to allow or drive misconduct.[64] It explained that supervisory role over culture for regulators as being to:

58 See David Wishart, Ann Wardrop and Marilyn McMahon, 'The Internal Autonomy of the Firm' (2018) 27 *Griffith Law Review* 131, 133, who also discuss its underlying assumptions: first, liberalism as freedom and, second, the need for competition, which is crucial to economic welfare.

59 Comino, (n 12) 322.

60 See also Prudential Report into CBA (n 28) 92, asserting that '[s]upervisors and regulators cannot determine culture'. But note discussion below, Culture *can* be assessed and supervised.

61 Hayne Royal Commission Final Report (n 3) 376 (citing Group of Thirty (G30), *Banking Conduct and Culture: A Call for Sustainable and Comprehensive Reform* (July 2015) 55).

62 Ibid. 376 (emphasis added).

63 Financial services entities are required to assess their culture under APRA's prudential standards (at least in relation to 'risk culture'): APRA, *Prudential Standard CPS 220* (April 2018) cl. 9(b).

64 Ibid. 376–377.

- assess the entity's culture;
- identify what is wrong with the culture;
- 'hold up a mirror' to the entity, and educate the entity about its own culture;
- agree with what the entity will do to change its culture; and
- supervise the implementation of those steps.[65]

Recent supervisory culture-oriented initiatives by regulators in the financial services sector have included ASIC's CCM Programme[66] and APRA's programme of pilot risk culture reviews undertaken in mid-2017.[67] The latter involved an independent assessment by APRA of the relevant organisation's culture through such means as interviews, surveys, document reviews, focus groups and observations.[68] Nonetheless, it was APRA's Prudential Inquiry into CBA in August 2017 that the Hayne Royal Commission described as marking a 'watershed' in APRA's handling of governance, culture and remuneration matters and stating that the Inquiry Report provides 'a very valuable, publicly available account' of how GCA failures can drive misconduct and how to address them.[69] APRA Chair Wayne Byres testified to the Commission, acknowledging that while the APRA supervision team dedicated to CBA had flagged multiple issues from 2016, its ordinary supervisory activity had not effectively dealt with these issues or facilitated cultural change at CBA.[70]

The terms of reference for the panel appointed to conduct the Prudential Inquiry into CBA were 'to examine the frameworks and practices in relation to governance, culture and accountability within the CBA group' in order to identify, assess and investigate certain identified issues and recommend what remedial action (in addition to that already undertaken by CBA) was required to be carried out.[71] It was the first time that APRA took public steps to scrutinise a regulated institution's GCA frameworks and practices. When the panel reported in April 2018, the Inquiry Report, which excoriated CBA's culture[72] made 35 recommendations. These concerned: the board and senior leadership; risk management and compliance; issue identification and escalation; financial objectives and prioritisation; accountability; remuneration; culture and leadership; and remediation initiatives.[73] An EU was subsequently reached between APRA and CBA with CBA agreeing to implement all of the

65 Hayne Royal Commission Final Report (n 3) 377 (citations omitted).
66 As noted above (n 15).
67 APRA, Information Paper, *Risk Culture* (October 2016), 24.
68 See Hayne Royal Commission Final Report (n 3) 384: Transcript, Wayne Byres, 30 November 2018, 7436.
69 Ibid. 384–386.
70 Ibid. 384–385: Transcript, Wayne Byres, 30 November 2018, 7438.
71 Prudential Report into CBA (n 28) 105.
72 Ibid. 3–4. It found that cultural failings, including a culture of complacency, reactiveness, insularity and overconfidence, lay at the heart of systemic problems, most notably inadequate stewardship of non-financial risks.
73 Ibid. 102–104.

recommendations,[74] which I maintain established a process to regulate the bank's culture.[75] That EU required CBA to develop a Remedial Action Plan (RAP) to rectify the problems that had been identified in the Inquiry Report, submit it to APRA and then to three-monthly reviews by an independent assurance provider (Promontory Australia) to report on its implementation, as well as apply a A$1 billion capital add-on to CBA's operational risk capital requirement. In December 2020, APRA also negotiated an EU from Westpac in similar terms and applied a A$1 billion additional operational capital overlay.[76] This followed various governance audits undertaken (both internally and externally) of Westpac in response to Australian Transaction Reports and Analysis Centre's (AUSTRAC) filing proceedings in November 2019 against Westpac for money laundering.[77]

As to the effectiveness of the processes, especially under these EUs, CBA appears to be a success story.[78] APRA and Promontory have been satisfied with the bank's progress in completing its RAP, with Promontory having issued its 13th and final report in September 2021 and announcing that, '[i]n many ways, CBA is now almost unrecognisable as the institution described in the Inquiry Report'.[79] In November 2021, APRA also halved the operational risk capital overlay, down to A$500 million, removing the balance A$500 million in September 2022.[80] Its approach in taking its time to remove the capital overlay suggests that APRA has been focused on whether the change at CBA is sustained and sustainable.

74 See EU, CBA and APRA (n 31).

75 As noted above (n 31). See also Comino, (n 12) 323; and Comino, (n 15) 23–24, arguing that this EU is an example of how EUs should be crafted to harness the potential to redirect and improve the culture of an organisation.

76 See EU, Westpac and APRA (3 December 2020), available on the APRA website; APRA, 'APRA Launches Westpac Investigation and Increases Capital Requirement Add-ons to $1 Billion' (Media Release, 17 December 2020).

77 In December 2019, APRA, e.g., had publicly announced that these proceedings had given it cause to initiate a risk governance review into Westpac: See EU (n 76) Recitals, [C].

78 Regarding Westpac, the picture is not as clear. While improvements have been made to address deficits in Westpac's risk culture, past attempts at remediation of weaknesses identified in its risk governance by the many reviews conducted have expressed concerns about the pace of remediation: see, e.g., Westpac's own 2020 Reassessment which found that the progress achieved since its 2018 self-assessment was only 'incremental': Westpac, Reassessment of Culture, Governance and Accountability Remediation Report (June 2020) 3.

79 See Promontory Australia, Independent Review of the Commonwealth Bank of Australia's Remedial Action Plan (30 September 2021) Executive Summary, 7–8 at https://www.rccol.vic.gov.au/sites/default/files/2021-07/RC415%20Letter%20from%20ABL%20to%20Minister%20for%20Consumer%20Affairs%20Gaming%20and%20Liquor%2C%202%20July%202021%2C%20tendered%206%20July%202021.pdf.

80 See APRA, 'APRA removes CBA's operational risk capital add-on' (Media Release, 30 September 2022).

In contrast, even though state gaming regulators have taken action against Crown and Star in the wake of findings that they were unsuitable to hold casino licences made by the recent inquiries into them, including the appointment of Special Managers (e.g., at Crown Melbourne in October 2021)[81] while these organisations undertake remedial action, culture change at these organisations and others in the gaming industry is much more elusive. This is mainly because it is unlikely that an EU like that agreed with CBA could be duplicated for them. One of the reasons is that state gaming regulators have less experience in overseeing systemic risk than APRA.

Culture of Regulators Problematic and 'Regulatory Capture'

There are also some other important problems that cannot be ignored in considering the ability and effectiveness of regulators themselves to tackle the issue of embedded cultures in corporations that have licenced and failed to prevent wrongdoing. Most prominent is that the culture of regulators, including ASIC and APRA, has been found to be problematic, with evidence of 'regulatory capture'.[82] Regulatory capture happens when regulators become too close or overly cooperative with the regulated community they are supposed to police, rendering them ineffective as enforcers. However, it is not limited to regulators. Regulatory capture can also occur when bureaucrats and politicians 'cease to serve some notion of a wider collective public interest and begin to systematically favour vested interests, usually the very interests they were supposed to regulate and restrain for the wider public interest'.[83] Crofts, in her work analysing wrongdoing at Crown, makes a powerful case that it is an example of 'state-corporate crime'.[84] In discussing the particularly close relationship between the Victorian government and Crown, it is revealing that Crown Melbourne was notoriously referred to as 'The Vatican'. This encapsulates the state's failure to investigate and/or enforce breaches of the law, such that it effectively authorised and legitimised Crown's activities where Crown was treated by Victorian politicians

81 Fines have also been levied (e.g., a fine against Crown of A$80 million in Victoria in May 2022 and A$100 million against Star in NSW in October 2022).

82 There is considerable evidence of regulatory capture of ASIC: see, e.g., Senate Economics References Committee, Parliament of Australia, *Performance of the Australian Securities and Investments Commission* (2014) xviii; Hayne Royal Commission Final Report (n 3) 424. Similarly, with APRA: see, e.g., Gill North and Therese Wilson, 'Has the Australian Prudential Regulatory Authority Done Enough to Meet its Legislated Objectives and Prepare Australia for the Next Financial Crisis?' (2020) 43 (2) *UNSW Law Journal* 552, 556.

83 Andrew Baker, 'Restraining Regulatory Capture? Anglo-America, Crisis Politics and Trajectories of Change in Global Financial Governance' (2010) 86 *International Affairs* 647, 648.

84 See Honni van Rijswijk and Penny Crofts, 'A case study of state-corporate crime: Crown Resorts' (2022) *Current Issues in Criminal Justice*, https://doi.org/10.1080/10345329.2022.2144899.

and police like an 'independent city-state where the normal laws of the land don't apply'.[85]

Conclusion

This chapter has highlighted that following the GFC and corporate and financial scandals since, such as by Australian banks unearthed by the Hayne Royal Commission, there has been growing awareness by regulators that simply focusing on regulatory reform and the rules will be ineffective if cultural deficits within corporations are not also addressed to prevent future wrongdoing. Despite 'corporate culture' being identified as *the* problem, namely the root cause of misconduct and unethical behaviour, I have also discussed the difficulties attendant on using 'corporate culture' as a regulatory tool, noting also that regulators, such as ASIC and APRA, are themselves beset by problems, such as capture. However, there is the arguable success story of the CBA. This was facilitated by APRA's thorough review and report into the bank's GCA frameworks and practices, and the EU that APRA secured from it which required a fundamental redesign of the organisation's policies, processes and controls, and independent monitoring to ensure its implementation. The hope is that this process, especially the EU, can provide a blueprint for other regulators to use so as to give formerly wrongdoing organisations a chance to 'mend their ways' and change the culture that caused the wrongdoing in the first instance. This is a tall order; however, for regulators in the gaming sector, the experience of Crown and Star has not only shown that state gaming regulators are not up to the task, but also, that along with state governments, they lack the will to deal with problems effectively. It is remarkable that all the inquiries into Crown and Star found that they were unsuitable to hold casino licences in the various states in which they operate due to money laundering and other illegal activities; yet these state regulators and governments seem more intent on allowing Crown and Star to continue in business. It is true that state regulators have appointed Special Managers and/or applied conditions while these organisations undergo remediation programmes.[86] However, it is telling, for example, that in June 2022 when Crown was given approval to open its Sydney casino (at Barangaroo), it was subject to conditions, but where unlike the EU between APRA and CBA, those conditions have not been made public.[87]

85 Ibid. 12 (citations omitted).

86 As noted above (n 81). Note also the second inquiry currently being undertaken into Star Casino Sydney referred to above (n 56), indicating that state regulators (at least in NSW) may be starting to take a harder line: see Elizabeth Knight, 'Casino Regulator Turns Predator with The Star on its Menu', *The Sydney Morning Herald*, 25 March 2024 (online: https://amp.smh.com.au/business/companies/casino-regulator-turns-predator-with-the-star-on-its-menu-20240325-p5ff22.html).

87 In June 2022, the takeover of Crown by the private equity firm, Blackstone, approved by shareholders, the Court and NSW, WA and Victorian gaming regulators was also completed.

Index

Made in the USA
Las Vegas, NV
19 September 2026

90fa52f8-ba5e-4d62-b9d2-38dde696612eR02